Popular Politics
and the American Revolution
in England

For this is not the liberty which we can hope, that no grievance should ever arise in the commonwealth: that let no man in this world expect; but when complaints are freely heard, deeply considered, and speedily reformed, then is the utmost bond of civil liberty obtained that wise men look for.

John Milton
Areopagitica
1644

To know *of any injury and to* redress *it are inseparable in the royal breast.*

Sir William Blackstone
Commentaries on the Laws of England
1765–1769

Popular Politics
and the American Revolution
in England

Petitions, the Crown,
and Public Opinion

James E. Bradley

MERCER

ISBN 0-86554-181-7

For my parents,
Clarence and Phyllis Bradley

Library of Congress Cataloging-in-Publication Data
Bradley, James E. 1944–
Popular politics
and the American Revolution in England
Bibliography: p. 237
Includes index.
1. Great Britain—Politics and government—1760-1789.
2. United States—History—Revolution, 1775-1783—
Foreign public opinion, British. 3. Public opinion—
Great Britain—History—18th century. I. Title.
DA510.B63   1986   941.07'3   86-5180
ISBN 0-86554-181-7 (alk. paper)

Contents

List of Tables

Abbreviations

Amer. Arch.	Peter Force, ed., *American Archives: A Documentary History of the English Colonies in North America*, 4th ser., 6 vols.; 5th ser., 3 vols. (Washington: M. St. Clair Clark and Peter Force, 1840-1853).
Burke Correspondence	*The Correspondence of Edmund Burke*, gen. ed. Thomas W. Copeland. Vol. 3, ed. G. H. Guttridge (Cambridge: Cambridge University Press, 1961).
City Addresses	*Addresses, Remonstrances, and Petitions to the Throne, Presented from the Court of Aldermen, the Court of Common Council, and the Livery in Common Hall Assembled: Commencing the 28th October, 1760, with the Answers Thereto* (London: Benjamin Pardon, 1865).
CJ	*The Journals of the House of Commons*
Commons, 1715-1754	Romney Sedgwick, *The House of Commons, 1715-1754*, 2 vols. (London: Her Majesty's Stationery Office, 1970).
Commons, 1754-1790	Sir Lewis Namier and John Brooke, *The House of Commons, 1754-1790*, 3 vols. (London: Her Majesty's Stationery Office, 1964).
Fortescue	*Correspondence of King George the Third from 1706 to December 1783*, ed. Sir John Fortescue, 6 vols. (London: Macmillan Co., 1927-1928).
HMC	Historical Manuscripts Commission
HO	Home Office
Parl. Hist.	T. C. Hansard, ed., *The Parliamentary History of England . . . to the Year 1803* (London: T. C. Hansard, 1806-1820).
PRO	Public Record Office
RG	Registrar General

NEWSPAPERS

Ann. Reg.	*Annual Register*
Bath Chron.	*Bath Chronicle*
Brist. J.	*Felix Farley's Bristol Journal*
Cam. Chron.	*Cambridge Chronicle*
Cumb. Pacq.	*Cumberland Pacquet*
Gen. Eve. Post	*General Evening Post*
Glos. J.	*Gloucester Journal*
Hamp. Chron.	*Hampshire Chronicle*
Kent. Gaz.	*Kentish Gazette*
Leeds Merc.	*Leeds Mercury*
Lond. Chron.	*London Chronicle*
Lond. Eve.-Post	*London Evening-Post*
Lond. Gaz.	*London Gazette*
Man. Merc.	*Manchester Mercury*
Mid. J.	*Middlesex Journal*
Morn. Chron.	*Morning Chronicle and London Advertiser*
North. Merc.	*Northampton Mercury*
Norw. Merc.	*Norwich Mercury*
Nott. New. J.	*Creswell's Nottingham and Newark Journal*
Pub. Adv.	*Public Advertiser*
Read. Merc.	*Reading Mercury and Oxford Gazette*
Sal. Win. J.	*Salisbury and Winchester Journal*
Shrews. Chron.	*Shrewsbury Chronicle*
Suss. Week. Adv.	*Sussex Weekly Advertiser*
Worcs. J.	*Berrow's Worcester Journal*
York Cour.	*York Courant*

Preface

This book originated in a search for new ways to measure the political influence of religion in a revolutionary setting. An exploratory survey of English newspapers revealed an entire array of hitherto unknown petitions to the Crown protesting the government's American policy, and this discovery necessitated a broader investigation into constitutional and social developments. As a constitutional monarchy, eighteenth-century England enjoyed the rule of law. But in all the monarchies of early modern Europe, the authority of kings was couched in mystical, quasi-religious terms. Even in England, trust in the king as the father and defender of his people continued to be a normal political expression long after 1689. Deference to royal authority was typically combined with widespread satisfaction with the Revolution settlement on the one hand and a general confidence in Parliament as a representative institution on the other. As a result, extraparliamentary avenues for the redress of grievance were slow to emerge. Studies in the development of the Constitution have revealed a great deal about the king's changing relation to the House of Commons and the cabinet, but the dynamic interaction between the people and the Crown remains an uncharted area of research.

Two channels of communication require particular attention in this regard, one ascending to the Crown, the other descending to the people. The way in which the popular will ascended to the Crown is the main subject of this study. The only approach the people had to their sovereign was the approach of dutiful children, and the only method of redress they possessed—short of violence—was the humble petition. Between the Stamp Act crisis in 1765 and the constitutional crisis over the Coalition in 1784, petitions with more than a quarter of a million signatures ascended to Parliament or the Crown. The way in which the king handled these appeals depended upon a second political trajectory descending from the central government to the people. The king received the people and their petitions at the levee, and the government's official pronouncements reached down to the populace through royal proclamations and notices in the government newspaper. These means of controlling and influencing public opinion turned out to be far more effective than the fragile instruments of liberty guaranteed by the Bill of Rights. Both the manner in which the petitions were received and the use of royal proclamations lend an element of truth to Thomas Paine's lament that when the English locked away the tools of tyranny, they presented the monarch with the key.

It is hardly surprising, however, that George III disregarded the petitions in favor of peace. Eighteenth-century monarchs were not in the habit of receiving advice from the populace in matters of colonial policy, and the theory that the king intended to subvert the Constitution has long since been disproven. But this is not to say that the actions of George III and his ministers were above criticism. In the period of the American Revolution, the executive utilized a variety of tactics that can only be called innovative and authoritarian. The government's control of public opinion is thus a second major concern of this book, although in such a brief compass it is only possible to introduce the petitions and raise some of the legal implications. Specialists in constitutional history will be able to assess with great precision the role of petitioning in the emergence of modern democracy.

Finally, this book attempts to show that the question of public opinion can only be addressed adequately through an analysis of political and social developments at the level of local history. The broad contours of English statecraft during the American Revolution are well understood, but among the many studies of the elite, one looks in vain for a survey of popular politics. Sir Lewis Namier's projected volumes on "England in the Age of the American Revolution" for the period 1775 to 1780 were never completed. London has attracted a great deal of attention, English radicals have received careful scrutiny, and an increasing number of scholars are making solid progress concerning popular politics in the provinces. But historians have almost completely neglected the provincial press in the 1770s, and the same is true of local politics. Consequently, the vitality of informed public opinion before 1780 has sometimes been discounted. In comparison to what we know about social and political reality in colonial America, and in revolutionary France, it is remarkable how little work has been done on the social composition of eighteenth-century England. Research on local interest groups and their social status, and the religious affiliation of individuals and their political behavior is still in its infant stages. Each petition to the Crown represented the voices of many individuals. Who were they? What place did they occupy in society? What motivated them? This book represents an initial attempt to answer these questions and, thereby, find a way across the gulf that is often assumed to exist between local politics and national issues.

I wish to thank Dr. Raymond Cooke and Dr. Thomas Andrews, formerly of Pasadena College, for introducing me to the study of the British Empire and for stimulating my interest in the Imperial school of historiography. Their encouragement at an early stage of my schooling strongly influenced the direction of my research. At the University of Southern California, I had the good fortune of studying with three mentors, each of whom specialized in a different aspect of eighteenth-century politics. Their respective areas are in some ways reminiscent of the political diversity of the period itself. John Schutz's biography of Thomas Pownell anticipated many of the insights brought to light by the neo-Whig school. This book appeared long before the seminal works of Caroline Robbins and Bernard Bailyn, and seminars with Professor Schutz grounded me in the "True Whig" tradition of English politics. Professor Donald Greene examined the period from a very different angle. His study of the politics of Samuel Johnson and his recent edition of Johnson's political writings have kept me in touch with the claims of the government and a conservative interpretation of the reign of George III. Finally, Professor Charles Ritcheson's work on the Anglo-American connection has left an abiding impression on me. The constructive attempts of English statesmen to save the Empire were first convincingly portrayed in his study of British politics. Dr. Ritcheson's examination of peacemaking among the elite served as an inspiration for my investigation of the support for peace among the people. I would like to believe that the influence of these teachers has enabled me to present both the defenders of coercive measures and the critics of the use of force in a fair and balanced way.

In the area of methodology I am especially indebted to two younger scholars. Professor John Brewer's work on popular politics, and in particular his examination of the provincial press in the 1760s, was highly influential. But my greatest debt is owed to Professor John Phillips. In recent publications Dr. Phillips has revolutionized our understanding of the unreformed electorate through an innovative methodology that has taken the study of popular politics a major step forward. He was the first to see the larger implications of the petitions to the Crown over America and the first to put them to good historical use. Although he knew there was more rich ore yet to be mined from these sources, he pointed me in the direction of the Public Record Office and encouraged me to make the same comparison between petitions and religious records that he had already made between registers and poll books. Both he and Dr. Charles Wetherell, the Director of the Laboratory for Historical Research at the University of California, Riverside, gave generously of their time and technical advice on another project, and their assistance enabled me to devote more time to this study. Without their support, this book could not have been written.

I wish to thank Dr. Frank O'Gorman of the University of Manchester, Dr. Paul Langford, Lincoln College, Oxford, and John Schutz for reading an early draft of the book and making numerous valuable suggestions; any errors of fact or interpretation that remain are my own. Janet Gathright worked long hours on the typescript, and she, with Amy Plantinga Pauw and Millie Aston, helped a great deal with editorial advice. Jack Balswick tutored me in basic statistics, and three other colleagues and friends, Donald Hagner, Richard Muller and James Butler, were constant sources of encouragement.

The librarians and staff of McAlister Library at Fuller Seminary, the Huntington Library, the Public Record Office, the Institute of Historical Research, and Dr. Williams's Library have all provided invaluable assistance in my research. The Public Record Office granted permission to reproduce the petitions to the Crown and allowed the citing of many nonparochial registers. The University of Nottingham permitted me to utilize the correspondence of the Duke of Portland, for which I am grateful. Portions of an article that appeared in the *Journal of British Studies* are found in chapters 6 and 7 and are used with permission. I am also indebted to the Institute for Humane Studies for financial assistance granted at an early stage of my research. James and Evelyn Allard of the Genealogical Library of Glendale, California, have been consistently gracious and helpful. Without the vital records provided on microfilm by the Genealogical Society of Salt Lake City and made available in Glendale and Pasadena, the research involved in this kind of study would have been infinitely more laborious.

Finally, my wife Diane was more than generous in her many expressions of support. To her and our children I am deeply grateful for the freedom they gave me to travel, to research, and to write.

Introduction

In an age of democratic revolution, politicians on both sides of the Atlantic expressed a lively interest in English public opinion concerning America. In England, Lord Camden observed in 1775 that "the common people hold the war in abhorrence," but he worried nonetheless about the "powerful assent" to the government's measures, both inside and outside Parliament.[1] As he watched English developments from America, Benjamin Franklin felt a similar ambivalence. He was persuaded that "the body of the British people are our friends," but he feared that the public was changeable and might even turn hostile.[2] In another era, Lord John Russell mused over the Opposition's poor showing in the House of Commons in 1775. A leader of popular revolt in his own time, Russell wondered whether the government's majorities in Parliament accurately reflected the response of the nation at large. "It would be very desirable to ascertain how far this great majority represented the opinion of the country." But he added, "we have not many indications to guide us." He surmised that Wilkes and the Middlesex election affair had "absorbed nearly all the popular sympathy in the country," but standing in the Whig tradition, Russell—like Camden and Franklin before him—wanted to believe that the common people opposed the war.[3]

The writings of W. E. H. Lecky and G. M. Trevelyan encouraged this pro-American perspective, but in the 1920s Lewis Namier's two volumes on mid-eighteenth-century politics radically reoriented the direction of English historiography. These works militated against serious interest in popular politics; in one of his more severe judgments, Namier compared the English people's mindless response to the American crisis to hordes of lemmings plunging into

---

[1]William S. Taylor and John H. Pringle, eds., *The Correspondence of William Pitt, Earl of Chatham*, 4 vols. (London: John Murray, 1838-1840) 4:401 (Lord Camden to the earl of Chatham, 12 February 1775).

[2]Leonard W. Labaree and William B. Willcox, eds., *The Papers of Benjamin Franklin* (New Haven: Yale University Press, 1982) 22:216 (Franklin to David Hartley, 3 October 1775).

[3]Lord John Russell, *The Life and Times of Charles James Fox*, 3 vols. (London: Richard Bentley, 1859) 1:82.

the sea.[4] Namier's accomplishments were so stunning that the study of English public opinion was truncated for a generation. Only rarely did modern students of popular culture venture into the terrain of former Whig historians. But J. H. Plumb found it "hard to believe," as so many since Namier had claimed, that "sympathy for America and strenuous adherence to liberal and radical sentiments" were restricted to the intellectuals.[5] Evidence for such popular opposition, however, remained fragmentary, and only recently has the topic of public opinion been taken up again with confidence.

Renewed interest in popular opposition to the government during the American Revolution is currently yielding new insights on radical ideology, pro-American sentiment, and the penetration of these views into the London populace.[6] The petitioning movements stimulated by Wilkes in 1769-1770 and by Wyvill and the Yorkshire Association in 1779-1782 are now thoroughly documented.[7] There was, however, another little-known popular agitation in

---

[4]Sir Lewis Namier, *England in the Age of the American Revolution*, 2d ed. (London: Macmillan Co., 1961) 41; *The Structure of Politics at the Accession of George III*, 2d ed. (London: Macmillan Co., 1957). The publication of John Robinson's papers in 1922 also contributed to this atmosphere. See John A. Phillips, *Electoral Behavior in Unreformed England: Plumpers, Splitters, and Straights* (Princeton: Princeton University Press, 1982) 8-16. In an early critique, Sir Herbert Butterfield examined the stultifying effect Namier's technique had upon research concerning public opinion, "George III and the Constitution," *History* 43 (February 1958): 33. For recent surveys that reassess Namier's achievement see John Brewer, *Party Ideology and Popular Politics at the Accession of George III* (Cambridge: Cambridge University Press, 1976); Frank O'Gorman, "Fifty Years after Namier: The Eighteenth Century in British Historical Writing," *The Eighteenth Century* 20 (Spring 1979): 99-120; John Cannon, ed., *The Whig Ascendancy: Colloquies on Hanoverian England* (New York: St. Martin's Press, 1981); and Phillips, *Electoral Behavior*.

[5]J. H. Plumb, "British Attitudes to the American Revolution," *In the Light of History* (New York: Dell Publishing Co., 1972) 74.

[6]Colin Bonwick in *English Radicals and the American Revolution* (Chapel Hill: University of North Carolina Press, 1977); Mary Kinnear, "Pro-Americans in the British House of Commons in the 1770s" (Ph.D. dissertation, University of Oregon, 1973) and "British Friends of America 'Without Doors' during the American Revolution," *The Humanities Association Review* 27:2 (1976): 104-19; John A. Sainsbury, "The Pro-American Movement in London, 1769-1782; Extra-Parliamentary Opposition to the Government's American Policy" (Ph.D. dissertation, McGill University, 1975) and "The Pro-Americans of London, 1769-1782," *William and Mary Quarterly* 3d ser., 35 (July 1978): 423-54; John Brewer, "English Radicalism in the Age of George III," in J. G. A. Pocock, ed., *Three British Revolutions: 1641, 1688, 1776* (Princeton: Princeton University Press, 1980) 323-67.

[7]Lucy Sutherland, *The City of London and the Opposition to Government, 1768-1774* (London: University of London, Athlone Press, 1959); George Rudé, *Wilkes and Liberty* (Oxford: Oxford University Press, 1962); Ian Christie, *Wilkes, Wyvill and Reform* (London: Macmillan Co., 1962); E. C. Black, *The Association* (Cambridge: Harvard University Press, 1963); and most recently John A. Phillips, "Popular Politics in Unreformed England," *Journal of Modern History* 52 (December 1980): 599-625.

the mid-1770s that allowed the English public to take an explicit stance for or against the government's American policy.[8] Beginning in January 1775, English merchants sent signed petitions to Westminster appealing for peaceful concessions, while others signed loyal petitions encouraging coercion. Later in the year, further appeals from numerous boroughs and counties ascended to St. James. In terms of numbers, geographical extent, and the importance of the constitutional issues involved, this popular activity compares favorably with the other petitioning movements of the decade.

The Middlesex election affair elicited petitions from eighteen English counties and twenty boroughs, while the drive for economic reform in 1780 was supported by petitions from twenty-six counties and eleven boroughs. Each movement is thought to have attained a number of petitioners equal to about one-fourth of the total electorate, though the actual number of signatures for the former stands closer to one-fifth at 53,100.[9] In the period 1775-1778, however, eleven English counties and forty-seven boroughs and towns sent signed petitions to Parliament or the Crown involving 44,000 petitioners, and the petitions from Scotland and Ireland bring the total to more than 50,000.

---

[8]In appeals to the Crown, in contrast to those to Parliament, it was common to distinguish between *petitions* for redress and *addresses* of support, though both might have signatures appended. In this study, the term *petition* is often used to include both petitions and addresses, but *addresses* will be restricted to documents that support the government. Fred J. Hinkhouse, *The Preliminaries of the American Revolution as Seen in the English Press, 1763-1775* (New York: Columbia University Press, 1926) 177-81, has a brief discussion of the movement in the fall of 1775, but Solomon Lutnick, *The American Revolution and the British Press, 1775-1783* (Columbia MO: University of Missouri Press, 1967), does not treat it. Dora Mae Clark, *British Opinion and the American Revolution* (New Haven: Yale University Press, 1930), provides the most extensive details to date, but she knows of only six conciliatory petitions from the boroughs to the Crown and only one from a county (82-85, 99). John Money, *Experience and Identity: Birmingham and the West Midlands, 1760-1800* (Manchester: Manchester University Press, 1977), has a good recent analysis of local petitioning activity, but he cites only the six conciliatory petitions that are germane to his regional study (199-206). Phillips, "Popular Politics," 611, examines four of the conciliatory petitions. Three articles treat the petitions from specific towns: B. D. Bargar, "Matthew Boulton and the Birmingham Petition of 1775," *William and Mary Quarterly* 3d ser., 13 (January 1956): 26-39; Peter Marshall, "Manchester and the American Revolution," *Bulletin of the John Rylands University Library of Manchester* 62 (Autumn 1979): 168-86; and Sainsbury, "The Pro-Americans of London." R. B. McDowell, *Irish Public Opinion, 1750-1800* (London: Faber and Faber, 1944), alludes to three petitions from Ireland, but offers no details on the numbers involved (43-44).

[9]Rudé obtains the figure of 60,000 by adding 5,000 for London and 4,000 for the other places for which no signatures have survived. The figures for the economic reform movement remain conjectural, since none of the petitions has survived, and the numbers are known for only five. On the size of the unreformed electorate see Phillips, "Popular Politics," 600. Petitioning activity in the eighteenth century was always small by comparison to the nineteenth century. Cannon, *Whig Ascendancy*, 109.

Unlike the movements of 1770 and 1780, this popular activity regarding America reflected serious political fissures in the nation. In the Middlesex election affair only two counties and four boroughs divided. In 1775, five of the eleven counties divided over whether conciliatory or coercive measures should be pursued; twenty-nine of the forty-seven boroughs and towns sent petitions for peace, and most of these were divided. Altogether, more than one-fifth of the parliamentary constituencies in England were involved in some form of popular expression concerning America. Further, while the addresses out-numbered the petitions, the majority of people who signed these documents favored peaceful concessions rather than coercive measures.[10]

The popular activity concerning America may be compared to the actual turnout of voters at general elections as well as to the potential electorate, which was always much larger. The number of voters in the second half of the century ranged from 47,600 in the general election of 1761, a notorious low, to no more than 97,600 in 1774, the most highly contested election of the period.[11] The Middlesex election affair, the American crisis, and the Association movement each elicited a popular political response that approximated that of a general election, but in 1775 alone was there widespread division. After the war the popular outcry against the Fox-North Coalition gave rise to petitions from 53,500 Englishmen, and this "massive demonstration of public disapproval" almost rivaled the turnout at the general election of 1784.[12] The agitation in 1775 is thus roughly comparable to a contested general election. In this case, however, the contest was highly divisive, it concerned the single issue of America, and most of the petitions are still extant.

In earlier studies, parliamentary election returns, evidence from newspapers, and unsigned petitions have served as the basis for making judgments concerning public opinion. The value of electoral data is increasingly recognized, but only a small number of printed poll books of contested elections during the American crisis have survived.[13] As guides to public opinion, newspapers are useful, but there are several characteristic drawbacks in all studies

---

[10]See ch. 3, tables 3.1-3.5 below. Petitions and addresses to the Crown are found in the HO Papers, series 55, the PRO, Kew, and are retained with their signatures; those to Parliament perished in the fire of 1834, but the written texts of these petitions without signatures may be located in the *CJ*.

[11]*Commons, 1754-1790*, 1:514. These figures are high since they are based on the total electorates for the boroughs that were contested and an estimate of the actual number of voters in the contested counties.

[12]John Cannon, *The Fox-North Coalition: Crisis of the Constitution, 1782-1784* (Cambridge: Cambridge University Press, 1969) 188.

[13]For example, twenty-nine printed poll books for the election of 1774 have survived (twenty borough and nine county contests), but, among these, America was raised as a political issue in only nine. See John Sims, ed., *A Handlist of British Parliamentary Poll Books* (Riverside CA: University of Leicester History Department and University of California, Riverside, 1984).

of the press. While an editor's political opinion is readily established, the opinion of the readership can, at best, only be inferred. In addition, it is impossible to place the readers of newspapers on a socioeconomic scale. Signed petitions, however, offer the possibility of providing a new perspective on the nature of eighteenth-century public opinion. By plotting the documents geographically, and thereby describing the extent of petitioning activity throughout the nation, one can determine whether or not opinion concerning America was genuinely public. By comparing the documents with other lists of names from political records in selected boroughs, one may answer the question of whether or not public opinion was genuine opinion. Comparative analysis based on record linkage illumines the issue of the political consistency of individuals over time, and it also provides a fairly precise identification of the levels of society from which these popular expressions arose.

The petitions, however, were largely ignored, both in 1775 by the politicians and since then by historians. The petitions were viewed by those who presented them as appeals to constituted authority, not as appeals to the nation. Unlike the coercive addresses that were systematically printed by the government organ, the *London Gazette*, the petitions for peace were not well publicized. In July 1775, George III determined to receive no more petitions concerning America while seated on the throne, that is, officially in his royal capacity. The government understandably did not wish widespread notice of opposition to its policy; accordingly, petitions were presented at the levee and thenceforth dropped from sight. With some justification, the *Public Advertiser* charged the administration with suppressing them.[14] Only one London newspaper made an attempt to print the petitions for peace, and the Public Record Office subsequently catalogued them under the misleading rubric "Condemnation of the American Rebellion by."[15]

These circumstances have resulted in a serious misunderstanding of the nation's reaction to the American crisis. "Pro-Americanism," writes George Rudé, "seems to have been confined to higher social circles and does not appear as an expression of popular opinion."[16] Nearly all other accounts of the public's re-

---

[14]Fortescue, 3:235 (George III to Lord North, 26 July 1775); *Pub. Adv.* (18 October, 7 November 1775). On charges of suppression, see also *Lond. Chron.* (14-17 October, 30 November-2 December 1775). On the *Gazette* as the instrument of the government, see Lutnick, *The American Revolution*, 20-22; the *Pub. Adv.* is considered "independent," 219. This same pattern of publishing the loyal addresses but not the petitions characterized the petitions concerning the Middlesex election affair. Sutherland, *The City and the Opposition*, 30 n. 1.

[15]See HO List B/20A x/L04508, at PRO, Kew. In the entire list, only three separate items are categorized in a way that implies they support peace: Middlesex (HO 55/13/2), Halifax (HO 55/16/3), and London (HO 55/16/4).

[16]George Rudé, "The London Mob of the Eighteenth Century," in *Paris and London in the Eighteenth Century: Studies in Popular Protest* (New York: The Viking Press, 1973) 315.

sponse to the administration's American policy agree with this conclusion since they necessarily rely upon the contemporary views of a select number of politicians, or upon the more widely known addresses for coercion. When combined with the administration's overwhelming majorities in Parliament, this evidence led to the widespread scholarly consensus that not only Parliament, but the nation at large, was united in recommending coercive measures against the colonists. "Coercion," it is said, "was a popular policy."[17]

In 1775 most Opposition leaders expressed little hope in the public's resistance to the government. Since this apparent absence of popular support was self-confessed, it has carried all the more authority. Lord Rockingham's negative assessment in mid-September is well known: "In this country," he wrote, "violent measures towards America, are fairly adopted and countenanced by a majority of individuals of all ranks, professions, or occupations."[18] Others, however, were less pessimistic. Temple Luttrell toured England in the summer of 1775; having canvassed "a multitude of persons widely different in station and description," he concluded before the House of Commons in October "that the sense of the mass of the people is in favor of the Americans." As late as 15 November Lord Camden agreed. In an attack upon the administration in the House of Lords he declared, "You have not half of the nation on your side," and he based his view explicitly on the number of conciliatory petitions he had seen.[19] The claims of Luttrell and Camden, however, were soon forgotten, while that of Rockingham became a stock reference. But neither the private nor the public viewpoints of the politicians provide adequate evidence for sustaining generalizations concerning national opinion.

Since private papers were of limited value in determining the nature of public opinion, some historians turned to the known conciliatory petitions to the Crown. However, no survey of the issue ever alluded to more than seven

---

[17]Clark, *British Opinion*, 92, 133-34, 216. Clark's conclusion appears to have shaped succeeding accounts. J. Steven Watson, *The Reign of George III, 1760-1815* (Oxford: Clarendon Press, 1959), refers to a "general conservative impulse" in the public (203). For similar views, see John C. Miller, *Origins of the American Revolution*, rev. ed. (Stanford: Stanford University Press, 1959) 201, 409; Bernard Donoughue, *British Politics and the American Revolution* (London: Macmillan Co., 1964) 155-56, 199, 238; Brewer, *Party Ideology*, 180; Paul Langford, "Old Whigs, Old Tories and the American Revolution," *Journal of Imperial and Commonwealth History* 8 (January 1980): 112, 124, 130 n. 69; and Edward Royle and James Walvin, *English Radicals and Reformers, 1760-1848* (Lexington: University Press of Kentucky, 1982) 26.

[18]*Burke Correspondence*, 3:215 (Rockingham to Burke, 24 September 1775). At Bristol, Richard Champion was similarly defeated. See G. H. Guttridge, ed., *The American Correspondence of a Bristol Merchant, 1766-1776: Letters of Richard Champion* (Berkeley: University of California Press, 1934) 59-60 (Champion to Willing, Morris & Co., 26 August 1775).

[19]*Parl. Hist.*, 18:759, 26 October 1775. Camden's remarks were not recorded in *Parl. Hist.;* for part of the text of the speech, see *Lond. Eve.-Post* (14-16 November 1775).

of these documents, and little attention was given to the number of signatures appended to them. The conciliatory petitions consistently gathered more names than the coercive ones, but since there were more unsigned addresses for coercion than signed petitions for peace, and since the addresses received more publicity than the petitions, the conclusion seemed irresistible: the government's decision to use force was welcomed by the people.[20]

The question of the public's response to the war has important historiographical implications. Differing interpretations of the Rockingham Whigs, the English Crown, and even the causes of the war itself are directly related to this issue. Americans at the time of the Revolution, and Whig historians since, wished to believe that the English people were sympathetic to the American cause. The Rockingham Whigs were applauded because they were believed to have interpreted correctly the will of the people, they opposed a corrupt administration, and they seemed to discern the future of imperial history more clearly than the king and Parliament. The villain of the story was George III, who was, as the Declaration of Independence asserted, a tyrant who did not deserve to rule over a free people. In this view, the English people suffered equally with the colonists under the evil influence of a coterie of "King's friends."[21]

Sir Lewis Namier provided the first modern departure from the Whig interpretation by demonstrating that George III did not control Parliament.[22]

---

[20]Even those who have specifically examined pro-Americans accept the idea based on the known petitions that public opinion in favor of coercion was a monolith behind administration; Rudé, *Wilkes and Liberty*, 197; Money, *Experience and Identity*, 187, 201; Sainsbury, "The Pro-Americans of London," 453; and Bonwick, *English Radicals*, 85. A few have held to a more widespread sentiment for conciliation. See Hinkhouse, *The Preliminaries*, 177; John R. Alden, *The American Revolution, 1775-1783* (New York: Harper and Row, 1954) 61-63; J. H. Plumb, "British Attitudes," 73; Frank O'Gorman, *The Rise of Party in England: The Rockingham Whigs, 1760-82* (London: George Allen & Unwin, 1975) 604 n. 3; and John Phillips, "Popular Politics," 603. But evidence for widespread popular support of conciliatory measures has heretofore been lacking.

[21]George H. Bancroft, *History of the United States of America from the Discovery of the Continent*, 6 vols. (Boston: Little, Brown and Co., 1876) 4:131, 134-35, 197, 494, 498; Richard Frothingham, *The Rise of the Republic of the United States* (Boston: Little, Brown and Co., 1872) 406-408; Esmond Wright, ed., *Causes and Consequences of the American Revolution* (Chicago: Quadrangle Books, 1966) 143-229; Merrill Jensen, "Historians and the Nature of the American Revolution," in Ray Allen Billington, ed., *The Reinterpretation of Early American History* (San Marino CA: The Huntington Library, 1966) 101-27; Jack P. Greene, "Revolution, Confederation, and Constitution, 1763-1787," in William H. Cartwright and Richard L. Watson, Jr., eds., *The Reinterpretation of American History and Culture* (Washington: National Council for the Social Sciences, 1973) 259-95.

[22]Namier, *The Structure of Politics*, 212-14, 218; and "King George III: A Study of Personality," in *Personalities and Powers* (London: Hamish Hamilton, 1955) 55.

Parliament, not the Crown, was responsible for the breach with America, and George III and his ministers were acting constitutionally in carrying out the will of Parliament. Far from a tyrant, the king was a defender of the legislative authority of Parliament and, thereby, the Revolution settlement of 1689. The conservative interpretation advanced a more sophisticated understanding of electoral history, it provided new insights into the role of the king's advisors, and it gave us a much-needed reappraisal of George III.[23] But the detailed investigation of political agents, their interests, and their relationship to the constituencies resulted in a general neglect of party ideology and popular political agitation.

Historians influenced by the conservative interpretation recently sought to explain the government's commitment to the use of force by reexamining the role of public opinion. The belief that the nation at large supported coercive measures is in harmony with previous studies, but because of the supposed unanimity of public opinion, it has become increasingly acceptable to argue that even had the government wished for peace, it could not have acted differently than it did.[24] The apogee of conservative historiography was reached when a volume written for the bicentennial of the Revolution put forth the sustained thesis that the nation's voice in support of Parliament and the king had ratified the decision to use force. "In the decision to crush rebellion the North ministry was carrying out Parliament's—indeed, the country's—will."[25] This first serious attempt to use public opinion to justify government policy represents the culmination of a conservative interpretation that finally rested its case in the will of the people. The appeal to popular opinion, and the use to which it was put, was remarkable for several reasons. First, conservative interpretations commonly viewed society as controlled by ties of deference, and public opinion was either disparaged or discounted. But here, in an attempt to explain the loss of the American colonies, popular opinion enjoyed a new place of importance. Second, the argument in this study was based ultimately on the judg-

---

[23]Above all, in Lewis Namier and John Brooke, *The House of Commons, 1754-1790;* Ian Christie, *Myth and Reality in Late-Eighteenth-Century Politics and Other Papers* (London: Macmillan Co., 1970) esp. 7-108; John Brooke, *King George III* (London: Constable and Co., 1972); Stanley Ayling, *George the Third* (New York: Alfred A. Knopf, 1972).

[24]Dorothy Marshall, *Eighteenth Century England,* 2d ed. (Thetford, Norfolk: Longman, 1974) 420, and John B. Owen, *The Eighteenth Century, 1714-1815* (London: Thomas Nelson and Sons, 1974) 217, 220. Although John Brooke recognized the importance of public opinion in 1780, the opinion of the mass of the nation is used to explain the slowness of the government's retreat from coercion in *Commons, 1754-1790,* 1:80.

[25]Ian Christie and Benjamin Labaree, *Empire or Independence* (Oxford: Phaidon, 1976) 234. "Behind the government stood the country. A great groundswell of opinion was rising against the apparent tendency of the Americans to seek their independence" (215). "As North was to claim long afterwards, the American war was truly the war of Parliament and of the British people" (257). See also pages 216, 232, 256.

ment of Lord North. Immediately following the war, North was out of favor and seeking to vindicate his ministry, and it was then that he claimed that the war was the war of the people. Hardly credible in 1783, such a thesis could only be advanced in the modern setting in an interpretative context dominated by a conservative ethos.

The use of public opinion as a point of departure for one's interpretation of the American Revolution has, with this argument, come full circle, but with exactly the opposite results. No longer the pro-Americans of Whig historiography, the English people themselves are asked to take final responsibility for plunging the nation into war. The paucity of evidence has allowed both interpretations to claim acceptance. Because of political presuppositions quite unrelated to the question of popular politics, neither could entertain the possibility that the nation was fundamentally divided.

In recent American scholarship the Whig interpretation has gained some acceptance. Studies by Caroline Robbins and Bernard Bailyn follow in the tradition of earlier work by scholars such as G. L. Guttridge, and they are generally construed as belonging to the neo-Whig school of thought.[26] These works illumine seventeenth-century "Commonwealthman" ideas and examine how they contributed to the ideology of revolution in eighteenth-century England and America. The emphasis upon ideology, however, has lacked some cogency, since there was so little evidence for the impact of the same ideas in England—a point readily admitted by the authors themselves.[27] If the Commonwealthman ideas were so important in America, why had they appealed to such a small minority of intellectuals in England? The neo-Whig interpretation is also weakened by an inability to measure the influence of progressive ideology, since it relies almost exclusively on literary sources. The Whig historians' proclivity for intellectual history thereby contributed to the general neglect of the study of popular political behavior.

The evidence from signed petitions, addresses, and poll books supplies what has been lacking in the neo-Whig interpretation. The petitions provide a new source of data that lends considerable support to the neo-Whig emphases. At the same time, the petitions are eminently quantifiable. Each signed petition presents the historian with a political statement that can be placed in an intellectual tradition, along with a number of signatures that can be analyzed from

---

[26]Caroline Robbins, *The Eighteenth Century Commonwealthman* (New York: Atheneum, 1968); Bernard Bailyn, *The Ideological Origins of the American Revolution* (Cambridge: Belknap Press, 1967); G. L. Guttridge, *English Whiggism and the American Revolution* (Berkeley: University of California Press, 1963).

[27]Robbins, *Commonwealthman*, 320; Bailyn, *The Ideological Origins*, 51; H. T. Dickinson, *Liberty and Property: Political Ideology in Eighteenth-Century Britain* (New York: Holmes and Meier, 1977), is more optimistic about the influence of ideas (206), but J. G. A. Pocock says that Whig ideas were "taken infinitely more seriously" in America than in England, cited in Patricia U. Bonomi, ed., *Party and Political Opposition in Revolutionary America* (Terrytown NY: Sleepy Hollow Press, 1980) 7.

a comparative standpoint. In a single document political opinion is connected to overt political behavior. The conspiratorial interpretation of the reign of George III has long been discounted, and the origins of the "Bute myth" can rightly be traced to the creative imagination of Opposition leaders. But belief in the myth cannot be dismissed, and the petitions concerning America provide new documentation for the discontent Burke believed he perceived in the nation. Ironically, there was even more discontent than Burke knew, though the Rockingham Whigs proved incapable of marshaling it. The petitions have implications for the alleged continuity in Whig party politics and the purported alliance with Nonconformity in the constituencies. They may also offer a new empirical grounding for the emergence of Whig historiography.

This study seeks to reassess the scholarly consensus by setting forth the number of petitions, examining their origins, and analyzing their content. A study of popular politics and public opinion in the widest sense of the word would embrace such phenomena as the new political clubs and societies, riots and popular disturbances, and radical ideology, but these topics will be mentioned only as they bear directly on petitions. Since only a small number of the available documents can be examined in detail, this book is necessarily an introduction. The chronological dimensions are set, on the one hand, by the beginning of petitioning activity in early 1775 and, on the other, by the already well-documented Association movement of 1779-1780 (although some attention will be given to the periods immediately preceding and following these dates). It cannot be concluded that peace was more popular than coercion, but it can be demonstrated that in many provincial settings people were seriously divided concerning the American crisis. Attention will be given to those places that sent both petitions for peace and addresses for coercion. The primary evidence for the political division is found in the petitions themselves, but it must also be determined whether these were the products of closed, corporate bodies, or whether they emerged from the population at large, and this will entail an examination of the provincial press and local histories.

The petitioning activity fell short of a movement because there was little centralized leadership; no significant organizational structure either preceded or followed the agitation. The rapid succession of petitions in 1775 was more intense than the movement concerning the Middlesex election affair. The emergence of petitions was thus a matter of popular agitation, and the energy of this agitation quickly dissipated through the neglect of the Opposition and the rapidly worsening political atmosphere. The petitions to the Crown were put forth in a political setting in which the king and Parliament had already declared the colonists in a state of rebellion. In such an environment, popular expressions of opposition had little hope of a receptive hearing, and they faced a good chance of being considered treasonous.

These documents, therefore, represent an outspoken variety of popular political opposition. The people had previously petitioned Parliament concerning colonial policy, but never before had they presumed to instruct a prince in matters of peace and war. The petitions to the Crown in 1775 thus represent the first modern example of a widespread popular protest against war. In this regard, the agitation over America was far more radical then the petitions to the Crown over the Middlesex election affair. The documents are also at variance with the dominant view of a passive and corrupt electorate. They depict a political nation in touch with issues of national importance, that, at considerable risk to itself, was willing to express its concerns. Further, since the agitation for peace involved thousands of freeholders from the counties and numerous petitioners from small towns, the opposition to the government was more widespread than the urban radical movement. While it can be shown that the agitation for peace was related to the emergence of nascent urban radicalism, it cannot be confined to the urban setting.

Traditional accounts of eighteenth-century English politics have isolated local politics too neatly from national issues.[28] Popular political activity is by definition local political activity, but to restrict agitation over America to the local context results in serious distortions. The controversy over the use of coercive measures brings an important fact to light: many people believed there was a fundamental unity between local political structures and national ones. Town corporations saw their security in the security of the great national corporation at Westminster, and local-interest groups that were excluded from power readily identified with the sufferings of their fellow citizens across the sea. The national crisis regarding America invested local concerns with a new, more universal scope; it raised local issues onto a higher, ideological plane. The clarity with which people in the provinces grasped the constitutional issues meant that the American conflict could not for them be reduced to merely a local matter of patronage or trade. It is true, that in any given setting, only a minority of people were concerned with political and constitutional matters, but these minorities are worth studying. Local issues, however, were important to everyone, and they can be distinguished in the language of the petitions themselves.

In 1775 two flurries of petitioning activity are discernible, one in the early months of the year to Parliament, and the other in the fall to the king, concluding in late December with the passage of the American Prohibitory Bill. Certain features, such as the way meetings were organized, connect the two periods of activity, but in other respects they must be carefully distinguished from one another. The first period has received the most attention to date, and it is generally thought that this was the last episode of popular agitation in favor of conciliatory measures.[29] The debate in Parliament over these documents led

---

[28]In Sir Lewis Namier and John Brooke, *The House of Commons, 1754-1790*, there is a sustained attempt to categorize issues as merely local in scope. A more balanced approach is taken by Brewer, *Party Ideology*, 164-65, and by Thomas R. Knox, "Popular Politics and Provincial Radicalism: Newcastle Upon Tyne, 1769-1785," *Albion* 11 (Fall 1979): 226, 238.

[29]Clark, *British Opinion*, 92, 98-99, Donoughue, *British Politics*, 156.

to the first clear separation of the issue of parliamentary supremacy from that of commercial policy. The entire subsequent conflict over petitions flows naturally from this turning point. The shift of petitioning activity away from Parliament to the Crown and the emergence of royal policy on petitions are consequences of Parliament's decision, and both developments are laden with constitutional implications.

The chronology of events sets the constitutional issue in its proper framework. The petitions to Parliament against the Coercive Acts were presented in the last week of January 1775. In response to these appeals, Parliament isolated the question of trade from the constitutional issue of political authority. Parliament's refusal to hear any petitions concerning trade was grounded in its determination to narrow the conflict to the single question of colonial submission. On 7 February Parliament declared the colonists in a state of rebellion, and this action resulted in a major change in the orientation of popular appeals. From March onward, petitions were sent to the Crown, not Parliament, but these early appeals were few in number and without effect. The king could not respond favorably to the petitions without coming into direct conflict with Parliament; accordingly, he refused to consider them at all. On 29 May news of the skirmishes at Lexington and Concord reached England, but it was not until 23 August that the king's proclamation of colonial rebellion was published throughout the land. Only then was it clear to the nation that the government might pursue its measures by force, and the proclamation stimulated numerous addresses in support of arms. These popular expressions prompted an equally strong popular reaction in favor of peace. Rumors of colonial advances into Canada reached England in November, the same month that the majority of these documents reached the throne. The petitions for peace thus arose when the conflict was well advanced and when all branches of government alike had declared the colonists in a state of rebellion.

No study of the constitutional issue of petitioning Parliament or the Crown exists. Yet on 11 February 1775, eighteen Opposition Lords protested that Parliament itself was acting unconstitutionally in refusing to hear petitions concerning America.[30] The Opposition then turned to the king, and the change in the petitioners' appeal from Parliament to the Crown goes to the heart of the issue. Since the Revolution of 1689 had established the supremacy of Parliament, petitioning the Crown against an act of Parliament raised the old specter of the king's suspending the law. The English petitioning agitation thus provides a new context in which to interpret colonial petitions to the Crown, and

---

[30]Constitutional historians have been unaware of the petitions concerning America. Cecil E. Emden, *The People and the Constitution, Being a History of the Development of the People's Influence in British Government*, 2d ed. (Oxford: Clarendon Press, 1956) 77; Sir David L. Keir, *The Constitutional History of Modern Britain since 1485*, 9th ed. (London: Adam and Charles Black, 1969) 397; E. Neville Williams, *The Eighteenth-Century Constitution, 1688-1815; Documents and Commentary* (Cambridge: Cambridge University Press, 1970) 408-409.

the emergence of royal policy toward English petitions explains much about the failure of the Olive Branch petition. Since these constitutional implications are reflected in the petitions themselves, an appendix is included with texts of selected English petitions to the Crown.

The petitions in the fall of 1775 were concerned primarily with the constitutional issue of authority, but they also bear upon the question of trade. It is widely supposed that English manufacturing centers with outlets on the continent of Europe were less opposed to the war than merchants in London and Bristol, who were more dependent on the American trade. However, the large petitions for peace from Lancashire and the West Riding of Yorkshire require that the trading thesis be highly modified or rejected. Many English pro-Americans were undoubtedly concerned with trade, but in an age of democratic revolution, commercial concerns were interpreted in a way that connected the freedom of trade with the rights of the individual. Some merchants felt that this connection was jeopardized and gave their support to petitions for peace. Others, in London, Bristol, and elsewhere, emphasized that respect for law was a necessary part of commercial enterprise, and since law was threatened, they took the side of the king and Parliament. Since the merchants themselves were divided, the polarization of English society cannot be explained on the basis of commercial matters alone.

The ideological context of the petitions must also be considered. Previous studies of English public opinion at the time of the American crisis have, with two notable exceptions, scarcely mentioned the provincial press, thereby confining public opinion largely to the opinion of the metropolis.[31] Generally, the press was not alert to the number of places that sent petitions, but many provincial newspapers recorded evidence of local differences concerning America. We learn, for example, that popular opinion in many of the leading cities that sent only addresses for coercion was also divided: there was pro-American sentiment in York, Liverpool, Manchester, Lancaster, and Gloucester. Newspapers illumine the local circumstances out of which the petitions arose, and they tell us much about the intellectual climate of the period. The pamphlets and broadsides listed in Thomas R. Adams's recent bibliographic survey of the American controversy in England adumbrate the wider intellectual context for this book. The vast literature published in opposition to government, the anti-government rhetoric in the provincial press, and the petitions that emerged in favor of peace are the principal grounds for arguing that the nation was divided over the use of force to secure colonial submission.

This study will also provide a taxonomy of popular protest by a comparative analysis of the petitions concerning the Stamp Act crisis, the Middlesex election affair, the American crisis of 1775, economic and parliamentary re-

---

[31]The exceptions are Money, *Experience and Identity*, and Brewer, *Party Ideology*, but Money's study is regional and Brewer's extends only to 1770. Hinkhouse, *The Preliminaries*, and Lutnick, *The American Revolution*, concentrate on the London press.

form, and the reaction to the Coalition in 1784. When ordered according to geographical region, the petitions from these six periods of agitation reveal that some areas were more prone to popular agitation than others. The geographical area most dominated by patronage was in fact the very area most involved in popular opposition to government. Further, it is possible to identify a number of little-known progovernment addresses from the Middlesex election affair. These documents of 1769 prepared the ground for the progovernment American addresses of 1775, and some of the strongest lines of continuity between the various periods of agitation turn out to be not radical but conservative, thereby lending further support to Whig fears of a rising authoritarianism.

It is one thing, however, to determine the number of petitions and analyze the local circumstances surrounding their origins; it is quite another matter to discover their political significance. Scholars have raised serious doubts concerning the value of signed petitions as indicators of public opinion, and there is thus a great need to test their validity as expressions of genuine public opinion. This is a controlling concern for the entire study, but the concluding chapters will give particular attention to it. A comparison of the addresses and petitions with subscriptions requesting financial relief for wounded soldiers and widows of those who fell in battle "while defending the constitutional rights of Great Britain" demonstrates consistency of behavior and gives added support to the serious intent of the petitioners. A comparison of the signatures in these documents with the names of voters in parliamentary elections indicates a high degree of correspondence between voting and petitioning.

Finally, the people who signed the petitions will be examined in the local setting. Studies of the press seldom deal with local political structures, and they tend to place ideology above local interests. Town corporations and Dissenting chapels are two examples of powerful interest groups whose influence cannot be ignored. Any attempt to answer the question of motivation must come finally to an analysis of the social, religious, and ideological status of individual petitioners. Petitioners and addressers in five medium and smaller boroughs will be identified in relation to local government officeholding, occupational status, and religious affiliation. Recent research points to a connection between conservative interest groups and the loyal addresses. In addition, fresh attention to the middling ranks of society and religious Dissent has suggested that socioeconomic rank and religion were important in stimulating progressive political behavior.[32] An analysis of individual petitioners in the local setting confirms and extends these findings, but no single explanation of motivation is forthcoming. In the American crisis, political behavior was re-

---

[32]Langford, "Old Whigs, Old Tories," 155-56; John Brewer, "Commercialization and Politics," in Neil McKendrick, John Brewer, and J. H. Plumb, *The Birth of a Consumer Society* (London: Europa Publications, 1982) 197-262; and Phillips, *Electoral Behavior*, 286-305.

lated to a complex interaction between wealth, ideology, religious affiliation, and local structures of authority and status.

Through documents of popular protest, this study will show that English politics in the age of the American Revolution were eminently engaging, not only to the king and ministry, not only to Parliament and the politicians, but also to the English people. By the use of quantitative data, it attempts to demonstrate in detail what a minority of social historians have already concluded about the vitality of English public opinion in this period.[33] The petitions to Parliament, the events leading up to the royal proclamation of colonial rebellion in August, and the subsequent petitions to the Crown suggest that the English people were politically informed, constitutionally astute, and deeply concerned about the authority of the British government on the one hand, and the rights of their American brethren on the other.

---

[33]Herbert Butterfield, *George III, Lord North and the People, 1779-80* (London: Bell, 1949) 9; Plumb, "British Attitudes," 73; Brewer, *Party Ideology*, 174; and Phillips, "Popular Politics," 603.

Petitions to Parliament and the "Committee of Oblivion"

Chapter I

Petitions were the time-honored means of introducing bills to Parliament.[1] A petition was designed to set forth the reasons for applying to Parliament; it was signed by the interested parties and presented to the House of Commons by one of its members. Following its reading, the petition was commonly sent to a committee along with a bill. Witnesses for or against the petition were heard, and the bill's ensuing progress followed clearly established channels through both Houses of Parliament. In addition to introducing legislation, petitions were also received against existing legislation, and in this case as well, committee action and the hearing of witnesses preceded all decisions.[2] When advising his Bristol constituents about what might be done concerning the administration's coercive policy in America, Edmund Burke penned a lucid account of the nature and value of petitions. Petitions were, said Burke, "the only peaceable and constitutional mode of commencing any procedure for the redress of public grievances. The presenting of a Petition was like bringing an Action; the beginning only, not the whole of the suit." He advised that "if they could not prevail on themselves to follow up their Petition by a regular solicitation, pursued through all the modes of civil resistance, and legal opposition, that they should not present it at all."[3] The wisdom of this advice, and the difficulty in practice of following it, are clearly illustrated by the merchants' petitions to Parliament.

The petitions to Parliament over the Coercive Acts are well known to students of English public opinion, but much uncertainty continues to surround this popular activity. Scholars are unclear about the number of petitions; the

---

[1]Shelia Lambert, *Bills and Acts: Legislative Procedure in Eighteenth-Century England* (Cambridge: Cambridge University Press, 1971) 52, 82, 87-105; and P. D. G. Thomas, *The House of Commons in the Eighteenth Century* (Oxford: Clarendon Press, 1971) 17-19; 57-60. Peter Fraser, "Public Petitioning and Parliament before 1832," *History* 46 (October 1961): 200-202. There were other means, such as a simple motion, or a report from a committee, but for private bills a petition was required.

[2]Thomas, *The House of Commons*, 17.

[3]*Burke Correspondence*, 3:208-209 (Burke to Rockingham, 14 September 1775).

petitions in favor of coercion are commonly believed to be as numerous as those that pled for conciliation.[4] In fact, fifteen of the seventeen places that petitioned urged peace. Further, this sentiment for peace is believed to have been motivated solely by concerns of trade with the result that the constitutional dimensions of the movement are neglected.[5] Whether or not the merchants supported conciliation is, in this view, dependent upon their principal place of trade; London and Bristol were tied to the older channels of commerce in the colonies and petitioned against coercion, while Manchester, Lancaster, and Liverpool had markets on the Continent and sent addresses in favor of force.[6] The merchants of London and Bristol, however, were thoroughly divided, and in early 1775, Manchester and Liverpool petitioned for conciliation rather than coercion. The number of petitions, their origins, and their ideological content therefore require renewed attention. The documents must be placed in the context of parliamentary procedure concerning petitions, examined in relation to divisions over America in the local setting, and viewed within a time frame that extends well into 1776 and links these expressions of public opinion with the petitions to the Crown.

I

In 1773 tensions between England and the colonies continued to mount as issues became revolutionary in Massachusetts. Boston's open defiance of British authority over the duty on tea led in the early months of 1774 to Parliament's passing a series of retaliatory measures designed to force the offenders to make compensation. The port of Boston was closed and legislation that restructured the government of Massachusetts followed almost immediately. Both of these bills were thoroughly debated in Parliament, but there was little effective opposition to them, and further legislation that protected English officers in America and allowed troops to be quartered in places that lacked barracks passed in April and May with equally impressive majorities. The Quebec Act received royal assent on 22 June. This sensible attempt to provide good government for the Northwest seemed to many Americans to be the copestone of a detailed plan of enslavement. Regardless of their intent, taken together, these laws demonstrated that both Houses of Parliament were determined to enforce

---

[4]Ian Christie and Benjamin Labaree, *Empire or Independence* (Oxford: Phaidon, 1976) 232; John Money, *Experience and Identity, Birmingham and the West Midlands, 1760-1800* (Manchester: Manchester University Press, 1977) 187.

[5]Dora Mae Clark, *British Opinion and the American Revolution* (New Haven: Yale University Press, 1930) 132-34. Clark also misses the conciliatory petitions from Wolverhampton and Huddersfield (83-84).

[6]Dorothy Marshall, *Eighteenth Century England*, 2d ed. (Thetford, Norfolk: Longman, 1962) 428; Peter T. Underdown, "The Parliamentary History of the City of Bristol, 1750-1790" (M.A. thesis, University of Bristol, 1948) 266; Christie and Labaree, *Empire or Independence*, 216.

colonial submission to English authority. The condition for reconciliation was submission to parliamentary supremacy.[7]

The "intolerable" acts of the English Parliament were the principal stimulus behind the calling of the first Continental Congress. It met in September and made plans for nonimportation, nonexportation, and nonconsumptive measures against the mother country. At the same time, a declaration of grievances to the English people was agreed upon, along with a petition to the Crown that protested the Coercive Acts. In the past, when the colonies sought redress of grievance, they had sent petitions to the king, though several individual colonies directed their appeals to the House of Commons. By 1774 the colonial radicals had given up hope of accomplishing anything through petitions, but the moderates held tenaciously to the value of petitioning. A recent detailed account of American attitudes toward their sovereign as protector and father has greatly illuminated the colonists' persistence in petitioning the king.[8] Accordingly, in the fall of 1774 and again in the spring of 1775, Congress agreed to further appeals to the king. The last appeal, the so-called Olive Branch Petition, arrived in England after the question of the handling of petitions had been thoroughly debated and its rejection cannot be understood apart from that debate. In England those who were sympathetic to the colonists would also eventually turn to the Crown, but in the early months of 1775, English merchants who sought a change in government policy made their first appeals to the House of Commons.

By January 1775 nearly a year had elapsed since the first Coercive Act had been passed, and some merchants had begun to perceive a decline in trade. Faced with the increasing threat of colonial trade restraints, the newly assembled Parliament attempted to balance sound commercial policy with legislative authority. At this date virtually everyone agreed on the desirability of reconciliation. The issue at stake was determining the best means to be used in achieving it, and coercion was viewed as one such means. The cabinet debated the question thoroughly; leaders remained at loggerheads over whether

---

[7]L. H. Gipson, *The Coming of the Revolution, 1763-1775* (New York: Harper and Row, 1954) 223-27; and Charles Ritcheson, *British Politics and the American Revolution* (Norman OK: University of Oklahoma Press, 1954) 158-65, and 165-68 for the distinction between the Coercive Acts and the Quebec Act.

[8]Jerrilyn Marston, "King and Congress: The Transfer of Political Legitimacy from the King to the Continental Congress, 1774-1776" (Ph.D. dissertation, Boston University, 1975) 29-42, 208, 232-34; Ritcheson, *British Politics*, 176-77. In addition to Congress, New York, New Jersey, and Georgia also petitioned. The House of Assembly in New York agreed to a "Representation and Remonstrance" to the House of Commons, but at the same time it agreed to a petition to the king and a memorial to the House of Lords (27 January 1775). *York Cour.* (7 March 1775). However, the petition from the inhabitants of Georgia to the king arrived even after the Olive Branch Petition. It was dated 14 July 1775 and presented to the king in late October. *Lond. Chron.* (28-31 October, 28-30 December 1775); *Gen. Eve. Post* (28-30 December 1775).

concessions could be granted while maintaining parliamentary supremacy.[9] The same debate was carried on in Parliament, and, at the popular level, the newspapers articulated opposing arguments. Serious divisions were thus found at all political levels. Every major spokesman in this period came forward with a plan for conciliation: Chatham on 1 February, North on 20 February, and Burke on 22 March. The Opposition, however, charged that the administration was not to be trusted, for at the same time that North was pursuing his Conciliatory Proposition, he won strong support from Parliament for an official recognition that the colonies were in a state of rebellion (7 February), and he pursued the policy of restraining colonial trade with vigor.[10] As the first session of Parliament convened, some statesmen still believed in the possibility of reconciliation without repeal of the Coercive Acts. Months would pass before the colonists finally declined to proceed with negotiations unless the acts were repealed. This development, combined with the Commons' refusal to consider their petitions, marked the end of the first agitation for peace, long before news reached England on 29 May of the battles at Lexington and Concord.

II

The agitation to petition Parliament began in the first week of January at a meeting of some 300 to 400 London merchants at the King's Arms Tavern, Cornhill. At the meeting of 4 January a committee was formed for the purpose of drafting a petition; letters were read from merchants in Bristol, Liverpool, Manchester, and Leeds expressing their desire to act in concert with the London merchants.[11] This meeting in turn stimulated interest in petitioning at Birmingham, Dudley, and Wolverhampton.[12] In the second week of January the merchants of Bristol and the Society of Merchant Venturers agreed to petitions. On 11 January the Birmingham merchants resolved to wait until they knew what the London merchants would do, and on 18 January they met at the Dolphin Inn and agreed to a petition.[13] By the third week in January, petitions were circulating in Norwich, Manchester, and Leeds, and by the fourth

---

[9]On divisions in the ministry itself, see Ritcheson, *British Politics*, 198-200, 203-205.

[10]Ibid., 183-89. The uncertainty about North is explicable: he worked for conciliation with William Eden in the fall of 1775 (201).

[11]For London see the accounts in *Lond. Eve.-Post* (31 December-1 January, 3-5, 10-12, 12-14 January 1775); *Mid. J.* (3-6, 7-10, 12-14 January 1775). The London traders to the West Indies were also actively debating what to do. *Mid. J.* (5-7, 7-10, 19-21 January 1775).

[12]Money, *Experience and Identity*, 199.

[13]*Brist. J.* (14 January 1775); *North. Merc.* (16, 23 January 1775); for Birmingham see B. D. Bargar, "Matthew Boulton and the Birmingham Petition of 1775," *William and Mary Quarterly*, 3rd ser., 13 (January 1956): 30; *Worc. J.* (19 January 1775); *Parl. Hist.*, 18:196.

week of the month, the principal hosiers at Nottingham had met at the Feathers Inn and adopted a petition "in favour of the Americans."[14]

The newspaper accounts of these events suggest that the activity in the boroughs and towns was only loosely coordinated with that in London, though a few of the leaders seem to have maintained connections between boroughs. Samuel Elam of Leeds was in close touch with the leaders in London and was also active in the meeting in Leeds. Thomas Wooldridge, prominent in London and in Staffordshire in the fall of 1775, may have been a liaison between London and his county in January. Connections between London and a number of other provincial towns have been drawn, but they remain loose—perhaps nothing more than the impact of the London papers.[15] There are no extant records from the committee that was apppointed by the London merchants; their organization never approximated the centralization of the movement organized to repeal the Stamp Act. In some cases, such as Nottingham and Whitehaven, the newspaper accounts imply that interest in petitioning Parliament arose spontaneously, and, in the case of Nottingham, it was not until later that the petitioners combined efforts with the Rockingham Whigs.[16] The activity of the first three months of the year is summarized in Table 1.[17]

---

[14]*Nott. New. J.* (28 January, 4 February 1775); *Leeds Merc.* (24, 31 January 1775).

[15]Money, *Experience and Identity*, 199. *North. Merc.* (15 February 1775); *York Cour.* (10, 31 January, 7 February 1775), for example, provided detailed accounts of petitioning activity.

[16]See *Burke Correspondence*, 3:21 (Burke to Mark Huish, 22 February 1775).

[17]Derived from *CJ*, 35:71, 73, 144, 151, 77, 80-81, 123, 86, 139, 164, 198, 82, 78, 89, 90, 108, 186, 141, 186, 124. The Huddersfield conciliatory petition is listed as the petition from Wakefield, Halifax, Bradford, and Huddersfield; it is almost identical to the Leeds conciliatory (124). The following conciliatory petitions to Parliament in early 1775 are not included in the table because they derive from smaller special interest groups and hence do not represent places, or are non-English: the Quakers (163-64; 28 March); Planters of his Majesty's Sugar Colonies (91-92; 2 February); Glasgow (74; 24 January); Belfast (139; 22 February); Waterford (Ireland) (171; 3 March). The Newcastle and Staffordshire petitions might be included in the category of small interest groups along with those from Nottingham, since the former are from shoemakers and manufacturers of felt hats and earthenware, and the latter from hosiers, but division here reached deeper into the populace than merely these groups, as is seen by the petitions from the same places in the fall. For the petitions from the Quakers see Arthur J. Mekeel, *The Relation of the Quakers to the American Revolution* (Washington: University Press of America, 1979) 21-22. Atherstone in Warwickshire also petitioned, but the petition is not recorded in *CJ*, and Whitney in Oxfordshire did not petition but expressed hopes for "amicable and conciliatory measures." *Worc. J.* (2 February 1775); *Leeds Merc.* (10 January 1775); *Mid. J.* (3-6 January 1775).

There were also petitions to Parliament concerning trade in the fall from the following places: Poole, Dartmouth, and Devonshire (2 November); Merchants trading to the West Indies (3 November); Westbury, Warminster, Trowbridge (16 November); Chester (22 November); London (23 November); Liverpool, Lancaster (5 December);

TABLE 1

PETITIONS TO PARLIAMENT CONCERNING AMERICA, JANUARY-MARCH 1775		
Boroughs/Towns/County Sending Conciliatory Petitions		
BOROUGH/TOWN*	SOURCE	DATE
London	Merchants, Traders Merchants, Traders	23 Jan. 23 Feb.
Bristol	Merchant Venturers Merchants, Traders	23 Jan. 23 Jan.
Norwich	Merchants, Manufacts.	25 Jan.
Dudley	Merchants, Manufacts.	25 Jan.
Liverpool	Merchants, Tradesmen	26 Jan.
Manchester	Merchants, Manufacts.	26 Jan.
Wolverhampton	Traders, Manufacts.	26 Jan.
Newcastle (Staffs.)	Manufacturers	31 Jan.
Staffordshire	Manufacturers	31 Jan.
Bridport	Principal Manufacts.	15 Feb.
Whitehaven	Merchants	22 Feb.
Boroughs/Towns Sending Coercive Petitions		
Poole	Merchants, Traders	28 Feb.
Trowbridge	Merchants	1 Feb.

Boroughs/Towns Dividing Over Conciliatory or Coercive Measures				
BOROUGH/ TOWN	SOURCE OF CONCILIATORY PETITION	DATE	SOURCE OF COERCIVE PETITION	DATE
Birmingham	Merchants, Factors	27 Jan.	Inhabitants	25 Jan.
Leeds	Merchants	1 Feb.	Mayor, Recorder	1 Feb.
Nottingham	Hosiers Hosiers	8 Feb. 9 Mar.	Aldermen, Sheriff ------------------------	22 Feb. --------
Huddersfield	Gentlemen, Merchants	9 Mar.	Merchants, Manufacturers	15 Feb.

*London, Bristol, Norwich, Liverpool, Nottingham and Bridport were parliamentary boroughs, the remainder were non-parliamentary towns. See *CJ*, 35:71-73, 144, 151, 77, 80-81, 123, 139, 164, 198, 82, 78, 89, 90, 108, 186, 141, 186, 124.

The Rockingham Whigs had been active in support of petitions over the Middlesex election affair, and in early 1775 Burke was, once again, the party's leading proponent of popular resistance.[18] As Member of Parliament for Bristol, Burke was vitally involved in the petitioning activity there; he provided the "heads" of the merchants' petition to Parliament and also had a hand in drafting the petition from the Merchant Venturers. His Bristol confidant, Richard Champion, kept him informed of local developments, and later in February, Burke was in close contact with Mark Huish, one of the promoters of the Nottingham petition.[19] He also may have had some contact with Samuel Elam, a leader of the merchants submitting the Leeds conciliatory petition, but it cannot be shown conclusively that Burke was the first mover in any of the petitions to Parliament except the Bristol petition.[20]

If the Opposition was behind a number of petitions for conciliation, the administration was involved in supporting several loyal petitions in favor of the Coercive Acts. Those taking the lead in Warwickshire, for example, worked in close cooperation with the administration, so much so that the wording of the loyal address from Birmingham was suggested by Lord Dartmouth.[21] A number of efforts were also made to oppose the conciliatory petitions,[22] but these endeavors met with little success, as the Opposition gained a clear majority of petitions to Parliament. Lord North watched the progress of popular opposition carefully and duly reported developments to George III.[23]

Planters of his Majesty's Sugar Colonies (7 December); Society of Merchant Venturers of Bristol (9 February 1776). See *CJ*, 35:417, 419, 447, 455, 458, 474, 476, 479, 539. These petitions plead specifically for permission to export goods and do not address the issue of the Coercive Acts directly. The two exceptions to this are the petition to Parliament from the city of London presented 27 October 1775 (*CJ*, 35:405) and the petition from Westbury, which will be treated in Chapter 3.

[18]Rudé, *Wilkes and Liberty* (Oxford: Oxford University Press, 1962) 107. At first, Burke was discouraged by the merchants' lack of interest in petitioning. *Burke Correspondence*, 3:95, 98 (Burke to Champion, 10 January 1775; Burke to Rockingham, 12 January 1775). Later, he worked hard to stimulate the movement. Richard Champion wrote concerning the petitions in January to Willing, Morris, & Co., "Mr. Burke's friends in particular have forwarded this Business . . . " G. H. Guttridge, ed., *The American Correspondence of a Bristol Merchant, 1766-1776: Letters of Richard Champion* (Berkeley: University of California Press, 1934) 40.

[19]*Burke Correspondence*, 3:96; 202, 121, 129, 131 (Richard Champion to Burke, 10 January 1775; Burke to Champion, 12, 20 January 1775; Burke to Mark Huish, 22 February, 9 March 1775; Burke to Champion, 9 March 1775).

[20]*Burke Correspondence*, 3:193 (Burke to Rockingham, 23 August 1775); see also 216, and Ritcheson, *British Politics*, 181.

[21]Money, *Experience and Identity*, 197, 202 n. 52. Bargar, "Matthew Boulton," 30-32.

[22]HMC, *Dartmouth Manuscripts*, 3 vols. (London: Her Majesty's Stationery Office, 1887-1896) 2:257-59, 263.

[23]Fortescue, 3:303, undated letter to George III.

The first petitions from London and Bristol were presented to the House of Commons on 23 January. The way they were handled sparked heated debate.[24] The London merchants hoped to have their petition referred to a committee of the whole House in order that it might be considered along with other papers pertaining to America. But with a large majority behind him, Lord North was able to isolate this and successive petitions in a committee that would handle the question of distressed trade separately from the crisis in America. Burke attacked this action as a tactic designed to avoid hearing evidence in favor of conciliation, and he aptly styled this committee the "committee of oblivion," since it would consign "everything the merchants could allege to entire oblivion."[25] Upon the presentation of each new petition, the Opposition dutifully recorded its disapproval of such tactics but was powerless to do more. The Commons' handling of the petitions was considered unfair by the Opposition, though it was consitutional.[26] Edward Gibbon explained the ploy to Holroyd in the following terms: "By the aid of some parliamentary quirks, they have been all referred to a separate inactive committee . . . and are now considered as dead in law."[27] As a result, Parliament never treated the petitions seriously as an expression of mercantile concern related to America.

The administration's political intention in refusing to hear the merchants' case for relaxing coercive measures was first made explicit by Lord Clare, former member of Parliament for Bristol. The issue of "the supremacy of parliament" must, said Lord Clare, be separated from the issues set forth in the "present petition." Lord North agreed; the London merchants' petition "could not, with the least colour of propriety, be considered with the [American] papers; one being simply an object of commerce, the other clearly a matter of policy."[28] The Commons was largely supportive of North's interpretation of the nature of the conflict as essentially political; the amendment that placed the petition in a separate committee was carried by a majority of 197 to 81. Nevertheless, debate in the ensuing week continued to center around the status of the merchants' petitions and how Parliament should handle them.[29]

Having already rejected five petitions from England, on 25 January the House refused to receive the petition from the American Congress.[30] Parlia-

---

[24]*CJ*, 35:80. *Parl. Hist.*, 18:172-73, 181. For the procedure on petitions from merchants, see Lambert, *Bills and Acts*, 71, 74, 85.

[25]*Parl. Hist.*, 18:173.

[26]Thomas, *The House of Commons*, 19, 59.

[27]J. E. Norton, ed., *The Letters of Edward Gibbon*, 3 vols. (London: Macmillan Co., 1956) 2:58 (Gibbon to J. B. Holroyd, 31 January 1775).

[28]*Parl. Hist.*, 18:174-75.

[29]See the debates on 23 January, *Parl. Hist.*, 18:168-81; 25 January, 181-82; 26 January, 184-94; 27 January, 194-95; and 31 January, 195-98.

[30]The petition from Congress went first to the king and was then sent to Parliament. Similarly the "Representation and Remonstrance" from New York to the House of Commons was rejected on 15 May since it "tended to call into question the unlimited rights of parliament." *Parl. Hist.*, 18:644.

ment's intransigence on every front provoked the London merchants to draw up a remonstrance stating that they in no wise wished their petition to be referred to a separate committee.[31] They pled that they or their agents might be heard before any further resolution on America was made and claimed that the petitioners had a "juridical right" to be heard.[32] Burke specifically addressed the separation of government policy from commercial matters. The reason given for refusing to send the petitions to the committee on the American papers "was of a most extraordinary and unheard of nature; it was, that the resolutions of that committee were to be solely on the grounds of policy, and that the commercial examination would delay the measures necessary for the coercion of America. This was to anticipate and predetermine the future proceedings in a committee, as a reason for keeping information from it."[33] Burke's logic, however, was unavailing.

The Commons' refusal to hear the petitions concerning trade narrowed the debate to the single issue of subordination to Parliament. The merchants' petitions to Parliament had thereby led the administration to the first explicit avowal that the conflict with the colonies was over parliamentary supremacy. This was a pivotal development for several reasons. First, as long as the crisis could be discussed in terms of commercial policy and schemes of taxation there was room for negotiation with the colonies. When the conflict was publicly reduced to the single issue of Parliament's supremacy, from that point forward there remained no possibility for compromise. Second, that North insisted on this approach, and that the lower House supported it, meant that in the future the king could comfortably find refuge in the opinion of his Parliament. Parliament's handling of petitions in early 1775 was a clear harbinger of how the king would treat the petitions in the summer and fall. Third, petitions from America were, at this juncture, irrevocably tied to English petitions, and they were doomed to the same fate. Finally, from the popular side, the politically literate public was well aware of the change to an insistence upon the political nature of the conflict. Newspaper editorials noted the "very remarkable" alteration in the administration's focus, and later petitions from the people would, as a result, come to center precisely on the question of political authority rather than that of trade.[34] By its own decision, however, Parliament had already guaranteed that it could not respond favorably to a public that differed from itself on the question of parliamentary authority.

The administration revealed the next step in its strategy on 2 February. In a speech lasting two hours, Lord North promised the House that the admin-

---

[31]To withdraw their petition was felt would be instrumental in "discouraging our manufacturing towns" from sending up further petitions to Parliament. *Mid. J.* (24-26 January 1775).

[32]*Parl. Hist.*, 18:184-86.

[33]Ibid., 18:189.

[34]*Brist. J.* (28 January 1775); *Leeds Merc.* (31 January 1775).

istration wished to adopt conciliatory measures, but that this was contingent upon colonial recognition of the supreme legislative authority of Parliament. New England, he urged, was "in an actual state of rebellion." Because of the rebellion, the House should present a humble address to the king pleading for him to "take the most effective measures to enforce due obedience to the laws and authority of the supreme legislature" and pledging their "lives and properties" to "stand by his Majesty, against all rebellious attempts, in the maintenance of the just rights of his Majesty and the two Houses of Parliament." The debate that followed centered around whether or not the colonies were in an actual state of rebellion. Burke, being "much indisposed," spoke only briefly, but he called the present moment "the true crisis of Britain's fate." The solicitor general reiterated the point that commerce was no longer the issue, but rebellion—and rebellion must be resisted. The vote in favor of the address was carried by a large majority, and the Commons thereby declared its agreement with the administration concerning the political nature of the conflict. This address from the lower House was to be the prototype for the addresses to the Crown in the fall.[35]

The action by the House of Commons led the London merchants to turn immediately to the House of Lords. The merchants met on 6 February; a petition was put forth, approved, signed, and left at the King's Arms Tavern until noon the next day. At this meeting William Baker said that the Americans "were contending only for their just rights and undeniable privileges," and it was agreed that petitioning the Lords was the "only alternative" before them.[36] The next day, the merchants and planters trading to the West Indies also agreed on a petition to the House of Lords. Since the Lords would debate the propriety of joining the Commons in its address to the Crown on the same day, the planters felt that no time should be lost in presenting a petition to the Lords. As Sir Philip Gibbes said, "it would be indecent to petition after any resolution against it had been taken."[37] Lord Rockingham presented both merchants' petitions that evening; he pled that they be heard before "any resolutions may be taken . . . respecting America" and hoped the petitioners would be able to lay their information before the House. The debate was long and heated, covering many of the same points raised previously in the Commons, but the Lords approved of the address to the Crown by a large majority, and the petitions were never heard.[38] Both Houses of Parliament had thereby rejected the petitions. The committee on petitions in the House of Commons made several reports in

[35]*Parl. Hist.*, 18:221-33. The propriety of the address was debated again on 6 February, and the issue of not hearing the merchants' petitions was brought up repeatedly in debate (223-64). The address was printed in the newspapers. *Mid. J.* (7-9 February 1775).

[36]*Lond. Eve.-Post* (4-7 February 1775); *Mid. J.* (4-7 February 1775); Clark, *British Opinion*, 86.

[37]*Lond. Eve.-Post* (7-9 February 1775); *Mid. J.* (7-9 February 1775).

[38]*Parl. Hist.*, 18:265-92.

late March, but these were futile, if not cynical, gestures. Following the joint address to the Crown, on 10 February the king promulgated a message for augmenting the armed forces, and this message was based explicitly on the address from both Houses of Parliament.

The action by the House of Lords led eighteen Opposition Lords to publish a protest. In the Opposition's view, the Lords' refusal to allow the merchants' petitions to be presented was "a proceeding of the most unwarrantable nature, and directly subversive of the most sacred rights of the subject." The Lords' rejection of the petitions was an "unconstitutional, indecent and improvident proceeding." A second protest attacked the address to the king as "an Address amounting to a declaration of war," which was "introduced by refusing to suffer the presentation of petitions against it (although it be the undoubted right of the subject to present the same)."[39] At the next two meetings of the London merchants the subject of debate was whether to proceed with a petition to the king. After considerable deliberation, the merchants decided to defer this ultimate action, and the topic was not raised again until the end of March.[40]

The rapidity with which events had transpired between 23 January and 10 February scarcely left the London merchants time to plan a coherent strategy, and it is little wonder that petitions from the provinces continued to be addressed to the House of Commons for some time to come. But in both Houses of Parliament the decision to enforce the Coercive Acts was settled by 7 February. However, the issue of how the petitions were handled continued to be the most useful point of departure for the Opposition's attacks on the administration. The Opposition at one point accused the administration of suppressing information concerning conciliatory petitions.[41] The constitutional implications of Parliament's refusal to consider the petitions were also thoroughly debated in the press.[42]

III

Since the number of signatures for most of these petitions was not recorded, their value as indicators of public opinion is difficult to assess. They certainly did not appear to pose a great threat to the government. A few shreds of information suggest that the petitions gathered hundreds of signatures, and this comports well with the movement in the fall. The meetings of the London merchants at the King's Arms Tavern normally involved 300 to 500 mer-

---

[39]Ibid., 18:292-96. On the increasing number of protests and their use to influence public opinion, see William C. Lowe, "The House of Lords, Party, and Public Opinion: Opposition Use of the Protest, 1760-1782," *Albion* 11 (Summer 1979): 151-53.

[40]*Lond. Eve.-Post* (7-9 February 1775); *Mid. J.* (9-11 February 1775). See ch. 2 on their petition to the king.

[41]*Parl. Hist.*, 18. See the Opposition's attack on 26, 31 January, 1, 8, 13, 28 February, 8, 13, 18, 20 March. See especially, 185-86, 189, 195-97.

[42]See, for example, the lengthy essays in *Lond. Eve.-Post* (4-7 February 1775) and *Mid. J.* (4-7 February 1775).

chants, and we know that the petition was signed by over 400 houses.[43] Similarly, the meeting of the West Indian merchants was attended by "upward of 200."[44] Matthew Boulton wrote to Dartmouth concerning the Birmingham coercive petition and noted that he "could have obtained several hundred more names to it, if I had persevered," implying that he had at least several hundred signatures.[45] Richard Champion claimed that the "Yorkshire petition"—apparently meaning those from Leeds and Huddersfield—"had many respectable Names."[46] This is confirmed by Samuel Elam. He published a letter in the London papers defending the Leeds conciliatory petition with a list of 80 master manufacturers of woolen cloth who signed their names, and an additional 273 noted, for a total of 353.[47] On the other hand, Champion admitted that the conciliatory petitions from Birmingham and Nottingham were "insignificant," and in the House of Commons, Edward Bacon claimed that only 48 genuine merchants signed the Norwich petition.[48]

The major preoccupation of each petition was, of course, the state of trade, but while praying generally for redress, the petitions seldom made specific recommendations to Parliament. Most of the petitions followed the lead of London; they listed the particular hardships under which they labored, then asked Parliament to "apply such healing Remedies as can alone restore and establish the Commerce between *Great Britain* and her Colonies on a permanent Foundation."[49] Many of the petitions were mildly worded, and they often left the form of relief completely up to Parliament. But previous treatments of this movement have overlooked an important point: no bill could go beyond the terms of the original petition, and since this rule was strictly enforced, the usual practice was to frame a petition in very general terms. At the first meeting of the London merchants, William Baker urged that "the prayer of that petition would be extremely guarded in pointing out the particulars of redress; as, in case of any one thing demanded or omitted, which may be afterwards found

---

[43]Thomas R. Adams, *The American Controversy: A Bibliographical Study of the British Pamphlets about the American Dispute, 1764-1783,* 2 vols. (Providence: Brown University Press, 1980) 1:305.

[44]*Lond. Eve.-Post* (3-5, 10-12, 19-21 January 1775); *Mid. J.* (5-7, 7-10, 19-21 January 1775).

[45]Cited in Bargar, "Matthew Boulton," 33.

[46]Guttridge, *American Correspondence,* 51 (Champion to Willing, Morris & Co., 13 March 1775).

[47]*Lond. Eve.-Post* (24-26 January 1775); the letter was answered by those who backed the coercive address, signed by 72 in the 2-4 February issue.

[48]Guttridge, *American Correspondence,* 51 (Champion to Willing, Morris & Co., 13 March 1775). *Nott. New. J.* (4 February 1775).

[49]*CJ,* 35:72.

necessary to add or expunge, the parliament may hold the petitioners to the direct letter, which perhaps would be insufficient to their general purpose."[50]

It should also be emphasized that the petitioners expected to be heard in Parliament, and the London merchants specifically left open the possibility of criticizing the Coercive Acts when their petition was read in the Commons. At the second meeting of the London merchants, some criticism was expressed because the Quebec Act was not mentioned. Those who drafted the petition responded that "there was left an open [i.e., opportunity] by the words 'the operation of all other acts' for the counsel at the Bar of the House to plead any inconveniences arising from the Quebec, or other acts; that the Boston Port and Massachusetts-Bay bills were omitted for the same purpose, yet were by no means precluded, (if the Committee should afterwards think proper to instruct their counsel so) from being remonstrated against, either in part, or in the whole."[51] This was the same tactic utilized by the merchants who had petitioned ten years previously over the Stamp Act.

The Bristol merchants' petition was a little more pointed than the London petition in its specific appeal to a return to the system that existed before the passage of the Coercive Acts. Nottingham hosiers gently reminded Parliament of their trust that "the faithful Depositories of the People's Welfare will find some temperate and honourable Means of conciliating the Differences of the *British* Empire." Whitehaven also went beyond most in praying humbly that "the House will take into Consideration the cause of these unhappy Disputes."[52] The only strongly worded conciliatory petitions were the second one from the London merchants of 23 February and that of the mayor, aldermen, and Common Council of a day later, against the restraining bill. Both petitions expressed sympathy for the grievances under which "our Fellow Subjects in America" labor, and they proceeded to list such hardships as the deprivation of trial by jury and the extension of the authority of Admiralty Courts and that of the Governor and Council of Massachusetts Bay. The petition of the London

---

[50]Mary Kinnear, "Pro-Americans in the British House of Commons in the 1770's" (Ph.D. dissertation, University of Oregon, 1973), for example, makes too much of Burke's statement concerning the failure of the petitions to criticize the government (121-22). See Thomas, *The House of Commons*, 57. *Lond. Eve.-Post* (3-5 January 1775); *Mid. J.* (3-6 January 1775).

[51]See the account of the meeting where this tactic is worked out. *Lond. Eve.-Post* (10-12 January 1775); *Mid. J.* (12-14 January 1775). Norwich, Dudley, Manchester, Wolverhampton, Liverpool, Birmingham, Leeds, Bridport, and Wakefield, *CJ*, 35:77, 80, 81, 82, 90, 123, and 124 are all mildly worded but may have had similar plans had the petitioners ever been heard. On the Stamp Act, see L. H. Gipson, "The Great Debate in the Committee of the Whole House of Commons on the Stamp Act, 1766, as Reported by Nathaniel Ryder," *Pennsylvania Magazine of History and Biography* 86 (January 1962): 10-41.

[52]*CJ*, 35:72, 108, 139.

Common Council was typically more radical, describing "several late Acts of Parliament" as evidently "partial and oppressive."[53]

For all of their differences, these petitions shared a single point: they implied a willingness, if not a desire, to retreat from the Coercive Acts, and it was precisely this willingness that was attacked by the coercive petitions. The issue of the wording of the petitions must, therefore, be understood in a specific historical context. The mildness of the majority of the conciliatory petitions on the question of parliamentary authority should be interpreted, first in the light of parliamentary procedure concerning the relationship between petitions and bills, and second in the light of the petitioners' expectation of being heard in Parliament. Vague language was probably also used for the purpose of attracting the support of people who opposed the colonists on ideological grounds, but who feared the further disruption of trade. The wording of the documents, however, is not fully explained by any of these concerns, as can be seen from developments in the local setting. In the provinces, opinion was already sharply divided on political grounds, and the possibility of remaining neutral on the question of authority was quickly disappearing.

Unlike the conciliatory petitions, five of the six coercive petitions explicitly raised the constitutional issue of authority, and, somewhat predictably, the strongest statements came from the four boroughs and towns that were divided. Far more than trade was at stake in the minds of the coercive petitioners. If the conciliatory petitions appeared almost passive by one standard, they were judged to be radical by those who opposed them. However they were intended, the press understood the conciliatory petitions as requesting the "repeal of the late American acts," and so did the coercive petitioners. Nottingham petitioners who favored the Coercive Acts expressed "great Concern and abhorrence" over "that seditious Spirit, which hath broken out with such Violence in the province of *Massachusetts Bay*" and they were "much surprised to find that Petitions have been repeatedly urged in their [i.e., the colonists'] Favour to the House, and in particular by some of the manufacturing Hosiers of the Town of *Nottingham*." They concluded that order would not be restored without a proper submission, "and therefore beseech the House to take such Measures as may seem most likely to secure and maintain the Supreme Authority, Honour, and Dignity, of *Great Britain*, enforce a due Obedience to her Laws, and restore Subordination, Order, and good Government."[54] In response, the supporters of the conciliatory petition at Nottingham presented their claims in a second petition and expressed "abhorrence" at the unjust representations of the coercive petition.[55]

The Leeds coercive petition similarly focused on the local setting and also expressed fears that the conciliatory petitions were put forth with the intent to

---

[53]Ibid., 35:144, 151.

[54]Ibid., 35:141.

[55]Ibid., 35:186.

repeal "several Acts of Parliament."[56] Birmingham and Huddersfield petitioners were more explicit in grounding their support for the Coercive Acts in the apprehension that if the laws were relaxed, commerce would eventually suffer, but the latter also drew out the constitutional issue: "any submission," wrote the Huddersfield petitioners, "to their unjust and unlawful Demands would be more prejudicial to the Petitioners, as well as to the Kingdom in general, as it would tend to make them more insolent, and totally to overthrow the lawful Authority which the King and Parliament must have over all its Dominions."[57] The Trowbridge petition well summarized both the question of trade and legislative authority: "the Petitioners conceive, that openly or tacitly giving up, in this Instance, the Authority of the Legislature of *Great Britain*, over the *American* Colonies, would be not only highly derogatory to the Honour and Dignity of the Crown and Parliament, but greatly injurious to the Welfare and Trade of *Great Britain*."[58] The Poole petitioners expressed support for the restraining bill and felt that any opposition to it was bound to work to "the general Prejudice of the Kingdom,"[59] and it is the only petition of the six that did not explicitly appeal for the enforcement of the law.

Eleven of the fifteen places that sent conciliatory petitions petitioned before 7 February, while only three of the six coercive petitions preceded the address from Parliament to the Crown (Trowbridge, Birmingham, and Leeds), and two of these cities were divided. It thus appears likely that the coercive petitioners were in part reacting to developments at Westminster. The local setting, however, was probably more influential in stimulating coercive petitions than the national setting.

The provincial press reveals how deeply the political differences were felt at the local level. In three of the four towns that divided (Huddersfield is the exception), the merchants' petitions preceded the conservative reaction, and, despite their mild wording, the petitions were largely instrumental in stimulating that reaction. This pattern was to be reversed in the fall of 1775 when addresses in favor of coercion provoked a reaction in support of peace. *Creswell's Nottingham and Newark Journal* followed the progress of petitions in other boroughs, and this agitation elicited a number of essays that took one side or the other of the debate. "A Manufacturer" condemned the petitioners in London and Bristol as people "with base spirits, whose meat and drink is to do evil, to pull down and lay waste, and to cry aloud that the danger is here."[60] The meeting in Nottingham at the Feathers Inn on 4 February provoked a "pretty warm debate," and the newspa-

---

[56]Ibid., 35:89.

[57]Ibid., 35:77-78, 186.

[58]Ibid., 35:198.

[59]Ibid., 35:164.

[60]*Nott. New. J.* (28 January 1775). See also "A Constant Reader," the rebuttal by "Moderatio," and the reference to "seeds of sedition" in the 18 February issue. *Nott. New. J.* (21, 28 January, 18 February 1775).

per accounts indicate that those who advanced the counter petition in favor of parliamentary supremacy were primarily concerned with the political question. When the original petitioners rebutted the counter petition with a second document, it was described locally as "a very angry Petition from a private Committee, in confirmation of the first."[61]

Local feeling over the contending petitions also ran high at Leeds,[62] but the constitutional issues were most sharply focused at Birmingham. "A Friend of Old England" published a series of queries defending the propriety of Birmingham's counter petition in favor of coercion. This lengthy statement examined the constitutional implications of opposition to Parliament and the Crown, the petitions' encouragement of rebellion in America, the right of representation in relation to taxation, and the charters of Massachusetts Bay. In conclusion, the author asserted that "every dissenting voice [to parliamentary supremacy] is an enemy to his country."[63] "An Old Correspondent" responded point by point to these queries and ranged over an equally wide array of constitutional matters. "The abettors or friends of the Americans, in this cause, are so far from favoring the worm of rebellion, that they consider it as no rebellion at all, but an honorable stand in all the Americans on behalf of their liberties, and an honorable testimony borne thereto by those their abettors." This author concluded with a series of his own penetrating queries: "whether the supreme power of Parliaments" being "JURE HUMANO, cannot possibly have any farther [sic] right than the constitution bestows, and the GOOD OF SOCIETY requires?" and whether there are "any rights belonging to the people that the Parliament cannot rescind and destroy?"[64]

There were hints of division in other boroughs that sent only one petition, or did not petition at all. Rumors of opposition to the merchants' petitions at Bristol and at Manchester can be accepted on the grounds of division evident in both places in the fall.[65] Norwich was also less than unanimous in its petition to Parliament; the majority of the Norwich corporation appears to have favored enforcing the Coercive Acts. One writer from Norwich expressed the opinion that those who defended the petitions to Parliament "have been the cause of spreading that licentious spirit which must prove fatal to those deluded people."[66] At York, "a very forcible speech" at the Guildhall on 13 February in favor of a petition to enforce the Coercive Acts was "quashed without a division."[67] The intensity of feeling expressed in the local setting, the inev-

---

[61]Ibid. (4, 11, 25 February, 25 March 1775).

[62]*Leeds Merc.* (17, 24, 31 January 1775).

[63]*Nott. New. J.* (18-25 February 1775).

[64]Ibid. (8 March 1775).

[65]*Brist. J.* (28 January 1775); *Leeds Merc.* (24 January 1775).

[66]*Nott. New. J.* (4 February 1775). According to this account, only two of the twenty-four aldermen signed the petition.

[67]Ibid. (25 February 1775).

itable extension of the issue to the question of authority, and the involvement of borough corporations on the side of the government were themes that would become far more prominent in the fall. The primary issue, inside Parliament and out, was whether or not the colonists were in actual rebellion, and on this point there were deep differences of opinion.

IV

Several attempts have been made to evaluate the significance of this first agitation for peaceful measures. One study of the English press claims that the petitions to Parliament were the chief topic of public discussion in the early months of 1775.[68] A survey of additional newspapers in the provinces confirms this.[69] Unlike petitions in the fall, the petitions to Parliament were thoroughly covered by the press. They were also the central point of focus in the Opposition's attack on the government, though this was without much effect. The importance of the number of petitions is difficult to assess, but a point overlooked by previous studies requires emphasis: only three of the six coercive petitions purported to come from merchants, and these were from the small towns of Poole, Trowbridge, and Huddersfield. By the fall of 1775, Poole and Trowbridge were divided over the government's policy, and thus even in these towns the merchants were not unanimously in support of coercion. The coercive petitions from Leeds and Nottingham represented corporate interests, whereas the petition favoring coercion from Birmingham originated from the "inhabitants." These considerations seem to underscore the strength of the merchants' agreement on conciliatory measures in the spring. Many corporations, of course, represented commercial interests, so the distinction between corporations and merchants should not be drawn too rigidly. But the identity between corporate and conservative interests that emerged in the fall of 1775 is evidently foreshadowed in the spring. In both periods of agitation, however, the merchants as a class were never perfectly united. Some merchants were apparently persuaded to support coercion by the argument that connected colonial disrespect for law with the unhappy prospect of the further destruction of property. It seems that concern for order, law, property, and status were dynamically related in many local settings. Further, since the merchants in at least some communities were divided, issues of trade alone do not account for every division over America.

While the petitions for conciliation outnumbered those for coercion, it is true that this appeal for peaceful measures represents no great public revulsion

---

[68]Fred J. Hinkhouse, *The Preliminaries of the American Revolution as Seen in the English Press, 1763-1775* (New York: Columbia University Press, 1926) 177.

[69]The thorough coverage of the petitions to Parliament by the press is easily proven. See *Leeds Merc.* (10, 17, 23, 31, January, 7, 14, 21 February 1775); *Nott. New. J.* (14, 21, 28 January, 4, 11, 25 February, 11 March 1775); *Worc. J.* (12, 19, 26 January, 2, 9, 16 February, 9 March 1775); *Brist. J.* (4, 14, 21, 28 January, 4, 11, 25 February 1775); *North. Merc.* (16, 23, 30 January, 13, 27 February, 6 March 1775).

over the general direction of the government's policy.[70] If the conciliatory petitions averaged 200 petitioners each, the total number of petitioners was quite small, and Parliament clearly was not impressed. It may be significant that eight of the seventeen places that petitioned were not represented directly in Parliament. (Those petitioners who were also freeholders were able to vote in contested county elections.) But while these towns may have more readily identified with the Americans who were unrepresented, the numbers are too small to advance generalizations about the issue of representation.

Dora Mae Clark's standard work on British public opinion during the American Revolution examined the number of boroughs and towns that sent petitions in January through March 1775. She then compared this petitioning activity to those petitions that emerged in 1765-1766 in favor of repealing the Stamp Act.[71] This comparison yielded a highly distorted picture because so little was known of the agitation in the fall of 1775. Poole and Trowbridge, for example, the only towns that appeared united against conciliation in February, had both by November submitted conciliatory petitions. A later chapter will examine the two movements in detail, but a secondary point emerging from Clark's comparison must be addressed here. The purported difference in the aggressiveness of the merchants in 1766 and 1775 is believed by Clark to be the explanation for why the former succeeded while the latter failed.[72] The merchants may have been somewhat less enthusiastic for conciliation in 1775 than they had been for repeal in 1766, but the number of places that petitioned and the aggressiveness of the merchants appear to have had little to do with the success or failure of the petitions. Recent studies of the Stamp Act clearly demonstrate that repeal was secured by the merchants' presentation of their evidence in the House of Commons, not by the mere reading of their petitions.[73] In fact, in 1766 two of the petitions from the larger trading centers arrived too late to be presented. But since the House had agreed to hear witnesses in support of the petitions, carefully amassed evidence from the remaining towns convinced a majority of M.P.s that repeal was necessary.[74]

---

[70]Ritcheson, *British Politics*, 190.

[71]Clark, *British Opinion*, 42, 85, 92.

[72]Ibid., 98. She also contends that "the loyal addresses completely destroyed the effect of the [conciliatory] remonstrances" (87), but this fails to take account of the fact that eight conciliatory petitions were presented before the second coercive petition arrived, and by that date Parliament's approach was already determined.

[73]Paul Langford, *The First Rockingham Administration, 1765-1766* (London: Oxford University Press, 1973) 173-85; P. D. G. Thomas, *British Politics and the Stamp Act Crisis: The First Phase of the American Revolution, 1763-1767* (Oxford: Clarendon Press, 1975) 216-25. Centralized leadership in the movement proved very effective. Barlow Trecothick sent a circular letter to thirty cities. Nothing approximating this organization took place in early 1775.

[74]Thomas, *British Politics*, 187-88.

Details of this campaign within doors contrast remarkably with the reaction of Parliament to the petitions presented in 1775, and they give added point to the London merchants' remonstrance that decried the parliamentary tactics used to silence the petitioners. The most important difference between the petitioning activity of 1766 and that of 1775 was Parliament's refusal to consider the merchants' petitions in the process of forming colonial policy. The press understood the issue well: "It has been remarked, in the affair of the Stamp Act, that the Ministry, with the Royal approbation, were for lenient, the Opposition for violent measures; the Ministry now, are for enforcing, the Opposition for declining, the authority of Parliament."[75] Parliament's decisive insistence upon the Coercive Acts, combined with a vote of confidence in the administration's view that the colonies were in a state of rebellion, strongly influenced the next development in popular opposition to the government. Parliament's refusal to deal with these early expressions of public opinion meant that petitioners would turn to the only other source of authority they knew. English appeals for peace followed exactly those of the colonies: when thwarted by Parliament, English petitioners, like the Americans, turned to the Crown.

The two agitations for conciliatory measures in 1775 were distinct in purpose and separated in time by a period of six months, but a number of developments in the earlier movement were harbingers of the petitions to the Crown. Nine of the seventeen places that petitioned Parliament in the spring later petitioned or addressed the Crown, and this repeated activity implies some continuity between the two periods of agitation.[76] Many of the same leaders were active in both movements.[77] While the earlier debate had centered around trade, in a number of cases it expanded to the larger question of the necessity of enforcing due obedience to law. The question of obedience to law was particularly prominent in those communities that were divided, and the issue of authority would become more pronounced in public debate, as colonial order disintegrated in the ensuing months. When the nine places petitioned or addressed again in the fall of 1775, the overriding concern was the constitutional one of authority, rather than the issue of trade. The merchant who for the sake of trade was willing to grant concessions to the colonies after observing colonial resistance to the Stamp Act and the Townshend Duties, might be expected to have a different perspective on authority than the merchant who, at all costs, insisted on the enforcement of the Coercive Acts. Beneath expressions of con-

---

[75]*Leeds Merc.* (17 January 1775); *Nott. New. J.* (21 January 1775).

[76]These are London, Bristol, Liverpool, Manchester, Staffordshire, Poole, Trowbridge, Leeds, and Nottingham.

[77]Edmund Burke, Thomas Wooldridge, and Samuel Elam have already been noted. William Baker and Alderman Hayley in London can be added to the list, as can Sir James Lowther of Cumberland. See *Parl. Hist.* 18:168, 186-87; on Baker, see Bernard Donoughue, *British Politics and the American Revolution* (London: Macmillan Co., 1964) 155; on Lowther, *York Cour.* (7 February 1775).

cern for trade one can detect, on the one side, a willingness to concede Parliament's error, and, on the other, an insistence upon submission to authority.

In light of this, one may ponder whether the American crisis had ever been perceived as merely a local matter of trade. The American question, rather, seems to have always involved both issues of trade and constitutional rights. In repeated cases, people readily identified what appeared to be strictly a local matter with the great national question of the colonial status of America. The press, for example, immediately interpreted Parliament's resistance to the conciliatory petitions as a constitutional issue. That national issues were interpreted through a local framework can also be seen in the response of town corporations that represented vested interests concerned with order. Later in the year, the preoccupation with order would become a clear characteristic of the petitions to the Crown. Resistance to authority in the colonies seems not so much to have produced divisions in England, but rather to have stimulated the more open manifestation of local social, religious, and political divisions that were already present. When Englishmen disagreed over the crisis in America, trade was always a part of the discussion. But if it had been the central issue, Parliament would have given more heed to the merchants. It is the burden of the following chapters to show that the most prominent question in the minds of the English people was submission to constituted authority on the one hand, or the recognition of constitutional rights on the other. Local circumstances often contributed to the sharpening of these differences, but divisions in the English populace cannot be reduced to local, material issues.

London Radicals, George III, and Royal Policy on Petitions

Chapter II

The right to petition the Crown for redress of grievances was part of the Revolution settlement guaranteed by the Bill of Rights.[1] Unlike petitions to Parliament, petitions to the Crown were an extraordinary form of political expression; the king was not appealed to unless other more common means of obtaining relief had proven futile. Appeals to the Crown regarding America in 1775 were similar in this regard to petitions concerning the Middlesex election affair. The refusal of the House of Commons to seat John Wilkes after he had been duly elected by a majority of Middlesex freeholders in 1769 led thousands of Englishmen to petition the king, the highest earthly authority and final defender of their constitutional liberties. In the eighteenth century, however, it was an established convention that the king accepted legislation passed by Parliament. The petitions to George III in 1769 and in 1775 were petitions against a decision of the House of Commons, and this raised a constitutional issue of the first importance.[2]

The right to petition the Crown was a right that at once looked to the past and pressed into the future.[3] It looked back in time by its recognition of the

---

[1]I Will. & Mary, sess. 2, c. 2. D. Pickering, ed., *The Statutes at Large from Magna Carta to . . . 1761; Continued* (to 1806) (Cambridge, 1762-1806) 9:67. E. Neville Williams, *The Eighteenth-Century Constitution* (Cambridge: Cambridge University Press, 1970) 28, 408-10. Lois G. Schwoerer, *The Declaration of Rights, 1689* (Baltimore: Johns Hopkins University Press, 1981) 14-16, 69-71. Sir William Blackstone, *Commentaries on the Laws of England*, ed. Joseph Chitty, et al. (London: W. Walker, 1826) 3:255. The immediate background to the fifth article of the Bill of Rights was the Seven Bishops' Case, in which the bishops petitioned the king against dispensing with the penal laws against Catholics and Dissenters. The right to petition the king and the issue of the royal prerogative in relation to law passed by Parliament were thus intimately linked. There exists no study of the constitutional implications of the petitions in 1769-1770 and 1775.

[2]John Sawbridge drew out the comparison between petitioning the king against Parliament regarding Wilkes and now appealing to the king concerning the acts of Parliament, since these acts were in both cases "unjust and oppressive." *Parl. Hist.*, 18:1007.

[3]Charles H. McIlwain, *The American Revolution: A Constitutional Interpretation* (Ithaca NY: Cornell University Press, 1923) 22-23, shows that when applied to a later and very different historical setting, the achievements of the Revolution settlement proved disastrous.

king's authority and his role as defender and protector of the people; it looked forward in that it took seriously the right of the people to be heard. The right to petition the king without fear of reprisal was thus a progressive concept that genuinely embraced individual rights.[4] But the authors of the Bill of Rights never envisioned a time when this avenue of redress would entail an appeal to the Crown against an act of Parliament.

If article five of the Declaration of Rights insisted on the right to petition, the first two articles pronounced the "pretended power" of suspending or dispensing laws "by regal authority without consent of Parliament" illegal.[5] For all it accomplished, the Glorious Revolution failed to provide any check upon the supremacy of Parliament. Whig doctrine "offered no more remedy against an oppressive parliament than the theory of divine right had offered against a despotic king, and that was only 'sighs and tears'."[6] The right to petition the Crown was never intended to function as a check upon Parliament, and this can be no more graphically illustrated than in the events of 1774 and 1775. The emergence of royal policy concerning the handling of petitions explains a great deal about the ineffectiveness of popular protest in England. The constitutional dilemma presented to Englishmen who opposed the Coercive Acts also sheds considerable light on the difficulties the colonists had in relating to King, Lords, and Commons. When applied as a check on Parliament, petitions to the Crown utterly failed not only the English, but also the Americans.

I

In early February, the London merchants knew they had reached an impasse. Their deliberations illustrated a sophisticated awareness of the constitutional implications of petitions to the Crown. Parliament's refusal to consider petitions in favor of conciliation led the merchants to weigh the value of appealing to the Crown, and on 8 February, the day after the House of Lords rejected their petition, they met once again. The committee informed the merchants of the fate of their petition in the Lords; speakers recounted their attempts to remove the fatal prospects before them, and they concluded with a motion for a petition to the Crown as the only measure "remaining unassayed." The motion, however, was opposed by several merchants. One felt the matter was of "such importance" that more time was needed, and David Bar-

---

[4]Schwoerer, *The Declaration.* 283. Schwoerer, however, notes that article five claimed "an *unlimited* right, whereas Restoration law permitted only a bonded right of subjects to petition the King" (71). That is, various restrictions were put on the right of petitioning by Restoration law, such as the requirement that the consent of the authorities be obtained to gather the signatures of twenty or more persons on the petition, and that no more than ten people could present it.

[5]Ibid., 59.

[6]McIlwain, *The American Revolution,* 158.

clay, a Quaker, believed it was such a "delicate question" that it should be weighed with exceeding care.[7]

In defending a cautious approach, Barclay developed the key issues that would frame the intellectual background of all the petitions to follow. His doubts about the propriety of petitioning the Crown arose from two paragraphs in Parliament's address to the king. One declared that " a part of the subjects in the Massachusetts Bay were in actual rebellion," and the other beseeched the king to "take the most effectual measures to enforce due obedience to the laws and authority of the Supreme Legislature." On these points Barclay made two pivotal observations: if a petition were presented to the Crown denying that a rebellion existed and beseeching the king "not to *enforce* but to *suspend* the laws, it might on one hand be unsafe to sign such a petition," and on the other hand, it might set a precedent that, "should it succeed in the present instance, might hereafter prove of a most dangerous tendency, lest a King should ever be on the British Throne who might follow such an example to act contrary to the joint opinion of his two Houses of Parliament." But if, Barclay concluded, the petition should contain less than a denial of rebellion in America, and less than an appeal to suspend the laws passed by Parliament, the document would be ineffectual.

Thomas Preston's reply to Barclay's speech swayed the opinion of the meeting. British subjects, he said, "had an undoubted right by the constitution to petition the King in all cases," and if they stopped short of "the ultimate act," their fellow subjects in both this kingdom and America would conclude that they had deserted the cause. The majority agreed with Preston, and the committee was requested to prepare a draft for the general meeting a week hence. But on 15 February the merchants decided not to petition the Crown, reasoning only that it was "expedient to defer the same for the present."

Three matters relative to the London merchants' deliberations should be emphasized. They considered turning to the Crown only after all other attempts to obtain redress had failed, and this alternative was approached with considerable reluctance. Second, as early as February 1775 the prospect of association with the colonists, if only on commercial grounds, was considered "unsafe," since Parliament and the Crown considered the colonists to be in a state of rebellion. The question of the petitioners' safety would only intensify with time. Finally, an appeal to the Crown over Parliament seemed inevitably to involve the merchants in a request for the king to suspend the law. The right of the subject to petition the king for redress was, in this case, bound to conflict with the primary achievement of the Revolution settlement, namely, the ultimate sovereignty of Parliament. Despite this, the merchants contended for the

---

[7]See the full account in *Mid. J.* (9-11 February 1775); *Lond. Eve.-Post* (7-9, 11-14 February 1775). On Barclay, see *Burke Correspondence*, 3:113. On the other speaker, Thomas Preston, see John Sainsbury, "The Pro-American Movement in London, 1769-1782: Extra-Parliamentary Opposition to the Government's American Policy" (Ph.D. dissertation, McGill University, 1975) 335.

right of a final appeal to the king himself. Burke, too, felt the importance of
maintaining this right, and even though he defended the Declaratory Act, he
and Lord Rockingham discussed the appropriateness of appealing first to the
House of Commons, then to the House of Lords, and finally to the king.[8]

II

The last petition to Parliament concerning the American issue was from
Trowbridge, presented on 15 March.[9] After this date, only London kept up
consistent opposition on the popular level. The transition to the petitioning activity in the fall centered around the activity of metropolitan pro-Americans,
with a distinct shift of focus from Parliament to the Crown. That there was a
discernible change in the orientation of petitioning activity about the middle
of March can be accounted for on the basis of several developments. On 16
March the House of Commons finally heard three speakers on the topic of the
petitions that were being considered by the "committee of oblivion." But further reports of the committee were twice deferred by the House, and on 3 April
the committee was dropped. Parliament's consistent commitment to enforcing
its own supremacy was thereby confirmed and petitioning activity brought to
a decisive conclusion.[10] Burke's brilliant speech for conciliation was soundly
rejected by the House on 22 March.[11] Instead of amending any of the previous
coercive legislation, new trade restrictions in the Restraining Bill were passed
into law with overwhelming majorities in both Houses of Parliament.[12] By the
end of March it was abundantly evident that there was no hope of effecting significant change through Parliament.

With yet further restrictive trade legislation pending, the London merchants finally turned to the king. At a meeting on 22 March they discussed again
the recent developments in Parliament. The merchants noted the progress of
the Restraining Bill, and the chairman presented a draft of a petition to the king.
This petition was presented the next day.[13] The Quakers, who, like the Lon-

---

[8]*Burke Correspondence*, 2:64 (Rockingham to Burke, 1, 3 September 1774); 3:101-
103 (Burke to the citizens of Bristol, 20 January 1775); 3:106-107 (Burke to Rockingham, 24 January 1775); 3:113-14 (Rockingham to Burke, 9 February 1775).

[9]This is not strictly so; a separate group from Trowbridge appealed to Parliament
on 16 November petitioning for conciliation as did the City of London on 26 October
and again at the opening of Parliament in 1776. *CJ*, 35:447; *Ann. Reg.* (1776) 252. Also
the New York petition was considered by Parliament in May. See also note 17 of chapter 1. In general terms, however, there was a clear reorientation.

[10]*Parl. Hist.*, 18:461-78; *CJ*, 35:200, 202, 209, 232, 255.

[11]*Parl. Hist.*, 18:478-540.

[12]Ibid., 18:399-457.

[13]*Lond. Eve.-Post* (21-23, 23-25 March 1775); *North. Merc.* (27 March 1775); and
York Cour. (28 March 1775) give detailed accounts. There was a debate at this meeting
regarding the mode of presenting the petitions, and it was finally agreed that the petition be presented to the king in the "most respectful manner."

don merchants, had petitioned Parliament in the past, now also turned to the Crown. They presented a petition to the king on 24 March, and it is the first petition not to mention trade; the Quakers simply appealed for a cessation of hostilities on the grounds of the desirability of peace.[14] Earlier, the colonists had anticipated this pattern of shifting attention from Parliament to the Crown. But in England, those who sympathized with the colonists were understandably more committed to seeking redress through Parliament than were the Americans.

These events have an instructive parallel in the earlier petitioning activity concerning the Middlesex election affair, and in both 1770 and 1775 the London radicals had a profound impact on subsequent developments.[15] The earlier movement had been more highly organized than that of 1775; it had centralized leadership, and many of the petitions were presented to the Crown within a period of several weeks of the first sitting of Parliament in 1770 in order to have a maximum impact at that critical juncture.[16] However, the petitions of 1769-1770 had little effect, since George III heartily endorsed Parliament's action against Wilkes. The way in which the petitions were ignored was related to how they were received. The petitions were presented to the king at the levee, or delivered to the lord in waiting.[17] In either case, the documents were easily laid aside, and with few exceptions they did not receive an answer.[18] This method of receiving petitions and refusing an answer did not pass unnoticed in the press, and in Opposition circles generally, it was severely censured. Also, in 1769-1770, the government capitalized upon the political

---

[14]Text printed in *York Cour.* (28 March 1775), also *Lond. Chron.* (5-7 September 1775) in an essay that praises it. Charles R. Ritcheson, *British Politics and the American Revolution* (Norman OK: University of Oklahoma Press, 1954) 190, notes that this was signed by sixty-one Quakers. See Arthur J. Meekel, *The Relation of the Quakers to the American Revolution* (Washington: University Press of America, 1979) 123.

[15]Lucy S. Sutherland, *The City of London and the Opposition to Government, 1768-1774* (London: University of London, Athlone Press, 1959) 25-26. In 1769-1770 the radical leaders in the metropolis were able to unite with the parliamentary opposition.

[16]A number of petitions were presented in 1769, but those from Yorkshire, Worcestershire, Devonshire, Derbyshire, Gloucestershire, Wiltshire, Wales, Bristol, Newcastle, Hereford, and the loyal petitions from Liverpool and Flint were all presented in the first two weeks of January 1770. See *Read. Merc.* (8, 15, 22 January 1770).

[17]Ibid. (15 January 1770). William S. Taylor and John H. Pringle, eds., *The Correspondence of William Pitt, Earl of Chatham,* 4 vols. (London: John Murray, 1838-1840) 3:448-65, deals at length with the constitutional issue surrounding the perceived threat to the right of petitioning. This matter is not dealt with by Sutherland or Rudé.

[18]Sutherland, *The City and the Opposition,* says they were ignored (32). The only loyal addresses to receive an answer were those from the Archbishop of Canterbury, the London merchants, and the City of London. *Lond. Gaz.* (4-7 February, 22 March 1769).

value of loyal addresses by publishing them in the *London Gazette*, whereas no space was given to the pro-Wilkes petitions.[19]

The king and his advisors thus had some practice in the handling of potentially damaging expression of public opinion, and their political acumen in this respect seems to have increased with the years. In 1772 a petition from Nonconformist ministers and schoolmasters praying for relief from the requirement to subscribe to the Thirty-Nine Articles was sent to the Commons. Lord North was aware of the importance of the Dissenting vote in returning some members to Parliament, and he concluded that the administration would be beaten if he opposed the petition openly, since those "whose elections principally depend upon Presbyterians must vote for this petition"; and "those, who have a few dissenting constituents would avoid voting at all."[20] He informed the king that he planned to allow the petition to pass through the House of Commons, since the Lords could be trusted to serve as a "longstop" and dispose of the unwanted document. The administration felt no scruple about using the House of Lords to control the potential influence of public opinion on the House of Commons.

Royal policy on petitions and the administration's attitude toward public opinion is further illustrated by a second incident in the House of Commons. On 8 March 1775 Governor Johnstone brought the existence of a petition from Jamaica to the attention of the House and pondered over why it was held back from the "public eye." Lord North responded that it had not been held back "designedly" and that it was currently under consideration by the Privy Council. Debate ensued concerning which papers the administration was required to lay before the House. Richard Rigby argued that there were only two ways of obtaining state papers; "one was to address his Majesty, which could only be done by taking the Sense of the House; the other was when his Majesty's Servants thought it necessary to lay certain Papers before them; but that in either event, Administration were still understood to be the sole Judges of what is and is not proper for public Inspection."[21] This interchange reveals the administration's method of minimizing the visibility of conciliatory petitions. It was the same tactic used later by George III.

When addresses to the Crown began to appear in profusion in the fall of 1775, Lord Suffolk advised the king that those who presented loyal addresses would be flattered to have the honor to kiss his Majesty's hand. But, he ob-

---

[19]Pauline Maier, *From Resistance to Revolution: Colonial Radicals and the Development of American Opposition to Britain, 1765-1776* (New York: Alfred A. Knopf, 1972) 206-207. The king's inattention to the documents led the City of London to remonstrate on three occasions. Fortescue, 2:133; Lord North to the king, 7 March 1770; 137, the king to Lord North, 20 March 1770. *Read. Merc.* (19 February 1770); *Lond. Gaz.* (4-7 February, 3-6 June 1769).

[20]Williams, *The Eighteenth-Century Constitution*, 136-37.

[21]*Parl. Hist.*, 18:400-405. A fuller account is found in the *York Cour.* (14 March 1775).

served, "a formal answer to these addresses does not seem requisite."[22] The same policy would apply to the petitions. In October the king wrote to Lord North that it was appropriate to prepare the lord in waiting to refuse even the introduction of the Petition of the Provincial Congress of Georgia. It came from a body he could not acknowledge, and "the treating all Provincial and General Congresses in that manner for the future will be proper."[23] The reason for rejecting colonial petitions was that they arose from illegal bodies; their introduction would imply a form of legal recognition. The same, of course, could not be said of English petitions. Here, the only line of recourse was for the king to appeal to the decision of his Parliament. By the summer of 1775, radicals in London had commenced a series of attacks that made this solution highly expedient.

III

While the petitions of 1770 had addressed the unseating of John Wilkes, in 1775 Wilkes was Lord Mayor of London. Before April 1775 the London radicals had not been prominent in the petitioning agitation.[24] But on 5 April, two weeks after the London merchants and the Quakers turned to the king, the radical elements of the London Livery met to prepare their own appeal to the Crown, an appeal that began a series of events that was to confirm the way in which the king handled future petitions related to America (see Table 2).[25] John Wilkes, together with some of the aldermen and liverymen, met at the Guildhall and agreed to a "Humble Address, Remonstrance, and Petition" to his Majesty against coercive measures in America. The liverymen not only rejected previous "oppressive" legislation, but claimed to discern malevolent intentions behind the law: the "real purpose" of Parliament's measures, they believed, was "to establish arbitrary power over all America." Having listed a series of grievous "oppressions," the petition concluded by appealing for a dismissal of those ministers who had, by their "secret advice," violated the constitution of the country.[26]

The king received this petition on 10 April while seated upon the throne, but he gave a blunt and ominous reply: "It is with the utmost astonishment that I find any of my subjects capable of encouraging the rebellious disposition

---

[22]Fortescue, 3:260 (Lord Suffolk to the king, 12 September 1775).

[23]Ibid., 3:273 (George III to Lord North, 23 October 1775).

[24]The one exception was the petition of the Common Council to Parliament on 24 February. John A. Sainsbury, "The Pro-Americans of London, 1769-1782," *William and Mary Quarterly*, 3d ser., 35 (July 1978): 434; Sainsbury, "The Pro-American Movement in London," 152-73.

[25]See the accounts in *Lond. Eve.-Post* (11-13 April 1775); *Lond. Chron.* (8-11 April 1775); *York Cour.* (11, 18 April 1775). Table 2 excludes one petition outside of our time from the Common Council, "Humble Address and Petition" against the Quebec Act of 11 June 1774 that was never answered. *City Addresses*, 31.

[26]Petition of 5 April 1775, in *City Addresses*, 34-36.

which unhappily exists in some of my colonies in North America." Placing his confidence "in the wisdom of Parliament," the king promised simply to pursue those measures which that council recommended.[27] George III's association of a strongly worded conciliatory petition with the positive encouragement of rebellion abroad clearly informed royal policy toward later petitions. It must be underscored that the king had, while seated on the throne, received this and three previous petitions from the London Livery no less radical.[28] Moreover,

TABLE 2

BODY PETITIONING	DOCUMENT	ISSUE	DATE	ANSWERED
UNSIGNED PETITIONS TO THE CROWN FROM THE CITY OF LONDON CONCERNING AMERICA				
Common Hall	Humble Address, Remonstrance, and Petition	Against Coercive Acts	5 Apr. 1775	10 Apr. 1775
Common Hall	Humble Address, Remonstrance, and Petition	Against Coercive Acts and Evil Advisors	24 June 1775	Never Presented
Common Council	Humble Address and Petition	Pleads for Conciliatory Measures	7 July 1775	14 July 1775
Common Council	Humble Address and Petition	Pleads for Mercy and Clear Statement of Terms to Precede Armament	14 Mar. 1776	22 Mar. 1776
Common Council	Humble Address and Petition	Pleads for Conciliatory Measures	4 Mar. 1778	13 Mar. 1778
Common Hall	Humble Address, Remonstrance, and Petition	Against Continuation of War and Evil Advisors	6 Dec. 1781	Never Presented

Source: *City Addresses*, 34-36, 40-42, 44-45, 45-47, 49-53, 60-62.

---

[27]*City Addresses*, 36. This avowal led the Common Council to turn back to Parliament in a petition of 26 October. *Gen. Eve. Post* (26-28 October 1775).

[28]The City of London did enjoy a privileged place with respect to petitions sent to Parliament. See P. D. G. Thomas, *The House of Commons in the Eighteenth Century* (Oxford: Clarendon Press, 1971) 19. On the radicalism of the Common Hall as contrasted to the Corporation see Sutherland, *The City and the Opposition*, 17. On the distinction between petitions from the Livery in Common Hall assembled and those from the Corporation in Common Council assembled, see the petition of 24 June 1769, in *City Addresses*, 15. Heretofore, George III had received petitions from both the Livery and the Common Council while seated on the throne. See the radical petitions from the Lord Mayor, Aldermen, and Livery of the City of London, in Common Hall assembled, on 6 March 1770, 24 June 1770, and 11 March 1773 with the king's answers (17-19; 26-28; 29-30). Horace Walpole commented that by receiving the petition of 10 April, the

the king's answers to these previous petitions had been published. Now, however, George III was to make a crucial distinction between petitions from a gathering of the Livery in Common Hall assembled, and the City of London in Common Council assembled. On 11 April, the day after the king received this petition, the Lord Chamberlain wrote to the Lord Mayor, "The King has directed me to give notice, that for the future His Majesty will not receive on the throne any Address, Remonstrance, and Petition, but from the Body Corporate of the City."[29] The more radical elements in the Livery had, in the king's estimation, taken the right of petition beyond its justifiable limits, and his reaction to their inflammatory language is understandable. Implicit in the king's distinction was an attempt to discriminate between the more respectable elements on the one hand, and the radical and less respectable elements on the other. But the king was, at the same time, breaking with a precedent that he himself had helped establish during the Middlesex election affair.

The new departure was clearly perceived by John Wilkes. During the Middlesex crisis, petitions from London were always denied, but never had they been turned away without a hearing. The petitions from the provinces in 1769-1770, however, had not been answered, and Wilkes seems to have learned a vital lesson from this previous episode. In his response to the Lord Chamberlain on 2 May 1775, Wilkes drew out the practical and constitutional implications of the king's decision with remarkable prescience. He reminded the Lord Chamberlain that the addresses of the Livery of London had in the past been received by the king on the throne, "both by the present Majesty and all his royal predecessors, the Kings of England." But more than broken precedent was at stake.

> The privilege, my Lord, for which I contend, is of a very great moment, and peculiarly striking. When His Majesty receives on the throne any Address, it is read by the proper officer to the King in the presence of the petitioners. They have the satisfaction of knowing that their Sovereign has heard their complaints. They receive an answer. If the same address is presented at a levee, or in any other mode, no answer is given. A suspicion may arise that the Address is never heard or read, because it is only received, and immediately delivered to the lord in waiting. If he is tolerably versed in the supple, insinuating arts, practiced in the magic circle of a court, he will take care never to remind his prince of any disagreeable and disgusting, however important and wholesome truths. He will strangle in its birth the fair offspring of liberty, because its cries might awaken and alarm the parent, and thus the common father of all his people may remain equally ignorant and unhappy in his most weighty concerns.[30]

There was no response to Wilkes's letter, yet his concern for the right of pe-

---

king "had established a precedent for what he now proscribed." A. Francis Steuart, ed., *The Last Journals of Horace Walpole*, 2 vols. (London: John Lane, 1910) 1:451. Actually, the precedent was set long before.

[29]*City Addresses*, 36-37 (Hertford to the Lord Mayor, 11 April 1775).

[30] Ibid., 38, 39 (Wilkes to the Earl of Hertford, 2 May 1775).

titioning was well founded. The only petitions known to have received an answer from the king after this date—and this includes all of those presented in the fall of 1775—were those from the city of London in Common Council assembled. The vast majority were "graciously received" at the levee. The king kindly thanked the petitioners, but none of them were in fact answered, and from there, as Wilkes predicted, the petitions dropped from sight.[31]

The London radicals saw the king's decision as but another instance of courtly corruption, and they set about to vindicate the right to petition. The caucus of the Livery met on 20 June and agreed to recommend an even more strongly worded petition, penned by Arthur Lee, to the forthcoming Common Hall meeting.[32] An estimated 2,500 liverymen assembled in Common Hall on Saturday, 24 June, discussed these developments, and proceeded to draft a number of resolutions. They resolved that those who advised his Majesty to refuse hearing petitions on the throne were "enemies to the right of the subject to petition the throne, because such advice is calculated to intercept the complaints of the people to their Sovereign, to prevent a redress of grievances, and alienate the minds of Englishmen from the Hanoverian succession" and that "unless His Majesty hears the petitions of his subjects, the right of petitioning is nugatory."[33] Technically, the right of petitioning was not denied by the king, but the London radicals clearly felt that the right was effectively denied by the way he received them. With only one dissenting voice, the Common Hall agreed to Lee's strongly worded petition and instructed the sheriffs to wait upon his Majesty to determine when he would be pleased to receive the "Humble Address" upon the throne.[34]

The meeting took place on 28 June. When asked when he would receive the address, the king replied, "You will please take notice that I will receive their Address, Remonstrance, and Petition, on Friday next, at the levee." Sheriff Plomer replied, "Your Majesty will permit us to inform you that the Livery, in Common Hall assembled, have resolved not to present their Address, Remonstrance, and Petition, unless your Majesty shall be pleased to receive it sitting on the throne." The king's response confirmed his earlier decision: "I am ever ready to receive addresses and petitions—but I am the judge where." The "Humble Address" was never delivered. The radical elements of the Livery were reduced to making yet further resolutions and com-

---

[31]Petitions and addresses were either presented at the levee (for the Gloucester and Winchester addresses see *Gen. Eve. Post* [3-5, 19-21 October 1775] and for the Worcester, Cambridge, and Taunton petitions see *Gen. Eve. Post* [7-9 November 1775]; and *Lond. Eve.-Post* [28-30 November 1775]; and *Pub. Adv.* [7 October 1775]) or to Lord Dartmouth, who gave them to the king (see for Liverpool and Beverley, *Lond. Chron.* [19-21 September, 3-5 October 1775]).

[32]Sainsbury, "The Pro-American Movement in London, 1769-1782," 166-67.

[33]*City Addresses*, 40.

[34]Sainsbury, "The Pro-American Movement in London, 1769-1782," 169-70.

posing instructions for their representatives in Parliament. In their minds, the refusal of the king to allow the reading of the petition in the hearing of the petitioners was tantamount to a "direct denial" of the right of petitioning.[35]

True to his word, George III was willing to receive petitions from the Common Council in its corporate capacity; on 14 July he heard a more mildly worded petition for peace while seated on the throne.[36] But for the king, this was to be the exception; the rule, by this date, was settled. He wrote to Lord North on 26 July: "By the minutes published by the Meeting at Guildhall, I see I should not be troubled with them, a Resolution being taken not to deliver the Remonstrance unless I receive it on the Throne, which shall never happen again."[37]

The constitutional issue raised by the specific mode of receiving petitions was thoroughly debated in the press. Some writers felt that Wilkes and the London radicals were correct in their analysis, while others defended the king's decision and marveled that the radicals were treated so mildly.[38] The issue persisted until the end of the war; while the Common Council was privileged with royal audiences and answers to their petitions for peace, throughout the war the Livery was refused.[39] When, in late 1781, the liverymen attempted to petition the throne, they met with the same denials they had faced in 1775. The sheriffs of the city, attended by the remembrancer, waited upon his Majesty on 7 December 1781 to inquire when the king would receive upon the throne their "Humble Address." The king replied that he would take time to consider "of the manner in which I shall receive it," and on 11 December the Lord Mayor received a letter from the Earl of Hertford. Here it was stated that the "settled custom" was for the king to receive addresses on the throne from the city only in its corporate capacity and that the petitions from the Common Hall would accordingly be received at the next levee.[40] The Lord Mayor, William Plomer,

---

[35]*City Addresses*, 40-44. Sainsbury rightly asserts that the radicals were overstating their case, "The Pro-American Movement in London, 1769-1782," 169.

[36]The petition of 7 July 1775, *City Addresses*, 44-45. See Fortescue 3:231, 233 (W. Brummell to North, 4 July 1775; George III to North, 5 July 1775). This milder petition caused some friction between the Common Council and the Common Hall that well illustrates the difficulty the Opposition had in presenting a united front against the government. See Sainsbury, "The Pro-American Movement in London, 1769-1782," 170-73. The Common Council was not even united as to whether or not the colonies were in a state of rebellion. Fortescue 3:233 (George III to North, 9 July 1775). See also *Lond. Eve.-Post* (11-13, 20-22 July 1775); *Lond. Chron.* (6-8 July 1775).

[37]Fortescue 3:235, 273 (George III to Lord North, 26 July 1775; George III to Lord North, 23 October 1775).

[38]In favor of the radicals, see *Lond. Eve.-Post* (23-25 May, 13-15 June 1775); in contrast see *Pub. Adv.* (1 July, 9, 28 August 1775).

[39]The petitions of 14 March 1776, 4 March 1778, and 9 April 1782 with answers, in *City Addresses*, 45, 49-53, 66.

[40]See the Humble Address of 6 December 1781, and Hertford's letter of 10 December. Ibid., 60-63.

rightly contested the question of custom—it had been "settled" only since July 1775—and he referred Hertford to the letter of John Wilkes of 2 May 1775. But the point was moot, and the petition was never delivered to the king.[41] The radicals in the Livery turned their attention to the Association movement that was by this date well underway.

By the end of July 1775, royal policy on how petitions were handled was firmly settled. The king's position was identical to that already taken by both Houses of Parliament. Parliament concluded its session on 26 May, three days before news arrived in London of the skirmishes at Lexington and Concord. One of the Commons' last acts was its refusal to hear the "Representation and Remonstrance" from New York. This was rejected on the grounds that Parliament could not possibly listen to any application for redress of grievances until its supremacy was first acknowledged.[42] This petition was also refused by the Lords for the same reason, and thus the king's approach to petitions for conciliation was in keeping with the other branches of government.

Legally the king's position was certainly correct. The law provided no details on the specific way in which a petition was to be received. Accordingly, from July forward, the king received petitions at the levee, or, as in the case of Georgia, they were not even introduced. A sympathetic public hearing of the petitions by the king, or any movement on the part of George III in favor of the petitioners, would have brought him into direct conflict with Parliament. His determination to abide by the decision of Parliament has rightly been construed as the final proof of his commitment to the Revolution settlement. But if it was constitutional, the king's handling of petitions was perceived as unconstitutional by the Opposition, and his actions provoked significant discussion both within Parliament and without.[43] Many people felt that their petitions were not answered, and this resulted in a heightened perception that basic liberties were threatened. George III was clearly not breaking any laws. However, just as Burke argued in 1769 that in the king's appointment of ministers he was acting against the "spirit of the constitution," so in the matter of petitions, his actions seemed to be contrary to the spirit of the constitution, and were, at a minimum, "improvident."

By the time the Olive Branch Petition arrived in England on 21 August, the king's approach to conciliatory petitions was completely determined. Therefore, when the London livery turned to the electors of Great Britain in their address of 2 October, they grounded much of the case against the administration on the refusal of the government to answer "repeated" petitions from

---

[41]Ibid., 64 (The Lord Mayor to Hertford, 12 December 1775).

[42]*York. Cour.* (23 May 1775). The New York petition was denied a hearing in the House of Commons on 15 May and in the House of Lords on 18 May. *Parl. Hist.*, 18:650.

[43]See the accounts in *North. Merc.* (10 July 1775); *York Cour.* (4, 11 July 1775). This issue of the king's rejecting petitions would later be raised in the House of Commons. See the debate on 27 November, *Parl. Hist.*, 18:1019.

the colonies "supported by many in this country." Similarly the protest of Opposition Lords on 6 November emphasized the evil of unanswered petitions.[44] But these charges had no effect on royal policy—a policy that determined the fate of the entire movement in the fall of 1775. The petitioners naively believed that their petitions would be taken seriously; the irony is that the interaction between the London radicals and George III had rendered this impossible. Later the Americans made much the same point as the pro-Americans in England, when, in the Declaration of Independence, they claimed "our repeated petitions have been answered only by repeated injury."

IV

The shift of popular agitation from Parliament to the Crown was motivated largely by the refusal of Parliament to consider petitions seriously. In reaction to the recalcitrance of Parliament, a small number of strongly worded petitions to the Crown helped, in turn, to confirm royal policy concerning how petitions were handled. Another incentive to petition the Crown came from North America. In July and August, as matters grew worse in the colonies, newspapers circulated notices of the advisability of sending loyal addresses of support to his Majesty. The same newspapers that reported fighting around Charlestown seem to have spontaneously responded to the crisis by seeking to elicit support for the government. In late July newspapers noted that a society of gentlemen in Manchester had agreed to present a loyal address to the king. Other papers printed a formal address consisting of four paragraphs in which those who were willing to participate dutifully pledged "their lives and fortunes" in order to maintain the king's honor. This "form" address had a blank space for the name of the county that would circulate the petition, and it was recommended that signatures could be added on separate parchments.[45]

The most important cause, however, of renewed petitioning activity was the royal proclamation of 23 August declaring the colonies in a state of rebellion. This proclamation for suppressing rebellion and sedition was based on the proclamation of 1715 and was designed to promote unity in England.[46]

---

[44]*Suss. Week. Adv.* (9, 13 October 1775). On the Lord's protest, see William C. Lowe, "The House of Lords, Party, and Public Opinion: Opposition Use of the Protest, 1760-1782," *Albion* 11 (Summer 1979): 151-53.

[45]*Gen. Eve.-Post* (3-5 August 1775); *Bath Chron.* (10 August 1775); *Glos. J.* (7 August 1775).

[46]HMC, *Tenth Report, Appendix, Part 6* (London: Her Majesty's Stationery Office, 1887) 10-12. There are also obvious parallels to the Royal Proclamation of 22 March 1769. This proclamation, "For the Suppressing Riots, Tumults, and Unlawful Assemblies," was published as a broadside "extraordinary" in the *London Gazette*, and it was reprinted in successive issues. Loyal addresses concerning Middlesex from eleven places appeared before 22 March. See *Lond. Gaz.* (4-7 February, 3-6 June 1769). The petitions in favor of Wilkes appeared after May. Compare George Rudé, *Wilkes and Liberty* (London: Oxford University Press, 1962) 105, 132, where he holds that the loyal addresses were prompted by the pro-Wilkes addresses.

(Months before, General Gage had read a proclamation in Boston that the colonists were in rebellion.[47]) Since the colonies were now in "open and avowed Rebellion" and "preparing, ordering, and levying War against Us," all the king's subjects in England were required to disclose any traitorous conspiracies, "against us, our Crown and Dignity." Parliament met on 26 October, and the king's speech to Parliament on the opening day was more strongly worded than his proclamation of 23 August. Like the proclamation, the speech was published in all the newspapers, and both documents served as a further stimulus to the outpouring of addresses and petitions. By 30 October there were rumors in England of the rebels' advance into Canada and the taking of St. Johns.[48] The date for this news is important since about half of the conciliatory petitions were sent to St. James after the middle of November.

It would be wrong to conclude from the king's reaction to the London radicals that he was uninterested in popular expressions concerning America. While he refused to give any public recognition to petitions for peace, and while the proclamation was designed to quell all vestiges of pro-American sympathy, he did in fact give his support to addresses of loyalty. There is substantial evidence that both the government and the Opposition were active in soliciting popular support for their respective measures. Numerous charges in the newspapers were leveled against the administration for promoting addresses through bribery.[49] While such accusations appear to be unwarranted, it is evident that the government was not averse to using less flagrant forms of influence in order to elicit at least some addresses. As early as July, the solicitor general, Alexander Wedderburn, urged Lord North to consider the utility of a royal proclamation against treason. He believed that "Addresses from the Country in support of Government, which are never worth solicitation, would soon follow unasked."[50] On 23 August the proclamation was published, and two days later, in writing to the king concerning possible ways of encouraging army recruitment, Lord North observed, "the cause of Great Britain is not yet sufficiently popular. . . . " By the first week in September, North had received loyal ad-

---

[47]Ian Christie and Benjamin Labaree, *Empire or Independence* (Oxford: Phaidon, 1976) 233.

[48]*Parl. Hist.*, 18:695-97; *Hamp. Chron.* (30 October 1775); *Read. Merc.* (30 October 1775).

[49]*Lond. Eve.-Post* (14-17 October 1775); *Bath J.* (2, 9, 23 October 1775); *Cumb. Pacq.* (19 October 1775, 4 January 1776); *Suss. Week. Adv.* (20 November 1775), where it was said that the Manchester address had cost £20,000 and that ministry would give £1,000 for an address from a borough, and £3,000 for one from a county. Many other charges of government influence not involving money were made; *Lond. Eve. Post* (26-29 August, 21-23, 28-30 September, 12-14 October, 18-21 November 1775); *Cumb. Pacq.* (7, 21 September 1775); *Suss. Week. Adv.* (16 October 1775). See also Sir Joseph Mawbey, *Parl. Hist.*, 18:1105, speech on 21 December 1775.

[50]HMC, *Tenth Report*, 9.

dresses from Manchester and Lancaster, and these prompted him to recommend to the king a positive program of encouraging addresses.

> As this spirit has sprung up spontaneously in Lancashire, Lord North submits to his Majesty whether it ought now to be encouraged, least [*sic*] the Lancashire addressers who have behaved so handsomely should think themselves neglected, and complain of being unsupported. If his Majesty is of that opinion, Mr. Robinson will privately endeavour to set on foot again the long projected address of the Merchants of London. One or two addresses may perhaps not be of much importance, but a general run of addresses just before the opening of Parliament will be of great service.[51]

The king's response to the idea of a general run of addresses was positive.

> It is impossible to draw up a more dutiful and affectionate Address than the one from the town of Manchester which really gives me pleasure as it comes unsolicited; as you seem desirous that this Spirit should be encouraged I will certainly not object to it; though by fatal experience I am aware that they will occasion counter petitions; one from the Merchants of London if Signed by a great Majority of the most respectable names in the City I should think highly proper as that would shew the Corporation of London have not been actuated by the Sense of the Merchants who are the respectable part of the Metropolis.[52]

The government's alertness to the value of support from the "respectable" part of the population is noteworthy, and the administration's involvement with the London merchants' address, if not other addresses from Lancashire, is thus beyond dispute. At this date there was also discussion of whether or not an "extraordinary Gazette" was necessary to publish the addresses from Lancaster and Manchester.[53]

Lord North worked through John Robinson, secretary to the treasury, and there are several threads of evidence that connect Robinson to a number of addresses. A draft of an address from the justices of the peace in Westminster was submitted to him, apparently for his approval, and a government agent at Kendal wished to know whether he should press to obtain an address there "at all Hazards," since the people were divided.[54] The First Lord of the Admiralty was active in obtaining the address from the University of Cambridge, and on two occasions he reported to Robinson concerning his progress. Lord Sandwich also worked through a government agent at Portsmouth in the hope of obtaining an address. While unsuccessful there, he met no such resistance in

---

[51]Fortescue, 3:249, 255 (North to George III, 25 August, 9 September 1775).

[52]Ibid., 3:256, 263 (George III to Lord North, 10 September 1775). See also regarding the London Merchants, North to George III, October 1775, and George III to North, 25 September 1775.

[53]Ibid., 3:260 (Lord Suffolk to George III, 12 September 1775).

[54]HMC, *Tenth Report*, 11-12. Sir S. Porten submitted a draft to Robinson on 6 October 1775, but there is no other record of this address. Dowker's report from Kendal was submitted through the Earl of Suffolk, 13 October 1775, 11-12.

his own pocket borough of Huntingdon.[55] Sir Thomas Dyke Acland was warmly encouraged by the government for his work in raising troops in Devonshire; he signed the addresses from the Devonshire justices of the peace and from the First Regiment of Devonshire Militia, and he may have been instrumental in promoting them.[56] Further research may reveal government activity behind the addresses from such boroughs as Plymouth, Barnstaple, and Rye, where the treasury held firm control.[57] It is no coincidence, as will be demonstrated in a later chapter, that the largest number of addresses came from boroughs and towns in Lancashire, a traditional Tory stronghold, and Hampshire, a county where politics was dominated by government patronage.[58] As in the case of Manchester, however, many of the loyal addresses arose as spontaneous expressions of patriotic support for the government's legislative authority, and a case will be made below for the independence of the majority of addressers.

Some addresses were promoted by individuals who may have had connections with the administration but who appear to have been acting in a private rather than an official capacity.[59] In Lancashire, Lord Stanley was the leading figure behind the massive county address, and Lord Derby, as lord lieutenant for the county, signed second after the sheriffs.[60] Titles of peers were predictably more prominent in the addresses from the counties than in those from the boroughs, though the precise influence of the nobility in promoting these addresses remains difficult to determine. Barrington's name heads the list for Berkshire, and Chandos and De La Warr were the first to sign the Hampshire address: all were steadfast supporters of court measures.[61] Dudley and Ward signed the Staffordshire address along with Lord Paget. Lord Gower was lord lieutenant of Staffordshire, and the editor of the *London Evening-Post* thought that this was certain evidence that this address was "the manufacture of the

---

[55]Ibid., 12-13, 19, 20 November 1775. On Portsmouth, see *Commons, 1754-1790*, 1:298. On Sandwich's control of Huntingdon, see *Commons, 1754-1790*, 1:312, and William T. Laprade, *Parliamentary Papers of John Robinson, 1774-1784* (London: The Royal Historical Society, 1922) 26-27, 6 September 1775, Sandwich to Robinson, about a vacancy at Huntingdon and American affairs. Sandwich was recorder of the borough and presented the address to the king along with the member of Parliament and one of the aldermen, HO 55/11/54.

[56]Fortescue, 3:249 (North to George III, 25 August 1775). HO 55/11/12; 11/17.

[57]See *Commons, 1754-1790*, 1:258, 251, 453, 294.

[58]Lancashire and Hampshire each sent six coercive addresses. For Hampshire and the place of government in borough politics, see Sir Lewis Namier, *The Structure of Politics at the Accession of George III*, 2d ed. (London: Macmillan Co., 1961) 67. See chapter 5 below, where the patrons connected to the unsigned addresses are treated.

[59]Regarding peers who normally supported the administration see *Lond. Eve.-Post* (5-7 October 1775).

[60]See HO 55/7/5; *Cumb. Pacq.* (16 November 1775); *Man. Merc.* (14 November, 12 December 1775); *York Cour.* (18 November 1775).

[61]See HO 55/12/8; 12/2.

Bedford party."[62] The names of Bateman, lord lieutenant of Herefordshire, and Oxford were prominent in the Herefordshire address, as was Lisburne in the address from Devonshire. The only anomaly in any of the county addresses is the signature of Plymouth on the document from Worcestershire; he was known to vote in opposition to court measures, and his signature seems out of place with the other names on this address: Dudley and Ward (the second address he signed), Sandys, Lyttelton, and Valentia.[63] Of all of the coercive addresses from counties, only Middlesex lacked the signature of a nobleman. Landed influence in the borough addresses is more difficult to detect, although the Earl of Warwick signed the address from Warwick, and the Duke of Beaufort was in attendance at the levee when the address from Gloucester was presented.[64]

V

If the government was interested in promoting loyal addresses, opposition groups spanning a wide political spectrum were equally involved with the petitions. The diversity of interests behind the petitions would, in the end, contribute not a little to the movement's ineffectiveness. Burke was always far more alert to the value of popular support than Rockingham, and by the fall of 1775 he was well versed in the petitioning process. On 23 August, the same day as the announcement of the royal proclamation, he attempted to persuade Rockingham of the importance of obtaining popular support before Parliament met. He offered specific suggestions of three leaders who "might feel the pulse of the people" and wondered whether it would be possible to do something "in the Counties and Towns." Rockingham's view of the usefulness of popular support stands in marked contrast to that of the king. In response to Burke, Rockingham expressed deep skepticism about the " generality of the public," and he proposed a conservative alternative: the only "proper" course of action

[62]*Lond. Eve.-Post* (12-14 October 1775).

[63]See HO 55/21/40; *Lond. Gaz.* (12-16 December 1775); HO 55/11/31; *Lond. Gaz.* (24-28 October 1775). Dudley and Ward may have been the leading force behind the Worcestershire address; at the meeting he read the document publicly before it was signed, *Shrews. Chron.* (28 October 1775).

[64]HO 55/9/1; *Lond. Chron.* (3-5 October 1775). Other possible connections between influential landed interests and coercive addresses can only be suggested here: the Bathhursts had a strong influence over local government at Cirencester, as did the Godolphin family at Helston. On the other hand, a number of boroughs that were heavily influenced by leading Whig patrons also sent coercive addresses. The Duke of Portland's influence at Wigan did not prevent an address, and neither did that of Lord George Cavendish at Derby. Lord Rockingham noted that Sir George Savile was mortified at the addresses from Kingston-upon-Hull. It is also possible, however, that the addresses from the inhabitants of these three boroughs were in part a reaction to the Whig influence upon the borough corporations, none of which addressed the Crown. But this is highly conjectural.

would be for Parliament to petition the Crown.[65] In mid-September Burke tried once again to persuade Rockingham of the importance of popular support through petitioning, and he candidly admitted that he had taken matters into his own hands at Bristol: "A Trusty secret Committee is formed to digest Business, and to correspond with other Towns." He did promise, however, not to proceed without his lordship's approval, a promise he later broke. In response, Rockingham appealed to his earlier tactic: nothing must be done until Parliament met.[66]

In spite of Rockingham's disapproval, Burke continued to work for obtaining as many petitions as possible. He himself drafted the Bristol petition to the Crown, and Richard Champion carried it about for signatures. He also worked closely with William Baker, the leader of the London merchants' petition.[67] Burke kept in close touch with Champion and Paul Farr at Bristol, and without Rockingham's knowledge, the local committee continued to seek petitions from other boroughs and towns.[68] Besides Bristol and London, it is possible to trace Burke's influence in the petitions from Westbury, Abingdon, Berkshire, Leeds, and possibly Nottingham and Bridgwater.[69] These documents are noteworthy for their moderate tone and their insistence on preserving the supreme legislative authority of Parliament—a hallmark of Burke's imperial theory. This, however, appears not to have satisfied many of those

---

[65]*Burke Correspondence*, 3:193-94, 205-206 (Burke to Rockingham, 23 August 1775); 205-206 (Rockingham to Burke, 11 September 1775). Rockingham's reservations in 1775 parallel exactly those he had in 1769. See George Rudé, *Wilkes and Liberty* (Oxford: Oxford University Press, 1962) 108, 120.

[66]*Burke Correspondence*, 3:207-209, 210, 214-16 (Burke to Rockingham, 14 September 1775; Rockingham to Burke, 24 September 1775).

[67]Ibid., 3:218-20 (Burke to Richmond, 26 September 1775).

[68]Champion sent detailed accounts of his own activity to Portland but, regrettably, no specific towns are ever mentioned. See Champion to Portland, 28 September, 5 October 1775, Portland Manuscripts, University of Nottingham, PWF 2, 715, 2, 718. *Burke Correspondence*, 3:223-24, 220-21, 230, 232 (Burke to Rockingham, 1 October 1775; Burke to Champion, 1, 17, 20 October 1775).

[69]*Burke Correspondence*, 3:234-35 (Rockingham to Burke, 2 November 1775). Lord Craven wrote to Burke concerning activities in Abingdon and Berkshire, and there was a "committee of correspondence" at Westbury that wrote to Burke on 21 November. See Ritcheson, *British Politics*, 228. Regarding the Earl of Abingdon's and Lord Craven's involvement with the Berkshire petition, see P. H. Ditchfield, ed., *The Victoria History of Berkshire*, 4 vols. (London: A. Constable and Co., 1906-1924) 2:164. Burke alluded at one point to contact with Samuel Elam of Leeds and Sir George Savile, who may have been involved in the petitioning activity at Halifax, and we know Burke had contact with Mark Huish at Nottingham in the spring. *Burke Correspondence*, 3:121, 194 (Burke to Mark Huish, 22 February 1775; Burke to Rockingham, 23 August 1775). The graceful prose of the petition from Wallingford also points to Burke. The petitions supported by Burke had an indirect influence on the broader movement; the wording of the Cambridge petition is clearly dependent on the petition from Bristol.

who wished to petition the Crown. The more radical political principles enunciated in other petitions demonstrate that the narrower interests of the Rockingham Whigs failed to encompass all the varieties of popular opposition to the government. Indeed, the differences in strategy within the Rockingham group itself meant that, unlike 1769, no central meeting was held and no centralized direction was given to the agitation. Burke was reduced to working behind his chief's back with results that were finally disappointing. He complained bitterly to Richmond and boldly called Rockingham's approach an "error."[70]

In contrast to the Rockingham Whigs, the London Association had no scruples about working with committees of correspondence.[71] Under the leadership of Thomas Joel, the society met regularly at the Globe Tavern, Fleet Street, and published resolutions concerning its grievances against the ministry and warnings against possible encroachments on the freedom of the press.[72] In late August, the association gained considerable notoriety for sending printed circular letters to a number of boroughs appealing for the organization of provincial associations designed to defend British liberties. The letter recommended the formation of committees of correspondence; while no specific appeal was made for petitions, loyal addresses were condemned as conducive to oppression.[73] It is impossible to determine how many conciliatory petitions the London Association may have elicited, but there is no doubt that it provoked a number of coercive addresses, and this, indirectly, stimulated some petitioning activity. The circular letters were addressed to the mayors, not the populace, of Nottingham, Worcester, Leicester, Lichfield, and Salisbury. The association appears never to have made a direct appeal to the people through handbills, though some of its deliberations were published in the newspapers.[74] The appeal to the mayors demonstrates the radicals' concern for the support of the more respectable elements in society. The circular letter also

---

[70]*Burke Correspondence*, 3:218 (Burke to Richmond, 26 September 1775). See Rudé, *Wilkes and Liberty*, 107.

[71]For a detailed discussion of the London Association, see Sainsbury, "The Pro-American Movement in London, 1769-1782," 208-22. Rumors of "Associations" forming throughout England to defend the people's liberties appeared in late July. See *Lond. Eve.-Post* (29 July–1 August, 5-7 August 1775).

[72]See *Lond. Eve.-Post* (9-12, 12-14 September, 26-28 October 1775); *Bath J.* (9 October 1775); *Suss. Week. Adv.* (9 October 1775).

[73]Printed in *Lond. Eve.-Post* (26-28 October 1775).

[74]For Nottingham see *Lond. Eve.-Post* (7-9 September 1775); *Man. Merc.* (12 September 1775); for Worcester, *Gen. Eve. Post* (5-7 September 1775); *Lond. Chron.* (5-7 October 1775); for Leicester, *North. Merc.* (18 September 1775); for Lichfield see HMC, *Dartmouth Manuscripts*, 3 vols. (London: Her Majesty's Stationery Office, 1887-1896) 2:376-77; for Salisbury, see *Sal. Win. J.* (11 September 1775). At Leicester, the association's appeal was almost certainly the main stimulus to the loyal address, and Dartmouth's tendering of thanks to the mayor of Lichfield may well have helped elicit the Lichfield loyal address. See HMC, *Dartmouth*, 2:380, 393.

reached Manchester, Blackburn, Kingston-upon-Hull, and Newcastle-upon-Tyne, and all of the boroughs known to have received the letter sent addresses supporting coercion to the Crown.[75] In Newcastle alone was an association actually formed, and of these nine cities, only Newcastle, Nottingham, and Worcester sent petitions for peace.[76] It is thus entirely possible that the net effect of the London Association's efforts was to promote more support for government measures than sympathy for the Americans.

A number of people who had no prominent position of leadership in the Opposition, or who seem to have been acting independently, expended considerable energy on behalf of obtaining petitions for peace. The petition against the Lancashire address was initiated and promoted by T. B. Bayley, Col. Townley, and J. Dobson, all of Liverpool. Abraham Rawlinson, Opposition Whig and later a member of Parliament for the county, was thought to have helped stimulate interest in this petition.[77] But the real counterpart to Lord Stanley and his dependents in Lancashire was the Rockingham Whig, Sir James Lowther, and his dependents in Cumberland. Against considerable odds, Lowther organized support for a petition in Cumberland, and he was also able to prevent an address from the Cumberland justices of the peace.[78] The opposition to the address from Staffordshire was led by Thomas Wooldridge, a London merchant who had a considerable estate in that county. Wooldridge had previous experience with the London merchants' petition, and at the county meeting he advanced a counter petition and later circulated it, ultimately obtaining a respectable number of signatures.[79]

The administration's plan of encouraging loyal addresses, when seen in conjunction with royal policy on unwanted petitions, suggests that the government had a coherent approach to public opinion. A later chapter will show how this approach was pressed to great advantage by an astute use of the government newspaper. George III's response to the suggestions of Lord North on the one hand, and Lord Rockingham's reaction to the plans of Edmund Burke

---

[75]For Manchester, see *Man. Merc.* (12 September 1775), for Blackburn, HMC, *Dartmouth*, 2:378, dated 28 August; for Hull, see *Burke Correspondence*, 3:216 (Rockingham to Burke, 24 September 1775); for Newcastle, see *Lond. Eve.-Post* (2-5 September 1775); *Lond. Chron.* (7-9 November 1775); *Bath J.* (11 September 1775). It was often observed in the newspapers that the loyal addresses were promoted in response to associations formed against the government. See, for example, *Glos. J.* (18 September 1775).

[76]On Wilkes's connection with Newcastle-upon-Tyne and, by extension, the London Association, see *Gen. Eve. Post* (31 October-2 November, 2-4 November 1775); *Lond. Chron.* (2-4, 4-7 November 1775).

[77]*Man. Merc.* (14 November 1775); *York Cour.* (21 November 1775).

[78]*Cumb. Pacq.* (2, 9, 16, 23, 30 November 1775; 18 January 1776).

[79]*Hamp. Chron.* (24-26 October 1775); *Lond. Eve.-Post* (12-14 December 1775). See John Money, *Experience and Identity; Birmingham and the West Midlands, 1760-1800* (Manchester: Manchester University Press, 1977) 204, on Wooldridge's leadership.

on the other hand, were to determine whether the policy of coercion appeared to be popular. Deeply concerned with the lack of public support for coercion, North believed that "a general run of addresses just before the opening of Parliament will be of great service."[80] The appearance of numerous addresses did in fact reflect at least one pole of public opinion. More importantly, the government's ability to present these addresses publicly actually *shaped* public opinion and proved the truth of North's statement.

The contrast to the Opposition could scarcely be greater. In late September, an anonymous newspaper article entitled "Popular Opposition to Government" lamented the impotence of the London petitions that resulted from the Court's contempt and urged in the place of petitions a "firm effectual opposition" that would be organized slowly, but deliberately.[81] Burke, however, remained convinced of the value of petitions, and in an attempt to convince Rockingham of the importance of popular support expressed in petitions, he observed, "A Minority cannot make or carry a War. But a Minority well composed and acting steadily may clog a War in such a manner, as to make it not very easy to proceed."[82] But the Rockingham Whigs were neither well composed nor able to act steadily. Their understandable aversion to radicalism and their abiding suspicion of popular support rendered the party almost totally ineffectual. An examination of the deep divisions in the English provinces suggests that the war might indeed have been clogged if the Rockingham Whigs had been able to marshal the popular support that emerged in reaction to coercion. The greatest indictment of the Rockingham Whigs lies in their failure to lead their party in popular agitation to petition the Crown. The agitation, however, proceeded in spite of them.

The thesis that national and local political issues coalesced around the American crisis receives considerable support by the general failure of nationwide leadership. Several attempts at centralized leadership did influence a few boroughs and counties, but what impresses one in the accounts of the provincial press is the spontaneity of both the addresses and the petitions. In his study of popular agitation in 1770, George Rudé was able to trace the origins of almost two-thirds of the pro-Wilkes petitions to the Rockingham Whigs or the Bill of Rights Society. But in the conflict regarding America, only about a third of the conciliatory petitions can be accounted for on the basis of the leadership

---

[80]Fortescue, 3:255 (North to George III, 9 September 1775).

[81]*Lond. Chron.* (30 September, 3 October 1775). The full title is "A Letter to John Sawbridge on Popular Opposition to Government."

[82]*Burke Correspondence*, 3:194 (Burke to Rockingham, 23 August 1775). On the oft-commented-upon inability of the Rockingham party to reach into the populace, see *Commons, 1754-90*, 1:289. On the inability of the Rockinghams, the followers of Chatham, and the London radicals to agree, see Mary Kinnar, "Pro-Americans in the British House of Commons in the 1770's" (Ph.D. dissertation, University of Oregon, 1973) 3, 33, 169-70, 283.

of the Rockingham Whigs.[83] Even in these cases, however, identifying the leaders of local agitation explains only the marshaling of public opinion, not its creation. There were, of course, various forms of indirect leadership, such as the government's use of the press. But in none of the five boroughs selected for further study below were the local leaders acting under the direction of either the government or the Opposition. In each case, leadership arose as an indigenous expression of popular politics, and these leaders won popular support through the ability to convincingly link local issues to the national crisis.

George III's delight over the spontaneity of the Manchester address appears genuine. The king's concern that addresses would of themselves elicit counterpetitions is itself a candid admission of the vitality of public opinion. Further, the Rockingham Whigs were divided on how to proceed, and this meant that their leadership would continue to be ineffective. The most outstanding feature, then, of the addresses and petitions in the fall of 1775 is that the majority of them emerged quite independently of direct centralized leadership. The petitions will next be analyzed through an examination of the divisions in the English provinces and the ideological content of the documents themselves.

---

[83]Rudé, *Wilkes and Liberty*, 211, table 7. Clear evidence for the influence of the Rockingham Whigs can be affirmed for London, Bristol, Westbury, Abingdon, Nottingham, Bridgwater, Leeds, and Berkshire. Direct government influence can be documented in only three cases: the London merchants, the University of Cambridge, and Huntingdon.

Petitions to the Crown: Division in the English Provinces

Chapter III

More than 200 separate appeals ascended to the Crown concerning America. The majority came from England alone, representing counties, towns, parliamentary boroughs, three groups of militia, and the Universities of Oxford and Cambridge.[1] The original manuscripts are retained in the Public Record Office. When combined with those printed in the *London Gazette* and the *London Evening-Post*,[2] they provide a reasonably complete survey of popular political activity. England, however, was not alone in expressing its wishes regarding the American issue: Scotland, Ireland, and Wales also sent numerous addresses to St. James (see Appendix 2). All but three of the Scottish counties sent loyal addresses to the king, as did the majority of parliamentary burghs. In Ireland only four constituencies addressed the throne, and in Wales there were three. In Scotland, Ireland, and Wales combined, the only cities to send petitions for peace were Dublin, Belfast, and Cork. The near-unanimous support of coercion from the north is of most interest to this study because it lent some support to the claim of the radicals that the government of George III was associated with Scotland and Stuart despotism.

I

Many of the most populous urban centers in England were divided regarding the American crisis. Some of the petitioners were also voters in parliamentary elections, but frequently more than half of the petitioners were not enfranchised. This underscores the popular dimension of the agitation, and the relationship between voters and petitioners is an important topic that will receive further attention below.[3] The total number of petitioners and the average number of voters in each borough is given in the following tables in order to

---

[1] There are 204 that can now be located: 109 from England, 89 from Scotland, Ireland and Wales (including the Isle of Man and the island of Guernsey) and six from London. See Appendices 1 and 2.

[2] References to these documents and the sources will be found in Tables 3.1-3.6 below.

[3] John A. Phillips, "Popular Politics in Unreformed England," *Journal of Modern History* 52 (December 1980): 611.

provide some index of the relative number of people involved. Since the nature of the franchise varied dramatically from borough to borough, the basis for the right to vote requires brief notice.

In eighteenth-century England there were 203 borough constituencies, most of which returned two members to Parliament.[4] The householder franchise granted the vote to any resident male who was the head of a household, and it was thus the broadest franchise of the five major types. While this franchise allowed poor people to vote, there were only eleven such boroughs in England. The freemen boroughs, by contrast, were the most numerous, comprising forty-five percent of the total, with electorates ranging from twenty to 7,000 voters. The basis for a person's municipal freedom varied considerably from borough to borough; some boroughs allowed the creation of nonresident honorary freemen while others did not. Often, the freeman boroughs with electorates of 200 or less were influenced by the corporation through its power to create honorary freemen, but the medium and large freeman boroughs were not so amenable to control, and among these were numbered the most respectable constituencies in England. The franchise for London was in the livery, a more restricted body than the freeman, but it is commonly classified with the freeman boroughs. The third borough type was the "scot and lot" variety in which the franchise rested in the inhabitant householders who paid the poor rate, thus excluding the poorest people. This group of boroughs was about a third as numerous as the freeman boroughs.

A much narrower franchise was found in the corporation borough where the vote was confined to members of the town corporation, normally the mayor and aldermen. Here as few as twelve and normally no more than twenty-four people possessed the vote. Finally, the franchise in the burgage borough was attached to the ownership of a plot of land rather than a person, and whoever owned a majority of burgages automatically controlled the nomination.[5] Corporation and burgage boroughs were therefore the quintessential pocket boroughs, since patrons often controlled and in some cases owned the right of election; combined, they account for about thirty percent of the English borough constituencies. Patronage was thus a significant part of eighteenth-century political life, and many elections were not oriented around political issues. In the general election of 1774, for example, sixty-nine boroughs were contested, but only about a fifth of these were divided concerning the American issue.[6] Tables 3.1-3.6, however, show that from the fall of 1775 through the

---

[4]Two boroughs returned four members each; five returned one member; the two universities returned two each. See *Commons, 1754-1790*, 1:513-19 for a list. The following discussion is based upon *Commons, 1754-1790*, 1:10-35.

[5]A subset of the burgage borough was the freeholder borough, where ownership of a majority of a borough's freehold properties gave a patron certain control at elections. There were six such boroughs.

[6]*Commons, 1754-1790*, 1:515-19. Bernard Donoughue, *British Politics and the American Revolution* (London: Macmillan Co., 1964) 177-200.

fall of 1776, fifty-two boroughs and six unrepresented towns, for a total of fifty-eight places, either addressed the throne in support of coercion or petitioned for peace, and to these a number of counties can be added. Clearly, by 1775 America had become an important issue and, in many ways, a divisive one.

Petitioning the Crown was a political act with a number of parallels to voting in parliamentary elections. Just as voting procedures differed from one constituency to the next, the structure of the meetings designed to address or petition the Crown varied dramatically from group to group. There were considerable differences in procedure, for example, between a university, a group of justices of the peace, a town corporation, a body of citizens in an urban setting, and a county meeting called for the purpose of petitioning.[7] Corporate bodies that did not seek support outside of a closed group obviously proceeded differently from those meetings organized specifically to obtain as wide a public response as possible. An address from a corporation was set forth at a regular meeting time, at a prescribed place, (normally the guildhall) and seldom met with serious opposition. In contrast, the organization of petitions and addresses in boroughs and counties was far more complex. Despite many variations, however, a pattern for putting forth petitions of the more popular variety did emerge, and it followed closely that of the Middlesex election affair. Leaders normally called for a public meeting weeks in advance by advertisements in local newspapers, and sometimes, depending upon the setting, by handbills.[8] Most advertisements made it clear whether or not the meeting was intended to organize support for the government's measures or support for peaceful measures. In this sense the meetings were partisan forums; they were intentionally designed to gather support for only one side of the debate.[9] This

---

[7]For brief discussions of how petitions circulated see Rudé, *Wilkes and Liberty* (Oxford: Oxford University Press, 1962) 119; Phillips, "Popular Politics," 606, 623. For descriptions of the organization of addresses and petitions from legal bodies, see the discussion in *Gen. Eve. Post* (23-26 September 1775); *Hamp. Chron.* (2 October 1775); *Glos. J.* (16 October 1775); from a corporation, *Read. Merc.* (6 November 1775); *Cumb. Pacq.* (21 September 1775); *Gen. Eve. Post* (14-16 September, 30 September-3 October, 21-23 November 1775); from borough inhabitants, *Lond. Chron.* (30 September-3 October 1775); *Morn. Chron.* (3-5 October 1775); and from the counties, *Glos. J.* (13 November 1775); *Gen. Eve. Post* (21-24 October 1775); and *Lond. Chron.* (21-24 October 1775).

[8]On the general pattern that follows, see the description of the proceedings of the London merchants, the Cambridge borough inhabitants, and the Lancashire freeholders, *Morn. Chron.* (5, 7, 10 October 1775); *Gen. Eve. Post* (11-14, 21-23 November 1775); *Man. Merc.* (14, 21 November 1775). On advertisements for meetings see, for London, *Lond. Chron.* (30 September-3 October 1775); *Pub. Adv.* (9 October 1775); for Bristol, *Gen. Eve. Post* (21-23 September 1775); for Newcastle-upon-Tyne, *Gen. Eve. Post* (26-28 October 1775); for the use of handbills at Cumberland, *Cumb. Pacq.* (26 October, 2 November 1775; 18 January 1776); and Cambridge, *Lond. Chron.* (10 November 1775).

[9]Advertisements for Lancashire, *Gen. Eve. Post* (21-24 October 1755); *Lond. Chron.* (21-24 October 1775) do not indicate which side will be taken; but it is clear for Her-

frequently led to a counterproposal, either in advance of the meeting or at the meeting itself, and since advertisements for both addresses and petitions commonly appeared in local newspapers at about the same time, a well-publicized choice was presented to the public.[10] In addition, the meetings sometimes provided an occasion for extended debate of the issues involved.

The order of business proceeded in a variety of ways, ranging from the highly stylized format of the London merchants, who had frequently petitioned, to the informal interchange of the Lancashire freeholders. In the former, the question was put whether or not the assembly wished to petition the Crown, and the question was then brought to a vote. The document itself was drafted ahead of time, read twice to the assembly, and voted upon. In the case of Lancashire, discussion was more open and the outcome of the meeting less certain. Once the assembly agreed to petition, it decided upon who would present the petition or address, and the document was signed by those present. For corporate and legal bodies there was seldom any public advertisement preceding the meeting, and agreement upon the content of the document normally concluded the process. With more open bodies there might then be some further discussion concerning the collection of signatures.[11]

In addition to advertising the time of the initial meetings, newspapers were used to publicize the proceedings and the place where the petitions lay for signing. As with the first advertisements, these notices commonly made the political orientation of the document very clear. The *Manchester Mercury*, for example, ran an advertisement for the Lancashire address that invited those who wished "to support the Legislative Authority" of Britain to sign it at Crompton's Coffee House in Manchester. In the same issue there was a notice inviting "all who wish a happy and speedy reconciliation between Great Britain and her colonies, without the further Effusion of Blood" to sign the peti-

---

efordshire, Worcestershire, Staffordshire, and Berkshire coercive, *Glos. J.* (13 November 1775), *Gen. Eve. Post* (21-24 October 1775), *Pub. Adv.* (9 October 1775), *Read. Merc.* (30 October, 6 November 1775); this is important in light of the fact that the turnout to address for these four counties was exceptionally low.

[10]For example, for Hampshire coercive, *Hamp. Chron.* (23, 30 October 1775); Hampshire conciliatory, *Lond. Chron.* (4-7 November 1775); for London, *Lond. Chron.* (30 September-3 October 1775). Regarding the debates at the meetings themselves, see the lengthy speech of Thomas Wooldridge at Staffordshire (*Shrews. Chron.*, 28 October 1775) and the extended discussion below in ch. 4 on Hampshire.

[11]Specifically who should be allowed to sign was sometimes discussed. The London Livery alone was to sign the Livery address, and the London merchants had to reside either in the city, in Westminster, Southwark, or the suburbs. *Cumb. Pacq.* (12 October 1775); *Morn. Chron.* (7 October 1775). The merchants in the spring had been equally careful. *Parl. Hist.*, 18:186-87 (26 January 1775). On the other hand, the Hampshire petition was "offered to all degrees and orders of people that are residents, without exception." *Lond. Chron.* (18-21 November 1775).

tion at Fletcher's Tavern.[12] The practice of depositing the document at some convenient public place to be signed during specified hours of the day was common. The London merchants even deputed a committee of twelve to oversee the signing of the document, but this appears to have represented exceptional care. The alternative method was for the leaders to carry the petition by hand from house to house, as Richard Champion did at Bristol. This was somewhat more open to criticism than placing the document in a public house; it was less objectionable than putting the document in one's own home for signing, as did Dr. Thomas Graham at Carlisle.[13] Some county petitions were also circulated throughout the county. The Lancashire petition, for example, was to lie at Manchester for a week and from there it was carried to Rochdale for more signatures and finally to London.[14]

Given the variety of circumstances surrounding public meetings, the differences of method in collecting signatures, and the strong political loyalties of the leaders, it is little wonder that the documents were denigrated by opponents. Nevertheless, based upon the literary evidence alone, a number of things could be said in favor of these efforts. The advertisements that solicited the public's involvement commonly stated that the purpose for meeting and petitioning was "to take the general sense of the county."[15] County meetings were modeled explicitly on the county caucuses that nominated knights of the shire to serve in Parliament. Later, when spokesmen came forward to defend the documents in Parliament, they claimed that those petitions that supported their views were the genuine expressions of the English public. Lord Craven, for example, said that "the sentiments of the people" were "faithfully collected and expressed" in the petition for peace from Coventry. Lord Stanley was equally certain that the address from Lancashire reflected "the sense of the freeholders at large."[16] At Cambridge "a Friend of Peace" answered charges against the conciliatory petitioners and defended at length the method of obtaining signatures, concluding that "every person that signed the Petition appears to have signed it with a full conviction of its propriety, and with a just sense of the importance of the request."[17]

---

[12]*Man. Merc.* (14, 21 November 1775). The London conciliatory lay at the King's Arms Tavern, and the coercive at the London Tavern, Bishopsgate Street.

[13]For Champion, see the letter to Portland, 5 October 1775, Portland Manuscripts, University of Nottingham, PWF 2, 718. "I have taken a great deal of Pains in going round the Town to procure the Signatures of Tradesmen which exertions might lead me to a greater knowledge of the Condition of Trade." On Graham, see *Cumb. Pacq.* (28 December 1775).

[14]*Man. Merc.* (14, 21 November 1775).

[15]See the Berkshire advertisement, *Read. Merc.* (27 November 1775).

[16]*Parl. Hist.*, 18:720, 758.

[17]*Gen. Eve. Post* (21-23 November 1775).

These assurances, however, are not in themselves convincing, for one could place alongside them an equal number of statements skeptical of the petitions' worth. The method of petitioning and the opinions of interested parties ultimately provide only ambiguous evidence regarding the question of the documents' validity. In terms of intent, organization, and method, petitioning activity represents a rough parallel to contemporary public-opinion polls, and yet the activity falls far short of modern standards. Given the highly polarized political atmosphere there is little hope of ever attaining a fully accurate picture of public opinion. At the same time, the way the signatures were collected does not preclude the possibility that the petitions reflected a reasonable level of validity. In those instances where specific locales were divided, the petitions allow for the possibility of a comparative approach that may be used to test political consistency over time. The consistency of individuals is a useful datum in drawing conclusions about validity, and this topic will be taken up in a later chapter.

II

The categorization of these documents under the simple rubrics "coercive" and "conciliatory" sometimes obscures nuances of thought, and in several cases may even be misleading. With few exceptions, however, the government was able to discern clearly whether or not an address supported its policy, and in the majority of borough and county cases there is little doubt about how a document should be classified. In his intensive regional study, John Money found that opinion in the west midlands was "sharply divided" concerning the American issue of whether or not to pursue coercive or conciliatory measures. But he was unaware of division in other parts of the country and concluded that the conciliatory petitions were "forlorn gestures rather than part of a campaign which had any hope of success."[18] This judgment, however, is controlled by the knowledge of subsequent events. The vigor of the reaction to addresses for coercion suggests that in the months of October and November the petitioners did not view their efforts as forlorn. The dating of the documents is important, because by the middle of October there were rumors in England that the provincials had invaded Canada, and by the first week in November these reports were confirmed. It cannot be proven that these developments were widely known to the conciliatory petitioners, but for those who made their presentations in late November and December it does seem likely.[19]

In the boroughs listed in Table 3.1, petitioning activity concerning America commonly involved between one-third and one-half as many people as voted in parliamentary elections, and at Newcastle-upon-Tyne and Great Yarmouth,

---

[18]John Money, *Experience and Identity: Birmingham and the West Midlands, 1760-1800* (Manchester: Manchester University Press, 1977) 200-201.

[19]See, for example, *Sal. Win. J.* (16 October, 6 November 1775).

the petitioners were approximately as numerous as the resident voters.[20] That America helped polarize the electorate in only fourteen borough constituencies in the general election of 1774 is sometimes seen as evidence for the unimportance of colonial affairs to the English public. But half of these boroughs were divided again a year later, and the colonies by this date had clearly be-

TABLE 3.1

					APPROXIMATE RESIDENT ELECTORATE
ADDRESSES AND PETITIONS FROM LARGE AND MEDIUM BOROUGHS					
	COERCIVE ADDRESS		CONCILIATORY PETITION		
BOROUGH*	SIGNATURES	DATE	SIGNATURES	DATE	TOTAL	
London (Merchants)	941	14 Oct.	1127	11 Oct.	2781	7000
(Livery)	1029	27 Oct.	--------	--------	--------	
Southwark	250	17 Nov.	756	29 Nov.	1006	2000
Bristol	901	7 Oct.	978	11 Oct.	1879	4000
Coventry	159	27 Sept.	406	20 Oct.	774	1900
	239	19 Oct. 1776	--------	--------	--------	
Newcastle-upon-Tyne	168	24 Nov.	1199	10 Nov.	1367	1500
Nottingham	230	21 Oct.	328 (Mayor)	1 Nov.	558	1400
	--------	--------		1 Nov.	--------	
Worcester	(Mayor)	25 Oct.	500	10 Nov.	500	1100
Colchester	125	9 Nov.	511	29 Jan. 1776	636	900
Taunton	191	6 Oct.	154	6 Oct.	345	500
Great Yarmouth	228	7 Oct.	344	17 Nov.	572	500
Southampton	56	18 Oct.	117	27 Oct.	173	400

* The franchise for London was in the Livery; Southwark was a large scot and lot borough; Taunton had a householder franchise; the remainder were freeman boroughs. The date is the day the petition was presented to the Crown, all in 1775, unless otherwise noted. For the Southwark conciliatory, see *Lond. Eve.-Post* (11-14 Nov., 2-5 Dec. 1775), *Suss. Week. Adv.* (20 Nov. 1775), *Pub. Adv.* (4 Dec. 1775); the Worcester conciliatory, *Lond. Eve.-Post.* (9-11 Nov. 1775), *Mid. J.* (11-14 Nov. 1775); the Great Yarmouth conciliatory and coercive, *Lond. Eve.-Post* (21-23 Nov. 1775), *Lond. Gaz.* (3-7 Oct. 1775), and *Norw. Merc.* (9 Dec. 1775). The remainder are in the PRO HO 55/7/3; 16/4; 9/12; 12/5; 11/9; 11/64; 11/6; 8/6; 11/65; 12/6; 28/19; 11/27; 10/18; 12/1; 8/10; 12/4; 9/4; 10/3; 8/3; 11/9; 11/20.

come more than a minor issue in Southwark, Newcastle, Worcester, and Great Yarmouth.[21] The coercive addressers outnumbered the conciliatory petitioners at Taunton, but in six cases the petitions for peace gathered more than twice as many signatures as those for coercion (the Worcester address alone lacking signatures). Since most petitions emerged in response to the addresses, it is likely that the leaders sought to obtain at least as many signatures on them as the addresses, so too much should not be made of this. Taunton is also of interest in that the electorate of 500 represented nearly a universal male suffrage, and the 345 petitioners and addressers thus involved a great majority of the population. Two large urban centers in Ireland—Dublin and Cork—sent signed petitions and addresses, and here too the petitions were much larger than the addresses with 2,986 as compared to 1,055 signatures on the former, and 500 to 160 on the latter. (See Appendix 2).

Similar patterns on a reduced scale are found in a number of smaller boroughs (listed in Table 3.2).[22] Here it is apparent that petitioning often involved a greater

---

[20]The total number of signatures for each address or petition is determined from the original document, when available, and otherwise from the newspapers. The total for the two London addresses (1654) and for the two Coventry addresses (368) counts only those who addressed once. For the 316 people who signed both the London merchants and the livery address, see John A. Sainsbury, "The Pro-American Movement in London, 1769-1782: Extra-Parliamentary Opposition to the Government's American Policy" (Ph.D. dissertation, McGill University, 1975) Appendices A and B. The address from Worcester was not signed, so it is somewhat questionable whether coercion was popular there; the unsigned Nottingham petition is also listed here, since the mayor, aldermen, and burgesses of Nottingham petitioned the Crown in addition to the inhabitants. The resident electorates are drawn from *Commons 1754-1775*, vol. 1, and from printed poll books, where available, rounded to the nearest hundred resident electors. The poll books are found in the collection of the Institute of Historical Research, University of London, unless otherwise noted, and resident electors alone are counted. *The Poll* (Bristol, 1774); *The Poll* (Coventry, 1780); *The Poll* (Newcastle, 1777); *The Poll* (Nottingham, 1774); *The Poll* (Colchester, 1768, 1780); *The Poll* (Worcester, 1761); *The Poll* (Southampton, 1774). *The Poll* (Great Yarmouth, 1777) is at Norwich Central Library, Norwich.

[21]*Commons 1754-1790*, 1:75. Donoughue, *British Politics*, 177-200. The boroughs that divided in 1774 and again in 1775 were London, Bristol, Southwark, Newcastle, Worcester, Great Yarmouth, Cambridge, and Southampton.

[22]The petition from Westbury, Warminster, and Trowbridge is to Parliament, not the Crown, but it was an explicit rebuttal to the petition to the king from Bradford, Trowbridge, and Melksham with 244 signatures and thus it is included here. See on this point *Lond. Eve.-Post* (18-21 November 1775.) A group of sixty addressers from Warminster, in turn, replied to the parliamentary petition in early December, *Bath Chron.* (26 October, 14 December 1775). Burke presented the Westbury petition to Parliament as part of his speech for conciliation on 16 November. For the resident electorates, rounded to the nearest ten electors, see *Commons 1754-1790*, vol. 1 and *The Poll* (Cambridge, 1774, 1776), Cambridge Central Library, Cambridge; MS poll book of the 1768 Poole election, Calcraft MSS, Dorset County Record Office; *The Poll* (Bridgwater, 1780); and *The Poll* (Abingdon, 1768) in the Guildhall Library, London.

proportion of the borough population in politics than in parliamentary elections. In the small freeman boroughs of Cambridge, Poole, and Lymington, the electorate was restricted in part because the corporation could manipulate it through its power to create honorary freemen. The petitioners faced no such restriction. The activity of large numbers of unenfranchised petitioners is most dramatically evident in the division of three nonparliamentary cities. With the exception of Dublin, the petition from Halifax collected more signatures than any other petition from an urban setting, a fact often remarked upon in the press. The larger numbers do not appear to be out of proportion to the concentration of population in these then rapidly industrializing areas. The connection with trade, however, is not as obvious as it was earlier in the year.

In light of what is now known about the origins of urban radicalism, petitions for conciliation from the large, independent boroughs listed in Table 3.1 might be expected, but there are some surprises with respect to the smaller boroughs. Wallingford, for example, was very venal; parliamentary elections

TABLE 3.2

ADDRESSES AND PETITIONS
FROM SMALL BOROUGHS AND UNREPRESENTED CITIES

BOROUGH*/CITY	COERCIVE ADDRESS		CONCILIATORY PETITION			APPROXIMATE RESIDENT ELECTORATE
	SIGNATURES	DATE	SIGNATURES	DATE	TOTAL	
Cambridge	96	27 Nov.	160	29 Nov.	256	80
Bridgwater	110	20 Oct.	150	27 Oct.	260	250
Poole	56	27 Sept.	144	31 Oct.	200	100
Lymington	74	20 Nov.	135	17 Dec.	209	50
Abingdon	115	27 Oct.	117	17 Nov.	232	220
Westbury, Warminster, Bradford, Trowbridge	244	21 Oct.	138	16 Nov.	382	69
Wallingford	----------	----------	80	17 Nov.	80	200
Unrepresented Cities						
Leeds (Yorks.)	264	1 Nov.	594	9 Nov.	858	
Halifax (Yorks.)	660	3 Nov.	1865	7 Nov.	2525	
Bolton (Lancs.)	1202	12 Dec.	751	16 Dec.	1953	

*Cambridge, Poole, and Lymington were freeman buroughs; Bridgwater, Abingdon, and Wallingford, scot and lot; and Westbury, burgage. For the Cambridge conciliatory, see *Cam. Chron.* (9 Dec. 1775); the Poole and Abingdon conciliatory, *Lond. Eve.-Post* (2-4, 18-21 Nov. 1775); the Westbury conciliatory, *Bath Chron.* (23, 30 Nov. 1775); the Bolton conciliatory, *Lond. Eve.-Post* (14-16 Dec. 1775). For the remainder, see HO 55/10/16; 11/24; 11/34; 8/2; 8/30; 11/56; 11/23; 11/15; 28/21; 10/5; 21/39; 12/3; 16/3; 10/17.

were often decided by money. A statement of high political principle was hardly in keeping with the borough's reputation. But Wallingford was under the influence of the Earl of Abingdon, an outspoken opponent of the government's American policy.[23] Lymington, like Wallingford, was also under the control of a patron, but Sir Harry Burrard was a placeman who always voted with the administration, and the pro-American petition there cannot be readily attributed to his influence.[24] These and other smaller boroughs raise the issue of the influence of patronage in an acute form. People in unrepresented industrial cities like Halifax and Leeds, however, were not as susceptible to influence, and the genuineness of the public division concerning America in these cities is less subject to doubt. The geographical distribution of the twenty-one cities (in Tables 3.1 and 3.2) was fairly wide; seventeen counties are represented, four of which had two boroughs or towns that divided.

Ten of the forty English counties sent up addresses or petitions to the Crown concerning America. In 1778 Norfolk sent a large petition to Parliament that cannot be justly considered a part of the earlier agitation. It did, however, reflect political divisions in the county and is included here in order to provide a complete listing.[25] Each county returned two members to Parliament and voting was based upon the possession of freehold property valued at 40 shillings.[26] Six of the ten counties made appeals for peace and five were divided concerning whether or not conciliatory or coercive measures should be pursued (see Table 3.3). Historians have assumed that if the trading centers expressed sympathy for America, the landed interests were uniformly behind the government.[27] The petitions for peace from the counties call for a thorough reevaluation of this generalization. With the exception of Middlesex and Lancashire, the number of county addressers was surprisingly small. Moreover, the counties that sent coercive addresses alone were not necessarily united. The *Kentish Gazette* of 1775 depicts widespread dissatisfaction with the govern-

---

[23]*Commons 1754-1790*, 1:212.

[24]Ibid., 1:295; 2:158-59.

[25]The meeting to petition was held in a tavern in Norwich though it was a county petition. Horace Walpole called this petition "a remonstrance from the county of Norfolk against the war," and notes that it was drawn up by "Mr. Windham of Felbry," A. Francis Steuart, ed., *The Last Journals of Horace Walpole*, 2 vols. (London: John Lane, 1910) 2:119. Hayes plays down the political significance of the document and seems oblivious to the fact that it collected over 5,000 signatures. B. D. Hayes, "Politics in Norfolk, 1750-1832" (Ph.D. dissertation, Cambridge University, 1958) 198-200. But this resistance to government resulted in contending parties, heated charges of disloyalty, and hints of treasonous activity. See *An Appeal to the People of England, on the Present Situation of National Affairs; and to the County of Norfolk, on Some Late Transactions and Reports* (London, 1778) 1, 5, 6.

[26]*Commons, 1754-1790*, 1:2.

[27]Dora Mae Clark, *British Opinion and the American Revolution* (New Haven: Yale University Press, 1930) 133.

ment in Kent, and in Devon there was some opposition expressed to the county address. Sir George Yonge made a spirited speech against addressing that met "with a very general applause," so that while the address was carried, "very few could be prevailed upon to sign it."[28] Finally, these data should be interpreted in light of the fact that at the general election of 1774, only eleven counties divided, and in 1780 only two went to the polls.[29]

III

This petitioning activity is distinguished from the movement in the early months of 1775 by its emphases on political principles, the consciences of the petitioners, and the constitutional issue of parliamentary supremacy. Only one-

TABLE 3.3

ADDRESSES AND PETITIONS FROM ENGLISH COUNTIES						
	COERCIVE ADDRESS		CONCILIATORY PETITION			APPROXI-MATE RESI-DENT ELECTO-RATE
COUNTY*	SIGNA-TURES	DATE	SIGNA-TURES	DATE	TOTAL	
Middlesex	613	21 Oct.	1033	21 Oct.	1646	3500
Berkshire	302	21 Nov.	853	23 Nov.	1155	3000
Hampshire	201	2 Nov.	2500	19 Dec.	2701	5000
Lancashire	6273	6 Dec.	4014	17 Dec.	10287	8000
Staffordshire	138	28 Oct.	900	11 Dec.	1038	5000
Conciliatory Only						
Cumberland	----------	----------	unknown		----------	4000
Norfolk (to Parliament)	----------	----------	5400	17 Feb. 1778	5400	6000
Coercive Only						
Herefordshire	380	16 Dec.	----------	----------	380	4000
Devonshire	240	25 Oct.	----------	----------	240	3000
Worcestershire	87	23 Oct.	----------	----------	87	4000
Kent	unknown	6 Dec.	----------	----------	----------	8000

*For the Middlesex coercive, see *Lond. Gaz.* (17-21 Oct. 1775); the Hampshire conciliatory, *Lond. Eve.-Post* (23-25 Nov. 1775), *Morn. Chron.* (19 Dec. 1775); the Staffordshire conciliatory, *Lond. Eve.-Post* (12-14 Dec. 1775); Cumberland, *Cumb. Pacq.* (23, 30 Nov. 1775); Norfolk, *Parl. Hist.*, 19:762, and *CJ*, 36:710-11; Herefordshire, *Lond. Gaz.* (12-16 Dec. 1775); Worcestershire, *Lond. Gaz.* (24-28 Oct. 1775); Kent, *Lond. Chron.* (2-5, 5-7 Dec. 1775), *Morn. Chron.* (7 Dec. 1775). For the remainder, see HO 55/13/2; 12/8; 12/9; 12/2; 7/5; 9/3; 21/40; 11/31.

[28]See the numerous antiministerial editorials in *Kent. Gaz.* (30 August-2 September, 2-6, 6-9, 9-13, 13-16, 16-20, 20-23, 23-27 September 1775); on Devon, see *Morn. Chron.* (1 November 1775).

[29]*Commons, 1754-1790*, 1:514.

third of the conciliatory petitions and less than a sixth of the coercive addresses to the Crown mention the condition of English commerce, and the petitions that do mention trade are still dominated by the question of political author- ity.[30] Another emphasis distinguishes these documents from those sent to Par- liament: one out of every three of the addresses for coercion explicitly condemns the domestic factions in England that aided, abetted, and encouraged rebellion in America.[31] This in itself suggests the reality of serious disunity in the En- glish populace. The change of emphasis to constitutional issues and the de- nunciation of domestic pro-American sentiment are clearly related, and both may be seen at least in part as a response to the king's proclamation. The pres- ence in England of "turbulent and dissatisfied minds"—men "void of all Prin- ciple" who have encouraged the "Flames of Sedition" and whose "machinations have driven headlong the Americans into a Rebellion"—is said to have been the principal reason behind the addressers' declaration of loyalty to the king and their urging the enforcement of coercive measures.[32] Addresses and peti- tions, however, have a number of points in common; both profess loyalty to the king and both are concerned about his honor. All the documents deal with parliamentary supremacy, and this theme is sometimes connected to hope for reconciliation, though the incompatibility of both supremacy and reconcilia- tion is occasionally perceived. The issue that divided the addresses from the

---

[30]These summary statements apply to all the English addresses and petitions in the fall, not just Tables 3.1-3.3. Six of the ten conciliatory petitions that mention the de- pressed conditions of English trade appear to have been arguing in response to the ad- dresses from the same boroughs that claim their trade was flourishing (Middlesex, Bristol, Worcester, Westbury, Leeds, and Bolton). The other four that deal with trade are London merchants, Nottingham, Coventry, and Staffordshire. Petitions from four additional boroughs allude fleetingly to the "valuable trade" with America: Abingdon, Southwark, Yarmouth, and Taunton. The eleven addresses that mention trade are from Manchester, Beverley, Worcester, Bewdley, Wigan, Leeds, Bristol, Bradford, Bolton, Blackburn, and Middlesex. Only six of the total of seventy-five addresses from Scot- land allude to commerce.

[31]Money, *Experience and Identity*, 202, noted the concentration on factions at home, and Paul Langford, "Old Whigs, Old Tories and the American Revolution," *Journal of Imperial and Commonwealth History* 8 (January 1980): 125, commented on the "sav- age" denunciation of the colonies in some of the coercive addresses. The addresses that mention domestic factions are those from Bristol, Coventry, Nottingham, Worcester, Taunton, Bridgwater, Poole, Halifax, Lancaster, Leicester, Beverley, Warwick, Hull, Shrewsbury, Winchester, Christchurch, Derby, Chester, Southmolton, Wigan, New Windsor, Sudbury, the counties of Devon and Stafford, the Devon justices of the peace, the justices of the peace of the Tower of London; the Northamptonshire Militia, and the Northern Regiment of the Devonshire Militia.

[32]The Leicester addressers make an explicit connection between their address, quelling domestic faction, and the king's proclamation. The phrases in the preceding sentence are taken from the addresses from Nottingham and Taunton.

petitions was twofold: whether or not the colonies were actually in rebellion and whether or not force should be used to reclaim them.

Sir Lewis Namier argued that by 1775 nothing approximating Whig and Tory parties subsisted in the nation at large, but even he admitted that the realities behind the old party labels were "latent in temperament and outlook, in social types, in old connections and traditions." Paul Langford recently traced expressions of support for coercive measures precisely to these old Tory connections and traditions. Through a detailed examination of Tory families, he demonstrated that the addressers were the "natural heirs" of the old Tories. Ideologically they differed in certain respects from the Tories of a generation past. They did not, for example, hold to passive obedience to the Crown. The addressers did, however, believe firmly in the absolute authority of Parliament, and Langford interpreted this as signifying the reality of a surprising ideological unity in conservatism over a period of years. In addressing the Crown during the American crisis "old Tories" had transferred their trust in the absolute sovereignty of the king to the absolute sovereignty of Parliament. Attitudes toward the divine right of properly constituted authority and the principle of nonresistance were now related to the king in Parliament, and according to Langford, this is accurately described as a new authoritarian viewpoint.[33] Further, the language of "abhorrence" was the same language used during the Exclusion crisis of 1679 when the Tories abhorred the Whig petitioners and stood steadfastly by the royal proclamation against tumultuous petitions.

The ideology of the addresses follows closely that of the address of both Houses of Parliament to the Crown in February. The rhetoric also has clear affinities to the addresses that emerged in support of the government during the Middlesex election affair. These earlier documents are almost indistinguishable in tone and content from those of 1775. The progovernment address from Bristol in 1769 declared "our utter Detestation and Abhorrence of those seditious Attempts, which have been lately made, to spread a Spirit of Riot, Licentiousness, and Disaffection, through the Kingdom, tending to destroy all Subordination to lawful Authority." The Liverpool addressers of 1769 registered their "utmost Abhorrence" of sedition. They promised to support all the king's measures to "re-establish due Order and Obedience among your Sub-

---

[33]Sir Lewis Namier, *England in the Age of the American Revolution*, 2nd ed. (London: Macmillan Co., 1961) 180. Langford, "Old Whigs, Old Tories," 8:106, 123, 125. Mary Kinnear, "Pro-Americans in the British House of Commons in the 1770s" (Ph.D. dissertation, University of Oregon, 1973) 89, found strong continuity between supporters of the administration's American policy in Parliament and the groups around Bute, Bedford, and the "King's Friends." This evidence supports J. A. W. Gunn, *Beyond Liberty and Property* (Kingston and Montreal: McGill-Queens University Press, 1983), on the persistence of high Tory ideas. Compare Ian R. Christie, "Was There a 'New Toryism' in the Earlier Part of George III's Reign?" in *Myth and Reality in Late-Eighteenth-Century British Politics and Other Papers* (New York: Macmillan Co., 1970) 196-213.

jects, and stop the progress of these factious Combinations" at the "Risque of our Lives and Fortunes." Coventry addressers in 1769 agreed: "We cannot, without Horror, reflect on that Spirit of Discontent and Disorder, which hath of late appeared among some of our misguided Fellow-Subjects," and they concluded, "we are ready to sacrifice every Thing that is dear to us in Defense of your Royal Person."[34] The same phrases are found repeatedly in the addresses of 1775.

The coercive addresses of 1775 expressed a fairly wide spectrum of sentiment, but a number of themes united them. The addressers agree with the Crown that the colonies are in a state of rebellion and are one in the conviction that the supreme legislative authority of Great Britain must be upheld. The addressers either recommend force, or, more commonly, pledge their lives and fortunes in the king's service to bring the colonies to due obedience to the law. The language used to express these ideas, however, differs considerably from address to address, ranging from bellicose to irenic. The mayor, burgesses, and inhabitants of Bristol, for example, expressed their "Astonishment" at the conduct of "a few disappointed men, whose sophistical Arguments and seditious Correspondence, have, in great Measure, been the occasion of deluding your American Subjects into open Rebellion." They testified to their "Abhorrence of this unnatural Rebellion" and expressed their "warmest wishes for the Success of those Measures your Majesty hath adopted in Support of the Legislative Authority of Great Britain over all your Dominion," concluding, "may your Majesty's Councils ever prevail to the extirpating of Licentiousness."[35] Support for George III and his administration was thus commonly wedded to an expression of belligerence towards the colonists, and the use of force was encouraged with promises of local assistance forthcoming if necessary.

Most addresses explicitly describe the reasons for advising the Crown to take coercive measures: the colonists are engaged in an "unnatural rebellion," and submission to the legislative authority of Great Britain is required of all British subjects. The coercive addresses from Newcastle-upon-Tyne, Southampton, Taunton, Cambridge, and Bridgwater either insisted upon the "undoubted rights" of the legislative authority of Great Britain or required "submission" to Parliament, and they all endorse the use of force for one reason: to secure this submission. The "right" of Parliament to enforce obedience is a common thread in all the addresses. Even when this is not stated concretely, it is inferred. At Colchester the coercive addressers lamented the fatal effects of the "unnatural contest" and pledged themselves to offer "due obedience to the Legislative Authority." At Coventry abhorrence is expressed at "those pernicious principles, which the patrons of sedition have industriously insinuated into the mind of your Majesty's deluded subjects," and support for "our admirable constitution in church and state" is affirmed. The same point

---

[34]*Lond. Gaz.* (14-18 March, 28 March-1 April, 4-8 April 1769).
[35]HO 55/11/14.

is made at Nottingham by rejecting the "Spirit of Faction and Rebellion" that is put forth in the colonies under the "Specious Pretense of Liberty."[36]

Several of the addresses draw directly upon the content, indeed even the language, of the Declaratory Act.[37] Others attempt to make finer discriminations. The city of Oxford, for example, grappled with the issue of taxation.

> We thought that America had reason to complain of the unconstitutional unlimited Right of Taxation claimed by the Parliament of Great Britain, but as the Grievance was, in our Apprehension, redressed by a Measure taken in the last Session of Parliament, and as America has contemptuously rejected this Redress absolutely, even without making it a Ground of Treaty, we cannot but think that She entertains Views totally inconsistent with the Subordination which she . . . owes to the Crown and Parliament of Great Britain.[38]

Of all the pro-administration addresses, only four equivocate on the use of force as the best policy. Cambridge declared the colonies to be in a rebellious state, but left it to the king to decide whether or not "coercion" or "indulgence" was best. The addresses from Plymouth and Exeter were so mild as to render their classification as coercive somewhat dubious. Hereford expressed a preference for conciliatory measures, but allowed for "vigorous" means.[39] All of these addresses permit the use of force, and the unifying theme throughout is the importance of insuring the submission of the colonies to the supreme legislative authority of Great Britain.

Seven of the coercive addresses were presented in late September, but the first conciliatory petitions did not appear until the early weeks of October. (See Appendix 1 for the texts of most of these documents.)[40] Most of the conciliatory petitions were put forth in direct opposition to the coercive addresses. In only two cases (London and Newcastle-upon-Tyne) were the petitions presented before the addresses. In fourteen out of twenty-six cases the petitions explicitly stated that they were being advanced in response to the misrepre-

---

[36]See HO 55/12/6; 11/19; 10/3; 10/16; 11/24; 12/4; 11/6; 11/27.

[37]See, for example, London, Cirencester, Exeter, Gloucester, Liverpool, Kingston-upon-Hull, and others (HO 55/7/3; 10/12; 11/7; 11/25; 28/20; 8/4).

[38]HO 55/10/8.

[39]For Cambridge (HO 55/10/16), and for Plymouth, Exeter, and Hereford (HO 55/10/10; 11/7; 10/7). *Lond. Eve.-Post* listed the address of the London Livery as conciliatory as did *Brist. J.* (28 October 1775), but it is more strongly worded than Plymouth and Hereford.

[40]The seven, in order of presentation, were Manchester, Lancaster, Leicester, Exeter, Coventry, Poole, and Liverpool.

sentations of the coercive addresses.[41] The petitioners intended to rectify the impression that the people were united in support of coercive measures. "We should not have presumed," wrote the Southwark petitioners, "to have troubled your Majesty . . . if the intention of some amongst us to encourage, as we apprehend an unnatural civil war between us and our fellow subjects in America had not made a declaration of our opinions absolutely necessary." Nottingham petitioners feared that the coercive measures that the addresses recommended "will lead to irrecoverable ruin," and Coventry petitioners rejected the loyal addresses that were falsely represented "as the genuine and general sentiments of the people of England."[42] "At a time when addresses of approbation are industriously sought by those interested men who have plunged an unhappy and united people into all the horrors of civil war," the petition from Newcastle-upon-Tyne asserted, "we should ill deserve the blessings of freedom and of commerce were we by our silence to give a sanction to their mischievous infatuation." Berkshire petitioners were opposed to the "inflammatory addresses" that had the effect of stimulating violence, and the petitioners from Leeds wrote that they "cannot approve the sanguinary measures, which have been recommended to your Majesty, in some recent addresses on the present unhappy disturbances in America." Lymington petitioners claimed, like the others, that they were petitioning in order that "Your majesty should be acquainted with the real voice of your people."[43] The majority of the petitions were thus motivated by a desire to avoid giving the king the impression that the people of England were unanimous in their support of coercive measures against America. This explicit intention of the petitioners was ignored at the time and subsequently forgotten.

In the petitions, as with the addresses, the spectrum of expression is fairly wide, while the essential political content is quite uniform. The Bristol, Bridgwater, and Berkshire petitions are moderate in their opposition to government. Influenced if not authored by Edmund Burke, their insistence upon the desirability of preserving the supreme legislative authority of Parliament is understandable. The Bristol petition, however, conceded that "the superiority can hardly be preserved by mere force"—a point that Burke had often made in Parliament—and the Berkshire petition pled for the "substantial and not nom-

---

[41]In a few settings, the meetings organized to facilitate petitioning activity were held before those that met to support coercive measures; Bristol, Nottingham, and Cambridge are examples. But even here, the earlier addresses from other boroughs undoubtedly played a role in stimulating conciliatory sentiment, and in the majority of boroughs that divided the coercive addresses were circulated before the conciliatory petitions. The fourteen that stated they were responding to addresses are: Bristol, Southwark, Newcastle, Coventry, Worcester, Nottingham, Cambridge, Great Yarmouth, Lymington, Westbury, Wallingford, Leeds, Berkshire, Lancashire. The petitions from Hampshire and Cumberland are not available, and that of Norfolk does not pertain.

[42]*Pub. Adv.* (4 December 1775); HO 55/12/1; *Lond. Eve.-Post* (21-24 October 1775).

[43]HO 55/28/19; 12/9; 21/39; 11/56.

inal assent of the subject in the granting of their own money." The petition from Bridgwater was so clearly insistent on the supremacy of Parliament that it won a place in the *London Gazette*, the only petition to be so honored. But even the most mildly worded conciliatory petitions sometimes contained pointed criticism of the government's policy. Halifax petitioners urged the king to accept their petition on the grounds that it "proceeds from motives solely tending to the re-establishing of that mutual confidence which ought always to subsist between the legislative body and the subject."[44]

Other petitions were also moderate in tone. The petitioners at Nottingham sagely attempted to defuse the constitutional issue from the English side by appealing to prudence and by reminding the king of the limits of sovereignty: "However just the claims of the British Parliament, however constitutional its sovereignty over every member of its extended empire, the situation of America we apprehend to be such, as renders it imprudent and of no advantage to the common welfare (the great end of sovereignty) to enforce all their claims." The conciliatory petitions from Cambridge and Colchester did not elaborate on constitutional questions, but the former made an appeal for "healing concessions" to avoid alienating the "affections of our fellow subjects in America" and the latter simply urged "conciliatory measures."[45] These conciliatory petitions generally recognized on purely pragmatic grounds that coercion was a shortsighted, ultimately disastrous policy, but in most of them constitutional issues were still prominent. All seven of these petitions pled for the adoption of lenient measures; none of them used the word *rebellion*, and they thereby witnessed against the king's earlier proclamation.[46]

While all of the petitions expressed their loyalty to the king, some were more progressive and represent a distinct step to the left of the Rockingham Whigs. The pro-American petitions from Southwark and Taunton did not mention parliamentary supremacy and asserted boldly the right of the colonists to be represented. The petitions from Newcastle-upon-Tyne, Southampton, and Lymington explicitly championed the "natural rights" as well as the "chartered rights" of the colonists. The latter three based their plea for benevolent measures on the importance of preserving such rights.[47] Others were remarkably candid in sympathizing with American grievances: "We are naturally led

---

[44]HO 55/11/64; 12/9; 11/34. That the petitions were scrutinized by the administration is suggested by Lord North's comment to the king concerning the London merchants' petition: "It were much better to have had no petition; but the petition intended seems as little inconvenient as any petition can be." Fortescue, 3:263 (North to the king, 25 September 1775.) This helps account for the admission of the Bridgwater petition in the *Gazette*.

[45]HO 55/12/1; *Cam. Chron.* (9 December 1775); HO 55/9/4.

[46]In addition, the petitions from Great Yarmouth, Abingdon, Bolton, and Lancashire were moderate in expression.

[47]*Pub. Adv.* (4 December 1775); HO 55/8/3; 28/29; 11/20; 11/56.

to believe," said the Coventry petitioners, "that they act from principle, and in consequence of self-conviction," and Leeds's petitioners acknowledged "the integrity and fidelity of our American brethren." The petitioners from Staffordshire agreed: "They think they are fighting in the sacred cause of liberty; and if mistaken, they ought on that account to be considered by Englishmen with indulgence." The Berkshire petitioners "lamented" the disorders in America and even blamed the colonists for them, but added, "We cannot think them unnatural, in those, in whom the love of freedom is united with the ordinary weakness and imperfection of human nature."[48]

London, Middlesex, Worcester, and Wallingford went beyond this pro-American sentiment by requesting that inquiry be made into the causes of the recent calamitous events. As was common in Opposition rhetoric, the king's advisors came under particular censure.[49] Although there was a two-year span separating these petitions, 5,400 people in the county of Norfolk expressed essentially the same point of view in their petition to Parliament: "We greatly fear that we . . . have been greatly deceived and deluded, with regard to the Nature, the Cause, and the Importance of the American Troubles . . . and, to speak with the filial confidence of free Subjects, we plainly declare ourselves unwilling to commit any more of our National Glory to Attaint."[50]

The ideological differences between petitions and addresses reflect considerable depth of feeling and illustrate how divisive the American issue had become. The differences were grounded in principle; if the addressers viewed the conflict as an "unnatural rebellion," the petitioners thought of it as an "unnatural civil war." Even at Bridgwater, where the conciliatory petition was moderate, deeply felt differences divided petitioners and addressers. The Bridgwater petitioners, while not wishing to impair "the supreme legislative authority of this country," were still preoccupied with the "enjoyment of the rights and privileges of a free people," and they pled for some "happy plan of conciliation, which may restore peace, and confidence in your Majesty's Government." By contrast, the deepest concern of the Bridgwater addressers was "the many inflammatory Methods used to alienate the Affections of Your Majesty's Subjects, to seduce them from their duty, and even to countenance and abet the most ungrateful and daring Rebellion in America," and it appears that they expressed their abhorrence of such "flagitious attempts" with one eye on

---

[48]*Lond. Eve.-Post* (21-24 October 1775); HO 55/21/39; *Lond. Eve.-Post* (12-14 December 1775); HO 55/12/9.

[49]HO 55/16/4; 13/2; *Lond. Eve.-Post* (9-11 November 1775); HO 55/28/21. The petitions from Westbury, Warminster, and Poole are also progressive. Occasionally, the use of foreign troops is criticized, as in the petition from Berkshire; the Coventry petitioners alone appeal to the king to give the Olive Branch Petition due attention as they firmly believe that it "proposes the foundation of a temple of concord." *Lond. Eve.-Post* (19-21, 21-24 October 1775).

[50]*CJ*, 36:710-11; *Parl. Hist.*, 19:762.

their more irenic fellow citizens.[51] Further examination of the provincial press will reveal how deeply felt these differences were.

IV

The twenty boroughs and towns and the five counties that sent contrasting addresses and petitions to the Crown (Tables 3.1-3.3, not including Wallingford) may now be compared to those counties and boroughs that sent only coercive addresses. The argument that the nation was united behind a policy of coercion must rest finally upon a comparison of those places that were divided with those that sent only coercive addresses. Similarly, the question of the popularity of government policy may only be answered by examining the number of addresses and the type of constituencies that appeared to be united in support of the Crown. Table 3.4 lists those boroughs and towns that sent only signed coercive addresses to the throne.

These seventeen addresses each stated explicitly that they were from the "inhabitants" or "principal inhabitants" of the borough or town, but nine of them also included local government office holders such as the mayor and aldermen. With the exception of Warwick and Cirencester, both medium-sized boroughs, this involvement of office holders was unique to the smaller boroughs. None of the five populous towns (Liverpool, Hull, Carlisle, Manchester, and Blackburn) mentioned local government, and neither did Derby and Sudbury. Moreover, the addresses from Warwick and Helston came with the common seal of the borough affixed. It thus appears plausible that the aldermen and burgesses took the lead in the seven smaller boroughs listed in Table 3.4 and in Axbridge. These seventeen boroughs and towns, combined with the four counties that addressed (noted in Table 3.3) are the only places that attempted to represent popular sentiment and were purportedly united. The argument that the English people were unified behind government measures hinges on these counties and boroughs, yet it has already been seen that several of the counties were not united, and it will be demonstrated below that many of the boroughs were also divided.

A number of additional addresses, however, arose from local government and smaller interest groups. In the popular debate over petitions in the fall of 1775, observers sometimes assumed that the coercive addresses came from the corporation boroughs. This is somewhat wide of the mark, since only three corporation boroughs and only eleven small freeman boroughs addressed, and six of these collected between fifty and 250 signatures. But a further distinction is necessary. Many of the larger freeman boroughs addressed the king only in their corporate capacity. Each of these addresses carefully identifies the addressers, and none of the following documents was circulated outside of a closed elite (see Table 3.5). While addresses were sent to the king from numerous larger boroughs, local officeholders in these instances were acting strictly in their corporate capacity. That a distinction between inhabitants and corpora-

---

[51]Compare HO 55/11/34 with 11/24.

tions was maintained can be observed in the eight cases where two virtually identical addresses were presented to the Crown: one from the inhabitants of the borough, and the other from local officeholders.[52] (Thus, Hull, Liverpool, Yarmouth, Taunton, and Leeds are found in previous tables and repeated in Table 3.5. None of the addresses listed in this table collected the signatures of the inhabitants, nor did they claim to represent more than the borough elite.)

TABLE 3.4

SIGNED COERCIVE ADDRESSES
FROM BOROUGHS AND UNREPRESENTED CITIES

BOROUGH*	SIGNATURES	APPROXIMATE RESIDENT ELECTORATE	DATE
Liverpool	472	2000	30 Sept.
Kingston-upon-Hull	171	1200	13 Oct.
Carlisle	308	1000	2 Jan. 1776
Derby	320	700	4 Nov.
Sudbury	140	800	10 Feb. 1776
Warwick	213	500	4 Oct.
Cirencester	174	800	13 Nov.
Wigan	245	100	2 Dec.
Plymouth	115	200	10 Nov.
Barnstaple	149	350	27 Oct.
Huntingdon	142	200	1 Dec.
Rye	68	40	22 Nov.
Arundel	64	200	17 Oct.
Helston	48	30	28 Oct.
Unrepresented Cities			
Manchester (Lancs.)	316	--------------------	16 Sept.
Blackburn (Lancs.)	227	--------------------	12 Dec.
Axbridge (Som.)	113	--------------------	29 Nov.

* Cirencester had a householder franchise; Warwick and Arundel, scot and lot; at Helston the vote was in the corporation; the remainder were freeman boroughs. For Blackburn, see *Lond. Gaz.* (9-12 Dec. 1775); for the remaining, see HO 55/28/20; 8/4; 11/58; 11/41; 11/1; 9/1; 10/12; 8/34; 10/10; 11/83; 11/54; 10/15; 10/4; 11/37; 18/45; 11/52.

---

[52]For Liverpool, compare HO 55/8/1 with 28/20; for Great Yarmouth, 10/2 with *Lond. Gaz.* (3-7 October 1775); for Taunton, 10/1 with 10/3; for Hull, *Lond. Gaz.* (10-14 October

TABLE 3.5

COERCIVE ADDRESSES FROM BOROUGH AND TOWN CORPORATIONS		
BOROUGH*	SOURCE	DATE
York	Mayor, Recorder	19 Oct. 1776
Beverley	Mayor, Aldermen	3 Oct.
Kingston-upon-Hull	Mayor, Recorder	14 Oct.
Lancaster	Mayor, Recorder	16 Sept.
Liverpool	Mayor, Aldermen	16 Sept.
Oxford	Mayor, Bailiffs	14 Nov.
Chester	Mayor, Recorder	11 Nov.
Gloucester	Mayor, Aldrman	28 Oct.
Hereford	Aldermen, Citizens	18 Nov.
Leicester	Mayor, Bailiffs	16 Sept.
Exeter	Mayor, Aldermen	25 Sept.
Great Yarmouth	Mayor, Aldermen	7 Oct.
Lichfield	Bailiffs, Citizens	31 Oct.
Taunton	Mayor, Justices	7 Oct.
Shrewsbury	Mayor, Aldermen	21 Oct.
Bewdley	Corporation	18 Nov.
Winchester	Mayor, Bailiffs	21 Oct.
New Windsor	High Steward, Mayor	4 Dec.
Andover	Bailiff, Steward	7 Nov.
Christchurch	Mayor, Burgesses	4 Nov.
Unrepresented Cities		
Leeds (Yorks.)	Mayor, Aldermen	4 Nov.
Maidenhead (Berks.)	Mayor, High Steward	25 Nov.
Southmolton (Devon.)	Corporation, Burgesses	18 Nov.

* New Windsor had a scot and lot franchise; Taunton, a householder; Andover and Christchurch were corporation boroughs; and the rest were freeman boroughs. For Beverley, see *Lond. Gaz.* (30 Sept.-3 Oct. 1775); for Hull, *Lond. Gaz.* (10-14 Oct. 1775). For the remainder, see HO 11/63; 11/2; 8/1; 10/8; 10/6; 11/25; 10/7; 11/3; 11/7; 10/2; 8/9; 10/1; 11/23; 8/23; 8/5; 11/67; 10/9; 11/28; 11/40; 10/14; 10/11.

The first eleven boroughs listed in Table 3.5 were large freeman constituencies. Eight of these addresses were agreed upon "in common council assembled," and in the cases of Oxford, Chester, and Leicester the addresses were given under the "common seal" of the borough. The addresses from Hereford and Lichfield refer to "citizens," but in the first instance the citizens were those "in council assembled," and in the second the address was agreed to "under our common seal at the guildhall." Similarly, the "commonalty" referred to at Oxford and Winchester is clearly the common council of the corporation.[53] Nevertheless, these twenty-three addresses for coercion represent the social and commercial elite of some of the larger freeman boroughs in England. While it is difficult to assess their importance with precision, in a deferential society such addresses with narrowly defined support undoubtedly carried considerable weight. In eight of the parliamentary boroughs that sent unsigned addresses from the corporation, the corporation was the most important force in parliamentary elections.[54] Here the mayors and aldermen were the local political power brokers; their statements in support of parliamentary supremacy are hardly surprising. The patrons of a number of these boroughs will be discussed in chapter 5.

The final list of addresses represents a number of diverse special-interest groups. As with the addresses from the borough corporations, these documents represented influential bodies, but not popular opinion, and are thus of limited value in establishing the popularity of the government's policy. Of the addresses in Table 3.6, the one from the justices of the peace and the Grand Jury of the Tower of London alone might be considered popular, since it also obtained the signatures of the "Gentlemen, Clergy, Freeholders, and Principal Inhabitants" of the Liberty of the Tower.

V

The boroughs and towns that sent both addresses and petitions concerning the imperial crisis in the fall of 1775 are significantly fewer in number than those that sent coercive addresses alone (twenty, as compared to thirty-five),[55] but there is evidence to suggest that public opinion in many of these apparently

---

1775) with 8/4; for Leeds, 11/40 with 10/5; for Nottingham compare 12/1 with 10/18; of the six English boroughs, Nottingham alone sent two conciliatory petitions. There were also two Scottish burghs that sent two each: for Perth, *Lond. Gaz.* (4-7 November 1775) with 8/18; for Dundee, 11/21 with 8/24. The Worcester address was from a corporation, but is listed in Table 3.1 above, as is the Nottingham petition that was unsigned.

[53]York and Lancaster also refer to the "commonalty," but each of the four set forth their addresses in common council, council chamber, or guildhall assembled. The signatures of these officeholders are given for three places; Lancaster with thirty, and New Windsor and Christchurch with twenty each.

[54]Oxford, Chester, Gloucester, Leicester, Exeter, Winchester, New Windsor, and Christchurch. See *Commons, 1754-1790,* 1:357, 221, 291, 323, 253, 302, 210, 294.

[55]Tables 3.1 and 3.2 compared to Tables 3.4 and 3.5.

unified towns was also seriously divided. This is nowhere more evident than in Lancashire. The addresses from Lancashire were the first to appear in the fall, and they provoked an immediate hostile response in the press that connected the current expressions of loyalty to the Crown with the disloyalty of Lancashire Tories in 1745.[56] "—Oh *Manchester! Manchester!* thy conversion is accepted with the exultation of *angels;* _____ There is joy at W _____ _____ll over one *village* that *repenteth,* more than over *ninety and nine* Cities which *need no Repentance.*"[57] While Manchester and Liverpool had sent signed petitions for peace to Parliament in January, the shift of support to coercion in September was not unanimous. Numerous appeals in the press appeared from both places contesting the impression of unanimity left by the coercive addresses.[58] But there is more than verbal evidence to establish the existence of popular opposition to the government in these cities.

Pro-American sentiment in Liverpool and Manchester was not strong enough to produce an independent petition for peace in the fall, but there is an

TABLE 3.6

COERCIVE ADDRESSES FROM ACADEMIC, LEGAL, MILITARY, AND COMMERCIAL BODIES					
UNIVERSITIES*	SIGNA-TURES	DATE	MILITIA	SIGNA-TURES	DATE
Oxford	----------	31 Oct.	Devonshire (First)	15	14 Oct.
Cambridge	----------	2 Dec.	Devonshire (Northern)	18	7 Nov.
			Northamptonshire	9	4 Nov.
JUSTICES OF THE PEACE	SIGNA-TURES	DATE	COMMERCIAL	SIGNA-TURES	DATE
Devonshire	20	14 Oct.	Trinity House, Kinston-upon-Hull	2	14 Oct.
Tower of London and Precincts	102	24 Oct.			

* For Justices of London Tower, see *Lond. Gaz.* (21-24 Oct. 1775).
For the remainder, see HO 55/11/32; 11/53; 11/12; 11/17; 11/26; 11/68; 11/4.

[56]*York Cour.* (19 September 1775) connects the Lancaster address with the Forty-Five; and *Cumb. Pacq.* (21 September 1775) does the same for Manchester. *Suss. Week. Adv.* (20 November 1775) makes a connection between the address from Montrose, Scotland and the previous rebellion.

[57]*Cumb. Pacq.* (21 September 1775).

[58]On Liverpool, see *Suss. Week. Adv.* (9 October 1775); *Gen. Eve. Post* (16-18 November 1775); on Manchester see *Cumb. Pacq.* (28 September 1775); *Gen. Eve. Post* (23-26 September 1775) and *Amer. Arch.* 4th ser., 3:648-49; 651.

obvious reason for this.[59] The massive Lancashire petition in favor of peace was circulated in both cities, and this had the effect of diminishing pressure to put forth an additional petition. A letter from Liverpool dated 13 November noted that "Party matters at present run very high here. A counter Petition and Address are both now handing about; the two parties to which are extremely inveterate against each other."[60] The "counter Petition" was the county petition that ultimately gathered over 4,000 signatures. At the same time Liverpool was recovering from a violent strike in the dockyards; it is thus little wonder that there was no separate petition for peace.

Opposing parties at Manchester were perhaps more hostile to each other than those at Liverpool. In late September it was reported that there was "a great riot and tumult" there occasioned by the coercive address "being smuggled up to the court, contrary to the voice and opinion of the people."[61] In October plans were made to obtain a counter petition. But just as at Liverpool, the circulation of the petition from the county in Manchester during the month of November came to be considered a sufficient expression of opposition to the government's policy.[62] A recent detailed analysis of the Lancashire conciliatory petitioners based upon city directories isolated 170 signatures of Manchester inhabitants, and undoubtedly there were many more. This study concluded that the political division regarding America was deep and unchanging in a city that was heretofore considered a bastion of Toryism.[63] Finally, a letter from Lancaster, signed "Philalethes," contended that the Lancaster address was misleading; the mayor was ridiculed by the citizens for his humble address, and the affections of the people, the author believed, were

---

[59]It was said that "Sir W.[illiam] M.[eredith] has laboured in vain for an address from Liverpoole." *Cumb. Pacq.* (21 September 1775); and at Manchester, it was said that "several very respectable inhabitants of that place are using their utmost influence to obtain a counter address and petition relative to the Colonies." *Cumb. Pacq.* (26 October 1775).

[60]*Gen. Eve. Post* (16-18 November 1775). The Liverpool coercive address was challenged by an essay in *Lond. Chron.* (2-4 November 1775).

[61]*Cumb. Pacq.* (28 September 1775). See also the lengthy essay in *Gen. Eve. Post* (23-26 September 1775) in regard to whether or not the Manchester address gave the true sense of the town, signed "Sandanis." In November the Manchester address was defended in *Man. Merc.* (7 November 1775) and attacked in *Lond. Chron.* (25-28 November 1775).

[62]For plans for a conciliatory petition from Manchester see *Cumb. Pacq.* (26 October 1775); *Hamp. Chron.* (16 October 1775).

[63]Peter Marshall, "Manchester and the American Revolution," *Bulletin of the John Rylands University Library of Manchester* 62 (Autumn 1979): 172-73. Clark, *British Opinion*, 112, had depicted Manchester as united in support of coercion. Later "Sandanis" still argued that the signatures for the Lancashire petition at Manchester had been obtained under the influence of pressure from landed patrons. *Gen. Eve. Post* (30 December 1775-2 January 1776).

alienated from the government.[64] Although Liverpool, Manchester, and Lancaster sent only coercive addresses, they, like the county itself, were deeply fragmented with regard to America.

Other boroughs in the north of England that sent only a single address were similarly divided. A lengthy letter from Carlisle in the *Cumberland Pacquet* attacked the idea that the Carlisle address represented the true sense of the borough; "many amongst us," claimed the author, opposed the address, and it met with "little success."[65] A letter by "Warwiciencis" claimed that many people at Warwick supported peace, and that the address "cannot by any means be the sense of the people."[66] York has been cited as a typical example of a large urban constituency "untroubled by political issues on the eve of the American War."[67] An attempt was made to gather support for a coercive address in the fall of 1775, but this provoked strong local opposition. It was not until a year later, and well into the war, that the corporation of York was sufficiently unified to address the Crown.[68]

In the west midlands, a person styling himself "an Inhabitant of Bewdley" argued that the Bewdley address was "strenuously opposed" by two of the nine officeholders who met to discuss it; it was solicited by Lord Lyttelton's agent and was not approved by the majority of the town—a majority, it was said, that desired the pursuit of peaceful measures.[69] William Lyttelton was member of Parliament for Bewdley and an outspoken champion of coercive measures in the Commons. A notice in the *Gloucester Journal* expressed disbelief that an address from Gloucester was ever presented to his Majesty, since "no person in this city ever heard of it before."[70] The conflict between the high Tory corporation of Leicester and an opposition party led by a core of Dissenters was endemic during the American Revolution. Moreover, the Earl of Denbigh's correspondence with the Leicester corporation concerning military appoint-

---

[64]*Lond. Eve.-Post* (3-5 October 1775) dated 26 September.

[65]*Cumb. Pacq.* (4 January 1776).

[66]*Morn. Chron.* (5 October 1775).

[67]*Commons, 1754-1790*, 1:79. Namier and Brooke are referring here to 1774.

[68]See *Gen. Eve. Post* (4-7 November 1775); *Bath J.* (18 September 1775); *Bath Chron.* (21 September 1775); See *A Speech intended to have been delivered to the Right Honorable the Lord Mayor, Aldermen, Recorder, and the rest of the Body Corporate of the City of York; endeavouring to show the Necessity of an Address to his Majesty, on the present Affairs in America; interspersed with Remarks on the Reasons advanced in Opposition to it; particularly those handed about, and signed by some Members of the Corporation* (York, 1775) which describes in 18 pp. the dispute within the corporation.

[69]*Lond. Eve.-Post* (14-16, 28-30 December 1775). Regarding the Lyttletons, see below, 132.

[70]*Glos. J.* (9 October 1775).

ments helps to establish the context for the corporation's loyal address.[71] A published letter from Exeter contested the idea that Exeter was united behind the government. Only eight of the chamber supported the address, and at the meeting during which the subject was broached, no such business had been expected; "if the sense of the people were fairly known," contended the author, a majority would have opposed the address.[72] People at Winchester were also at odds concerning America. An anonymous correspondent listed the names of the officeholders who were behind the address, but claimed to know of "about fifty people" in Winchester who opposed it.[73]

In these eleven towns listed in Tables 3.4 and 3.5, at least some local feeling was clearly against coercive measures. If they are added to those boroughs that sent conciliatory petitions, it could be argued that there were more places contending over the use of force in America than were purportedly united. There is thus documentary evidence to suggest that about one-third of the boroughs (in Tables 3.4 and 3.5) were divided, and while literary evidence alone would not be convincing, when read in the light of what is known about political division in other boroughs, it seems highly credible.

Some of the special-interest groups (listed in Table 3.6) were also less than united. The senate at the University of Cambridge decided in favor of an address by a large majority, but the vote of eighty-four to forty-six proves that a minority of masters and scholars did not wish to encourage the government in coercion.[74] In London at a "numerous meeting" of the students of the various Inns of Court at the Devil Tavern on 14 November, a proposal was made to address the throne with expressions of approbation of the administration's conduct towards the colonies; "but it appearing repugnant to the sense of a great majority of the Gentlemen present, it was dropped by the proposer."[75]

Other boroughs (not treated in the tables above) were also divided. When Thomas Binstead, an agent of Lord Sandwich, sought to obtain a loyal address from Portsmouth, he found the corporation divided, seventeen to eighteen, and felt that if he were to attempt to solicit an address from the inhabitants, "we should meet with great opposition if not a defeat." The project was accordingly dropped.[76] At Kendal, Westmorland, the Earl of Suffolk found the people "much divided" in their opinion concerning America, and at Appleby there was "general applause" for a speech by Sir James Lowther regarding the

---

[71]Marion Balderston and David Syrett, eds., *The Lost War: Letters from British Officers during the American Revolution* (New York: Horizon Press, 1975) 6, 7, 23, 48, 55, 62-63.

[72]*Morn. Chron.* (13 October 1775).

[73]*Lond. Eve.-Post* (19-21 January 1776).

[74]Reported in *Glos. J.* (27 November 1775); *Bath Chron.* (30 November 1775); there was also a considerable amount of opposition to the Chancellor leading up to the vote.

[75]The *Lond. Chron.* (14-16 November 1775); *Suss. Week. Adv.* (16 November 1775).

[76]*Commons, 1754-1790,* 1:298.

American crisis and local support for a conciliatory petition.[77] Rumors of an address from King's Lynn prompted Crisp Molineux, member of Parliament for the borough, to make a public declaration denying that such an address had been made, and he claimed that nothing was "more foreign to the sentiments of our constituents."[78] An address "to carry on the war against the Americans" was proposed at Ludlow, but at a meeting of burgesses it met such opposition that it was no longer pursued.[79] Salisbury was similarly divided; the promotion of an address, it was thought, would lead inevitably to a counter petition, and there is no surviving record of either an address or a petition.[80] Birmingham had sent two petitions to Parliament in January, one for peaceful measures and one for force, but in September the city was still divided. An attempt to obtain a petition for peace met with opposition and failure.[81]

To these seven towns that were divided but neither addressed nor petitioned can be added a number of constituencies that divided in the general elections of 1774 and 1780. The results of general elections should not, however, be interpreted as comprehensive measures of public opinion. Traditional accounts of the popular reaction to the war have been unduly influenced by the fact that comparatively few constituencies divided on the issue of America in the general election of 1774.[82] This interpretation relies too heavily upon a single general election held before the true dimensions of the conflict were well

---

[77]On Kendal, see HMC, *Tenth Report, Appendix Part 6* (London: Her Majesty's Stationery Office, 1887) 12; on Appleby, see Brian Bonsall, *Sir James Lowther and Cumberland and Westmorland Elections, 1754-1775* (Manchester: Manchester University Press, 1960) 149. *Gen. Eve. Post* (13-16 January 1776) alludes to a "Westmorland Petition." This was probably the Cumberland petition that circulated in Westmorland.

[78]*Lond. Chron.* (12-14 October 1775); *Lond. Eve.-Post* (10-12 October 1775). Another letter from an inhabitant of King's Lynn also denied the address and there is no known record of any such document; *Gen. Eve. Post.* (7-10 October 1775).

[79]*Lond. Chron.* (26-28 October 1775); *Lond. Eve.-Post* (14-26 October 1775); *Morn. Chron.* (23 November 1775).

[80]*Hamp. Chron.* (23, 30 October 1775).

[81]*Lond. Eve.-Post* (26-28 September 1775); *Lond. Chron.* (28-30 September 1775). John Money also notes "the serious division caused by the American War" in Birmingham. "Birmingham and the West Midlands, 1760-1793: Politics and Regional Identity in the English Provinces in the Later Eighteenth Century," *Midland History* 1 (Spring 1971): 10. There are hints that Wolverhampton, divided in the spring, was still divided in the fall. See John Money, *Experience and Identity*, 198 and HMC, *Dartmouth Manuscripts*, 3 vols. (London: Her Majesty's Stationery Office, 1895) 2:378 (James Perry to Lord Dartmouth, 10 September 1775). There was also evidence of a division of opinion in Scotland; at Edinburgh, *Lond. Chron.* (12-14 October 1775); at Aberdeen, *Gen. Eve. Post* (14-16 September 1775); *Cumb. Pacq.* (21 September 1775); and Glasgow, *York Cour.* (17 October 1775); *Gen. Eve. Post* (12-14 October 1775).

[82]*Commons, 1754-1790*, 1:75. Namier and Brooke do recognize the growth of opposition in 1775, but no means of measuring this opposition has been available heretofore.

known. If the election had occurred in the fall of 1775, the public response might have been different. Similarly, the involvement of France and Spain in the war against the colonies greatly confused the American issue in the general election of 1780. Daniel Parker Coke, for example, was a steadfast opponent of the government's American policy, but when America became "the confederate of the House of Bourbon," Coke said that he saw "no medium between unconditional submission to the enemy and the most spirited exertions."[83] Nevertheless, a survey of elections in which America became an issue provides a useful supplement to the evidence from petitions.

Support for candidates who opposed the government's American policy is found in at least seventeen elections in 1774, and in 1780 the Opposition actually gained a number of seats in the Commons.[84] In light of the care with which the government prepared for these elections, its losses, especially in the counties, are noteworthy. The counties had a relatively broad franchise, and despite the possible influence of patrons, the large number of voters rendered them less susceptible to corruption. County constituencies were thought to reflect public opinion more accurately than many boroughs, although the representative nature of Parliament was the subject of much debate both then and now. In a detailed study of pro-American members of Parliament and their constituencies, Mary Kinnear found it remarkable that "more than half of the eighty county members of Parliament were pro-American [in the Parliament of 1774-1780] and nearly a quarter of all pro-Americans represented English counties, as compared with only seven percent of the other [progovernment] members of Parliament."[85] Kinnear observes that this naturally reinforced the Whigs' contention that the government's majorities could be traced to the use of influence. Further evidence in support of this claim is found in the large freeman boroughs with constituencies of more than 1,000 electors. When these are combined with the counties, forty-four percent of the 207 pro-American members of Parliament identified by Kinnear sat for populous constituencies with more than 1,000 voters, compared to only twenty percent of the progovernment members of Parliament. This was exactly reversed for the small boroughs with electorates of less than 100; forty-four percent of the progovernment

---

[83]*Commons, 1754-1790*, 2:233.

[84]In addition to the eight listed in note twenty-one above, Westminster, Rochester, Seaford, Dover, Milborne Port, Maidstone, Surrey, Essex, and Kent may be added for 1774. Donoughue, *British Politics*, 195-97; John A. Phillips, *Electoral Behavior in Unreformed England: Plumpers, Splitters and Straights* (Princeton: Princeton University Press, 1982) 143-44 on Maidstone. For 1780, see Ian R. Christie, *The End of North's Ministry, 1780-1782* (London: Macmillan Co., 1958) 156-61.

[85]Kinnear, "Pro-Americans," 71. Kinnear defines "pro-American" members of Parliament on the basis of three parliamentary division lists of 1775 and 1778. By locating these members of Parliament on eight other division lists, she argues for a high level of ideological consistency among pro-Americans. They were "aware of the arguments justifying the course taken, and that that course was consistent," 104.

members of Parliament compared to twenty-two percent of the pro-Americans sat for small boroughs.[86]

More research is needed studying the provincial press and local politics in order to determine the exact nature of pro-American sympathy in the contested boroughs and counties in 1780. At Bristol, Liverpool, Newcastle-upon-Tyne, and Norwich, it is not the case that "local interests were the determining factor" in the contests of 1780, nor were these elections fought "with little or no reference to national politics."[87] The published handbills and songs at Bristol indicate that at least a minority of electors was vitally interested in the war. At Liverpool the American conflict was also a prominent political issue.[88] The broadsides and squibs of these two elections depict America as a major concern of the voters, yet no reference to such popular forms of literature is found amid the denials of the political nature of these contests. A recent analysis of the electorate at Newcastle-upon-Tyne demonstrates that radical issues dominated the election, and it can now be shown that America was a central issue at the Norwich contest of 1780.[89] These examples suggest that electoral history in this period needs to be rewritten from the perspective of popular culture. Further study of the electorate, and especially minorities within the electorate, should concentrate on the ideological interests of the voters and show how these concerns were related to their local and material interests.

County and borough by-elections of the period 1775-1783 are another untapped source of information concerning the popular reaction to the American crisis. The Dissenters were behind the opposition to the government in Leicestershire in 1775, and although this hard-fought contest was lost, the struggle may reveal a connection between Dissent and pro-American sentiment. A study of the extensive election literature of the 1776 by-election in Gloucestershire is also needed.[90] The victory of the opposition in Hampshire in 1779 and Kent in 1780 (uncontested) is of particular interest because antigovernment agitation in these counties had characterized popular politics for years.[91] At a by-

---

[86]Kinnear, "Pro-Americans," 72-73, 298.

[87]Christie, *The End of North's Ministry*, 83, 128, 142, 153. Regarding Norwich, see *Commons, 1754-1790*, 1:342.

[88]"Bristol Elections, 1774-1790. Addresses, Squibs, Songs," Ref. B6979, ff. 201, 205, 209, 211, 213, 231, 238, 243, 251, 253, 258, 259. For Liverpool, see *A Collection of Papers, Addresses, Songs etc., printed on all Sides during the Contest for Representatives in Parliament for the Borough of Liverpool* (Liverpool, 1780) 24, 27, 67, 72, 74.

[89]Thomas R. Knox, "Popular Politics and Provincial Radicalism: Newcastle-Upon-Tyne, 1769-1785," *Albion* 11 (Fall 1979): 224-25. Hayes, "Politics in Norfolk," 208; Phillips, *Electoral Behavior*, 44-45, 171; contrast *Commons, 1754-1790*, 1:86.

[90]*Commons, 1754-1790*, 3:304; 1:282. A poll book for the Leicestershire election is available and the election literature for Gloucestershire is at the Bristol Central Library. These sources were not used in the *History of Parliament*, yet it is maintained that Gloucestershire was contested on mainly local issues.

[91]*Commons, 1754-1790*, 1:283, 312.

election at Reading in 1782, a contemporary noted that Richard Aldworth Neville was called on "to vote against the American war," and in his first reported vote in Parliament he followed the instructions of his constituents.[92] Finally, the agitation regarding economic reform in 1780 was related geographically to the agitation concerning America, and the ideology of petitions in 1780 can occasionally be seen to reflect the American conflict (see chapter 5).

If parliamentary elections provide further evidence for the division of society with respect to America, much remains to be explained concerning the government's overwhelming majorities within Parliament. Prosopographical analysis of the 207 pro-American members of Parliament who sat in the Parliament of 1774-1780 and their 484 progovernment counterparts is not greatly illuminating; only minor differences in age, religion, social background, and education distinguished these two groups.[93] The pro-Americans' repeated failure to win over the independent country gentlemen has been carefully chronicled and convincingly explained: the belief that a strong central authority was needed to maintain an extended empire prevailed, and for the majority, the use of force was a legitimate tool of mercantilist theory.[94] But another consideration—often overlooked—must have influenced many members of Parliament who voted in favor of coercive measures.

The numerous addresses for coercion from borough and town corporations suggest an additional, more ideological reason for the government's majorities. The nearly unanimous support given to Parliament and the king by corporate bodies throughout the land underscores the heightened interest in law and order that such bodies were almost bound to express in a revolutionary setting.[95] By the spring of 1775 Parliament had narrowed the American question to the single issue of its own absolute supremacy. Eighteenth-century corporations, both local and national, were naturally concerned to maintain their privileged status and authority. Aldermen, common councilmen, and a majority of members of Parliament felt that in defying the laws of Parliament, the colonists were challenging Parliament's very identity. Indeed, any group whose identity was established by law perceived developments in America as threatening. The clergy of the established Church, for example, responded uniformly with the justices of the peace, the corporations, and Parliament: Parliament's supremacy was to be upheld at all costs. Confidence in England's mixed form of government, the prominent place of law in the English constitution, and the rule

---

[92]Ibid., 1:233.

[93]Kinnear, "Pro-Americans, " 74-76.

[94]Ibid., 279-84.

[95]On the conservatism of eighteenth-century corporations, see the fine discussion in Hendrik Hartog, *Public Property and Private Power: The Corporation of the City of New York in American Law, 1730-1870* (Chapel Hill: University of North Carolina Press, 1983) 22-25, 31-32, 42-43. Property defined the nature of the corporation.

of social elites made any other course of action on the part of Parliament unthinkable. But these conditions may also suggest that the only body of people less capable of truly reflecting public opinion concerning the colonists than Parliament was the city corporation. In this respect, the government's majorities in the early years of the war represented the opinion of a small minority of the English public. Parliamentary majorities did reflect more than the interests of this ruling elite, but division lists should not be accepted as the sole means for gauging English public opinion any more than loyal addresses from city corporations.

If the evidence from all of these sources is combined, can it be determined which side represented the majority of the politically literate public? The answer can only be ambiguous, since different forms of "popular" response are being compared. This much can be said with certainty: the nation was not united in support of the Coercive Acts and the use of force. The American crisis divided Parliament; it led to bitter debate in parliamentary elections; and it gave rise to popular agitation among thousands of citizens who had never obtained the right to vote. The significance and historical value of these different forms of the public's response will undoubtedly remain debatable. The question of the popularity of coercive measures in the political nation at large, however, may be pursued further through an examination of the provincial press. The government's greatest source of influence was not to be found in patronage, nor in its use of money; it was found instead in its control of the press. The *London Gazette*, not the secret service funds of George III, became the principal instrument by which the king and his ministers shaped the nation's understanding of the war.

Political Ideology
in the Metropolitan
and Provincial Press

Chapter IV

The Middlesex election affair and the American crisis transformed many newspaper printers into editors, and as editors they became vitally involved in the events they described. Provincial papers such as the *Kentish Gazette,* the *Salisbury and Winchester Journal,* and the *Leeds Mercury* took a pronounced pro-American stance in 1775. The editors of these papers wrote not only to inform, but to influence public opinion, and they did more than write. James Bowling, the printer of the *Leeds Mercury,* contributed radical editorials, and when in November an address and counter petition were circulated in Leeds, he signed his name to the petition for peace.[1] Numerous pro-government newspapers were also published in the mid-1770s; the *Manchester Mercury,* the *Hampshire Chronicle,* and *Creswell's Nottingham and Newark Journal* are three examples among many. Samuel Creswell, stationer, bookseller, and printer of Nottingham, was as committed to the use of force against the rebels as Bowling was to the colonists' rights—a fact to which his many editorials attest. When opposing documents circulated in Nottingham, Creswell added his signature to those who wished for the government's success.[2] There was evidently a vital link between the writing of politically oriented editorials and making a public declaration of one's viewpoint in a petition. The shaping of public opinion and

---

[1] *Leeds Merc.* (10, 17, 24, 31 January 1775); compare to HO 55/21/39. The petitioners referred to the colonists as "our American brethren" and viewed the conflict as an "unnatural civil war." A common ethnic, cultural, mercantile, and religious heritage united the colonies to England, and these bonds explain much about English pro-Americanism. The works of Franklin Wickwire and Michael Kammen on subministers and agents, J. R. Pole and Alison Olson on politics and parties, and Bernard Bailyn and Carl Bridenbaugh on ideology and religion provide the needed context for our understanding of Anglo-American relations in the decades preceding the war. Most accounts of the Revolution, however, concentrate on explaining the widening breach between England and America, and this has resulted in a neglect of those elements that sustained the unity of the empire for so many years. Further research is needed to account for the reluctance of moderates on both sides to accept the drift into war, but here we will examine merely the immediate ideological and political context of the petitions and addresses.

[2] *Nott. New. J.* (28 January, 11, 18 February 1775); compare to HO 55/11/27.

popular political behavior were thus intimately connected in the persons of newspaper editors. Indeed, the provincial press was so politically charged in 1775 that had there been no petitions at all, a comprehensive survey of newspapers alone would have led scholars to the conclusion that the nation was divided over America.

Petitions to the Crown emerged from a complex ideological milieu, and they were forged into shape by local leaders who were themselves products of the contemporary intellectual climate. Any attempt to account for the origins of petitioning activity must, therefore, examine the ways in which the prominent ideas of the age were disseminated. Since the Rockingham Whigs were not highly successful in organizing popular opposition to the government, the need to explain the intellectual origins of the petitions becomes all the more pressing. English newspapers published the most important documents from the American Congress and thereby stimulated widespread pro-American sentiment. But in the end, the government was able to control the press in such a way that the loyal addresses not only reflected public opinion, they helped to create it.

The editors of local newspapers formed in themselves a kind of elite leadership of popular opinion, but the editors were sometimes influenced in turn by the metropolitan press, and therefore the use to which newspapers were put must also be examined. In addition, the meetings called to organize the petitions depended for their success upon public advertisements in the press. The use of the press in organizing, marshaling, and shaping public opinion into specific petitions and addresses is a topic of equal importance with that of ideological origins. In the use of the press, just as in the area of leadership, the contrast between the administration and the Opposition could hardly be more striking. Particular attention will be given in this chapter to how the former succeeded in influencing public opinion, while the latter failed so completely.

I

The intellectual setting of the petitions and addresses can be examined at three levels. The Commonwealthman tradition constitutes a long intellectual foreground. True Whig ideology provided a sweeping critique of government; John Locke's perspective on the Glorious Revolution was brought up to date by Thomas Pownall's *Principles of Polity* (1752) and reprints of John Trenchard's and Thomas Gordon's *The Independent Whig* and *Cato's Letters* (1754-1755).[3] Later, these and other progressive statements were balanced by a mod-

---

[3]John A. Schutz, *Thomas Pownall: British Defender of American Liberty* (Glendale CA: The Arthur H. Clark Co., 1951) 28, 47; and Caroline Robbins, *The Eighteenth-Century Commonwealthman* (New York: Atheneum, 1968). On Trenchard and Gordon, see David L. Jacobson, ed., *The English Libertarian Heritage* (Indianapolis: Bobbs-Merrill Co., 1965) xxxi; the best recent survey is Colin Bonwick, *English Radicals and the American Revolution* (Chapel Hill: University of North Carolina Press, 1977). For the influence of these thinkers in America, see Bernard Bailyn, *The Ideological Origins of the American Revolution* (Cambridge: Belknap Press, 1967) 35, 51.

erate portrayal of the Whig heritage in the works of Edmund Burke, notably his *Thoughts on the Cause of the Present Discontents* (1770) and his contributions to the *Annual Register*.[4] The government also had its defenders in such well-known writers as Samuel Johnson. In *The False Alarm* (1770), for example, he articulated the Ministry's position concerning the Middlesex election affair, and he attempted to discredit the Opposition in *The Patriot* (1774).[5] Such a spectrum of progressive, moderate, and conservative ideology undoubtedly informed the thought of many petitioners, but it is rarely possible to trace the ideology of the petitions to any of these treatises. The brevity of the documents and the general terms in which they were couched preclude fruitful comparative analysis. The most that can be claimed is that these and similar writings helped influence attitudes toward the government that may have contributed to a person's willingness to petition.

The months immediately preceding the outbreak of hostilities provide a second, intermediate context of ideas, a context that is more specific with respect to colonial matters. The American Revolution was a war of political pamphlets. The literary output increased in direct proportion to the increase in hostility; in 1773, fourteen pamphlets on the American crisis were published; in 1774 there were eighty-eight; in 1775, 160; and in 1776, the peak was reached with 169. Thereafter the number of pamphlets dropped significantly.[6] The highest intensity of literary productivity thus coincided directly with the agitation surrounding petitioning and addressing. The connection between some of these pamphlets and the popular response in petitions is also readily established. For example, early in 1775 Catherine Macaulay published her progressive *An Address to the People of England, Scotland, and Ireland, on the Present Alarming Crisis of Affairs*. Some months later, in the very midst of the petitioning movement, John Wesley's *A Calm Address to our American Colonies* appeared.[7] The latter was a plagiarized version of Samuel Johnson's *Taxation No Tyranny*, and it was published as a pamphlet in addition to appearing in many

---

[4]G. H. Guttridge, *English Whiggism and the American Revolution* (Berkeley: University of California Press, 1963) still provides a fine overview, 41-45.

[5]Donald J. Greene, *The Politics of Samuel Johnson* (New Haven: Yale University Press, 1960) 204-19. Also, see Donald J. Greene, ed., *Samuel Johnson's Political Writings* (New Haven: Yale University Press, 1977) for these pamphlets, and 411-55 for *Taxation No Tyranny*.

[6]In 1977 there were approximately 103; in 1778, 120; in 1779, 113; in 1780, 95; in 1781, 75; in 1782, 102; and in 1783, 96. Thomas R. Adams, *The American Controversy: A Bibliographical Study of the British Pamphlets about the American Disputes*, 2 vols. (Providence: Brown University Press, 1980).

[7]The second edition of Macauley's pamphlet is advertised in *Brist. J.* (21 January 1775). Wesley's *Calm Address* was printed in numerous newspapers and sometimes as an extra sheet, provided gratis. *Man. Merc.* (24 October 1775); *North. Merc.* (23 October 1775). The pamphlet provoked considerable debate. *Brist. J.* (7 October, 2, 16, 23 December 1775).

newspapers. In some cases it is possible to establish the number of pamphlets that were printed, but it is difficult to determine how widely they were disseminated to the literate public.

The published sermon was a specialized form of popular expression. A recent survey analyzed 156 fast and Thanksgiving Day sermons that were delivered in England during the course of the war.[8] Of these, ninety-eight dealt with the conflict specifically in political terms. While the majority supported the government, nineteen, or one in five of these sermons, expressed opposition to the government's coercive measures. In each case the sermons were preached before they were published, and thereby they reached all levels of society, including the illiterate. In addition, far more sermons were delivered from the pulpit than ever reached the press. Just as with newspaper articles and pamphlets, both oral and printed sermons faced the possibility of appearing treasonous. Given the government's perspective on rebellion, the proportion of sermons that took a stance against the government would seem to reflect considerable popular opposition.

The shorter variety of essay or sermon that could be printed separately as a pamphlet, but more often appeared in newspapers, constitutes the most solid evidence for establishing the ideological origins of the petitions. This third and more immediate intellectual context can be shown to have had a direct impact on popular agitation. Newspapers are more geographically specific than pamphlets, and it may be assumed that the entire literate public, as well as many nonliterate people, were exposed to their contents. In order to demonstrate that the petitions reflected genuine awareness of political issues possessing national importance, one must show how well informed the public was of developments in America. The provincial press reveals how this awareness was developed at the local level of English politics and nurtured in settings traditionally considered inimical to political principle. An investigation of this area is especially needed in light of the fact that previous studies of public opinion have concentrated almost exclusively on metropolitan newspapers.[9]

---

[8]Henry Ippel, "British Sermons and the American Revolution," *The Journal of Religious History* 12 (December 1982): 198.

[9]With the exception of John Money's regional study, *Experience and Identity: Birmingham and the West Midlands, 1760-1780* (Manchester: Manchester University Press, 1977), K. G. Burton, *The Early Newspaper Press in Berkshire (1723-1825)* (Reading: University of Reading, 1954), and John Brewer, *Party Ideology and Popular Politics at the Accession of George III* (Cambridge: Cambridge University Press, 1976), no study of the provincial press exists for the period 1760-1790. See G. A. Cranfield, *The Development of the Provincial Newspaper, 1700-1760* (Oxford: Clarendon Press, 1962); Donald Read, *Press and People, 1790-1850: Opinion in Three English Cities* (London: E. Arnold, 1981) and *The English Provinces, c. 1760-1960: A Study in Influence* (London: E. Arnold, 1964). See Brewer, *Party Ideology*, 16-18, and John A. Phillips, *Electoral Behavior in Unreformed England: Plumpers, Splitters and Straights* (Princeton: Princeton University Press, 1982) 15-19 on the increased political importance of the press. Brewer has given particular attention to the provincial press in the 1760s (174-76).

In the early 1780s there were approximately fifty provincial newspapers. Reliable circulation figures are difficult to obtain and even more difficult to interpret, but editors occasionally did comment upon their sales. The *Salisbury and Winchester Journal* reported that it sold between 4,000 and 5,000 newspapers weekly, and Thomas Wood, the editor of the *Shrewsbury Chronicle*, claimed that "from the increasing sale of this paper, upon a moderate computation they [advertisements] are read by ten thousand persons."[10] In the eighteenth century a newspaper's readership extended considerably beyond the number of copies printed. Nonliterate and semiliterate people assimilated the news through discussions at inns and public houses. It would seem to be a conservative estimate to suggest that many provincial newspapers reached five thousand people on a weekly basis.

Metropolitan and provincial papers alike were financially dependent upon advertising revenue. Consequently, the impact that a political stance could have upon a newspaper's income was carefully taken into account. In an editorial of 6 January 1776, Thomas Wood of the *Shrewsbury Chronicle* noted first his attempt "with respect to politics" to be as "impartial as possible"; second, the extent of his readership; and third, the advantages of "advertising herein." Accordingly, Wood published Wesley's *Calm Address* in one issue, and in subsequent numbers he printed Caleb Evans's detailed reply to Wesley.[11] Other newspapers such as the *Kentish Gazette* were equally dependent upon advertising and yet were anything but impartial concerning the American crisis. Evidently not all editors feared that radical editorials would offend potential customers, although it would be too much to assume that in each case they viewed their entire readership as supportive of their politics.

By the 1770s newspapers carried extensive accounts of parliamentary debates. In addition to making public the arguments of Opposition leaders, the press also printed such documents as the Opposition Lords' protest of the address to the Crown at the opening of Parliament.[12] Numerous statements of the

---

[10]*Sal. Win. J.* (8 January 1776); *Shrews. Chron.* (6 January 1776); see also Brewer, *Party Ideology*, 142-43, 148, 157, for a fine discussion on literacy and readership. The *York Chronicle* had sales of 2,000 in the 1770s (144).

[11]*Shrews. Chron.* (21 October, 7, 18, 25 November, 9 December 1775; 6 January 1776); see also Brewer, *Party Ideology*, 174, 176.

[12]P. D. G. Thomas, "The Beginnings of Parliamentary Reporting in Newspapers, 1768-1774," *English Historical Review* 74 (October 1959): 623-36; Ian Christie, "British Newspapers in the Later Georgian Era," 311-33, in *Myth and Reality in Late-Eighteenth-Century British Politics* (London: Macmillan Co., 1970). Regarding the Lords' protest, see *Suss. Week. Adv.* (13 November 1775); *Hamp. Chron.* (13 November 1775); *York Cour.* (24 November 1775); and in many other papers too numerous to note. These and the following citations are not exhaustive but are representative.

London radicals were also widely publicized.[13] These materials, however, were probably less important in shaping public opinion than the American documents themselves. It is a fact of some importance that English newspapers made the colonial interpretation of events in America accessible to the English public in precisely those terms that Congress thought most convincing. In its first petition to the Crown, Congress explicitly planned a public relations campaign in England in the hope of eliciting public support for its actions. Congress directed its agents in London to present the petition to the king and then added, "We wish it may be made public through the press, together with the list of grievances. And as we have hope for great assistance from the Spirit, virtue, and justice of the nation, it is our earnest desire, that the most effectual care may be taken, as early as possible, to furnish the trading cities and manufacturing towns throughout the United Kingdom, with our memorial to the people of Great Britain."[14] The English press cooperated in this effort with surprising unanimity; even those editors who were hostile to the colonies consistently printed the most important American papers.

In January 1775 the petition from Congress to the king was printed in several newspapers, but the first American document to receive widespread newspaper coverage in the late summer of that year was the "Declaration of the Causes and Necessity of Taking up Arms." At about the same time, the English press gave equal attention to the colonial appeal to the English public styled "The Twelve United Colonies to the Inhabitants of Great Britain."[15] This detailed list of grievances appeared just before the royal proclamation on rebellion. In both the metropolitan and the provincial press, hostile as well as friendly editors printed the full texts of these documents, sometimes with, and sometimes without, editorial comment. Other documents were intended to have an

---

[13]For the "Address to the Electors of Great Britain," see *Suss. Week. Adv.* (9 October 1775); for other related statements of the London radicals, see *Bath J.* (2, 23 October 1775); *Cumb. Pacq.* (5 October 1775); *Hamp. Chron.* (13 November 1775); *Brist. J.* (30 September 1775); and *Sal. Win. J.* (2 October 1775).

[14]Printed in *Brist. J.* (21 January 1775), dated Philadelphia (26 October 1774).

[15]For the petition, see *Leeds Merc.* (24 January 1775); *Brist. J.* (28 January 1775); for the declaration, *Lond. Eve.-Post* (15-17 August 1775); *Gen. Eve. Post* (15-17 August 1775); *Pub. Adv.* (16 August 1775); *Morn. Chron.* (17 August 1775); *Hamp. Chron.* (4 September 1775); *Bath J.* (21 August 1775); *Sal. Win. J.* (21 August 1775); *Brist. J.* (19 August 1775); and *Glos. J.* (21 August 1775); for the appeal to the inhabitants of Great Britain, *Pub. Adv.* (17 August 1775); *Morn. Chron.* (18 August 1775); *Brist. J.* (19 August 1775); *Read. Merc.* (21 August 1775); *Sal. Win. J.* (21 August 1775); *Hamp. Chron.* (18, 25 September 1775). A companion document directed to the people of Ireland appeared later. *Lond. Eve.-Post* (14-16 September 1775); *Morn. Chron.* (18 September 1775); *Brist. J.* (23 September 1775).

appeal to specific groups, such as the letter from Congress to the Lord Mayor and Livery of London, and these too found their way into many newspapers.[16] But of all the American documents designed to influence public opinion, the Olive Branch Petition received the widest attention. Within three weeks of its arrival on 21 August, this final appeal to the king for conciliation was spread throughout the land.[17] By the time it was made public, however, the king had already declared the colonies to be in a state of rebellion, and most papers that printed the petition noted that the government had determined that no answer would be given to it.

The motives of the colonists in sending the petition were understandably called into question. Some papers published a letter from Thomas Johnson, Jr. to Horatio Gates, adjutant general of the American forces, in which the former expressed the hope that the petition would "unite America and divide Britain."[18] While it is extremely difficult to determine what influence this document may have had on English public opinion generally, in one notable instance, it is possible to demonstrate a significant impact. The petition to the Crown from 406 inhabitants of Coventry pled as late as 20 October that his Majesty "recommend to your Parliament to consider with all due attention the petition from America lately offered to be presented to the Throne, which we firmly believe proposes the foundation of a temple of concord, sacred to the mutual interests of Great Britain and America." This is the only English petition that alluded directly to any of the American documents, but it seems reasonable to conclude that the publication of these papers helped shape public opinion in favor of conciliatory measures. The American papers also prompted

---

[16]*Hamp. Chron.* (2 October 1775); *Bath J.* (2 October 1775); *Read. Merc.* (2 October 1775); and *Brist. J.* (7 October 1775). American documents such as the petition from the committee of New York to the Lord Mayor, Aldermen, and Court of Common Council of London were also published. See *Lond. Eve.-Post* (25-27 July 1775); *Gen. Eve. Post* (15-17 August 1775); *Bath Chron.* (17 August 1775); *Hamp. Chron.* (18, 25 September 1775); and a notice of it in *Glos. J.* (21 August 1775).

[17]It is printed, for example, in at least two papers that were hostile to the colonies, *Suss. Week. Adv.* (11 September 1775); *Man. Merc.* (12 September 1775). See, in addition, *Lond. Eve.-Post* (2-5 September 1775); *Lond. Chron.* (2-5 September 1775); *Pub. Adv.* (5 September 1775); *Morn. Chron.* (6 September 1775); *Hamp. Chron.* (11 September 1775); *Glos. J.* (11 September 1775); *Brist. J.* (9 September 1775); *Read. Merc.* (11 September 1775); *Hamp. Chron.* (11 September 1775); *Sal. Win. J.* (11 September 1775); *York Cour.* (12 September 1775); *Cumb. Pacq.* (28 September 1775); *Shrews Chron.* (9 September 1775); and segments in *Bath J.* (12 September 1775). For a discussion of its origin, see Charles Ritcheson, *British Politics and the American Revolution* (Norman OK: University of Oklahoma Press, 1954) 193-95.

[18]*Gen. Eve. Post* (18-21 November 1775); *Pub. Adv.* (20 November 1775).

the supporters of the government to address the Crown, and these addresses were, in turn, an important stimulus to the petitions.[19]

II

The publication of the American papers was accompanied by notices in the press that associations were forming in various parts of England to defend the people's liberties.[20] The number of associations actually organized was in fact quite small. The most well known of these groups was the London Association, which met regularly at the Globe Tavern, Fleetstreet, and published resolutions concerning its grievances against the Ministry, with warnings about possible encroachments on the freedom of the press.[21] Appeals went forth from this body for the organization of additional associations, but the only other city known to have actually formed an association was Newcastle-upon-Tyne.[22] The country club organized by the Hampshire County petitioners was likened by its opponents to the association in the metropolis, but little is known concerning its proceedings.[23] Well-publicized rumors of this movement, however, appear to have been influential. The *Gloucester Journal*, for example, reported that it was expected that cities throughout the land would address his Majesty "in order to discountenance the association that is now forming against Government."[24] The frequency with which the coercive addresses referred to seditious factions in England attests to the importance of such notices. The address to the Crown from the county of Devon went so far as to request the punishment of the London Association, since it defied the tenets of the royal proclamation.[25] The publication of the American documents, combined with the fear of pro-American associations, can be said to account for at least several loyal addresses.

The royal proclamation of 23 August in support of suppressing rebellion and sedition was, however, the most important positive stimulus in eliciting loyal addresses. In this document the colonists were stated to be in "open and avowed

---

[19]For the Coventry petition, see *Lond. Eve.-Post* (19-21 October 1775). Other documents such as the London Livery's address to the electors of Great Britain referred in detail to the Olive Branch Petition and complained that it was not answered. *Suss. Week. Adv.* (9 October 1775).

[20]Rumors of associations forming throughout England appeared as early as July. See *Lond. Eve.-Post* (29 July-1 August; 5-7 August 1775); *Sal. Win. J.* (11 September 1775); and *Read. Merc.* (2 October 1775).

[21]For a discussion of the London Association, see above, 55-56. See also *Lond. Eve.-Post* (9-12, 12-14 September; 26-28 October 1775); *Bath J.* (9 October 1775); *Suss. Week. Adv.* (9 October 1775).

[22]See *Lond. Eve.-Post* (2-5 September 1775); *Lond. Chron.* (7-9 November 1775); *Bath J.* (11 September 1775).

[23]*Sal. Win. J.* (27 November; 11 December 1775); *Read. Merc.* (27 November 1775).

[24]*Glos. J.* (18 September 1775).

[25]See *Lond. Eve.-Post* (26-28 October 1775).

Rebellion," and full information was demanded of "all Persons who shall be found carrying on Correspondence with, or in any Manner or Degree aiding or abetting the Persons now in open Arms and Rebellion against our Government." The proclamation was printed in all of the country's newspapers and read publicly in the larger urban centers.[26] Editors explicitly stated that they expected a flood of loyal addresses in response to the publication of this document.[27] The prediction proved accurate; the unanimity of the loyal addresses concerning the rebellious state of the colonists demonstrates both the influence of the proclamation and the efficiency of the press. The king's speech to Parliament on 26 October reiterated the government's fundamental commitment to the use of force. The speech argued that the rebellion was escalating into a general war—a war "manifestly carried on for the purpose of establishing an independent empire," and this document also received widespread coverage in the press. Subsequently, two of the petitions promoting peace referred to the "late speech from the Throne" to both Houses of Parliament.[28]

If the royal proclamation provided the greatest incentive to address the Crown, the publication of the loyal addresses in newspapers all across the country was, in turn, the most important stimulant to the petitions for peace. The earliest coercive addresses were printed many times over in both the metropolitan and provincial press. By the third week in September, the coercive addresses from Manchester, Lancaster, and Liverpool were widely dispersed to the literate public, and in the following weeks a steady stream of printed addresses supporting the royal proclamation continued to appear.[29] The address

---

[26]Printed, for example, in *Lond. Gaz.* (22-26 August 1775); *Lond. Eve.-Post* (24-26 August 1775); *Lond. Chron.* (22-24 August 1775); *Pub. Adv.* (25 August 1775); *Morn. Chron.* (25 August 1775); *Man. Merc.* (29 August 1775); *Hamp. Chron.* (28 August 1775); *Suss. Week. Adv.* (28 August 1775); *Glos. J.* (28 August 1775); *York Cour.* (29 August 1775); *Hamp Chron.* (28 August 1775); *Sal. Win. J.* (28 August 1775); and *Brist. J.* (26 August 1775). It was read in several parts of the cities of London, *Lond. Chron.* (29-31 August 1775); Bath, *Bath J.* (4 September 1775); Bristol, *Gen. Eve.-Post* (7-9 September 1775).

[27]*Gen. Eve.-Post* (24-26 August 1775); *Bath Chron.* (31 August 1775).

[28]It was printed, for example, in *Lond. Gaz.* (24-28 October 1775); *Suss. Week. Adv.* (30 October 1775); *Man. Merc.* (31 October 1775); *Bath Chron.* (2 November 1775); *Glos. J.* (30 October 1775); *Cumb. Pacq.* (2 November 1775); and virtually all the other papers. For the petitions of Abingdon and Middlesex, see *Lond. Eve.-Post* (18-21 November 1775); and HO 55/13/2.

[29]The address from Manchester was printed in *Gen. Eve.-Post* (12-14 September 1775); *Lond. Chron.* (12-14 September 1775); *Hamp. Chron.* (18 September 1775); *Cumb. Pacq.* (21 September 1775); the Lancaster addresses appeared in *Gen. Eve.-Post* (14-16 September 1775); *Lond. Chron.* (14-16 September 1775); *Cumb. Pacq.* (21 September 1775); *Man. Merc.* (19 September 1775); the Liverpool address appeared in *Gen. Eve.-Post* (16-19 September 1775); *Lond. Chron.* (19-21 September 1775); *Man. Merc.* (19 September 1775).

from Manchester, for example, was printed at Newcastle-upon-Tyne, and there it met stout opposition. It was reported that "the generality of people" expressed "much indignation" at the address; they went so far as to threaten a boycott of manufactured goods from Manchester. Some animus toward this address was also expressed in a letter from Carlisle.[30] The petitions for peace, however, provide the strongest evidence for the importance of the publication of the addresses in the newspapers. The fear that the addresses for coercion would be construed by the king as accurate portrayals of public opinion prompted those who supported peaceful measures to react. This is clearly established by the texts of the petitions themselves. Over half of them explicitly opposed the idea that the addresses accurately represented public feeling. Apart from the prominence given to the addresses by the newspapers, this response in favor of peace would be difficult to imagine.

In addition to publishing the texts of the addresses, newspapers gave considerable space to commentary upon them. After a number of the conciliatory petitions were printed, and thereby publicly contrasted to the loyal addresses, the differences of opinion stirred further debate, and this interchange depicts popular politics at its best. The *London Chronicle*, for example, printed only a few of the addresses and petitions, but it ran a series of essays on the documents that spanned the political spectrum.[31] This single newspaper provided more opinion on petitions and addresses than any other paper, and though the essays were written in reaction to the earliest published petitions, these polemical statements appear to have stimulated further petitioning activity. Many of these short articles were merely impassioned pleas either for or against the addressers and petitioners. In the essays that opposed the conciliatory petitions, the colonies were commonly assumed to be in a state of rebellion, and it was feared that rebellion might spread to England. Furthermore, these polemicists believed that the petitions for peace were actually an incentive to rebellion.

Those who opposed the petitions often favored the addresses. The addresses were viewed by progovernment writers as essential means to strengthen the government and secure good order. The theme of order was the dominant emphasis of those who wrote in support of the addresses. "Unanimity among ourselves, the combined voice of the sensible and virtuous in addresses to a justly-beloved Sovereign," wrote "Hermes," "will effectually strengthen the nerves of Government, restore order and obedience to the laws in our Colonies, and the triple-headed hydra [of opposition in England] will shrink into its original obscurity and nothingness."[32] The value of loyal addresses as one means of helping restore order was the central thrust of the essays written by

---

[30]*Sal. Win. J.* (2 October 1775).

[31]See *Lond. Chron.* (28-30 September, 30 September-3 October, 24-26, 28-31 October, 2-4, 4-7, 7-9, 9-11, 16-18, 25-28 November, 12-14 December 1775).

[32]*Lond. Chron.* (21-24 October 1775).

"A Loyalist," "An Old Citizen," "Anti-Faction," and "S.S."[33] Given the perception that addressing the Crown would contribute to quelling rebellion, it is not surprising to find a "Loyal Subject" even appealing for more addresses to the Crown: "to be silent now," urged the author, "is to be criminal."[34]

The progovernment writers were answered by an equal number of essays written in favor of the petitioners. These writers wished to support the rights of the subject and claimed that the addresses were giving unthinking consent to arbitrary power. The notion that the colonies were in a state of rebellion was typically rejected. "Veritas," for example, construed the "real principles" of the addressers to be passive obedience to the king's sovereignty; addressers were indifferent to the liberty of the subject, and what was really at stake in the American conflict was the right of "self-defense and self preservation."[35] Writers under the pseudonyms "Independent," "A Royalist," and "An Old Briton" associated the addresses of 1775 with the "fulsome" addresses to James II, or loyalty to the Stuarts in the "Forty-Five"—"who, mingling, in the sordid, servile train, Address alike, if George or Charley reign."[36] Other editorials defended the propriety of petitioning and condemned the addressers who hoped by their expressions of loyalty to "gain or keep a portion of the Ministerial loaves and fishes."[37] Writers who favored the conciliatory petitions denied that the loyal addresses reflected the considered opinion of the people, and just as progovernment writers appealed for more addresses, these authors pled with the public to send more petitions to St. James. "Should there be no other Addresses or Petitions presented to the King, but what countenance these *bloody* Measures, may not our gracious Sovereign conclude that the present Civil War in America is the general Voice of his People?"[38]

A number of essays that appeared in the press went beyond the charges of disloyalty on the one hand, and servility on the other, and attempted to deal intelligently with the issues presented in the petitions. A lengthy essay by "Anti-Vesanus" and another by "A Manufacturer" rebutted the London merchants' petition point by point. The former argued cogently that upholding the law necessarily entailed the use of force, and the latter made a case for the injustice

---

[33]*Lond. Chron.* (24-26, 26-28 October, 9-11 November 1775); *Gen. Eve. Post* (23-25 November 1775).

[34]*Lond. Chron.* (28-30 September 1775). There is another unsigned essay in favor of addresses in *Lond. Chron.* (4-7 November 1775). "A Wiltshire Freeholder" also appeals for more addresses. *Sal. Win. J.* (18 October 1775).

[35]*Lond. Chron.* (28-31 October 1775), dated Manchester (18 October 1775).

[36]*Lond. Chron.* (28-30 September, 25-28 November 1775).

[37]*Cumb. Pacq.* (19 October 1775); *Suss. Week. Adv.* (2 October 1775).

[38]*Gen. Eve. Post* (28-30 September 1775); regarding appeals for more petitions, see "An Old Englishman," *Pub. Adv.* (3 August 1775) and essays in *Sal. Win. J.* (16 October 1775); *York Cour.* (24 October 1775).

of the mother country bearing the burden of taxes alone.[39] "A. B." wrote a substantive, two-part response to the Bristol petition. Here, as in other essays disputing the petitions, it is argued that the colonies were aiming at independence; and since all previous attempts at conciliation by the government had proven ineffectual, if British rights were to be secured, the authors of the rebellion must be brought to "condign punishment."[40] "Opifex" also wrote a detailed response to the Bristol petition that concentrated on the necessity of the Americans bearing their just share of taxation. Virtual representation was also defended: "the notion of the necessity of representation to constitute the right of taxation is ill-founded, and not true, in fact, it is a novel opinion; upon the same principle the greater part of the people here might refuse payment of taxes."[41] Parliamentary supremacy, in this view, had to be maintained by "compulsive force," and all four essayists stressed the connection between this supremacy and the security of property.

One of the most insightful essays against the loyal addresses was written by an anonymous author who attacked the notion of virtual representation and absolute parliamentary supremacy. He argued that the heart of the trouble could be found in the "new mode of taxation" that was forced upon the colonists "without their consent." "Passive obedience and non-resistance" as espoused in the Liverpool address could not be the duty of British subjects when "the Revolution and the principles on which it was founded" denied such views. If the supremacy of the legislature meant that there were no liberties that could not be rescinded or destroyed, then the supremacy of the legislature had to be held up as a sufficient plea "to justify everything that has been, or may be enacted, or inflicted by law." If, however, there were liberties that even it could not destroy, then the extent of the supremacy of Parliament would be open to debate.[42] "J. N." similarly attacked the addresses as "inflammatory" since they encouraged civil war, and pled for mercy to be shown the Americans since they were only "asserting the rights of Englishmen, not to be taxed but by their own representatives."[43]

In addition to the debate concerning the issues raised by the petitions and addresses, the press printed articles on the constitutional question regarding the right of petitioning. Even though progovernment writers believed that the petitions encouraged American resistance, attacks on the right of petitioning were rare. "Junius" held that the public meetings in London for the purpose of petitioning were illegal, and the corporation of London was specifically censured. "The idea of a Corporation's controlling or interfering with the author-

[39]*Lond. Chron.* (24-26 October, 7-9 November 1775).

[40]Ibid. (16-18, 18-21 November 1775); see also *Gen. Eve. Post* (16-18 November 1775).

[41]*Lond. Chron.* (28-31 October 1775).

[42]Ibid. (2-4 November 1775).

[43]*Gen. Eve. Post* (9-12 December 1775).

ity from whence it holds its charter, is really monstrous."[44] (Unlike most corporations, London derived its charter from Parliament rather than the king.) Edmund Burke's attack on the addresses from the Devonshire Militia and the University of Oxford provided the counterpart to "Junius's" criticism of London. Burke styled these two documents the addresses "military" and "ecclesiastical" and he, along with John Dunning, proceeded to denounce them as inappropriate. This elicited a strong response in the press. "Observator" declared that "those have a right to address, whose Addresses the King chooses to receive," and several others also defended the legitimacy of these addresses.[45] Finally, that the petitions were "unanswered" was condemned on constitutional grounds. It is no exaggeration to say that the primary burden of the Common Hall of London's "Address to the Electors of Great Britain" was the evil of unanswered petitions, both those from America and "many in this country."[46] Similarly, the Lords' Protest of 2 November, against the address of loyalty to the king from the House of Lords, attached great significance to the government's lack of attention to petitions. This document construed the colonists as "fellow-subjects" who were "driven to resistance by acts of oppression and violence." It was signed by nineteen Lords and its printing in many newspapers cannot have been without effect.[47]

III

These essays concerning addresses and petitions comprise only a fraction of those that were printed. The intensity of feeling expressed concerning this activity is further illumined through an examination of the provincial press and local politics. When the petitions are read in isolation, the measured cadence of the prose sometimes obscures the strength of local political antagonism. Vituperative political exchanges in the weekly newspapers added another dimension to the sharp divisions in the nation. The picture of contending parties that emerges from the provincial press is even more vivid than that derived from the petitions. This fact has been thoroughly documented in the west midlands;[48] the same divisions can be seen in two southern and two northern counties.

Newspapers in Hampshire and Wiltshire provide a good illustration of the role of the provincial press in relation to the petitions. The *Hampshire Chronicle* took a pro-Ministry position while the editor of the *Salisbury and Winchester Journal* supported the Opposition. Differences with respect to America in

---

[44]*Cumb. Pacq.* (19 October 1775).

[45]*Gen. Eve. Post* (11-14, 16-18 November 1775); *Lond. Chron.* (12-14 December 1775).

[46]Printed in *Suss. Week. Adv.* (9 October 1775).

[47]Printed in *Suss. Week. Adv.* (13 November 1775) and *Sal. Win. J.* (13 November 1775). Parliament's unwillingness to answer petitions in the spring was criticized by "Curtius," *Lond. Eve.-Post* (25-27 July 1775).

[48]Money, *Experience and Identity*, 199-206.

Hampshire surfaced on 12 October during a meeting at the audit-house in Southampton. One observer commented: "This has caused a great stir and dissensions among us; when they will end, or which side will prevail, at present it is difficult to say."[49] Charges and countercharges concerning the social status and political principles of both addressers and petitioners appeared immediately in the *Hampshire Chronicle*.[50] The coercive address was printed with signatures, the petition without, and successive issues of the *Chronicle* record the rancorous debate that surrounded these popular expressions.[51] This interchange was spirited, and yet sometimes finer constitutional discriminations were made in the provincial press than in the petitions themselves. An essay by "A Native of Southampton" stated that the petitioners aimed at a "total subversion of the constitution, both in church and state," but a "Lover of Peace and Harmony" penetrated into the issues by citing Lord Camden, the late high chancellor, on the problem of taxing the colonies.[52] "A Lover of Peace and Harmony" was attacked in turn by "Libertas" who referred to him as a "crazy zealot" and a "political Bedlamite."[53] "Cataline," in response, wrote in favor of the petitioners.[54]

Local concern about addressing the Crown soon extended to the county, and some of the leaders in the borough were also involved with the Hampshire address. On 2 November a meeting of Hampshire freeholders at the County Hall, Winchester, led to a "warm debate" over whether or not "it was the Sense of the Meeting to have an Address."[55] A rough draft of an address was presented, and the meeting's detailed consideration of each point reveals a great concern for the constitutional issue of parliamentary supremacy on the one hand, and the claims of the colonists on the other.[56] The address was agreed upon by a vote of about

---

[49]Accounts in *Hamp. Chron.* (16 October 1775); *Sal. Win. J.* (16 October 1775); *Gen. Eve. Post* (14-17 October 1775).

[50]*Hamp. Chron.* (16, 23 October 1775). Later, the integrity of the Southampton petitioners was defended by "A Lover of Peace and Harmony" in *Sal. Win. J.* (27 November 1775) and challenged by "Libertas," *Hamp. Chron.* (18 December 1775).

[51]For the address, see *Hamp. Chron.* (23 October 1775); for the petition, ibid. (6 November 1775) and *Sal. Win. J.* (13 November 1775).

[52]*Hamp. Chron.* (23, 30 October 1775); *Sal. Win. J.* (27 November 1775).

[53]*Hamp. Chron.* (6, 27 November, 4 December 1775).

[54]Ibid. (18 December 1775).

[55]See the advertisements preceding the meeting in *Hamp. Chron.* (23, 30 October 1775); *Sal. Win. J.* (30 October 1775), along with the partial accounts in *North. Merc.* (13 November 1775) and *Man. Merc.* (14 November 1775) which state that 200 supported an address and only seven opposed it, with no further indication of the later county movement in support of peace.

[56]Accounts in *Hamp. Chron.* (6 November 1775); *Sal. Win. J.* (6 November 1775). The high sheriff read the addresses two or three times and many specific expressions were debated.

100 to 8, and this led, just as at Southampton, to a movement to petition for peace. On 18 November a meeting numbering about 100 freeholders met at the George Inn, Winchester, and agreed to a county petition for "lenient and peaceful measures with the Americans." The intelligence of the debate in the newspapers over the division in the county is noteworthy. One author referred his readers to "the acts of 7 and 8 Will. III c. 22 and 6 Geo. III c. 12" and claimed they would find these "sufficiently conclusive as to the supreme authority of Parliament over the colonies in all cases whatsoever."[57] "A Lover of Peace and Harmony" countered by arguing that these acts gave Parliament no right to tax the Americans without representation: "Taxation and Representation are *coeval* with, and *essential* to this Constitution."[58]

Charges concerning the *Hampshire Chronicle*'s reluctance to report on the Winchester meeting of 18 November led to a bitter exchange between the editors of the *Salisbury and Winchester Journal* and the *Hampshire Chronicle*.[59] In Wiltshire fewer boroughs were divided, but the debate in the newspaper regarding the petition and address from Westbury, Warminster, and Trowbridge was possibly more extensive than any other single newspaper debate in the fall of 1775. When on 16 November Burke introduced his speech supporting conciliation with the petition from Westbury, he attempted to legitimize his views with the weight of popular opinion. This use of the petition gave it more publicity than the petitions to the king, and this resulted in widespread debate in the press.[60]

The provincial press occasionally recorded local divisions that were unknown to other newspapers. For example, apart from the *Cumberland Pacquet*, the support for peace in two northern counties would have remained virtually unknown. The agitation for peace in Cumberland and Westmorland provides a good example of the false impression that could be left by the one surviving address for coercion. The address from Carlisle was signed by 308 people who promised to "exert ourselves to the utmost, in supporting the rights of the Crown, and the authority of Parliament; and that nothing on our part shall be wanting, to counteract the frantic and nefarious machinations of aristocratic or republican traitors."[61] But Carlisle and the counties of Cumberland and Westmorland were not united in support of coercion. A letter from Carlisle signed "A. Z." claimed that this address had "not met with that success which was

[57]*Hamp. Chron.* (20 November, 4 December 1775).

[58]*Sal. Win. J.* (11 December 1775).

[59]Ibid. (27 November, 11 December 1775); *Hamp. Chron.* (4, 25 December 1775).

[60]See the numerous essays on the Westbury, Warminster, Trowbridge petition in *Sal. Win. J.* (13, 20, 27 November, 4, 11, 18, 25 December 1775; 1 January 1776); *Bath Chron.* (9, 30 November; 14, 21, 28 December 1775). See also the London press, *Gen. Eve. Post* (18-21, 23-25 November; 5-7 December 1775); *Lond. Chron.* (9-11, 25-28 November; 7-9, 26-28 December 1775).

[61]Printed in *Cumb. Pacq.* (28 December 1775).

expected, nor seems to have been blessed with those sanctions which were spoken of." The author urged that "many amongst us" do not share the sentiments of the addressers that the colonists are traitors.[62] This claim was substantiated by the circulation of a conciliatory petition in both counties. Although this petition has not survived, the *Cumberland Pacquet* provides a relatively complete picture of its evolution.

The petitioning movement began with notices in the *Cumberland Pacquet* calling for a county meeting at Cockermouth to prepare a loyal address to the king.[63] The sheriff subsequently canceled this meeting and only later took pains to explain his motives.[64] On 9 November, the very day that the county meeting was to have been held, Sir James Lowther "very unexpectedly" arrived at Cockermouth with a petition to his Majesty regarding "the present disturbances with the colonies" and "the impropriety of taking Hanoverian troops into British pay."[65] While the text of the petition is not extant, another editorial remarks that it pled with the king to put an end "to an unnatural and destructive war."[66] A meeting was held at the Moot Hall, and the petition was read and signed by "as many as thought proper." These events elicited numerous letters to the *Cumberland Pacquet* that the editor summarized in three categories: those who wished to thank Sir James for his unwearied diligence; those who wished a new county meeting would be called to "prove the preference they give to plain and public proceedings, when suddenly opposed by secret and ambiguous attempts"; and a third group that condemned both addressing and petitioning.[67] About two weeks later Lowther took his petition to Whitehaven and left it at the Court House for signing. The next day, Tuesday, 28 November, it was "handed about" the town and carried as far south as Appleby, Westmorland.[68] After the election at Appleby on 7 December, Lowther made a speech on the American dispute "which gained him general applause. . . . At the same time a petition to His Majesty, praying a reconciliation with

---

[62]Ibid. (4 January 1776).

[63]Ibid. (26 October; 2 November 1775).

[64]Ibid. (9 November 1775). Anthony Benn, sheriff, explained that he was informed that on the one side a number of people "of considerable property" did not then choose to interfere with Parliament and on the other side there was a group of people who were determined to support the measures of government but were unable to attend on 9 November. One wonders if Sir James Lowther was not more directly behind the cancellation. *Cumb. Pacq.* (18 January 1776).

[65]Ibid. (16 November 1775).

[66]Ibid. (23 November 1775).

[67]Ibid. (23 November 1775).

[68]Ibid. (30 November 1775). "What number of names were added to it here, [i.e., Whitehaven] we have not learnt yet," nor was this ever reported.

the Colonies, was concluded upon."[69] Division at Kendal, Westmorland, as noted in a previous chapter, may indicate that the petition was circulated there as well. It was not until the end of December that the competing Carlisle address was placed in the house of Dr. Thomas Graham, to be signed between the hours of three and ten. Graham himself later presented the address to the king "and had the honour to kiss his Majesty's hand."[70]

In January 1776 fifteen justices of the peace attended upon the bench in the Sessions in Cockermouth, and it was proposed by the sheriff that they put forth a loyal address to his Majesty. Five of the justices were in favor of such an address, but ten were against it, with Sir James Lowther at the head.[71] A subsequent comment in the *Cumberland Pacquet* explained that while the majority who were against an address were loyal to the king, they were opposed to the "ruinous and coercive measures adopted by administration" and for that reason opposed to an address.[72] Earlier, in defending his cancellation of the county meeting, the sheriff went so far as to say that "a considerable number of respectable Freeholders" believed that an address to the Crown would be "unseasonable."[73] It seems certain that Sir James Lowther influenced the opinion of his fellow justices of the peace and probably swayed the views of many lesser property holders; his influence in the county must be given its due weight. But it would certainly be wrong to conclude from the one surviving address from Carlisle that the county was unanimously behind the coercive measures of the government.

IV

Only by looking at many different local newspapers has it been possible to reconstruct a relatively complete picture of popular division regarding America. Developments in Cumberland and Westmorland, for example, were almost completely unknown to the metropolitan press and have subsequently been passed over by historians. But while local newspapers provide many details concerning local antagonisms, on the whole the press failed to print the petitions, and it neglected to portray the extent of support in favor of peace. In contrast to this paucity, newspapers gave remarkably wide coverage to the coercive addresses, and it is this imbalance in publicity that has led to a distorted picture of public opinion concerning America. The dimensions of this

---

[69]Brian Bonsall, *Sir James Lowther and Cumberland and Westmorland Elections, 1754-1775* (Manchester: Manchester University Press, 1960) 149, drawing upon the *Newcastle Journal* (16 December 1775). See also *Gen. Eve. Post* (13-16 January 1776), where "Observator" attacks the "Westmorland" petition.

[70]*Cumb. Pacq.* (28 December 1775, 18 January 1776).

[71]Ibid. (18 January 1776). Their names are recorded. Those in support of the address include one clergyman; those against it include two.

[72]Ibid. (25 January 1776).

[73]Ibid. (18 January 1776).

distortion are seen by surveying the number of petitions and addresses that were printed in eighteen metropolitan and provincial newspapers.[74]

The *London Gazette* was the official instrument of the government, and it printed the texts of all the coercive addresses.[75] The average *Gazette* was four pages in length, two columns per page, and it appeared twice a week. The addresses normally occupied one-half to a full column of text, but the *Gazette* also transcribed and printed all of the signatures, and this required numerous additional pages. In the three-month period from 12 September to 12 December 1775, the twenty-seven issues were enlarged to accommodate the printing of the loyal addresses to an average of six pages in length, and since normal reportage was reduced, over half of the entire coverage was given to printing the coercive addresses with signatures.[76] In the 3 October issue, for example, seven addresses and the names of over 1,200 people took up seven of the eight pages of the *Gazette*, leaving only half a page for the price of corn. This tactic of printing the names of loyal supporters was important; the visual impact of thousands of printed names left a strong impression of widespread support for the government. The signatures of the Lancashire address alone filled nearly ten pages of the *Gazette* and caused some marvel among contemporaries.[77]

The only paper that attempted a comprehensive listing of the petitions for conciliation was the radical *London Evening-Post*, and while it printed the text of nineteen of these petitions, it transcribed the names of only eight. The *London Evening-Post*, as most other papers, listed all the coercive addresses that appeared in the *Gazette*, but since the *Gazette* in turn gave no notice to the conciliatory petitions, it was charged with suppressing them.[78] The *Public Adver-*

---

[74]The six metropolitan papers surveyed from 1 August-31 December 1775 are *Lond. Gaz.*, *Lond. Eve.-Post*, *Lond. Chron.*, *Gen. Eve. Post*, *Morn. Chron.*, *Pub. Adv.*; the twelve provincial papers are *Sal. Win. J.*, *York Cour.*, *Bath Chron.*, *Glos. J.*, *Bath J.*, *Hamp. Chron.*, *Brist. J.*, *Cumb. Pacq.*, *Man. Merc.*, *Read. Merc.*, *Suss. Week. Adv.*, and *North. Merc.*

[75]Concerning the *London Gazette* as an organ of the administration and discussion of its highly biased reportage, see Solomon Lutnick, *The American Revolution and the British Press, 1775-1783* (Columbia MO: University of Missouri Press, 1967) 20-22. The *London Evening Post, London Chronicle, Morning Chronicle, Middlesex Journal,* and *Crisis* were antigovernment papers; *The General Evening Post* was progovernment and the *Public Advertiser* was independent. See ibid., 219, 224-25.

[76]Some 87 of a total of 172 pages are taken up with the addresses. For the average, 12-16 September through 12-16 December 1775 was compared to 17-20 June through 9-12 September 1775 and 16-19 December 1775 through 16-19 March 1776.

[77]*Bris. J.* (16 December 1775).

[78]The *London Gazette* did print a few conciliatory petitions; the Bridgwater petition for conciliation was printed apparently because it took such a strong stand in defense of the Declaratory Act, as was that of the London Livery, which equivocated on the use of force, *Lond. Gaz.* (24-28 October 1775). The *Lond. Eve.-Post* also considered the Livery petition conciliatory (28-31 October, 4-7 November 1775). Later, the conicilia-

tiser, which took neither a government nor Opposition stance, referred to the scandalous partiality of the *Gazette* in refusing to print petitions for peace, and later it noted that while the "court Gazette" continued to treat petitions with contempt, it was intended by the publishers that the addresses for coercion should "prove the Opinion of the Nation."[79] Other papers also noticed the failure of the *Gazette* to give any place to the petitions and claimed the truth was being suppressed.[80]

The *London Gazette*, however, was not the only metropolitan paper that gave a highly biased picture of petitioning activity. Next to the *London Evening-Post*, the *Morning Chronicle* printed the greatest number of petitions with five; the other three papers surveyed printed four each. In contrast, the *London Chronicle* and the *General Evening Post* printed fourteen and fifteen coercive addresses respectively. While these two papers refer to a number of additional petitions, many of these references are fleeting allusions to a "petition" presented to the king. One would not even know that the petition was for conciliatory measures apart from the contempoary usage that associated "petitions" with a desire for change, and "addresses" with an approval of current policy.[81] The petitions from Taunton, Nottingham, Worcester, and Bolton, listed in the *General Evening Post*, would be quite lost to the reader unless he were alert to this distinction, as would those from Cambridge, Southwark, and Worcester in the *London Chronicle*.[82] As evenhanded a paper as the *General Evening Post* was far more careful to print coercive addresses than conciliatory petitions, and this sometimes led to serious distortions. In the 14-17 October issue the *General Evening Post* noted that Southampton was divided with respect to America, but on 19-21 October it reported only the presentation of the coercive address; in failing to mention the petition for peace, it left the impression that Southampton supported the government.[83]

Numerous London newspapers circulated in provincial towns and boroughs. Since the *London Evening-Post* alone gave detailed attention to the pe-

---

tory petitions of the Lord Mayor and Aldermen of London were also printed, *Lond. Gaz.* (19-23 January 1776). It is questionable whether or not the address for Exeter can be called coercive and it also was printed, but these are the only exceptions, *Lond. Gaz.* (26-30 September 1775).

[79]*Pub. Adv.* (18 October, 7 November 1775).

[80]*Lond. Chron.* (14-17 October 1775); *Lond. Eve.-Post* (7-10, 14-17 October, 30 November-2 December 1775). See also the *Middlesex Gazette* noted in *Amer. Arch.*, 4th ser., 3:981. Sir James Lowther attacked the *Gazette* on 3 November in the House of Commons for its biased reporting of American affairs, as did the Duke of Manchester on 18 December in the House of Lords, *Parl. Hist.* 18:828, 1904.

[81]Regarding this usage, see the essay in *Cumb. Pacq.* (19 October 1775); *Lond. Eve.-Post* (2-4 November 1775).

[82]See *Gen. Eve. Post* (10-12, 26-28 October, 7-9 November, 16-19 December 1775); *Lond. Chron.* (9-11, 11-14 November 1775).

[83]*Gen. Eve. Post* (14-17, 19-21 October 1775).

titions for peace, it would be necessary to read this specific paper in order to discover the true dimensions of popular opposition to the policy of coercion. More important than the circulation of London papers was the dependence of provincial papers on news items drawn directly from the London press. Citations from the *London Evening-Post*, the *St. James Chronicle*, and the *London Gazette* appeared in the *York Courant;* and the *Public Advertiser* and the *London Gazette* were cited by the *Sussex Weekly Advertiser*. But in the provinces, no metropolitan paper received as much coverage as the *London Gazette*. It was cited in almost every issue of every provincial paper. Whereas other news stories from other London papers were occasionally noted, provincial papers drew major news items directly from the *Gazette,* and they regularly devoted their most prominent columns to this official government source. Deference to this source had a profound impact on public opinion.

Two-thirds of the provincial newspapers surveyed listed all of the addresses as they appeared in the *London Gazette*. They also commonly printed a number of coercive addresses that were ready at hand, having already been conveniently transcribed by the *Gazette*. By contrast, the only petitions that were regularly printed in the provinces were the same ones that were repeatedly printed by the London press, which were, in order of frequency: London, Bristol, Coventry, Nottingham, Newcastle-upon-Tyne, Halifax, and Westbury-Warminster-Trowbridge. Of these, Newcastle and Halifax seem to have attracted attention because they were so large, and the petition from Westbury was more prominent because Burke presented it to Parliament.[84] The fragmentary nature of the coverage is seen in that none of the twelve provincial papers surveyed listed all seven of these petitions, and not one provincial paper printed more than four petitions for peace.[85]

The amount of attention given to the petitions for peace predictably reflected the political stance of the paper. The *Manchester Mercury* and the *Bath Chronicle*, for example, were strongly proadministration;[86] the former printed the texts of seven coercive addresses and the latter printed eleven, which was matched only by Felix Farley's *Bristol Journal*. The *Manchester Mercury*, however, printed only one conciliatory petition and the *Bath Chronicle* printed only three, though it can be demonstrated that the editor of the *Bath Chronicle* read the *London Evening-*

-----

[84]The prominence of these petitions in the London press appears to have been the data base for Dora Mae Clark's study. She knew only of the London, Bristol, Nottingham, Halifax, Westbury-Warminster-Trowbridge, Leeds, and Staffordshire petitions.

[85]*York Cour.*, for example, printed the Halifax and Leeds petitions; *Bath Chron.* printed the Trowbridge petition and noted the one from Taunton; *Cumb. Pacq.* followed the movement of the Cumberland petition.

[86]The orientation of the papers can be established independently on the basis of editorial comment. For *Man. Merc.*, see 15 August 1775 and for *Bath Chron.* 10 August, 21 September 1775.

Post and so had access to most of the petitions.[87] Conversely, the *Bath Journal* and the *Salisbury and Winchester Journal* were both sympathetic to the American cause.[88] Yet even these editors gave more attention to the addresses than the petitions; the *Bath Journal* printed two petitions and two addresses, while the *Salisbury and Winchester Journal* printed three petitions and seven addresses, though the editor of the latter also clearly read the *London Evening-Post.*[89] It seems fair to conclude that the political orientation of the provincial papers influenced the handling of petitions and addresses. In this they merely followed the example of the *London Gazette* on the one hand, or the *London Evening-Post* on the other. But the former was far more influential than the latter. The provincial papers that were favorable to Opposition politics made little effort to provide a full listing of the petitions in favor of peace, and this has contributed to a distinctly one-sided viewpoint of English public opinion.

The impact of the aggressive publishing program of the *London Gazette* and the subsequent partiality of other newspapers can be explicitly demonstrated in the few cases where an overall evaluation of the number of addresses and petitions was attempted. Here the editors must have assumed that the number of petitions and addresses, not the number of signatures, was the critical factor in linking these forms of popular expression to public opinion. In the 31 October-2 November issue of the *London Chronicle,* the three petitions supporting conciliation from London, Bristol, and Coventry were interpreted as "the clearest proofs imaginable of the abject state to which sedition is reduced." This report seemed to imply that they were the only petitions produced.[90] In the next issue of the *London Chronicle* (2-4 November), an editorial that subsequently appeared in provincial newspapers claimed that an "immense Majority" of the men of property and character in England supported coercive measures. As evidence for this generalization, and proof of "the abhorrence" with which the colonists' conduct was held by "their European fellow subjects," the author listed sixteen boroughs and towns in England that had sent addresses to the Crown in favor of coercion.[91] The article failed to note that six

---

[87]See the reference to *Lond. Eve-Post* in *Bath Chron.* (5 October 1775). Evidence for this connection between political orientation and the printing of addresses could be multiplied. The *Suss. Week. Adv.* (7, 14 August 1775) and *North. Merc.* (23 October 1775) were proadministration papers; neither of them printed any conciliatory petitions. Instead, they printed three and five coercive addresses respectively, and listed many from the *Gazette.*

[88]*Bath J.* (21 August, 11 September, 2 October 1775); *Sal. Win. J.* (16 October 1775).

[89]See *Sal. Win. J.* (11 September, 2 October 1775).

[90]*Lond. Chron.* (31 October-2 November 1775).

[91]*Lond. Chron.* (2-4 November 1775); the sixteen are: London, Manchester, Liverpool, Bristol, Coventry, Lancaster, Leicester, Poole, Taunton, Exeter, Warwick, Kingston-upon-Hull, Great Yarmouth, Southampton, Winchester, and Trowbridge-Bradford-Melksham. This same essay was printed in *North. Merc.* (13 November 1775) and *Man. Merc.* (7 November 1775) with the addition of Chester in the latter.

of the sixteen places were by this date divided and had sent conciliatory petitions as well as coercive addresses. Furthermore, by the same day that this editorial was published, petitions for peace from a total of twelve places had already appeared in the pages of the *London Evening-Post*.[92] Thus while the addresses were in the majority, the listing of sixteen addresses compared to twelve petitions was hardly a matter of an "immense majority." In the next issue of the *London Evening-Post*, another commentator, basing his observation on only six conciliatory petitions, observed that "the tide of addressing begins already to turn."[93] Later, a few correspondents concurred; one depicted the people pleading for reconciliation, and another alluded to the "numerous petitions in favour of the Americans."[94] But this was not the predominant opinion.

The *London Gazette* and influential editorials like that in the *London Chronicle* of 2-4 November created the prevailing impression that the great majority of people were in favor of coercion.[95] Horace Walpole, for example, despaired of any substantial popular opposition to the government. He listed seventeen addresses for coercion from England alone. He knew of only three for conciliation; therefore, he must have been ignorant of the *London Evening-Post*.[96] The *London Gazette* had done far more than reflect public opinion; it had created it. The newspapers that were sympathetic to the Opposition not only failed to report the extent of pro-American public opinion that was present; by their silence they contributed to the impression of a nation united behind the government.

V

It is difficult to assess with precision the degree to which the political atmosphere of August through December may have hindered expressions of sympathy for peace. Equally difficult is the question of whether or not the political setting contributed to the highly selective treatment of the conciliatory

---

[92]By 2-4 November 1775 the *Lond. Eve.-Post* had printed the petitions from London, Bristol, Poole, Taunton, Southampton, Coventry, Middlesex, Staffordshire, Newcastle, Nottingham, Leeds, and Halifax.

[93]*Lond. Eve.-Post* (4-7 November 1775); the six were Middlesex, Livery of London, London Merchants, Bristol, Nottingham, and Coventry.

[94]*Lond. Eve.-Post* (5-7 December 1775); *Gen. Eve. Post* (4-6 January 1776). For the view that the addresses do not represent "the voice of the nation," see also *Sal. Win. J.* (16 October 1775) and an anonymous resident of London to a gentleman in Virginia dated 21 December 1775 in *Amer. Arch.*, 4th ser., 3:369.

[95]For further statements based on the addresses that claimed the "majority of the nation" was behind the government, see *Hamp. Chron.* (2 October 1775); *Lond. Chron.* (28-31 October 1775); *Man. Merc.* (26 September, 3 October 1775).

[96]Walpole's list seems to be based on a somewhat faulty memory. He recorded an address from Suffolk and one from Dover for which there is no corroborative evidence. A. Francis Steuart, ed., *The Last Journals of Horace Walpole*, 2 vols. (London: John Lane, 1910) 1:474-79. The three conciliatory petitions he knew of were those from London, Middlesex, and Bristol.

petitions found in the press. That the royal proclamation of 23 August stimulated many loyal addresses can be clearly demonstrated. Can the converse be shown, that the proclamation stifled the emergence and publication of petitions for peace?

Before any English petitions were printed, both Houses of Parliament and the king had declared the colonies in a state of rebellion. The proclamation demanded full information of "all Persons who shall be found carrying on Correspondence with, or in any Manner or Degree aiding or abetting the persons now in open Arms and Rebellion against our Government." Whether or not the clause concerning "aiding and abetting" extended to those who wished to petition the Crown in favor of peaceful measures was unclear, and there ensued a lively debate in the press over the exact meaning of the proclamation. Generally it was agreed that royal proclamations by themselves did not have the force of law; "nor," said "Philo-Regis," "are we liable to the pains of misprision of treason for disobeying them." "A Lawyer," however, warned that any "minority meetings" that "either directly or indirectly" tended to encourage the American subjects of Great Britain were, on the basis of the proclamation, "clearly guilty of treason." Another correspondent feared that if a Common Hall in London were called "for the *professed* purpose of remonstrating *against* the measures *now carrying on in respect to America*," it would come under the description of the late proclamation.[97] The debating club at the Robin Hood in London addressed the question of whether or not it was "repugnant" to the constitution for the freeholders of a county to meet for the purpose of consulting on "political national affairs."[98] The freedom to meet and petition, and the freedom of the press, therefore, could not be taken for granted. Uncertainty about how to interpret the proclamation remained pervasive.[99]

In April George III had already associated conciliatory petitions with encouraging a "rebellious disposition" in the colonies, and the uncertainty in the minds of pro-Americans about how strictly the Crown might construe the proclamation seems to have been enough to discourage activities that hinted of support for the Americans. In the meeting that was called to organize a petition at Bristol, one of the opponents resisted the project on the grounds that there was a "disinclination in his Majesty to receive petitions respecting the American dispute."[100] This objection did not deter the petitioners, but there can be

---

[97]*Lond. Eve.-Post* (26-29 August 1775); *Gen. Eve. Post* (30 September-3 October 1775); *Morn. Chron.* (31 August 1775).

[98]*Morn. Chron.* (30 September 1775).

[99]*Lond. Eve.-Post* (24-26 August, 5-7, 9-12 September 1775); *Gen. Eve. Post* (9-12 September 1775); *Lond. Chron.* (7-9 September 1775); *Morn. Chron.* (8, 9, 12 September 1775); *Pub. Adv.* (1 September 1775); *Brist. J.* (2, 16 September 1775); *Bath J.* (4 September 1775); *Cumb. Pacq.* (31 August 1775). "L. G.," for example, directed his questions to the printers of the *London Gazette*, Sir Charles Eyre and William Strahan. *Lond. Eve.-Post* (26-29 August 1775).

[100]*Brist. J.* (30 September 1775); *Lond. Chron.* (28-30 September 1775).

little doubt about the accuracy of the perception. It is not unlikely that similar fears hindered some printers in the publication of the petitions. Historically there was some precedent for the notion that publishing a petition to the Crown was tantamount to sedition, but this argument seems never to have been explicitly raised by the press.[101] The London Common Hall's progressive "Address to the Electors of Great Britain" of 29 September has, in light of the king's proclamation, been recently judged a "bold document,"[102] and the same kind of evaluation could with equal justice be applied to the petitions for peace.

The connection between petitioning and sedition was never legally spelled out in 1775. Whether petitioning was considered seditious depended upon an individual's political viewpoint. Many observers believed that even opposition in Parliament was an encouragement to rebellion abroad.[103] The central argument against Burke's speech supporting conciliation in November was that the more Great Britain showed a disposition towards conciliation, the more rebellious the colonists would become.[104] To judge from notices in the press, it was widely believed that petitions supporting conciliation would mislead people in the colonies, and many associated conciliatory petitions explicitly with the encouragement of rebellion.[105] Conversely, it was often held that coercive addresses would help stanch the rebellion.[106]

The circulation of rumors contributed to the uncertainty of the political atmosphere. In early October there was widespread news coverage that another

---

[101]In the Seven Bishops Case (1688), the publication of the bishops' petition to the king was considered the grounds for its being seditious libel, though in this instance "publication" had to do principally with proof that the petition was merely presented to the king. See *The Proceedings and Tryal in the Case of the Most Reverend Father in God William, Lord Archbishop of Canterbury, and the Right Reverend Fathers in God* (London, 1689) 72-74, 78-79, 82-85, 91-92, 136-37. But the issue of intent was related indirectly to the question of publication in a broader sense. In the summation, the prosecution made its case hinge on whether or not the petition was intended as a petition to the king only, or intended to stir up sedition by inciting the people against the government. There was also opinion expressed that the petition should have been presented in Parliament.

[102]John Sainsbury, "The Pro-American Movement in London, 1769-1782; Extra-Parliamentary Opposition to the Government's American Policy" (Ph.D. dissertation, McGill University, 1975) 177, who also thinks that it may have been the proclamation that kept the Common Hall from replying to a letter from Congress to the city of London.

[103]*Lond. Chron.* (2-4, 23-25 November 1775); *Gen. Eve. Post* (1-3 August, 12-14 September 1775); *Cumb. Pacq.* (17 August 1775); *Suss. Week. Adv.* (4 September 1775).

[104]*Bath Chron.* (23 November 1775). *Parl. Hist.*, 18:982, 991.

[105]*Suss. Week. Adv.* (9 October 1775); *Lond. Chron.* (28-31 October, 18-21 November 1775); *Pub. Adv.* (13 September 1775); *Gen. Eve.-Post* (30 September-3 October 1775); *Cumb. Pacq.* (17 August, 13, 19 October 1775); *Brist. J.* (30 September 1775); *Read. Merc.* (4 December 1775).

[106]*Lond. Chron.* (23-26 September 1775); *Gen. Eve.-Post* (23-26 September 1775); *Bath Chron.* (9 November 1775); *Hamp. Chron.* (11 December 1775).

proclamation was about to be issued, "which will be particularly calculated to prevent any public Meetings being held for abetting the cause of the Americans," and this illustrated at once the ambiguity of the proclamation of 23 August and the courage of those who met to petition the Crown.[107] There were also rumors that after the meeting of Parliament an act would be passed to suspend the Habeas Corpus Act.[108] Newspapers, however, were generally uncertain about whether conciliatory or coercive measures were going to be pursued, and contradictory positions were found in a single paper from one issue to the next.[109] Rumors of a possible accommodation persisted through this period, as did preparation for war; notices appeared in the provincial press calling the deputy lieutenants and the militia to forthcoming meetings.[110] This uncertainty is most clearly reflected in the petitions and addresses themselves. As late as December 1775, there was still some uncertainty about whether or not the government would actually follow through with coercive measures.

The public uncertainty concerning the government's use of force abroad was related to the insecurity respecting possible political reprisals for the expression of pro-American sentiment at home. The actual policy of the government toward the press contributed directly to this atmosphere of uncertainty. On the one hand, the policy appeared lenient enough. The government allowed the seditious publication entitled the *Crisis* to continue publishing well into 1776, and this represents a remarkable instance of toleration.[111] On the other hand, John Horne Tooke was prosecuted for advertising a subscription for the relief of the widows and orphans of those Americans who had fallen at the hands of the king's troops at Lexington and Concord. At about the same time as the publication of the royal proclamation, newspapers carried notices that the nine papers that had printed Horne Tooke's advertisement were served

---

[107]*Hamp. Chron.* (2 October 1775); *Bath. Chron.* (2 October 1775); *Suss. Week. Adv.* (2 October 1775); *Man. Merc.* (3 October 1775); *Cumb. Pacq.* (5 October 1775); *Sal. Win. J.* (9 October 1775).

[108]*Gen. Eve. Post* (23-26 September 1775); *Pub. Adv.* (6 October 1775); *Cumb. Pacq.* (28 September 1775); *Man. Merc.* (3 October 1775); *Bath J.* (9 October 1775).

[109]See *Man. Merc.* (26 September, 24 October 1775) for contradicting reports in the same issues, and also as late as 14 and 21 November.

[110]Rumors of conciliation can be seen in *Hamp. Chron.* (25 September, 9, 23 October 1775) and then notice of the use of the "utmost" power to subdue them (27 November 1775). See the same uncertainty in *Sal. Win. J.* (11, 18 September, 20 November 1775). For the militia, see *Read. Merc.* (6 November 1775).

[111]Only one issue was condemned before October 1776. See Lutnick, *The American Revolution*, 3. Sainsbury surmises that this may have been more a matter of prudence than liberality, since a riot followed the burning of *Crisis* no. 3. Sainsbury, "The Pro-American Movement in London," 155.

with writs.[112] In late October there was also extensive news coverage of Stephen Sayer's arrest on charges of treason.[113] Actual and threatened prosecution for sympathy shown to the Americans may have contributed to a reluctance on people's part to sign petitions for peace, and such threats almost certainly contributed to a reluctance among some printers to publish them. For example, printer John Keene of the *Bath Journal*, while clearly favoring the Americans, on three occasions published his misgivings about possible prosecution, and proceeded, apparently against his conscience, to print more coercive addresses than conciliatory ones.[114] The failure of the press to provide a balanced coverage of petitions and addresses seems to reflect a prudent reluctance to oppose the government publicly. The tendency of the provincial press to publish only those petitions that the London press published suggests that the London press served as a political litmus test for provincial editors.

If newspaper editors were influenced by the political atmosphere, it is still necessary to account for why other leaders were also reluctant to take an aggressive part in petitioning the Crown. Opposition groups of every political hue failed to utilize the press as effectively as the government. A number of things contributed directly to this failure, not the least of which was the threatening political atmosphere. It may have been this atmosphere that prompted the London Association to seek support among the more respectable elements in society. All the circular letters that the association printed were directed to mayors and town corporations, and yet with the advantage of historical hindsight, one can confidently conclude that this tactic was singularly unsuited to elicit support for peaceful measures. As bastions of order and good government, corporate bodies across the country were almost unanimous in sending addresses of approval to the Crown. The rabidly pro-American paper the *Crisis* gave only passing notice to the petitions in support of peace. It appears to have erred on the opposite side of the London Association by appealing only to ultraradical malcontents who had given up all hope of influencing the king.[115] These more radical factions experienced little success in cooperating with each

---

[112]See Sainsbury, "The Pro-American Movement in London," 163-65 and Ritcheson, *British Politics*, 223. The first notice of plans for prosecution of London papers appeared in *Lond. Eve.-Post* (17-19, 26-29 August 1775); see also *Read. Merc.* (21 August 1775); *York Cour.* (5 September 1775); *Suss. Week. Adv.* (4 September 1775); *Brist. J.* (9 September 1775).

[113]See John Sainsbury, "The Pro-Americans of London, 1769-1782," *William and Mary Quarterly* 3rd ser. 35 (July 1978): 437. *Suss. Week. Adv.* (4 September 1775).

[114]*Bath J.* (21 August, 11 September, 9 October 1775).

[115]See *Crisis* (23 September, 2 December 1775) in which five addresses are mentioned. The reason why the editor did not encourage petitioning is patent: "At such a CRISIS an appeal lies only to the PEOPLE; they and they only are proper to be addressed—The Right of a King exists no longer than he acts as a King." "Present Yourselves to his Majesty, not as Petitioners, introduced by Lord Hertford, or some other servile Courtier, but as ENGLISHMEN." *Crisis* (30 September 1775).

other, and in most cases their appeals for popular support betrayed strategies that were finally ineffective.[116]

If the radicals lacked wisdom in tactical matters, the cause of popular opposition was hindered even further by the attitude of the Rockingham Whigs. Burke saw the folly of limiting political activity against the government's American measures to Parliament alone, and he worked hard to stimulate petitioning activity.[117] In contrast to his involvement during the Middlesex election affair, however, he refused to cooperate with the radicals and defended his own forays into popular politics in terms of channeling popular sentiment away from the London demagogues. "My sole motive for attempting anything there, [in London]," Burke wrote, "was to keep the City, now and forever, out of the hands of the Wilkes, Olivers, Hornes, Mascalls, and Joels—perhaps even out of the talons of the Court."[118] This conservative impulse doomed all hope of cooperation with the radicals, and it fatally weakened any chance of a unified and hence strong opposition to the government's measures. The division is illustrated in the way that the ideological content of the petitions stimulated by the Rockingham Whigs contrasts with the more radical expressions from Southampton and Newcastle-upon-Tyne. The Rockinghams not only refused to work with the radicals, they were fundamentally divided; in boroughs where Burke was able to organize popular support, he was forced to work without Rockingham's knowledge or approval.[119] Moreover, the confidence Burke himself placed in the government may have contributed to yet another basic weakness in the petitioning movement.

VI

Burke, other leaders of the party, and the organizers and signers of petitions themselves appear to have rested their hopes too narrowly upon the king's response to their petitions, rather than seeing the value of the petitions as stimulating further public opposition. Little effort was made to publicize even those petitions that were known. While in the process of petitioning the Crown, the value of using the press occurred to Richard Champion, but he failed to take aggressive action. In a revealing letter to Portland, he told how he had sent a narrative of the proceedings of the Bristol addressers to London for insertion

---

[116]Sainsbury illustrates this by citing alderman Oliver's ill-timed attempt in the House of Commons on 27 November to discover who advised the king on the American measures. This resulted in a general debate and division among the radicals. Sainsbury, "The Pro-American Movement in London," 179.

[117]*Burke Correspondence*, 3:219, 220, 233 (Burke to Richmond, 26 September 1775; Burke to Champion 1, 23 October 1775).

[118]Ibid., 3:225 (Burke to Rockingham, 1 October 1775). Sainsbury argues that this inability of the Rockinghams to unite with the radicals contributed a great deal to the failure of effective opposition, "The Pro-American Movement in London," 156-58, 178.

[119]*Burke Correspondence*, 3:207-10; 220-21, 230, 232 (Burke to Rockingham, 14 September 1775; Burke to Champion, 1, 17, 20 October 1775).

in the papers; "but to my great mortification it was not. . . . I could have wished the Papers were more accessible, as I should have been glad to have had this narrative circulated throughout the kingdom. I must endeavor, if possible, to find out a method of obtaining a place in the London News, as it may be of Service."[120] Champion seems never to have followed up on his own suggestion. Burke's attempts to persuade Lord Rockingham of the value of petitioning the Crown before Parliament met proved fruitless.[121] The Rockingham organ, the *Annual Register*, later recorded only one petition in support of peace, and this illustrates, once again, that the self-imposed aristocratic orientation of the party guaranteed its inability to use effectively popular support.[122] Well might "a Friend of the People" criticize the Rockinghams' "devotion to Prerogative."[123] An understandable desire to avoid the imputation of sedition or treason, combined with the related need to obtain respectable backing, led the Rockingham Whigs and the London Association to a fundamental impasse.

The contrast with the administration could not be greater. Three facets of the administration's activity must be seen together. First, the government controlled the petitions for conciliation; they were always presented to the king, either privately to the lord in waiting, or at the levee. By contrast, petitions to Parliament were a matter of public record, and the press covered them with far greater ease. On balance, the *London Evening-Post* did remarkably well by printing the texts of most of the petitions, and it is not surprising that other papers gave very fragmentary accounts of petitioning activity. In a few cases, such as Cumberland and Lymington, no known copies of the petition ever appeared in print. Second, on the positive side, George III, Lord North, and their agents encouraged the putting forth and signing of loyal addresses, though this can be explicitly documented in only a handful of cases. Finally, the king and his ministers initiated a major campaign to see the coercive addresses published, and nationwide dependence upon the *London Gazette* represented a political advantage that no opposing party could even approximate. It appears that the administration had learned an important lesson about petitions from the Middlesex election affair, for by 1775 the government was far more adept at exploiting popular opinion than the Opposition. The printed names of those in favor of coercion were paraded before the public, page upon page, week after week, and the overwhelming impression one receives from the *London Gazette* is that the nation was united behind the government. In a fundamentally deferential society, the loyal support of dozens of corporate bodies was perhaps more impressive than the mere listing of names. Nevertheless, the government saw the value of listing names—whether respect-

---

[120]Champion to Portland, 5 October 1775; Portland Manuscripts, University of Nottingham, PWF 2,718.

[121]*Burke Correspondence*, 3:208 (Burke to Rockingham, 14 September 1775).

[122]Two petitions, if one includes the London Livery. See *Ann. Reg.* for 1775, 267-69, 271-72.

[123]*Pub. Adv.* (5 December 1775).

able or not—and it made its major public campaign in the fall the creation of an impression of national support. As a controller of public opinion, the government proved itself far superior to the feeble attempts of the Opposition. Its success in convincing the nation of the popularity of the use of force through its own newspaper is one of the most striking instances of successful government propaganda in modern times.

The petitions supporting peace had little effect on public opinion because the king had determined as early as April that they would not be recognized. Following the royal proclamation, some printers seem to have believed that it was impossible to publicize them without appearing treasonous, and in other cases printers were simply ignorant of their existence. The strategy of the American Congress to make public its appeals to English leaders was not followed by those who wished for peace in England. As a result, the strength of English support was never fully grasped. Benjamin Franklin's comment concerning the state of English public opinion was at least half true: "I am persuaded the body of the British people are our friends"; but, he continued, "they are changeable, and by your lying Gazettes may soon be made our enemies."[124] The visual impact of the *London Gazette*, with its expressions of loyalty and its thousands of signatures was far more compelling than anything the friends of America ever attempted. The intended result was achieved: both the nation and historians have seen only one pole of a distinctly divided public opinion.

---

[124]Leonard W. Labaree and William B. Willcox, eds., *The Papers of Benjamin Franklin* (New Haven: Yale University Press, 1982) 22:216 (Franklin to David Hartley, 3 October 1775).

Popular Opposition to Government during the American Crisis

Chapter V

From the Stamp Act Crisis until the Peace of Paris, widespread popular agitation in England erupted every five years, and on three of these occasions it involved approximately 60,000 people. If the popular reaction to the Fox-North Coalition is included in this earlier period, the petitions to Parliament and the Crown collected more than a quarter of a million signatures. This is roughly comparable to the number of people who voted in parliamentary elections during the same period of time; about 315,000 English voters went to the polls in the general elections of 1768, 1774, 1780, and 1784.[1] Surprisingly similar patterns between popular and electoral politics are also found by comparing the national distribution of parliamentary seats to the regional concentration of cities that petitioned the Crown. In the age of the American Revolution, extraparliamentary politics rivaled electoral politics in demographic terms, if not in influence.

A substantial minority of Englishmen felt that the government was unresponsive to the ensuing course of events and viewed the traditional channels of political expression as inadequate. They assumed, or at least hoped, that petitioning was a viable alternative that might influence the policy of the national government. The petitioners, however, made little attempt to influence public opinion at large. Their pleas were easily ignored by the authorities, and in the case of America, neglected by the Opposition. Historians have carefully studied the Middlesex election affair and agitation in regard to parliamentary reform. But since the decade of the 1770s was thought to be largely free from domestic disturbance, the movements of 1770 and 1780 were not connected to the American crisis. Seen separately and in isolation, these episodes of popular agitation were sometimes viewed as evidence that the political nation was uniformly conservative, apathetic, or corrupt. However, when the petitions concerning America are placed in the mid-1770s, hitherto unperceived regional

---

[1] *Commons, 1754-1790*, 1:514. Counting the total voting constituency for contested English boroughs and adding the approximate number of voters for the contested counties, the turnout for the general elections was 66,000 for 1768, 97,600 for 1774, 71,700 for 1780, and 79,900 for 1784, for a total of 315,200. These estimates are undoubtedly high, and many voters polled in more than one election.

and ideological connections become apparent. Taken together, these movements challenge the notion of a moribund national will.

Historians have differed markedly as to what constitutes a significant expression of public opinion.[2] The petitions from the Middlesex election affair, for example, were first dismissed as unimportant, but subsequently considered "impressive" displays of public opinion.[3] While differences of interpretation concerning the importance of popular agitation will continue, a comparative approach is needed that will embrace the Stamp Act Crisis of 1765-1766, the Middlesex election affair of 1769-1770, the American crisis of 1775, economic reform in 1780, and parliamentary reform in 1782-1783. The geographical and ideological similarities of these periods of agitation will offer a new framework in which to view contemporary political rhetoric. This applies to the conservative addresses as well as the petitions supporting change. A comparison of the regional provenance of loyal addresses to the king in successive periods provides substantive evidence for the reality of a perceived threat to the constitution. Repeated popular expressions of loyalty to the king also help explain why the Whigs thought they discerned a new authoritarianism that demanded a response with petitions of their own. Patterns discovered through an examination of the national dimensions of popular agitation will serve as points of departure for further investigations in the local setting.

I

Previous attempts at a comparative approach to popular politics have lacked a comprehensive character. In her standard account of English public opinion, Dora Mae Clark made a rudimentary comparison of the Stamp Act Crisis to the petitioning agitation of 1775. Since the petitions of 1765 were influential in effecting repeal, they were treated as a useful gauge in judging the significance of public opinion in other decades. The Stamp Act, however, was repealed because the administration supported repeal; accordingly, the petitioners were free to present their case to the House of Commons.[4] In contrast, the petition-

---

[2]Compare Dora Mae Clark, *British Opinion and the American Revolution* (New Haven: Yale University Press, 1930) 132, and Ian Christie and Benjamin Labaree, *Empire or Independence* (Oxford: Phaidon, 1976) 232.

[3]For a negative evaluation, see Lucy Sutherland, *The City of London and the Opposition to Government, 1768-1774* (London: University of London, Athlone Press, 1959) 30, and Caroline Robbins, *The Eighteenth-Century Commonwealthman* (New York: Atheneum, 1968) 320; George Rudé, *Wilkes and Liberty* (Oxford: Oxford University Press, 1962) 135, thought the petitions impressive, and John Cannon, *Parliamentary Reform, 1640-1832* (Cambridge: Cambridge University Press, 1973) 63, 69, takes a moderate approach. Through an examination of popular literature, John Brewer has extended Rudé's research in *Party Ideology and Popular Politics at the Accession of George III* (Cambridge: Cambridge University Press, 1976) 163-200.

[4]Edmund S. Morgan, *The Stamp Act Crisis: Prologue to Revolution* (New York: Collier Books, 1963) 331, 346.

ers of 1775 were never heard by the Commons. Clark did not recognize this distinction and proceeded to make the entire focus of her argument dependent upon the number of petitions that were presented. A serious mistake in arithmetic also contributed to this disadvantageous comparison. "On January 17," Clark wrote, "the House of Commons received ten petitions for the repeal of the Stamp Act; on the twentieth, seven more; and by February 27, eight more—thirty-five in all." Clark then compared "the thirty-five petitions presented in 1766" to the mere fifteen that were presented in 1775, and this erroneous comparison contributed to her conclusion that "coercion was a popular policy."[5] In fact, twenty-five, not thirty-five, English towns sent petitions for repeal of the Stamp Act, and while this represents eight more places than petitioned for conciliation in January-March of 1775, it is less than the number that petitioned for peace in the fall of 1775. Since the true dimensions of the petitioning movement in the fall have heretofore been so little understood, other historians as well were confined to comparing the agitation for the repeal of the Stamp Act to the merchants' petitions to Parliament.[6] A comparison of the petitions in the two movements served as the basis for concluding that as colonial matters worsened in the decade 1765-1775, public opinion in England turned against America.[7] Scholars have expended much energy in explaining why the commercial centers that petitioned for repeal in 1765 did not oppose coercion in 1775,[8] when in fact the same centers did petition in both periods.

Historians have also made serious errors when calculating the number of places that petitioned during the Middlesex election affair. The early study by Lucy Sutherland made a fleeting allusion to the addresses of loyalty to the king, but in an extended survey of the petitions of 1769-1770, George Rudé mentioned only two addresses in support of law and order.[9] These analyses resulted in the impression that the popular outcry against the unseating of Wilkes was almost unanimous. In fact, five English counties and twelve boroughs (in addition to some twenty-six Scottish counties and thirty-three burghs) sent addresses in support of the government's position.[10]

---

[5]Clark, *British Opinion*, 42, 85, 92. The book was reprinted in 1966 by Russell and Russell, and the errors remain.

[6]Bernard Donoughue, *British Politics and the American Revolution: The Path to War, 1773-75* (London: MacMillan Co., 1964) 152; B. D. Bargar, "Matthew Boulton and the Birmingham Petition," *William and Mary Quarterly* 3rd ser., 13 (January 1956): 27.

[7]Donoughue, *British Politics*, 156, 199-200, 238, 289.

[8]Ibid., 147-53.

[9]Sutherland, *The City of London*, 30 n. 1; Rudé, *Wilkes and Liberty*, 112, 128, mentions the loyal addresses from Bristol and Liverpool, but this seriously underestimates the extent of loyal support. Brewer, *Party Ideology*, 175, 179, also examines only the pro-Wilkes petitions.

[10]The counties are Essex, Kent, Salop, Surrey, and Cumberland; the boroughs are London, Bristol (three addresses), Norwich, Liverpool (two addresses), Leicester,

Pivotal historical conclusions have thereby evolved from the apparent paucity of loyal addresses in 1769 and the supposed absence of conciliatory petitions in 1775. Scholars have made important claims for the representative nature of the petitions in 1765 and 1769-1770. Concerning the Stamp Act Crisis of 1765, P. D. G. Thomas stated, "nearly all the ports and industrial towns" petitioned Parliament for repeal.[11] John Brewer's recent examination of the provincial press during the Middlesex election affair revealed widespread opposition to the government. On the basis of petitions, counties that considered sending petitions, popular demonstrations over Wilke's release, and gifts presented to him, Brewer concluded that "the phenomenon of Wilkes was one of nationwide scope."[12] A comparative analysis of both movements with the agitation in 1775 is needed, since the former dealt specifically with colonial policy, and the latter was the only other issue in the period during which differences in public opinion resulted in counter petitions.

II

Any division of England into geographical units for the purpose of political analysis will result in some distortion. Since individual counties seldom provide meaningful guides to distinctive political areas, the grouping of counties will obscure important differences within a single region. The value of geographical analysis, however, is readily apparent. In discussing the representative nature of the petitions, for example, it is useful to know that the eight counties that sent neither addresses nor petitions in 1775 were sparsely populated; combined, they made up only about eleven percent of the population of England.[13] If the limitations of an extensive geographical framework are fully recognized, and if conclusions are advanced tentatively with an eye to the in-

---

Coventry, Lancaster, Kingston-upon-Hull, Great Yarmouth, Huntingdon, Carlisle, and Whitehaven. In addition, loyal addresses came from the archbishop, bishops, and clergy of the Province of Canterbury and the two universities. See *Lond. Gaz.* (4-7 February— 23-27 May 1769). Of these, the number of signatures are noted for the London merchants' address with 854 and Liverpool with 450; the remaining addresses were also apparently signed, claiming to come from the inhabitants of the various places, with the exception of the one from Leicester, which purports to come from the corporation. In addition to the twenty-six Scottish counties and thirty-three burghs, St. Andrews University and the University of Glasgow addressed along with two other colleges, and there were also eight groups of Presbyterian ministers who addressed against Wilkes. (31 March-1 April—3-6 June 1769).

[11]P. D. G. Thomas, *British Politics and the Stamp Act Crisis: The First Phase of the American Revolution, 1763-1767* (Oxford: Clarendon Press, 1975) 188.

[12]Brewer, *Party Ideology*, 174.

[13]No petition concerning America emerged from the following counties or boroughs within these counties: Co. Durham, Lincs., Rutland, Northants., Beds., Herts., Bucks., and Mon. Regarding the population, see Phyllis Deane and W. A. Cole, *British Economic Growth, 1688-1959: Trends and Structure*, 2d ed. (Cambridge: Cambridge University Press, 1967) 103, table 24, col. 3b.

tensive study of local politics, the ordering of petitions by region may enhance our understanding of popular politics during the American crisis.

England is conveniently divided into four roughly equivalent areas: the southeast, with seven counties, and the southwest, midlands, and northeast, with eleven counties each.[14] The distinguishing features of these regions were classically described in the early studies of Sir Lewis Namier. He viewed the midland Tories of 1761, for example, as "genuine reactionaries, heirs to the Counter-Reformation, to the authoritarian High Church, and the Jacobites," and he proceeded to demonstrate the truth of this judgment by comparing the votes of midland Tory members of Parliament regarding General Warrants with the less-consistent votes of Tories from the southwest.[15] Namier's analysis underscored the provincial character of English politics, a point that was also made in Rudé's study of the Middlesex petitioners. Rudé remarked upon the strong Puritan heritage of the southwest and believed he could discern "the authentic flavour of the 'Puritan Revolution' of the Seventeenth century" in the names of Somersetshire and Gloucestershire petitioners.[16]

John A. Phillips has recently given critical attention to the distinctive electoral structure of these four areas. His study shows that generalizations about the influence of patronage must be geographically specific, since the type of borough and its potential for influence varied so radically from region to region. Almost half (45.2%) of England's parliamentary boroughs were concentrated in the southwest, yet the majority of these boroughs were small and highly susceptible to influence. Moreover, the increase in patrons' influence in the late eighteenth century was greater in this region than in the other three areas.[17] Judgments concerning the nature of influence in individual cases will vary, but these statistical differences are great enough that any comparative analysis of popular political activity should have constant recourse to both the political traditions and the electoral structure of these four regions.

Table 5.1 provides a comprehensive listing of places that expressed popular political concerns in the period 1765-1784 by arranging the six most im-

---

[14]Sir Lewis Namier, *England in the Age of the American Revolution*, 2nd ed. (London: Macmillan Co., 1961) 199-201; John A. Phillips, "The Structure of Electoral Politics in Unreformed England," *Journal of British Studies* 19 (Fall 1979): 84-88; Linda Colley, *In Defiance of Oligarchy: The Tory Party, 1714-1760* (Cambridge: Cambridge University Press, 1982) 119-20. The southeast encompasses Mdx., Herts., Essex, Suff., Kent, Suss., and Surr.; the southwest, Berks., Hants., Wilts., Dorset, Som., Devon, Cornw., Mon., Herfs., Worcs., and Glos.; the midlands, Lancs., Cheshire, Derbys., Salop, Staffs., Leics., Warws., Northants., Oxon., Bucks., and Beds.; the northeast, Northumb., Cumb., Westmld., Co. Dur., Yorks., Notts., Lincs., Rutland., Norf., Hunts., and Cambs.

[15]Namier, *England in the Age of the Revolution*, 200-202; see also *The Structure of Politics at the Accession of George III*, 2d ed. (London: Macmillan Co., 1957) 235.

[16]Rudé, *Wilkes and Liberty*, 146.

[17]Phillips, "The Structure of Electoral Politics," 19:84-86.

portant disturbances in the four traditional geographico-political regions.[18] It is organized for the purpose of illustrating the geographical distribution of popular agitation, and therefore boroughs and counties that sent signed petitions are combined. The table does not include towns that sent unsigned addresses or petitions from special interest groups.[19] Nor, since the purpose is to relate actual popular agitation to geographic locale, does it note the places that were reportedly divided, but for which no document exists.[20] The petitions and addresses regarding America sent to Parliament in the spring of 1775 and those to the Crown in the fall are combined; the length of time separating these two periods of agitation was about the same as that which separated the earliest from the latest petitions during the Middlesex election affair. This results in a net gain of ten in the conciliatory row and two in the coercive row. Of these ten, however, we know that there was still support for conciliation in the fall of 1775 in Liverpool, Manchester, Birmingham, Wolverhampton, Whitehaven, and possibly Norwich.[21]

---

[18]The Stamp Act petitions are found in *Parl. Hist.*, 16:133-36 and *CJ*, 462-611. The Middlesex petitions and addresses are derived from Rudé, *Wilkes and Liberty*, 133, Appendix 7 (211), and n. 10 above. The American petitions are from Tables 1 and 3.1-4. The petitions for economic reform are from *Parl. Hist.*, 20:1370-72 and *CJ*, 37:581-724, which adds Hampshire (586). The petitions in support of parliamentary reform are from Ian Christie, *Wilkes, Wyvill and Reform* (London: Macmillan Co., 1962) 169 n. 4. The petitions from 1784 are found in *Lond. Gaz.* (13-17 January—25-29 May 1784), but with only the tally of signatures, not the signatures themselves. The Public Record Office, Kew, retains only forty-eight borough and six county addresses concerning the Coalition. The frequency of contested elections and the proportion of borough votes is drawn from *Commons, 1754-1790*, and Cannon, *Parliamentary Reform*, 280-89. This election data does not count by-elections and the figures for the borough voters in 1774 are the maximum possible and for the counties they are an estimate of the actual turnout. The figures on population are derived from Deane and Cole, *British Economic Growth*, 103, table 24, col. 3b.

[19]The corporations that addressed the Crown concerning America will be discussed below; they serve to strengthen the geographical peculiarities shown in Table 5.1.

[20]Eighteen such places that were concerned with America are noted at the end of ch. 3, and Rudé records agitation regarding Middlesex at Lincoln, Norfolk, Northampton, Oxford, Canterbury, and Glamorgan, plus the counties of Essex, Hampshire, and Nottinghamshire (*Wilkes and Liberty*, 130-33). But none of these boroughs actually produced a petition, and they are not considered here.

[21]A number of boroughs that petitioned in support of government in January-March sent both conciliatory and coercive documents in the fall (Poole, Trowbridge, Leeds, and Nottingham), and so Poole, for example, is counted as one in the coercive row, as one in the conciliatory, and as one in the "total" row. Liverpool sent only a conciliatory petition in the spring and only a coercive address in the fall, and so is counted as one in each row. In addition, Norwich, Dudley, Manchester, Wolverhampton, Bridport, Whitehaven, Newcastle (Staffordshire) were conciliatory in the spring, and Birmingham and Huddersfield sent both coercive and conciliatory petitions in the spring. These last two are thus added as coercive as well as conciliatory. Of the ten, one is from the southwest, six from the midlands, and three from the northeast.

The twenty-seven petitions for conciliation in the fall of 1775 exceeded the number that appeared in favor of repeal of the Stamp Act in 1766, and were equal to the number that appeared in favor of Wilkes in 1770. When combined with those in the spring of 1775, the petitions for conciliation exceeded those of 1766, 1770, and 1782, and equalled those of 1780. In terms of the number of signed petitions, only the reaction to the coalition in 1784 exceeded the agitation regarding America.

The largest number of petitions concerning America came from the southwest and the west midlands, which on the surface confirms the notion of geopolitical realities. Provincial politics were tradition-bound, and the channels of local political loyalty were deep and abiding. The large number of addresses supporting coercion from the west midlands is thus not surprising, since it was a traditional Tory stronghold and a prominent center of the Forty-Five. Similarly, one might have predicted that a large number of petitions in favor of peace would arise from the southwestern counties—counties traditionally as-

TABLE 5.1

DISTRIBUTION BY GEOGRAPHIC REGION OF COUNTIES AND BOROUGHS THAT SENT SIGNED ADDRESSES OR PETITIONS TO THE CROWN OR PARLIAMENT									
	SOUTHEAST		SOUTHWEST		MIDLANDS		NORTHEAST		TOTAL
Repeal of Stamp Act	1	4%	10	40%	9	36%	5	20%	25
Middlesex:									
Pro-Wilkes	6	16.2%	11	40.7%	4	14.8%	6	22.2%	27
Pro-Government	4	23.5%	1	5.9%	5	29.4%	7	41.2%	17
Total Places	7	18.4%	11	28.9%	7	18.4%	13	34.2%	38
America:									
Conciliatory	4	10.8%	13	35.1%	10	27%	10	27%	37
Coercive	8	16.3%	19	38.8%	11	22.4%	11	22.4%	49
Total Places	8	14.3%	21	37.5%	14	25%	13	23.2%	56
Economic Reform	9	24.3%	13	35.1%	4	10.8%	11	29.7%	37
Parliamentary Reform	12	35.3%	14	41.2%	2	5.9%	6	17.6%	34
Opposition to the Coalition	14	13.6%	47	45.6%	26	25.2%	16	15.5%	103
Boroughs that divided in 1774	16	23.2%	30	43.5%	9	13%	14	20.3%	69
Proportion of borough voters in 1774		43.5%		22%		10.4%		24.1%	100%
Counties that divided in 1774	4	36.3%	2	18.2%	2	18.2%	3	27.3%	11
Proportion of county voters in 1774		45.3%		20.3%		18.8%		15.6%	100%
Proportion of the population in 1781		24.4%		25%		24.7%		25.9%	100%

sociated with Elizabethan Puritanism. In the seventeenth century the south-west was the home of Monmouth's uprising and the site of William's landing. Of the four areas, the southwest appears to have had the highest concentration of Dissenters in 1775; Presbyterians, Congregationalists, and Baptists combined made up about five percent of the population during the American Revolution.[22] The presence of religious Dissenters in specific centers of popular protest thus becomes a subject of some interest. But the largest number of coercive addresses also came from the southwest, and this raises the question of the relation between popular politics and patronage.

Of the four geographical areas, the southwest was the most controlled by patronage, and one might have suspected that it would be the least susceptible to popular politics. The reverse is in fact the case. The petitions for peace tended to follow chronologically the coercive addresses, and the fact that there was a strong response to coercive addresses in the southwest suggests that there was considerable popular feeling below the level of patronage-dominated politics. Popular agitation concerning America was most frequent in the area where there was the largest number of political contests, that is, where there was a high level of political activity. The same area, however, had a low proportion of voters, a fact that is illustrated by the general election of 1774. Since there was a disproportionately large number of boroughs in this region, the greater number of contests is not surprising. However, from 1761 to 1790, eighty percent of the nation's increase in the influence of patronage occurred in the southwest,[23] and it is this increase, combined with the low proportion of voters, that holds the most promise for explaining the unexpected regional concentration of petitions and addresses.

Agitation with respect to America in 1765 and again in 1775, regarding Wilkes in 1770, economic reform in 1780, and parliamentary reform in 1782 implies that instead of stifling popular activity, patronage may have actually stimulated it by encouraging popular reaction.[24] The concentration of popular agitation in the southwest during the period of the American crisis may be construed as partly the product of a fortuitous distribution of parliamentary seats; the higher proportion of boroughs in the area meant that there was a greater

---

[22]The midland Dissenters comprised perhaps just over four percent of the population; the southeast had less than four percent and the northeast a little more than three percent. See James E. Bradley, "Whigs and Nonconformists: Presbyterians, Congregationalists, and Baptists in English Politics, 1715-1790" (Ph.D. dissertation, University of Southern California, 1978) 127-41.

[23]Phillips, "The Structure of Electoral Politics," 19:84-85.

[24]Popular agitation concerning Wilkes that went beyond the petitions also seems to bear a regional stamp. Of the seventy-one places that demonstrated upon Wilkes's release in April 1770, 31 percent were in the southwest, 15.5 percent in the midlands, 19.7 percent in the southeast and 33.8 percent were in the northeast. Brewer, *Party Ideology*, 175. Before Wilkes, resistance to the cider tax was concentrated in the "cider counties" of the southwest.

number of political contests at regular intervals, and this, in turn, may have resulted in a general heightening of political awareness. But in the same area there was less opportunity for people to vote, and patrons were progressively reducing even the existing level of popular participation in politics. Private patronage in the southwest increased by seventeen percent in the period from 1761 to 1790, and it is highly likely that this constriction of political freedom was a cause of the popular reaction. The greatest number of addresses and petitions came precisely from the southwestern county most influenced by government patronage, namely Hampshire. While Tory electoral influence was most reduced in this region in the period 1715-1761, the prominence of Dissent in the southwestern counties may have also contributed to popular opposition.[25] A detailed examination of local politics will be necessary in order to determine the exact nature of the influence of patronage. The relation between petitioning and religious, or quasireligious, convictions will require investigation into the role of high church Anglicans and Nonconformists in popular politics. In broad terms, however, the geographical distribution of petitions suggests that popular support for the government during the American crisis was related to private and governmental influence, and popular opposition was stimulated at least in part by a reaction to this prevailing pattern of patronage and deference.

This thesis derives further support from the popular reaction to the Fox-North Coalition. The addresses of 1784 provide us with an illustration of what a spontaneous outpouring of conservative opinion looked like when there was little risk of political reprisal against popular agitation.[26] Charles James Fox's India Bill was viewed by many as a direct attack on vested interests, and the addresses to the king accordingly thanked his Majesty for dismissing his late ministers and their adherents. Wallingford addressers, for example, "felt for the rights" of their own "ancient borough"—indeed, they claimed to feel for the rights of "every corporate Body in the Nation."[27] As with the other periods of agitation, these addressers were heavily concentrated in the southwest, but unlike the previous petitions, more than half of the addressers in this region arose from the heavily encumbered counties of Devon, Wiltshire, and Cornwall.

All but two of Devon's eleven parliamentary boroughs addressed (with an average of 250 signatures each), and never before, or probably since, have so many rotten boroughs in the counties of Wiltshire and Cornwall acted in concert concerning their corporate rights. Tregony and Penryn were so anxious to declare their loyalty that they each sent two addresses in rapid succession. In

---

[25]Regarding patronage, see Phillips, "The Structure of Electoral Politics," 19:85; Namier, *The Structure of Politics*, 67, treats the dominance of government in Hampshire politics; Hampshire vied with Lancashire for the largest number of coercive addresses. Concerning Tories in the southwest, see Colley, *In Defiance of Oligarchy*, 120.

[26]For a general discussion, see John Cannon, *The Fox-North Coalition: Crisis of the Constitution, 1782-1784* (Cambridge: Cambridge University Press, 1969) 188.

[27]*Lond. Gaz.* (2-6 March 1784).

these two counties alone, sixteen boroughs and towns (averaging 170 signatures each) protested the high-handed behavior of the Coalition and pledged their support for the king's prerogative. This provides graphic evidence of the concentration of political power and privilege in the southwest. It might, of course, be argued that the number of signatures is evidence that the majority of the inhabitants were satisfied with the local patron-client arrangements, and perhaps they were. What is impressive, however, is not the number of signatures, which was almost uniformly small in this area, but the number of patron-dominated boroughs that addressed. The contrast with the paucity of addresses from the relatively open political environment of the eastern counties is particularly striking.

Of the four geographical areas, the southwest was the most divided regarding America, with eleven places sending both conciliatory and coercive documents. These two counties and nine boroughs represent about a third as many contests as occurred in the same area in the general election of 1774, which was the most highly contested election of the second half of the century. John Money argued that the west midlands were sharply divided during the American Revolution, and yet, because of the dominant interpretation, he believed that was exceptional. Now it can be demonstrated that the southwest was even more riven than the midlands, and these two regions combined account for half of England.

The southeast and the northeast were more open politically, and these areas were generally less susceptible to popular agitation than the southwest and the midlands. The only exceptions were the northeast during the Middlesex election affair and the southeast during the period of parliamentary reform. Less popular activity in these areas may reflect more apathy, but it could also be accounted for on the basis of less politicization, or less perceived need to resist the inroads of government and private patrons. In the American crisis the north experienced considerable division in the cases of Cumberland and Westmorland; in Yorkshire, Leeds and Halifax were divided, as was Newcastle-upon-Tyne in Northumberland. The only areas that did not experience popular agitation were the east midlands and the southeast. The counties of Northamptonshire, Bedfordshire, and Buckinghamshire demonstrated little popular response either way. But the absence of petitions cannot in each case lead to the conclusion that there was no opposition to the government. The concentration of pro-American members of Parliament in several of these apparently less-divided counties is noteworthy. Eight of Norfolk's twelve parliamentary seats were occupied by pro-Americans, and it is conceivable that this lessened the pressure for popular opposition. In the southeast pro-Americans were returned for more than half of the twenty-two seats of Sussex. The *Kentish Gazette* was exceptionally hostile to the government, and we may suppose that its readership was influenced by the numerous pro-American editorials.[28] The re-

---

[28]Mary Kinnear, "Pro-Americans in the British House of Commons in the 1770s" (Ph.D. dissertation, University of Oregon, 1973) Appendix A, 289-93. In Norfolk, Ed-

lationship, then, between parliamentary politics, patronage, types of borough constituencies, and popular politics will require considerable scrutiny.

The unsigned addresses for coercion from borough and town corporations not listed in table 5.1 confirm these general patterns. These documents have been excluded from the discussion to this point because they arose from corporate bodies and cannot be considered valid expressions of popular politics. There were no unsigned addresses for coercion from the southeast and only two from the northeast; but ten came from the patron-bound southwest and six from the midlands. Of the ten coercive addresses from southwestern corporations, six can be accounted for on the grounds of the traditional Tory orientation of the corporation or the progovernment sympathies of the dominant patrons.[29] Similarly, in the midlands, the Oxford and Leicester corporations

---

ward Astley, Thomas Coke, and Wenman Coke for Norfolk: Harbord Harbord, Norwich; Crisp Molineux and Hon. Thomas Walpole, King's Lynn; Charles Fitzroy Scudamore, Thetford; and Hon. Richard Walpole, Great Yarmouth. In Sussex, Lord George Henry Lennox for Sussex; Thomas Brand and George Lewis Newnham, Arundel; Thomas Conolly and William Keppel, Chichester; Thomas Edward Freeman and Filmer Honywood, Steyning; Thomas Hay and Sir Thomas Miller, Lewes; Charles Goring, New Shoreham; William Needham, Winchelsea; and Thomas Thoroton, Bramber. The other most heavily represented county was Yorkshire, with eighteen pro-American members of Parliament in 1774-1780, a tribute, no doubt, to the influence of Lord Rockingham. The overall distribution of pro-American members of Parliament was not significantly different than the distribution of seats with 19.1 percent in the midlands, and 26.6 percent in the northeast.

Regarding the radicalism of the *Kentist Gazette*, see the essays by "Richelieu" and "Publicola," *Kent. Gaz.* (30 August-2 September 1775), and "an Englishman" and "a Patriot" (2-6 September 1775); unsigned editorial comment is consistently antigovernment and there is a strong defense of the London Association (6-9, 9-13 September 1775).

[29]See Table 3.4 above. Hull, Liverpool, Yarmouth, Taunton, and Leeds are not counted here since they also sent signed petitions. The two from the northeast were York and Beverley. See *Commons, 1754-1790*, 1:253, 290-91, in regard to the dominant Tory influence in the corporations of Exeter and Gloucester; the Duke of Beaufort was present at the levee when the address from Gloucester was presented. *Lond. Chron.* (3-5 October 1775). At Hereford, the Symons family had a strong interest. John Symons (member of Parliament, 1768-1784) was always with the government. *Commons, 1754-1790*, 2:426, 3:515. At Bewdley, Thomas Lyttelton and William Henry Lyttelton were two of the strongest advocates of coercive measures; William seconded the address to the Crown of 26 October 1775, *Commons, 1754-1790*, 1:76-77, and it was remarked in the press that Lyttelton was behind the address. *Lond. Eve.-Post* (5-7 October, 14-16, 28-30 December 1775). At Winchester, Henry Penton was consulted by North on Hampshire affairs, and the Duke of Chandos worked through Lovell Stanhope, who was a strong supporter of North (*Commons, 1754-1790*, 3:265, 463). The government also had a dominant influence at Christchurch, *Commons, 1754-1790*, 1:294, but the connection between the government, the patrons, and the addresses at New Windsor and Andover remains less clear. At New Windsor, John Montagu had government support in 1772 but voted with the Opposition; and while Sir John Griffin at Andover

were notoriously conservative bodies, and the dominance of the Grosvenor family at Chester and the Gower family at Lichfield may explain, in large measure, the emergence of these coercive addresses.[30] Conversely, the paucity of petitions appealing for change from the midlands, especially with respect to the Wilkes affair and economic and parliamentary reform, is in keeping with the conservative orientation of this area. The near absence of unsigned addresses supporting coercion from the politically open areas of the northeast and southeast indirectly corroborates the idea that support for coercion was related to governmental and conservative interests. The fewer conciliatory petitions from these areas may also reflect less felt need to petition for redress.

From 1765 to 1783 only 18.1 percent of all the signed petitions in support of change came from the midlands, whereas 38.1 percent came from the patron-dominated southwest.[31] In discussing the progovernment addresses of 1775, Paul Langford observed that "the deployment of traditional Tory emotions and beliefs in the service of parliamentary omnicompetence was carried out much more smoothly than the channeling of old Whig energies in a radical or reforming direction."[32] The prominence of petitioning activity in the southwest, however, suggests that there were abiding continuities between Dissenting religion and popular opposition to the government. At least in broad terms, the geographical location of the petitions and addresses appears to be consistent with time-honored and geographically defined centers of distinct political orientation. Despite the influence of patronage, indeed perhaps because of it, there was a strong popular outcry in opposition to the government's policy of coercion. While it is true that politics were still provincial, the provinces did respond to the great national issues of the time in a way consistent with their political history. In the age of the American Revolution, provincial politics can no more be isolated from national politics than can local politics.

One index of how deeply an issue polarized the populace would be whether or not the same towns and counties divided repeatedly over a period of time

---

equivocated regarding coercive measures, Benjamin Lethieullier tended to support the Opposition. But the Earl of Portsmouth was conservative and may have influenced the address from Andover (*Commons, 1754-1790*, 2:665, 444; 3:37). Maidenhead and Southmolton were nonparliamentary.

[30]With respect to Oxford and Leicester, see *Commons, 1754-1790*, 1:357, 323-24. Regarding the Tory background of the Grosvenor family and the Gower family and the Bedford faction see *Commons, 1754-1790*, 1:558; 2:500, 557; 3:38-39. The political loyalties of the corporations of Lancaster and Shrewsbury, however, were less clear. At Lancaster Lord Richard Cavendish was, with his family, consistently in opposition, though the Reynolds family and Sir George Warren were government supporters. Perhaps at Shrewsbury the interest of Baron Clive won over that of William Pulteney. *Commons, 1754-1790*, 2:206, 228, 608; 3:341-42, 351.

[31]Twenty percent came from the southeast and 23.8 percent from the northeast.

[32]Paul Langford, "Old Whigs, Old Tories and the American Revolution," *Journal of Imperial and Commonwealth History* 8 (January 1980): 124.

on related topics of national importance. A comparison between the Stamp Act petitions and the American crisis of 1775 is revealing in this regard. During the Stamp Act Crisis, "all the key trading and industrial areas"[33] of England petitioned for repeal; a decade later, sixteen of these twenty-five places (64%) appealed once again for conciliation. The only large trading centers that petitioned in 1765-1766 and failed to do so in 1775 were Lancaster, Leicester, and Sheffield.[34] While it is true that the opening of new European markets changed the economic situation in 1775,[35] and that trade was not the predominant issue in the petitions to the Crown, the same centers of trade did in fact petition for the right of free trade relations with America and for peace. This does not suggest that the merchants were united in favor of conciliation in 1775, for in fact they were not. However, the difference between the course of events in 1765 and 1775 was not related solely to a change in public opinion, but to Parliament's separation of the issue of commercial policy from the issue of its own sovereignty, whereby both Parliament and the Crown refused to consider public opinion.[36]

Since petitions concerning the Middlesex election affair concentrated on the rights of freeholders, the movement was dominated by the counties, and points of comparison with the American agitation are fewer. Yet a comparative analysis of towns and counties reveals a high level of continuity between the places that sent loyal addresses concerning Middlesex and those that addressed the Crown concerning America. The loyal addresses that Sutherland and Rudé overlooked thus provide a link between the issue of electoral rights and parliamentary sovereignty. This is a connection in which historians have shown increasing interest, and several large urban centers illustrate considerable overlap between supporters of Wilkes and the pro-Americans.[37]

If one looks at both movements in their entirety, however, the strongest connections appear to be between those places that repeatedly voiced strong

---

[33]Paul Langford, *The First Rockingham Administration, 1765-1766* (London: Oxford University Press, 1973) 121.

[34]The sixteen places are: London, Bristol, Liverpool, Halifax, Leeds, Manchester, Birmingham, Coventry, Newcastle-upon-Tyne, Nottingham, Worcester, Wolverhampton, Dudley, Taunton, Bradford, and Melksham. The six remaining towns that did not petition again in 1775 were small: Frome, Macclesfield, Minehead, Chippenham, Whitney, and Stourbridge.

[35]Donoughue, *British Politics*, 153.

[36]See ch. 1.

[37]Pauline Maier, "John Wilkes and American Disillusionment with Britain," *William and Mary Quarterly* 3d ser., 20 (July 1963): 373-95; John Sainsbury, "The Pro-Americans of London, 1769-1782," *William and Mary Quarterly* 3d ser., 35 (July 1978): 423-54; Thomas R. Knox, "Wilkism and the Newcastle Election of 1774," *Durham University Journal* 72 (1979-1980): 23-37. At Southwark, Sir Joseph Mawbey was involved in both agitations, as was Lord Montagu at Southampton, and many other connections can doubtlessly be drawn out. Donoughue, *British Politics*, 196-98.

support for law, good order, and the government. Of the seventeen English boroughs and counties that sent loyal addresses regarding Middlesex, eleven (65%) also sent coercive addresses concerning America.[38] The ideological similarities in these two sets of documents have already been noted. The London and Liverpool loyal addresses were signed, and it is possible that further comparison of signatures with the American documents may reveal additional lines of continuity at the level of individual behavior. This apparent continuity of opinion in favor of law and order is to be contrasted with only seven of twenty-seven places (26%) that petitioned in support of Wilkes in 1769-1770 and for conciliation in 1775. The same affinities can be found in Parliament. In an analysis of parliamentary division lists, Mary Kinnear discovered some correlation between the minority that supported Wilkes and the pro-American minorities. But there was a "clearer correlation between those who opposed Wilkes and those who later supported North."[39] In some settings such as Newcastle-upon-Tyne, there were important connections between the pro-Wilkes and pro-American movements in terms of leadership. However, agitation concerning the Stamp Act and the Middlesex election affair, even when combined, did not embrace all of the areas that sent expressions for conciliation in 1775. Of the thirty-seven places that sent conciliatory petitions in 1775, fully twenty had never petitioned before.[40]

The Association movement of 1780, like the Middlesex election affair, was concentrated in the counties, so the correlation of specific places that petitioned in 1775 and 1780 was inconsiderable.[41] The petitions of 1780, however, referred almost unanimously to an "expensive and unfortunate war," and some of the documents were even more pointed in their criticism of the administration. The Bristol petition alluded to the "unhappy and destructive contest," and the mayor and burgesses of Nottingham viewed the present moment as the "Height of National Calamity." Buckingham petitioners believed that the Crown "has acquired a great and unconstitutional Influence, which, if not checked, may soon prove fatal to the Liberties of this Country," and the petitions from Hereford and Kent also opposed the influence of the Crown.[42] But

---

[38]Of the twelve boroughs that sent loyal addresses in 1769, ten sent loyal addresses in 1775; only one of the counties sent a loyal address in both periods. London, Bristol, Liverpool, Lancaster, Coventry, Leicester, Carlisle, Great Yarmouth, Kingston-upon-Hull, Huntingdon, Kent.

[39]The seven places that petitioned in both 1769 and 1775 are Middlesex, London, Southwark, Bristol, Worcester, Coventry, and Newcastle-upon-Tyne. Kinnear, "Pro-Americans," 94.

[40]The twenty are: Colchester, Berkshire, Abingdon, Wallingford, Hampshire, Southampton, Lymington, Poole, Bridport, Bridgwater, Lancashire, Bolton, Staffordshire, Newcastle (Staffordshire), Cumberland, Whitehaven, Huddersfield, Great Yarmouth, Norwich, Cambridge. Fifteen of these were first in the fall of 1775.

[41]Five of the twenty-six counties had petitioned in 1775, and six of the eleven boroughs.

[42]*CJ* 37:581, 757, 702, 761.

there was resistance to these sentiments in the borough of Nottingham and the county of Kent, and these expressions of support for the government are evidence that political issues raised by the American Revolution were still being debated in the provinces.[43] In an attempt to avoid such conflict, the Association movement sought to minimize political issues, but the ideological affinities with the petitions of 1775 can now be appreciated.

A related point emerges from this comparative analysis. Of all the popular movements of the period, the government's coercive policy was by far the most divisive. The only other popular agitation that resulted in the appearance of numerous petitions at cross purposes was the Middlesex affair, but while there were twenty-seven places that sent pro-Wilkes petitions versus seventeen places that sent progovernment addresses, only two counties and four boroughs were divided.[44] During the American crisis, however, the conciliatory petitions from thirty-seven places and the signed coercive addresses from forty-nine places actually divided five counties and twenty-one boroughs; this is more than four times as many places as divided concerning Wilkes.

The identity of specific places that petitioned more than once in the period from 1765 to 1782 therefore seems to connect popular interest in repeal of the Stamp Act with sympathy toward America in 1775 on the one hand, and progovernment supporters concerning Middlesex in 1769 with progovernment opinion in 1775 on the other hand. The connection is less strong between pro-Wilkes sentiment and pro-American feeling, and there appears to be about the same low consistency of response in places that petitioned regarding Wilkes or America and parliamentary reform.[45] In light of the fact that the Middlesex election affair dealt primarily with the rights of freeholders, it was far less radical than the American issue; it also seems to have won the support of more of the landed elements in society than America ever did.

III

In addition to counting the number of places that petitioned, contemporary observers were also interested in the actual number of signatures appended to the documents, although here too their attempts were far from comprehensive. The *Manchester Mercury* and the *Cumberland Pacquet*, for example, counted the number of signatures for three or four addresses each, and the editor of the

---

[43]Ibid., 37:614, 761.

[44]Surrey, Kent, London, Bristol, Liverpool, and Coventry. For the division regarding America, see Tables 3.1-3.3 in ch. 3. In 1780 Kent alone sent up a loyal address, but there was oposition to the petitions reported at Nottingham, and in nine counties. *CJ*, 37:761, 614. *Parl. Hist.*, 20:1372.

[45]Only 24 percent of the places that petitioned over the Stamp Act also petitioned in favor of Wilkes; 26 percent of the places that petitioned in support of conciliation with America also petitioned in favor of parliamentary reform; but 37 percent of the places that petitioned in support of Wilkes also petitioned in support of parliamentary reform.

Bath Chronicle was most conscientious, with thirteen.[46] Since these papers were dependent on the *London Gazette*, and since the *Gazette* listed the names, but did not provide totals, it is evident that the editors added up the signatures themselves. Sometimes the opposing documents from the same locale were printed in a single issue for the sake of comparison.[47] The larger number of signatures on the conciliatory petitions compared to the coercive addresses was noted for at least eight boroughs; but in a single paper, this comparative evaluation was made for only three boroughs at most.[48] A few contemporary observers were thus interested explicitly in the popularity of these issues. More important, they tied a comparison of the number of signatures to the issue of popularity.

The agitation regarding the use of force in America elicited about as many signatures as did the other movements of the period. Each of the protests for which there is reliable evidence involved between 50,000 and 60,000 petitioners. In the Middlesex election affair it is possible to count 53,095 signatories, and Rudé estimates that at least 5,000 should be added for the pro-Wilkes petition from London.[49] In light of what is known about the response of London on the other issues, this latter figure may be exaggerated, but the signatures of fifteen of the seventeen loyal addresses would probably add substantially to these numbers. The movement in support of economic reform in 1780 is also thought to have involved about 60,000 petitioners, though the evidence to substantiate this claim is not strong.[50] In the fall of 1775, agitation regarding the American

---

[46]*Man. Merc.* (10 October 1775); *Cumb. Pacq.* (12 October 1775); *Bath Chron.* (26 October, 2 November 1775). Totals vary somewhat from paper to paper; *Man. Merc.* has 909 for Bristol and 212 for Warwick; *Cumb. Pacq.* has 912 for the former and 220 for the latter.

[47]*Cumb. Pacq.* printed both from London, with the number of signatures noted, and *Lond. Eve.-Post* (14-17 October 1775) printed both with signatures. *Norw. Merc.* (9 December 1775) printed both from Yarmouth with signatures also printed (9 December). *Lond. Eve.-Post* (2-4 November 1775) printed both from Southampton, but *Gen. Eve. Post* did best with printing the coercive and conciliatory petitions from three places: London, Bristol, and Coventry, though only the London petitions were printed in the same issue: (30 September-1 October, 7-10, 12-14, 14-17, 21-24 October 1775).

[48]For an explicit comparison of the total number of signatures on conciliatory petitions versus coercive addresses from London, Bristol, Taunton, Southampton, Southwark, Halifax, Abingdon, and Coventry, see *Lond. Chron.* (26-28 October, 2-5 December 1775); *York Cour.* (17 October 1775); *Bath Chron.* (12, 19 October 1775); *Hamp. Chron.* (6 November, 11 December 1775); *Lond. Eve.-Post* (2-4, 18-21 November, 2-5 December 1775).

[49]This includes 50,681 signatures, 1,110 "marks," and the signatures from the Liverpool and London loyal addresses that are not totaled by Rudé (450 and 854 respectively). See *Wilkes and Liberty*, 128, 211, and *Lond. Gaz.* (22, 21-25 March 1769).

[50]Christie, *Wilkes, Wyvill and Reform*, reconstructs numbers for four counties and one borough—Yorks. (8,000), Notts. (3,500?), Kent (3,500), Cambs. (1,200), and Westminster (5,000)—but relies finally on Rockingham's phrase "upwards of 60,000." (97 n. 1, 122).

crisis prompted at least 44,619 people in England, Ireland, Scotland, and Wales to sign their names to petitions or addresses. If the large petition from Norfolk in early 1778 is added, the total comes to 50,019 people.[51] This figure does not include any of the petitions to Parliament in the spring of 1775, nor does it include any estimates for the counties of Cumberland (conciliatory) and Kent (coercive). In contrast, the movement in support of parliamentary reform in 1782 concluded with about 20,000 signatures.[52] The popular outcry against the Coalition in 1784 resulted in signed addresses from ninety-five English boroughs and towns and eight counties totaling 53,539 addressers.[53] The American crisis, however, was unlike the other popular protests in that it divided the number of signatures between those who favored coercion and those who wished for conciliation. The number of conciliatory petitioners including those from Ireland and Norfolk comes to 28,740, which is about a third greater than the number of those who petitioned concerning parliamentary reform, but far less than those who petitioned in favor of Wilkes or against the Coalition.

Normally the conciliatory petitions gathered more signatures than the coercive addresses. In a few instances, such as Newcastle-upon-Tyne, Colchester, Halifax, Hampshire, and Staffordshire, the differences were dramatic. However, at Bolton, Westbury, Warminster, and Lancashire, the coercive addressers greatly outnumbered the petitioners. In the fall of 1775 petitions in support of conciliation from twenty-one English boroughs or towns and five counties numbered 19,854 signatures, while addresses in support of coercion from thirty-seven boroughs or towns and nine counties numbered 18,511. While the petitions thus gained the majority of signatures, the addressers held the majority of corporations, and these bodies represented the social and commercial elite of many large cities. Even if one were to relate popularity directly to numbers, it would be inappropriate to suggest one side was more popular than the other since this would involve a comparison of different forms of public response. Numbers were so evenly divided that the contest must be considered inconclusive.

---

[51]These totals are drawn from Tables 3.1-3.6 and Appendix 2. With respect to the conciliatory side there are 19,854 from boroughs and counties, 3,486 from Ireland and 5,400 from Norfolk. Concerning the coercive side, there are 18,511 from boroughs and counties, 735 from Scotland, 1,770 from Ireland and Wales, 97 from the Isle of Man and the Island of Guernsey, and 166 from special-interest groups.

[52]Christie, *Wilkes, Wyvill and Reform*, notes that Yorkshire had a petition with more than 10,000 signatures, but Somerset had only 601, and he credits Lord North's estimate of 20,000 total (167, 169 n. 4, 173).

[53]*Lond. Gaz.* (13-17 January—25-29 May 1784). Seven boroughs sent two or more signed addresses, and six boroughs sent a second unsigned address from the corporation (counted as one in the total of ninety-five). In addition, seven counties sent unsigned addresses, and twenty boroughs and towns sent unsigned addresses, plus the grand juries of Buckinghamshire and Essex. Fifteen counties and twenty boroughs and towns in Scotland, Ireland, and Wales also addressed the Crown concerning the Coalition.

The Middlesex election affair provides a useful comparison to the agitation concerning America. While the two periods of agitation involved almost exactly the same number of people, there was a different response in the boroughs as compared with the counties. In the earlier movement the great majority of support came from fifteen counties with 38,177 signatories versus 14,918 from the boroughs (not including London, pro-Wilkes); this contrasts with 17,534 petitioners and addressers from ten English counties in 1775 (not including Norfolk) and 20,831 from boroughs and towns.[54] The American documents were almost exactly divided between conciliatory and coercive signatories; there were 9,300 petitioners from five counties versus 8,234 addressers from nine counties, and there were 10,554 petitioners from twenty-one boroughs and towns versus 10,277 addressers from thirty-seven boroughs and towns. The counties were therefore far more involved with Middlesex and the boroughs with America.[55]

The differences concerning America have sometimes been thought to reflect a distinction between an old order that looked to the traditional agricultural economy and a new order that invested in trade and commerce.[56] While the greatest activity in 1775 centered in the boroughs, the numbers from the counties in favor of peace are fairly impressive and invalidate any notion of a landed interest united in favor of coercion. It is true that fewer counties petitioned in support of peace than those that addressed. The larger county petitions supporting conciliation, like those from Lancashire with 4,014 and from Hampshire with 2,500, must be held in tension with the greater number of counties that sent up less-well-supported coercive addresses. The feeble support for the government in Berkshire (302), Hampshire (201), Staffordshire (138), Herefordshire (380), Devonshire (240), and Worcestershire (87) is notable in this regard, especially since the meetings held to address the Crown were advertised well in advance. On the basis of these addresses, one cannot argue that the propertied interests favored coercion. The number of county signers of conciliatory petitions also has implications for the notion that pro-Americanism had a unique affinity to urban radicalism.[57] Considerable pro-American sentiment can be located in counties and boroughs where there is no known evidence of radicalism at all.

---

[54]This discussion does not presuppose a strict separation between county and borough petitions. It is known, for example, that many Lancashire petitioners were from Manchester.

[55]The reaction to the Coalition was more akin to that of America in this regard with 41,173 addressers from boroughs and towns and 12,366 from the counties.

[56]Clark, *British Opinion*, 133. This was a popular opinion in the eighteenth century. Lord Camden believed that the landed interest was "almost altogether anti-America." William S. Taylor and John H. Pringle, eds., *The Correspondence of William Pitt, Earl of Chatham*, 4 vols. (London: John Murray, 1838-1840) 4:401 (Lord Camden to the Earl of Chatham, 12 February 1775).

[57]*Commons, 1754-1790*, 1:16-17.

The petitioners involved in the Wilkes affair and those involved in economic reform are customarily compared to the entire electorate. If one adopts
the figure of 105,000 for potential borough votes and 177,000 for potential
county votes (282,000 total) these movements, as well as the agitation regarding America, involved a number equal to about one-fifth of the total electorate.[58] The turnout at general elections was, of course, substantially less than
the total potential electorate. The number of borough and county voters that
went to the polls, therefore, provides another useful point of comparison. The
general election of 1774 saw more borough (69) and county (11) contests than
any other general election in the second half of the eighteenth century; the election elicited a turnout of no more than 65,660 borough voters and 32,000 county
voters.[59] The borough petitioners in the Wilkes affair thus comprised a group
equal to about twenty-three percent of the turnout at the general election of
1774, while the petitioners from the counties exceeded the number of county
voters in that year. In the crisis over America, the petitioners and addressers
from all boroughs and towns in England combined totaled a number equal to
at least thirty-two percent of the borough voters in 1774, and the county signatories amounted to a number equal to fifty-five percent of the county voters.
Those that petitioned in support of peace, however, equaled only about sixteen
percent of the borough voters and twenty-nine percent of the county voters.
While small by comparison to the general election, this public response revolved around the single issue of war or peace with America. These figures
represent only the vocal expressions of opposition and do not embrace all the
pro-American sympathy of the nation. How far such sympathy actually extended must, however, remain speculative.

Addresses in favor of the king and against the Fox-North Coalition appeared
only months before the general election of 1784. These documents have been called
a "massive demonstration of public disapproval," and they were followed immediately by an election in which some 100 parliamentary seats were lost by the
Coalition.[60] The addresses represented two-thirds as many people as turned out

---

[58]Ibid., 1:16-17, and John A. Phillips, "Popular Politics in Unreformed England,"
Journal of Modern History 52 (December 1980): 600 n. 3. For comparison of the peti-
tioning movements to the total electorate, see Rudé, *Wilkes and Liberty*, 105; Christie,
Wilkes, Wyvill and Reform, 97 n. 1.

[59]These are the maximum number of borough voters possible, calculated from each
constituency history in *Commons, 1754-1790*, 1. There were actually only about 32,000
county voters in 1774, which is the figure used in the introduction, giving a total of
97,600. It should also be kept in mind that the 7,000 borough voters in London and
12,000 in Westminster tend to inflate the total, and skew the figures for the southeast
in Table 5.1. Borough contests run: 1754 (55); 1761 (42); 1768 (62); 1774 (69); 1780
(64); 1784 (69); 1790 (68); 1796 (50); the number of counties contested are: 1754 (5);
1761 (4); 1768 (8); 1774 (11); 1780 (2); 1784 (7); 1790 (8); 1796 (4). Cannon, *Parliamentary Reform*, 279, 289, has 70 contests for 1774; *Commons, 1754-1790*, 1, lists 69.

[60]Cannon, *The Fox-North Coalition*, 188.

for the election in April. This number of addressers therefore might be considered illustrative of what could be expected in terms of the extent of agitation throughout the nation when an issue was genuinely popular. However, many of these addresses represented closed, vested interests, and whether or not the government's victory at the polls was a true reflection of the nation's political will is still the subject of much debate.[61] John Phillips has recently advanced the discussion by comparing addressers to voters and demonstrating a high level of political consistency between the popular agitation of 1784 and the general election.[62] To be sure, the issue of political consistency provides only a partial answer to the question of a movement's representative nature, but it is a necessary first step in determining the genuineness of public opinion. If the reaction of more than 50,000 people to the Coalition may be considered a significant display of English public opinion—and the evidence is increasingly pointing in this direction—then so may the agitation concerning America.

In a number of specific instances it can be demonstrated that the issue of peace or war with America stirred the population as deeply as the Middlesex affair and somewhat more than the reaction to the Coalition. Table 5.2 lists the seven cities and three counties that petitioned regarding Wilkes and also sent petitions and addresses concerning America in 1775.[63] At Southwark, Coventry, Newcastle-upon-Tyne, and Worcester the response of the populations concerning America was about as great as it was with respect to Wilkes—but there were notable differences at London, Bristol, and Liverpool. Liverpool, however, sent an additional petition regarding America in the spring of 1775 for which there are no numbers. The average petition in the Wilkes affair for these boroughs gathered 1,400 signatures, compared to 1,100 in the American crisis.[64]

---

[61]John A. Phillips, *Electoral Behavior in Unreformed England: Plumpers, Splitters, and Straights* (Princeton: Princeton University Press, 1982) 10-13, cites all of the pertinent literature. See J. A. W. Gunn, *Beyond Liberty and Property: The Process of Self-Recognition in Eighteenth-Century Political Thought* (Kingston and Montreal: McGill-Queen's University Press, 1983) 279-84, for a discussion of the constitutional implications of the general election.

[62]Phillips, *Electoral Behavior*, 32-33.

[63]For these figures, see Rudé, *Wilkes and Liberty*, 128, 131-32, and the totals from Tables 3.1-3.3 above. The figure for London is a guess on Rudé's part, and that for Liverpool includes 450 proadministration petitioners; it is known that there were at least 854 progovernment addressers in London. *Lond. Gaz.* (21-25 March 1769). Another way of gauging how deeply the popular agitation penetrated the populace is to look at the two householder boroughs that sent petitions and addresses. At Taunton and Cirencester, the franchise extended to most adult males. The petitioners and addressers at Taunton thus represent approximately 69 percent of the adult male population, and at Cirencester the addressers alone involved perhaps 22 percent of the male population.

[64]In Tables 5.2 and 5.3 the largest and the smallest petition were excluded from each group and the averages are rounded to the nearest ten.

In the reaction to the Coalition, more boroughs were involved than the agitation concerning Wilkes or America, but these documents often gathered fewer signatures. In those places where a direct comparison can be made, more people petitioned concerning America than responded to the Coalition (see Table 5.3). The average number of petitioners in these boroughs and towns in 1775 was 480, and in 1784 the average was 410. However, the petitioning activity concerning America contrasts in a number of ways with both the Middlesex election affair and the Coalition, and these differences help account for the smaller public response in 1775. The petitioning activity with respect to America was far more intense than it was regarding the Middlesex election affair. In the former movement it was spread over a nine-month period. In the agitation concerning America, petitions to Parliament and the Crown extended over an eleven-month period, but almost all of them were presented in the two, much briefer periods from 23 January-15 March and 21 October-31 December 1775.[65] The Wilkes petition from Bristol, for example, was in circulation for five months, whereas the signatures on both coercive and conciliatory documents at Bristol were collected in two weeks. A mere month

TABLE 5.2

BOROUGH	WILKES PETITIONERS AND ADDRESSERS	AMERICA		
		PETITION	ADDRESS	TOTAL
MIDDLESEX ELECTION PETITIONS AND ADDRESSES COMPARED WITH PETITIONS AND ADDRESSES OVER AMERICA				
London	(5000?)	1127	941 1029	2781
Southwark	1200	756	250	1006
Bristol	2445	978	901	1879
Coventry	900	406	159 239	774
Newcastle-upon-Tyne	900	1199	168	1367
Worcester	650	500	---------	500
Liverpool	1550	---------	472	472
COUNTY				
Middlesex	1565	1033	613	1646
Worcestershire	1475	---------	87	87
Herefordshire	475	---------	380	380

[65]Sutherland notes it took months to collect signatures in the Middlesex election affair. Sutherland, *The City of London*, 30.

separated the meeting for the massive Lancashire petition supporting peace from its presentation at St. James.[66] While it is true that the addressers had an equally

TABLE 5.3

COALITION PROTEST ADDRESSES COMPARED TO PETITIONS AND ADDRESSES OVER AMERICA				
		AMERICA		
BOROUGH/TOWN	COALITION	PETITION	ADDRESS	TOTAL
Bristol (2)	4944	978	901	1879
Coventry	1150	406	159 239	774
Newcastle-upon-Tyne	1020	1199	168	1367
Worcester	480	500	------------	500
Colchester	151	511	125	636
Taunton	188	154	191	345
Great Yarmouth	312	334	228	572
Southampton	223	117	56	173
Poole	142	144	56	200
Abingdon	167	117	115	232
Westbury, Trowbridge (2)	225	138	244	382
Wallingford	165	80	------------	80
Leeds	669	594	264	858
Halifax	656	1865	660	2525
Liverpool	812	------------	472	472
Kingston-upon-Hull	535	------------	171	171
Carlisle	225	------------	308	308
Sudbury	138	------------	140	140
Warwick	154	------------	213	213
Plymouth (2)	381	------------	115	115
Barnstaple	192	------------	149	149
COUNTY				
Berkshire	1103	853	302	1155
Staffordshire	1809	900	138	1038
Devonshire	2797	------------	240	240

---

[66]*Read. Merc.* (8 January 1769); *Glos. J.* (2 October 1775); *Brist. J.* (14 October 1775); *Cumb. Pacq.* (16 November 1775); *Lond. Chron.* (16-19 December 1775).

short period of time to circulate their documents, the number of signatures on the petitions was considered by some to be related to the press of time. One observer noted that while the ministerial party might argue that "not a hundredth part of the Freeholders of England have signed the petitions," yet he concluded, "so large a majority has signed as might well be expected on so short a call, and ought, on account of their property and numbers, to have all due respect paid to them."[67] This may account in part for the discrepancy in size between the Wilkes petitions and those concerning America.

The intensity of petitioning activity in 1775 and in 1784 was, however, very similar. Just as with America, the majority of petitions in 1784 were presented over a three-month period; the average number of signatures gathered in these two periods was accordingly almost identical. The petitioning activity in 1775 and 1784 was also relatively spontaneous. In comparison to the petitioning movements in 1769 and 1780, there was an evident lack of centralized organization in 1775. Most petitioners were especially handicapped in this regard, since unlike the addressers, the petitioners did not have access to traditional structures of government such as corporations and quarter sessions.

A final and more important characteristic distinguishes the American agitation from both the Middlesex election affair and the reaction to the Coalition. The petitioners in 1775 pled for peace at a time when, in some people's minds, the king and Parliament had made such expressions tantamount to treason. The petitions supporting peace were, in this respect, far more radical than the petitions concerning Wilkes and economic reform, and they were in stark contrast to the addresses of 1784, which were uniformly conservative in orientation. When people petitioned in favor of peace, they not only appealed against stated government policy, they took a stance against their friends and neighbors. The addressers were more secure from the viewpoint of possible political and social reprisals. By comparison to the structure of electoral politics, by comparison to the voting public during general elections, and by comparison to the other petitioning movements of the decade, the American crisis in England stirred widespread attention and became a highly divisive political issue.

IV

Further insight into the nature of this popular agitation can be acquired by determining the identity of individual petitioners. The most pressing question in this regard is whether or not individual petitioners were also voters. Since some of the people who petitioned the Crown did vote in parliamentary elections, in those boroughs where voting records were retained it is possible to link identical names in two or more otherwise unrelated lists. Printed poll books thus hold out the possibility of locating electors who were also petitioners and

---

[67]*Read. Merc.* (8 January 1776).

thereby determining their political orientation. This will provide evidence that illumines the issue of political consistency over time.[68]

Previous studies of popular protests assumed that virtually all the petitioners involved in the Middlesex election affair and in the agitation concerning economic reform were also electors. This interpretation was recently overturned, and it now can be shown conclusively that petitioning offered an avenue of political expression to a considerable number of people who were not enfranchised. In an examination of six large freeman boroughs, John Phillips found that an average of 51.8% of the signers were not voters in parliamentary elections.[69] We have seen that the number of petitioners actually exceeded the number of voters in many of the smaller boroughs, and numerous nonvoters were obviously involved in the nonparliamentary towns. A comparison of poll books to petitions in two medium-sized and three smaller boroughs further confirms Phillips's findings. The proportion of signers who did not vote in parliamentary elections in these boroughs ranges from 81.6% at Poole to 31.2% at Southampton; Cambridge, Yarmouth, and Bridgwater had 79.7%, 71.6% and 49.2% nonvoters respectively. On average, 62.7% of all petitioners and addressers in these five medium and small boroughs were nonvoters.[70] While approximately half of those who signed petitions

---

[68]The method of record linkage utilized here is dependent upon the following studies: E. A. Wrigley, ed., *Identifying People in the Past* (London: E. Arnold, 1973); W. A. Speck, W. A. Gray, and R. Hopkinson, "Computer Analysis of Poll Books: A Further Report," *Bulletin of the Institute for Historical Research* 48 (May 1975): 64-90; and John A. Phillips, *Nominal Record Linkage and the Study of Individual-Level Voting Behavior* (Iowa City: University of Iowa Laboratory for Political Research, 1976).

[69]Phillips, "Popular Politics," 52:611. For the coercive addresses, the proportion of unenfranchised signers in Colchester was 53.1 percent; in Coventry (two addresses), 28.1 percent and 30.8 percent; in Bristol, 41.4 percent; in Liverpool, 83.6 percent and in Nottingham, 42.7 percent; for conciliatory petitions, Newcastle was 46.1 percent; Colchester, 87.9 percent; Coventry, 43.3 percent; and Bristol, 61.6 percent.

[70]In the petitioning agitation only rarely were petitioners identified as voters. The Southwark petitioners do call themselves electors of the borough, *Pub. Adv.* (4 December 1775), and Abingdon petitioners are called voters, *Lond. Eve.-Post* (18-21 November 1775). The signers of the Middlesex and Berkshire petitions distinguish themselves as freeholders, but the Lancashire petitioners were criticized precisely because the document was not limited to freeholders, *Gen. Eve. Post* (26-28 December 1775). More poll books have survived from freeman boroughs than from other borough types so we are limited in our analysis. See nn. 20 and 22 in ch. 3 above for the poll books. The poll books for 1774 at Great Yarmouth and at Poole are no longer extant, so it is necessary to use the 1777 and 1768 poll books respectively, and the 1780 poll book for Bridgwater. There were ninety-three resident electors at Poole in 1768, and in the seven-year period between the election and the petitioning agitation in 1775, there would be some loss of electors due to mortality. Similarly, a small number of the potential electors who petitioned at Bridgwater in 1775 would have died by 1780. Thus the proportion of electors who were also petitioners and addressers would be slightly greater for Poole than 18.4 percent, and slightly less for Bridgwater than 50.8 percent, but these losses would

and addresses from large, medium, and small boroughs were not voters, they were interested enough in the political issues raised by the conflict between the colonies and Parliament to risk signing their names to documents that were sometimes considered seditious.

This fact raises an important question about the value of these documents as expressions of political opinion. Addresses from corporations might be regarded as respectable, for the social status of aldermen and burgesses commonly elevated them above the suspicion of corruption. The most important question concerning the origins of these documents has to do with the leadership that may have influenced them. If approximately half of the signatures on the addresses and petitions came from the unenfranchised, can their signatures have been freely given apart from influence or corruption? Since there is some evidence that both the government and the Opposition were active in soliciting popular support for their respective measures, the petitions on either side have naturally been called into question concerning whether or not they were valid expressions of public opinion.

That the administration, Opposition, and local magnates used their influence to initiate addresses and petitions in several boroughs and counties is beyond dispute. The actual impact of their influence upon those who signed the documents, however, was the subject of much debate. The role of leaders in organizing and marshaling public opinion has always been controversial—and no politician in the eighteenth century worked with the detachment of a modern pollster. Yet legitimate leadership may certainly be distinguished from undue influence. Despite the apparent clarity of the issues presented by the two options in the addresses and petitions, a number of contemporary observers were doubtful as to whether or not the petitions reflected genuine political conviction. Inside Parliament and out, critics asserted that such influence invalidated these documents as genuine expressions of popular opinion.

The question of the petitions' validity was one of the most frequently raised topics in both houses of Parliament in 1775. Critics of the administration's American policy were especially vocal in disparaging the value of the progovernment addresses. They were considered invalid as expressions of political opinion since the signatures were believed to have been obtained by unfair means under the influence of progovernment interests. Opposition speakers who could not agree upon a positive program against the government were at one in their attempt to dis-

---

affect the proportions only marginally. For a discussion on mortality rates, see Phillips, *Electoral Behavior*, 90-91. As with the larger boroughs studied by Phillips, the proportion of nonvoting petitioners was greater than the proportion of nonvoting addressers, but the differences, with the possible exception of Yarmouth and Poole, are not great enough to make valid generalizations about the disaffection of the unenfranchised. They are as follows: Yarmouth, conciliatory 77.3 percent, coercive 63 percent; Southampton, conciliatory 35 percent, coercive 23.2 percent; Cambridge, conciliatory 83.8 percent, coercive 72.9 percent; Poole, conciliatory 93.8 percent, coercive 50.9 percent; Bridgwater, conciliatory 46.7 percent, coercive 52.7 percent.

credit the validity of the loyal addresses.[71] Horace Walpole was particularly outspoken in condemning the addresses; he appears really to have believed that the signers were bribed with money or military contracts.[72] The implication in most of these charges is that the influence of money was more important in gaining a person's support than his own political orientation. Newspapers also reported the debate in Parliament and sometimes provided further negative commentary upon the validity of the addresses.[73]

Conversely, those on the side of the government denigrated the anti-administration petitions and claimed that signatures were often obtained by "interested persons" with artifice enough to induce others to sign them.[74] It is not surprising that those in opposition saw this most representative form of political expression as being manipulated from the powers above, while those in power feared that they were the product of the rabble below. The political bias of all contemporary commentators, however, is beyond dispute; each party defended those petitions that supported its views as genuine expression of public opinion. The apologies for the validity of the addresses and petitions were equally as vociferous as the condemnations.[75] The judgment of Edward Gibbon, for example, must be compared with that of Horace Walpole. Gibbon believed that the addresses were genuine expressions of heartfelt support for coercive measures; "no arts no management whatsoever have been used to procure the *Addresses which fill* the Gazette."[76] On the whole, however, Walpole's reservations were the more influential, and the Whig interpretation of the government's influence has dominated the scholarly interpretations. These

---

[71]In the fall, John Dunning (2 November 1775), and Sir Joseph Mawbey (21 December 1775), *Parl. Hist.*, 18:847, 1105-1106. In the House of Lords, Lord Craven spoke against the addresses on 26 October 1775 (*Parl. Hist.*, 18:719-20).

[72]W. S. Lewis, ed., *Horace Walpole's Correspondence* (New Haven: Yale University Press, 1967) 24:77, 89, 132 (Walpole to Horace Mann, 25 January, 17 April, 10 October 1775). See also A. Francis Steuart, ed., *The Last Journals of Horace Walpole*, 2 vols. (London: John Lane, 1910) 1:474-75.

[73]*Lond. Chron.* (26-28 October, 2-4 November 1775); *Lond. Eve.-Post* (28-31 October, 14-16, 16-18 November 1775); *Bath J.* (20 November 1775); *York Cour.* (31 October 1775).

[74]Sir George McCartney (23 January 1775); Hans Stanley claimed the same (26 January 1775); *Parl. Hist.*, 18:175, 186.

[75]Alderman Hayley (26 January 1775), Lord Craven, Tempell Luttrell (both 26 October 1775), Edmund Burke (16 November 1775), and Lord Camden (15 November 1775), *Parl. Hist.*, 18:187, 720, 759, 965; *Bath J.* (20 November 1775) in defense of opposition petitions. Col. Acland, William Bagot (both 2 November 1775), Lord Stanley (26 October 1775), and Thomas Egerton, *Parl. Hist.*, 18:851, 854, 758; *Man. Merc.* (7 November 1775) in defense of administration addresses.

[76]J. E. Norton, ed., *The Letters of Edward Gibbon*, 3 vols. (London: Macmillan Co., 1956) 2:88-89 (Gibbon to J. B. Holroyd, 14 October 1775).

documents, it is held, "prove little as to public opinion" largely because of purported government influence.[77]

The question as to the validity of petitions and addresses as genuine expressions of public opinion may be debated at different levels. The issue was first introduced by locating the documents in specific geographical areas. This regional survey suggested that there existed a significant relationship between an area's political characteristics and the majority of popular documents. These hints at continuity between a political tradition and political behavior were, however, vague and general at best. The validity of the addresses and petitions was also examined by looking at the loyalties of the leaders of the petitioning agitation and determining how this related to the geographical areas in which they were influential. For example, the support of unsigned addresses by conservative patrons appears to be significant. Similarly, in promoting the Bristol petition Burke was clearly acting in accord with his stated political convictions, as was Lord Stanley in supporting the Lancashire address. A number of leaders who presented the conciliatory petitions had distinguished careers in both local and national politics, and their support of conciliatory measures cannot have surprised anyone. Lord Rockingham's countryman and friend, Sir George Savile, presented the petition from Halifax. The Worcester petition was delivered by Sir Watkin Lewes and Lord Viscount Mahon. The Earl of Abingdon saw the petitions from Wallingford and Abingdon through from beginning to end, and Lord Craven presented the petitions for Berkshire and Coventry. The role of Lord George Cavendish in the petitioning activity at Bolton is unknown, but he presented the document to the king and thereby lent the weight of his family name to the cause of peace.[78]

An examination of less-prominent members of Parliament, obscure political managers, and local supporters of the documents takes us a step below the national leaders and illustrates additional elements of political consistency. A recent survey of the names of those who presented the coercive addresses to George III demonstrates that there was a high level of behavioral consistency among conservatives. Paul Langford has shown that many old Tory members of Parliament who never spoke in the House of Commons were entrusted with presenting the coercive addresses to the king.[79] These were the same country gentlemen who had voted against the repeal of the Stamp Act, and they were the ideological successors of the "Tories." This identity is established not only by family members, but by geographical location and high Anglican religious affiliation. The term *Tory* had, of course, lost its currency by this time, but the former commitment to passive obedience to the king was transformed into trust in the sovereignty of Parliament—or, more exactly, the king in Parliament. The

---

[77]Clark, *British Opinion*, 132. She appears to have followed Walpole. See also 133, 164.

[78]*Lond. Eve.-Post* (4-7 November 1775); *Mid. J.* (11-14 November 1775); *Lond. Eve.-Post* (18-21 November 1775); HO 5/8/6; *Lond. Eve.-Post* (14-16 December 1775).

[79]Langford, "Old Whigs, Old Tories," 8:123-24 n. 69.

colonial crisis thus provoked the rise of a new authoritarianism precisely among those who traced their family lineage to their Tory fathers. These men not only sustained North's American policies in Parliament, they were the intermediate-level organizers and supporters of coercive addresses to the Crown.[80]

A distinct counterpart to this exists in the less-well-known leaders and presenters of the conciliatory petitions. Local organizers of meetings in favor of petitioning had long been associated with opposition politics in general, and the Rockingham Whigs in particular. In London, for example, the merchants' conciliatory petition depended a great deal on the energy and organizational skills of William Baker, a confidant of the Rockinghams and a longstanding leader in city politics in his own right.[81] Similarly, at Bristol, Richard Champion, Paul Farr, and Thomas Hayes distinguished themselves as local Whig politicians long before they became involved in working on behalf of conciliation.[82] Samuel Elam of Leeds was known for his support of local efforts against the government's American measures in the spring of 1775. When there was talk of petitioning once again in the fall, it was natural for Burke to appeal to him.[83] This is not to argue that the Whigs alone opposed the government, nor that the Tories alone supported coercion, but only that the activity of local self-styled Whig leaders on behalf of conciliation was consistent with their past behavior. In some cases their support for conciliation also comported well with their religion; Richard Champion and Samuel Elam were both Quakers.

There were other local Whig leaders who also espoused a consistent political orientation over a period of time. At Newcastle-upon-Tyne, George Grieve had been active in radical causes for years, and in 1775 he was a leading force in the movement that supported conciliation with the colonies.[84] What part the Presbyterian common councillor, Mark Huish, may have played in the leadership of the Nottingham petition to the Crown is unknown, but his prominence in the earlier appeals to Parliament suggests a large role.[85] Similarly, the precise involvement in the petitioning agitation of Posthumous Lloyd and Jacob Dalton, Dissenting ministers of Coventry, has not been discovered. Both of their names appear at the head of the petition, not far below those of Craven

---

[80]Ibid., 106, 121, 123-24, 127.

[81]*Burke Correspondence*, 3:219 (Burke to Richmond, 26 September 1775).

[82]G. H. Guttridge, ed., *The American Correspondence of a Bristol Merchant, 1766-1776* (Berkeley: University of California Press, 1934) 40 (Champion to Willing, Morris, & Co., 17 January 1775). *Burke Correspondence*, 3:95, 220, 230, 232 (Burke to Champion, 10 January 1775, 1, 17, 20, 23 October 1775); 3:220-21, 229 (Burke to Paul Farr, 1 October 1775; Burke to Thomas Hayes, 11 October 1775).

[83]*Lond. Eve.-Post* (24-26 January 1775); *Burke Correspondence*, 3:194 n. 3 (Burke to Rockingham, 23 August 1775).

[84]Knox, "Wilkism and the Newcastle Election," 30-31; HO 55/29/19.

[85]*Burke Correspondence*, 3:129, 131 (Burke to Mark Huish, 22 February, 9 March 1775); HO 55/10/18.

and Archer, and this suggests that their ministerial offices were put to use in the cause of their "American brethren."[86] Patterns of consistent political behavior can be demonstrated among little-known leaders in other boroughs. The Hurrys at Great Yarmouth, the Bernards at Southampton, and the Jolliffs at Poole were Dissenting families with a long tradition of commitment to the Whig cause, and they all provided active leadership for the petitions supporting peace.[87] The activity of obscure local leaders on the one hand, and prominent national magnates on the other, is exactly what would be expected; in each case there is a close correspondence between a political tradition, a political identity, and political behavior.

These observations, however, appear tautological, except insofar as they demonstrate the political consistency of leadership over a period of time. In any case, they do not address the more important issue of whether or not these leaders influenced petitioners to act against their political convictions, assuming, of course, that the signers were politically literate. The question of validity can only be addressed satisfactorily by looking at local leaders and local political structures in more detail. Leadership, interest groups, and local networks of influence may then be related to the political behavior of individual petitioners through an analysis of petitions and pollbooks. In these lines of inquiry, the purpose will be to discover as much as possible about the political consistency of the leaders in relationship to the petitioners themselves. There is no doubt that undue influence was exerted on some petitioners. The question that must now be determined is whether or not the use of influence invalidates the documents or whether it can be isolated and evaluated accordingly.

---

[86]*Lond. Eve.-Post* (21-24 October 1775); "A View of English Nonconformity in 1773," in *The Transactions of the Congregational Historical Society* 5 (1911-1912): 375.

[87]Regarding the Hurrys, *Commons, 1754-1790*, 1:340. Ian R. Christie, "Great Yarmouth and the Yorkshire Reform Movement," in *Myth and Reality in Late Eighteenth-Century British Politics* (London: Macmillan Co., 1970) 284. *Norw. Merc.* (9 December 1775). For the Bernards, *Commons, 1754-1790*, 1:300. *The Poll* (Southampton, 1774); *Hamp. Chron.* (16 November 1775). Regarding the Jolliffs, *Commons, 1754-1790*, 1:269-70; 2:120; RG 4/2290.

Political Consistency
among Petitioners,
Subscribers, and Voters

Chapter VI

Popular agitation concerning America was as widespread in the English provinces as other popular protests in the 1770s and 1780s. The petitions also penetrated deeply into the populace; frequently more than half of those who petitioned were not qualified to vote in parliamentary elections. Political concern regarding America involved enough people in extra-parliamentary politics to lead one recent study of petitions to conclude that Burke's estimate of a "political nation" of 400,000 people was fundamentally accurate.[1] If the agitation concerning America qualifies as public agitation, many contemporaries nevertheless remained skeptical about the validity of these documents as indicators of genuine opinion. In an aristocratic age, the opinion of the people was often viewed with disdain. Even leaders such as Lord Rockingham, who might have benefited from appealing to the public, doubted the validity of popular opinion and scorned its political utility.

Historians as well have questioned the representative nature of public opinion, and this skepticism has arisen in part because of an unfortunate division of scholarly labor. Traditional studies of public opinion and political thought tend to suspend ideology above the level of the material, local interests of the people.[2] Conversely, those who have done the most to advance our knowledge of local political structures have not given adequate attention to newspapers and the vast

---

[1]John A. Phillips, "Popular Politics in Unreformed England," *Journal of Modern History* 52 (December 1980): 599, 615.

[2]This is true of studies of the press: Fred J. Hinkhouse, *The Preliminaries of the American Revolution as Seen in the English Press, 1763-1775* (New York: Columbia University Press, 1926) and Solomon Lutnick, *The American Revolution and the British Press, 1775-1783* (Columbia MO: University of Missouri Press, 1967); and studies of ideology: Colin Bonwick, *English Radicals and the American Revolution* (Chapel Hill: University of North Carolina Press, 1977) and H. T. Dickinson, *Liberty and Property: Political Ideology in Eighteenth-Century Britain* (New York: Holmes and Meier, 1977). Even George Rudé, with the exception of his examination of London, does not relate petitioning activity to the local structures of politics, *Wilkes and Liberty* (Oxford: Oxford University Press, 1962).

pamphlet literature of the period.[3] Eighteenth-century political ideology has, as a result, seemed impotent, and it has seldom been taken seriously as a cause of social change. Some recent work has begun to bridge this gap, but much research is still needed to illumine the interaction between ideas and local interests.[4] Historians need to know, for example, precisely what it was that led members of corporations to articulate a conservative ideology and identify their interests with the Crown. Local political antagonisms, religious affiliation, and material interests are sometimes assumed to stand behind conservative ideology, but the inner connection between ideology, status, and wealth needs to be drawn out. Implicit in any such attempt are assumptions about the fundamental rationality and consistency of human behavior.

The validity of public opinion may be tested by examining the consistency of an individual's behavior in discrete political acts over a period of time. If petitioners acted consistently with their previous and subsequent political behavior, it becomes difficult to dismiss their opinions as invalid. The concentration of coercive addresses in the traditional Tory stronghold of the west midlands, and the preponderance of conciliatory petitions in the Puritan southwest pointed to one form of political consistency. But the behavior of individual petitioners is further illumined by comparing these documents to subscription lists and poll books. This will necessitate setting forth the political history of five parliamentary boroughs in some detail. These local studies will serve as an introduction to the issue of political motivation and the relation of ideology to interest that is taken up in the next chapter.

I

One test of the political consistency of addressers and petitioners is found by comparing the petitions to lists of subscribers to funds that supported wounded English soldiers and their families. A subscription was begun in London on 18 October 1775 and approved by the king. This subscription remained open through 15 January 1777 and was designed to aid those soldiers who were employed in his Majesty's service in America, and "for succouring the distressed Widows and Orphans of those brave Men who have fallen or may

---

[3]*Commons, 1754-1790*, for example, gives little attention to political squibs and newspapers.

[4]Three examples are John Brewer, *Party Ideology and Popular Politics at the Accession of George III* (Cambridge: Cambridge University Press, 1976); John A. Phillips, *Electoral Behavior in Unreformed England: Plumpers, Splitters, and Straights* (Princeton: Princeton University Press, 1982); and Paul Langford, "Old Whigs, Old Tories and the American Revolution," *Journal of Imperial and Commonwealth History* 8 (January 1980): 106-30.

fall in defending the Constitutional Government of this Country."[5] The names of subscribers were printed every week in the London papers along with the amount they subscribed, and prominent among them were such distinguished leaders as Lord North (£100), Lord George Germain (£105), and John Robinson (£21). On 22 November, £17/11 was "collected at Bethnal Green Church, after a Sermon preached by the Rev. Mr. Wesley."[6] The political nature of the subscription was obvious; the funds were used to support the war effort directly. From the final report of expenditures it is clear that more than two-thirds of the £20,000 that was finally raised was used to supply troops with articles of clothing at Boston, Halifax, Quebec, and New York. The remaining third was used for sick and wounded soldiers, women, and children.[7]

The subscription at Bristol was equally political in its orientation. Begun on 18 December, it solicited contributions for the widows and orphans of those brave men who have fallen or may fall "in the Defense of the inherent Rights of the Mother Country," and by the time it concluded on 13 April 1776, the citizens of Bristol alone had contributed £1806.[8] The Bristol committee was in correspondence with the London committee, and the former also wrote to General Burgoyne, who responded in a public letter. The general wrote that he was honored to be "considered a Fellow Zealot in maintaining the Constitutional Rights of Great Britain," and he felt that benefactions founded on such true principles "could hardly fail of making an Impression on public Opinion."[9] Here, as in London, more than two-thirds of the money collected was used to provision troops in Boston "engaged in suppressing a Rebellion against the just and inherent Rights of their country."[10] Subscriptions from Manchester, Leeds, Nottingham, Poole, Portsmouth, and numerous other places were also printed. At an early stage in the period of subscribing, the political implications of these subscriptions were drawn out, as was the connection between subscribing and addressing. At Manchester, for example, "Philanthropos" attempted to stir up support for the local subscription and at the same

---

[5]*Pub. Adv.* (25 October 1775). In the spring of 1775 the London merchants opened a subscription at the London Tavern "to contribute to the relief of the Americans," and it was said that £15,000 was raised in less than half an hour. No lists of names in support of this subscription have survived. It was just such a scheme that led to the arrest of John Horne Tooke. *Brist. J.* (25 February 1775); *Leeds Merc.* (21 February 1775).

[6]*Pub. Adv.* (15, 22 November 1775).

[7]The total reported was £19,532/8/11 of which £15,618/14/16 went directly to supplies for soldiers. *Pub. Adv.* (29 January 1777).

[8]*Brist J.* (23 December 1775-13 April 1776). The subscription at Portsmouth was collected for those involved "in the just defense of the constitutional government of this kingdom." *Sal. Win. J.* (11, 18 December 1775).

[9]*Brist. J.* (24 February 1775).

[10]Ibid. £1,500 of the £2,047/19 collected by 24 February went to supplies for soldiers. This total includes some funds from places other than Bristol, not included in Table 6.1 below.

time stanch rumors concerning the possible governmental influence of addressers: "By this Subscription you will silence these malicious Heralds of sedition, who have as impudently as falsely asserted that you were forc'd or instigated to Address his Majesty, by the retainers of Administration."[11]

The subscriptions throughout the country were related directly to the agitation concerning addressing and petitioning. Not only were the same leaders who supported the addresses active in promoting the subscriptions, at least twenty of the same English boroughs and towns that sent loyal addresses to the Crown in the fall also collected funds for the subscription.[12] Conversely, only ten that had not addressed in the spring or fall of 1775 sent in subscriptions.[13] Two groups stood out in the subscription: Anglican clergymen and town corporations. During the first month of the London subscription, some thirty Anglican clergy had contributed to the fund, and this seems to have represented a political orientation as well as charitable concern.[14] The other feature of these lists that strikes the reader is the number of corporations that subscribed; altogether some sixteen corporations wished to make their financial support of the government's colonial policy known to the public.[15] The identity of interests between corporations and the government in defending constituted authority was graphically portrayed for a second time.

The relationship between the subscriptions and the addresses and petitions is also established by their chronological proximity. In the early months of 1776, there was a dramatic curtailment of support for the subscriptions, despite the fact that appeals for aid continued to be published.[16] Whereas there had been 1,170 London subscribers in the two-month period from 18 October to 27 De-

---

[11]*Man. Merc.* (7 November 1775). Conversely, an author opposed to the government connected twenty subscribers directly to the government. *Pub. Adv.* (4 November 1775).

[12]At London, for example, Isaac Hughes was prominent in both, as was George Daubeny at Bristol. These boroughs, in order of appearance in the London papers, are London, Bristol, Exeter, Manchester (twice), Rye, Nottingham, Poole, Blackburn, Liverpool, Shrewsbury (twice), Southmolton, Great Yarmouth, Cambridge, Newcastle-upon-Tyne, Southampton, Bolton, Kingston-upon-Hull, Leicester, Carlisle, and reported in *Brist. J.* (13 April 1776), Melksham. To these might be added Birmingham, which had sent an address in the spring of 1775, and York, which had not yet addressed. In addition, Carmarthen, Edinburgh, and Guernsey also subscribed.

[13]Scarborough, Boston, Stockport, Weymouth and Melcombe Regis, Chepstow, Corfe Castle, Harwich, Bocking, Eye, Falmouth. Most of these were small cities; of the ten subscriptions, four were from corporations.

[14]*Pub. Adv.* (25 October—22 November 1775).

[15]Scarborough, Exeter, Boston, Rye, Corfe Castle, Shrewsbury, Southmolton, Great Yarmouth, Harwich, Cambridge, York, Newcastle-upon-Tyne, Kingston-upon-Hull, Leicester, Carlisle, Eye.

[16]For instances of continuing appeals for aid, see *Gen. Eve. Post* (16-18, 20-23 January 1776, 27-29 February, 11-13 April 1777); *Brist J.* (24 February, 2, 9 March 1777).

cember 1775, in the next three months (28 December—13 April 1776) there were only ninety-six subscribers from London. In the nine-month period from 14 April to the conclusion of the subscription on 15 January 1777, only fifty-three additional persons subscribed. Thus 89 percent of the London subscribers were enrolled in the fall of 1775 when the agitation concerning petitioning and addressing was at its height. Similarly, at Bristol 223 or 86.8 percent of all subscribers responded in the first month and a half (18 December 1775—3 February 1776) of the four-month period in which the subscription was active. Moreover, those who had signed loyal addresses at London and Bristol subscribed at a slightly faster rate than all the subscribers considered together.[17] The period of vigorous activity in collecting funds for the government corresponds generally to the highest literary output of political pamphlets dealing with the war, and it corresponds specifically to the period when addresses and petitions were presented to the Crown. By the spring of 1776 public awareness of the magnitude of the war effort may have dampened enthusiasm for what could be accomplished by private benevolence.

By comparing the names in the subscription lists to those that appeared on the coercive addresses and conciliatory petitions, one can determine the extent to which addressers and petitioners actually supported the use of force.[18] Table 6.1 demonstrates beyond a reasonable doubt that many who addressed the Crown in favor of coercive measures were in fact willing to support the use of force with their fortunes, if not their lives, while the conciliatory petitioners, on the whole, were not. In the five boroughs examined, between twenty-two and seventy percent of all subscribers also addressed the Crown (an average of forty-six percent) and of all those who addressed, an average of twenty-four percent subscribed to the government fund. Popular support for coercive measures seems to have been given freely, one could even say enthusiastically, since addressers who also subscribed responded sooner than all contributors considered together. The handful of conciliatory petitioners who subscribed in London does not fall into any meaningful pattern with regard to the time that they

---

[17]In London, 96.5 percent of all subscribers who were also addressers had subscribed by 27 December 1775, and at Bristol 91.5 percent of all subscribers who had also addressed had subscribed by 3 February 1776.

[18]The subscription lists supply names, amount given, and residence; they are compared to the addresses and petitions from London, Bristol, Leeds, Nottingham, and Poole. In the list of total subscribers, companies are counted as one except when the partners appear separately on the addresses or petitions, in which case they are added separately. This happened in twelve cases in the London address, one in Bristol, two in Leeds, two in Nottingham, and one in Poole. The figures for London exclude eighty-four subscribers who explicitly gave a residence other than London and an additional thirty-nine places other than London that sent their subscriptions to London. At Bristol, forty nonresidents are excluded and five at Leeds. A small percentage of the matches are of common names and probably do not refer to the same person, but the number of such mismatches should be roughly equal for both addressers and petitioners.

subscribed. In London and Bristol the subscriptions went on over a period of months, and this allows for an analysis of data that spans a period of time. In neither city is there evidence for a gradual erosion of conviction among the signers of conciliatory petitions. Rather, the near absence of their names from the subscription lists suggests the seriousness of their considered opinion on the inappropriateness of coercive measures.

II

The rise of urban radicalism in large parliamentary boroughs was an important characteristic of late-eighteenth-century politics. Well-organized political parties in places such as Bristol and Norwich produced an impressive output of popular literature at election time, and this stimulated early expressions of public opinion in matters of national importance. Such developments, however, were less likely in smaller boroughs. The influence of patrons and the lure of guineas hindered the emergence of political parties and often stifled expressions of popular opinion. The study of popular issues in these smaller settings is especially needed precisely because public opinion was more susceptible to various forms of influence and control.

The following examination of the political consistency of individual petitioners is based on an analysis of two medium- and three small-sized parliamentary

TABLE 6.1

ADDRESSERS, PETITIONERS, AND SUBSCRIBERS

BOROUGH AND DATE OF SUBSCRIPTION	NUMBER OF SUBSCRIBERS	AMOUNT (£) SUBSCRIBED	SUBSCRIBERS† WHO ADDRESSED OR PETITIONED NUMBER	%	AMOUNT SUBSCRIBED £	%	PROPORTION OF ADDRESSERS AND PETITIONERS WHO SUBSCRIBED
London (18 Oct. 1775– 15 Jan. 1777)	1319	11,832/7/3	Coer 286 / Conc 38	21.7% / 2.9%	1,862/5/6 / 268/5	15.7% / 2.3%	30.4% / 3.4%
Bristol (18 Dec. 1775– 13 April 1776)	257	1806/11	Coer 165 / Conc 2	64.2% / 0.8%	1008/16 / 10/10	55.8% / 0.6%	18.3% / 0.2%
Leeds (Reported 7 May 1776)	155	467/6/3	Coer 63 / Conc 4	40.6% / 2.6%	197/8 / 9/16/6	42.2% / 2.1%	23.9% / 0.7%
Nottingham (to 12 Dec. 1775)	45	153	Coer 32 / Conc 1	71.1% / 2.2%	104/9/6 / 1/1	68.0% / 0.7%	13.9% / 0.3%
Poole (to 27 Dec. 1775)	64	146/19/3	Coer 21 / Conc 5	32.8% / 7.8%	33/1/6 / 4/4	22.8% / 2.7%	35.7% / 3.5%

† Coer = Coercive; Conc = Conciliatory.
* For London, see *Pub. Adv.* (25, 31 Oct.; 4, 8, 15, 22, 29 Nov.; 12, 27 Dec. 1775), *Gen. Eve. Post* (16-18 Jan.; 6-8, 27-29 Feb.; 11-13 Apr.; 7-9 May; 13-16 July; 17-19 Sept. 1776), *Pub. Adv.* (15-29 Jan. 1777); for Bristol, *Brist. J.* (23-30 Dec. 1775; 6, 13, 20, 27 Jan.; 3, 10, 17, 24 Feb.; 2, 9, 16 Mar.; 13 Apr. 1776); for Leeds, *Gen. Eve. Post* (7-9 May 1776); for Nottingham and Poole, *Pub. Adv.* (12, 27 Dec. 1775).

boroughs. Politics in these boroughs often revolved around the interaction between conservative interests such as corporations on the one hand, and potentially disrupting groups such as the Dissenters on the other. The progressive political ideology of the Dissenting elite is thoroughly documented in studies of English radicalism. Their progressivism is also sometimes attributed to their exclusion from municipal office holding by the Test and Corporation Acts, though the frequency of conformity in order to qualify for office has seldom been appreciated. In the period between 1715 and 1790 the Dissenters held mayoral or corporate office in at least thirty parliamentary boroughs, or one out of every five boroughs they inhabited.[19] Nevertheless, there was considerable discontent in their ranks concerning the legal obstructions they faced in order to obtain office. This discontent often led to political rivalry between the Dissenters and Anglican-dominated corporations. Apart from such interest groups and their political orientation, the behavior of individual petitioners cannot be properly understood. Each of the boroughs selected for study has ample data from poll books and nonparochial registers to answer questions one might ask concerning the economic and religious background of the petitioners.

The boroughs of Great Yarmouth and Cambridge were influenced by government interests in the eighteenth century, and there were organized attempts in both to wrest control away from the government. Yarmouth and Cambridge were the only cities situated in the northeast that petitioned concerning the American crisis and also petitioned regarding economic and parliamentary reform in the 1780s. In the southwest, opposition to the government's American policy will be studied in three boroughs. A movement in support of political independence emerged in the 1770s at Southampton, a borough that had links with America through Lord Charles Montagu, governor of South Carolina. Bridgwater is of interest because, despite its reputation for venality, Charles James Fox was one of the contestants during the election of 1780. Finally, the small borough of Poole gained a notorious reputation during the American crisis by opposing the repeal of the Coercive Acts in the spring of 1775. Accordingly, it has been treated in the past as an outstanding example of a trading center that stood in support of coercive measures. In fact, it too was divided with respect to America. Each of the cities reflects a core of government supporters backing coercive measures who came into conflict with an indigenous movement sympathetic to the pursuit of peaceful measures. A survey of the political interests and prominent leaders in each of the five boroughs will provide the necessary context for a comparative statistical assessment of individual petitioners.

---

[19]James E. Bradley, "Whigs and Nonconformists: Presbyterians, Congregationalists, and Baptists in English Politics, 1715-1790" (Ph.D. dissertation, University of Southern California, 1978) 111-15 has some of these data. This subject will be treated at length in a subsequent study. For the best survey of the legal issue, see K. R. M. Short, "The English Indemnity Acts, 1726-1867," *Church History* 42 (September 1973): 366-76.

GREAT YARMOUTH

Great Yarmouth was a medium-sized borough with a freeman electorate, and although there were some 800 voters, the corporation played an important part in borough politics. The corporation in turn was influenced by the Townshend and Walpole families who dominated borough politics from 1722 to 1784. Frequent political contests illustrate the existence of a viable opposition element that, though active, was kept under control through the port's heavy dependence on patronage. The corporation systematically excluded those whose politics ran counter to the government. Opposition to the corporation party in the second half of the century was organized by the Nonconformists.[20]

The attempt to take the control of patronage from the Townshend-Walpole monopoly and the corporation began in 1768 and extended through 1784. The opposition faction was organized by ten of the town's leading Dissenters, headed by the prominent Hurry family. Thomas Hurry and his sons were hemp and iron merchants with numerous ships and extensive warehouses in Queen Street.[21] A small coterie of disaffected corporation members constituted the Anglican side of the faction. In 1769 this group presented a remonstrance to the sitting members of Parliament that attacked John Ramey, the Townshend-Walpole agent, for neglecting their own special interests. The opposition, deriving nearly half of its force from the Dissenters, was threatening enough to cause Ramey's resignation, but little else was accomplished.[22] In the general election of 1774, the opposition put forth Sir Charles Saunders, a friend and supporter of Rockingham, and William Beckford, son of the well-known London radical. At a by-election in 1777 they backed Beckford again, but in both elections they made a poor showing at the polls.[23] In 1780 the independents signed a petition for economic reform, and in 1782 and 1783 attempts were made to change the prevailing channels of patronage by means of further appeals for parliamentary reform.[24] In their last attempt, the Yarmouth independents

---

[20]*Commons 1715-1754*, 1:290; *Commons, 1754-1790*, 1:340. B. D. Hayes, "Politics in Norfolk, 1750-1832" (Ph.D. dissertation, University of Cambridge, 1958) 121.

[21]Thomas Hurry-Houghton, *Memorials of the Family of Hurry* (Liverpool: C. Tinling and Co., 1926) 9.

[22]Hayes, "Politics in Norfolk," 151. According to Hayes, the Dissenters were "rigidly excluded" from the corporation (124). *Commons, 1754-1790*, 1:340; Lewis Namier, *The Structure of Politics at the Accession of George III*, 2d ed. (London: Macmillan Co., 1957) 453 n. 1; Ian Christie, "Great Yarmouth and the Yorkshire Reform Movement, 1782-1784," in *Myth and Reality in Late-Eighteenth-Century British Politics and Other Papers* (London: Macmillan Co., 1970) 284.

[23]*The Poll* (Yarmouth, 1777). Although Richard Walpole was in opposition to North, he had acquiesced to the local patronage arrangement and was, as a result, opposed by the opposition faction. Christie, "Great Yarmouth," *Myth and Reality*, 290.

[24]Regarding the petition of 1780, see *Parl. Hist.*, 20:1370-72; Christie, "Great Yarmouth," *Myth and Reality*, 284-92; and Christie, *Wilkes, Wyvill and Reform* (London: Macmillan Co., 1962) 160 n. 4.

turned to the Reverend George Walker, the Presbyterian minister, as their spokesman. In his various approaches to Lord Shelburne, Walker was also unsuccessful, but when Pitt's government pronounced against the sitting members at the general election of 1784, the opposition won both parliamentary seats. At this point, the independents themselves became the main channel of government patronage to local placemen.

Although the Dissenting interest at Great Yarmouth was not large, all four of the major denominations were represented. The Goal Street Presbyterian Chapel was the most prominent in size and influence, and it was the chosen home of the Hurry family. There was a Congregational chapel of unknown size, and in the course of the eighteenth century a second Baptist meeting was added to the existing one. A small Quaker assembly rounded out the full complement of Dissenting options, but none of the meetings put forward a single prominent clerical leader during the years of the American crisis.[25] Of the four known Dissenting ministers who might have supported conciliation in 1775, only one in fact did.[26]

What was lacking in the clergy, however, was supplied by the laity. The Hurry family had taken the initiative against the local monopoly in the 1760s, and they, with a number of their brethren, provided constant leadership for opposition politics. The Presbyterian baptismal register graphically illustrates the family's connection to the independent faction. In 1762 William Hurry named his first son Edmund Cobb. Cobb's namesake was, like Hurry himself, a leading Yarmouth independent. In 1777, when the opposition party put up William Beckford against the government interest for the second time, Hurry named his fourth son Beckford, after William Beckford, thereby symbolizing the family's longstanding attachment to radical causes.[27] Five of the six Hurrys who voted in this election voted for Beckford.[28] After the American crisis the family continued to take politics seriously. In the late 1780s, Thomas and Thomas Hurry, Jr., Samuel and Samuel Hurry, Jr., George and William Hurry

---

[25]John Evans, "List of Dissenting Congregations and Ministers in England and Wales (1715-1729)," MS. 38.4, 83-85. Josiah Thompson, "List of Protestant Dissenting Congregations in England and Wales (1772-1773)," MS. 38.6, 25. Hayes, "Politics in Norfolk," 123. Baptismal and birth registers survive for the Presbyterian chapel (RG 4/1973; 2473) and the Quaker meeting (RG 6/1570; 1473; 1410; 689; 597; 557; 1482; 558; 507).

[26]The four are Thomas Howe, John Whiteside, George Walker, and John M. Benyon, of whom only the latter signed the conciliatory petition. See "A View of English Nonconformity in 1773" in *The Transactions of the Congregational Historical Society* 5 (1911-1912): 271, which provides a list of ministers who petitioned Parliament in 1772 for relief from subscription to the Thirty-Nine Articles. RG 4/1973.

[27]RG 4/1973.

[28]*The Poll* (Yarmouth, 1777). The father, Thomas, and his four sons acted together; John Hurry alone voted for Townshend. Charles John Palmer, *Memorials of the Family of Hurry* (Norwich: Miller and Leavins, 1875) 21.

all purchased freeholds at Norwich for the purpose of voting in Norwich elections, and in the contest of 1786 they all voted for the opposition candidate.[29]

The leaders of the independent party were also prominent in the local resistance to the government's American policy.[30] The agitation regarding America began on 26 September 1775 when the mayor called the corporation together for the purpose of addressing the Crown in favor of coercive measures. Four days later a second coercive address was circulated among the population and it ultimately gained 227 signatures. Among the signers was John Ramey, the former agent of the Townshend-Walpole interest—who was by this date placated by a government pension—and his successor as government agent, William Fisher. Both addresses supporting coercion were presented by the faithful supporter of North and sitting member of Yarmouth, Charles Townshend of Honingham. It was not until six weeks later that a conciliatory petition reached London. It had collected 347 signatures. While only one of the Presbyterian ministers signed this petition, the leadership of the Dissenting laity in the petitioning activity is likely in that seven of the first ten signatures were Presbyterian and five members of the Hurry family also signed the document.[31] The American crisis had provided yet another occasion for the local opposition faction to express its disaffection toward the government, but it can be argued that the plea for peace illustrated something more exalted than pique over their exclusion from political perquisites.

CAMBRIDGE

In 1774 the borough of Cambridge had been uncontested for nearly forty years, and the county had lain dormant under the weight of patronage for more than half a century. With the approach of the American war, there was thus no tradition of party rivalry in Cambridgeshire—even the university was considered little more than one of Newcastle's pocket boroughs. Between 1737 and 1774 the corporation of this small freeman borough returned government candidates for a fixed fee. The sitting members in 1774 were staunch supporters of measures to tax the colonists, and one of them, Soame Jenyns, had written

---

[29]Hurry-Houghton, *Memorials of the Family of Hurry*, 11.

[30]Continuity between the opposition in 1775 and support for reform in 1782 can be demonstrated by comparing the earlier document to the leadership of the committee that applied to Lord Rockingham. In the memorial of April 1782, six of the ten leaders had signed the petition supporting peace in 1775, and in the memorial of June 1782, seven of the twelve had signed. Of the thirteen different leaders in 1782, nine were Presbyterian. For the lists of leaders and the leadership of the Hurrys in 1782, see Christie, "Great Yarmouth," *Myth and Reality*, 290-91. These lists were compared to RG 4/1973.

[31]*Lond. Chron.* (30 September-3 October, 5-7 October 1775); *Lond. Chron.* (3-5 October 1775); *Pub. Adv.* (19 October 1775); *Lond. Eve.-Post* (21-23 November 1775); *Norw. Merc.* (9 December 1775). In order of appearance, the Presbyterians are Henry Gooch, Thomas Scratton, John Morris, Joseph Bridgewell, Thomas Hurry, George Errington, and John Fowler. Hayes, "Politics in Norfolk," 198, only makes a passing allusion to this petition.

a pamphlet that defended virtual representation. For some years there had been discontent expressed in the corporation concerning the government's monopoly of local office.[32] The division in the corporation was more extensive here than in Great Yarmouth, and unlike Yarmouth, a handful of Dissenters did sit on the corporation.[33] This openness, however, was not adequate to assuage discontent, and Anglicans and Dissenters alike began to organize a party against the government candidates.

At the general election of 1774 the new party put up two candidates against the government. Robert Robinson, the minister of St. Andrew's Street Baptist Chapel, published a broadside addressed to the corporation exhorting it to consider the importance of supporting the opposition candidates.[34] The independent party held a meeting in the Guildhall and required its candidates to sign a statement that committed them to back parliamentary reform, to support "an enlarged toleration to Protestant Dissenters of every denomination and persuasion," to oppose the government's repressive American policy, and to agree not to accept any place or pension from the Crown while representing Cambridge. The ensuing election was exceedingly turbulent, and in the end the opposition candidates, supported by the Dissenters, were defeated by thirty votes. One observer of this election commented on the social status of the independent faction, observing that the movement was comprised of "Riffe-raffe."[35]

The issue of America was not prominent in the borough elections of 1776 and 1780. The newspaper accounts and the drop in the poll (from 153 voters in 1774, to 135 in 1776, to 107 in 1780) indicate that political issues generally were less important in these two elections than they had been in 1774.[36] The same, however, was not true of the county. Cambridge joined the Yorkshire Association movement supporting reform in the early months of 1780, and the Dissenters once again were actively involved. In February a petition was circulated that called for a county meeting and urged cooperation with other

---

[32]James E. Bradley, "Religion and Reform at the Polls: Nonconformity in Cambridge Politics, 1774-1784," *Journal of British Studies* 23 (Spring 1984): 55-78. *Commons, 1715-1754*, 1:200-202; *Commons, 1754-1790*, 1:210, 217-21; 2:164, 681. J. Milner Gray, *Biographical Notes on the Mayors of Cambridge* (Cambridge: W. Heffer and Sons, 1922) 49. Helen Cam, "Quo Warranto Proceedings at Cambridge, 1780-1790," *The Cambridge Historical Journal* 8:2 (1945): 156-57.

[33]Four generations of the family of Purchase held the office of mayor at Cambridge, beginning in 1760, and at least the first two were professed Presbyterians. Gray, *Biographical Notes*, 48, 51, 55-57. Four other Dissenters also held office, for a total of at least six in the period 1760-1790. See Additional Manuscripts, 5855, f. 140; 5813, ff. 131, 137.

[34]The Baptist Church Books, f. 18.

[35]William Cole, Add. MSS. 5823, f. 986.

[36]*The Poll* (Cambridge, 8 October 1774); *The Poll* (Cambridge, 7 November 1776); *The Poll* (Cambridge, 6 September 1780); *Cam. Chron.* (28 September, 9, 16 November 1776; 9 September 1780).

counties. A local correspondent observed that when he first saw the petition there were about twenty signatures, and they "appeared to me to be those of no great consequence, most of them Presbyterian [Dissenters]." Eight of the nineteen signatures at this early stage of circulation can be identified as Dissenters, and this suggests that they were taking the lead.[37] The meeting at the Town Hall on 9 March agreed on a petition to Parliament that lamented an expensive and unfortunate war and urged a correction of all abuses in the expenditure of public money. The address was signed by 100 petitioners, of whom twenty-three can be identified as Dissenters, and eight of these were members of St. Andrew's Street Baptist meeting.[38] Later, when the two sitting members for the county refused to present the Cambridgeshire petition in support of economic reform, the reformers put up an opposition candidate. This provoked the first election in the county to be pressed to a poll in more than fifty years. The Dissenters not only provided the leadership for this county contest (a point that is beyond dispute), but they appear to have voted a fairly disciplined party line, with the result being that the opposition candidate won an easy victory. Two years later a mere threat of opposition from the Dissenters led the new candidate for the county to become a steadfast proponent of parliamentary reform, and in the ensuing years the second county member was also won over to reform.[39]

Presbyterians, Congregationalists, and Baptists were all represented at Cambridge, but the denominational complexion of the borough was fundamentally altered in the 1770s by the evangelistic efforts of Robert Robinson. He singlehandedly made St. Andrew's Street Baptist meeting the largest and most influential Dissenting chapel in the area. By 1775 there was a weekly attendance of 600-800, and the lectureships that Robinson organized in the surrounding villages were even more well attended. At the same time, the Congregationalists at Hog Hill flourished under the ministry of Joseph Saunders, but the Presbyterians at Green Street dwindled and finally closed the chapel doors. Altogether, the Dissenters within the borough numbered 1,000

---

[37]Ewin to Hardwicke, February 1780, Add. MSS. 35626, ff. 117-18. Ewin consistently equated Presbyterians with Dissenters. The list of names given by Ewin are compared to Cole, Add. MSS. 5855, ff. 140-41; the Baptist Church Book and the Trust Deeds of 1764 and 1795 of St. Andrew's Street Baptist Church and the Congregational Register, RG 4/3870.

[38]*Cam. Chron.* (11 March 1780). Cole lists the 100 names and identifies eighteen Dissenters, seven and possibly eight of whom can be confirmed from the church book. Add. MSS. 5855, ff. 140-42. From the church book and registers it is possible to match five more for a total of twenty-three. The eight from Robinson's congregation are Richard Foster, William Hollick, William Lyon, Charles Finch, John Gifford, Ebenezer Hollick, Sr., and Ebenezer Hollick, Jr., and William Curtis. The first six were trustees.

[39]The *County Poll* (14 September 1780); compared to the Baptist Church Book; The Congregational Register, RG 4/3870. *Commons, 1754-1790*, 1:218; 3:273, 682-85; *Cam. Chron.* (15 April 1780; 1, 15 June 1782) Add. MSS. 5855, f. 134.

in a population of about 7,000. From 1774 until well into the 1780s Robinson was the most visible leader of liberals in Cambridgeshire, and he, along with Joseph Saunders and a third Dissenting minister, Joseph Robinson, was clearly sympathetic to the American cause. Robinson, the Hollick family in his church, and another church member, Richard Foster, worked consistently for conciliation with the colonists, and they all signed the petition for peace.[40]

Just as at Yarmouth, the agitation in Cambridge concerning America was part of an ongoing struggle for power. The conflict, however, cannot be reduced to a contest between those in office and those out of office, because at Cambridge the corporation was divided with respect to America. The mayor and the common council sided with those who wished for peace; political principles and the meaning of the American crisis as it affected the nation seem to have been considered important. The initiative was taken by the pro-Americans on Wednesday, 8 November at the Rose Tavern. The mayor took the chair and a petition in support of peace was presented, agreed upon, and signed by most of those present, ultimately acquiring 160 signatures. One critical observer of these proceedings noted some of the petitioners' occupations and questioned what he considered to be their low social standing, but "A Friend of Peace" defended the "respectability" of the signers, and concluded that "every person that signed the Petition appears to have signed it with a full conviction of its propriety, and with a just sense of the importance of the request."[41] A week later handbills were circulated in Cambridge notifying the inhabitants that all who were inclined to subscribe to a dutiful and loyal address to his Majesty could do so at the Shire Hall. The address was signed at the hall on Friday and Saturday from ten o'clock in the morning until three in the afternoon, and it attracted ninety-six signatures altogether, including most of the aldermen and the two sitting members of Parliament, Cadogan and Jenyns.[42]

---

[40]Benjamin Flower, ed., *Miscellaneous Works of Robert Robinson* (Harlow, England: Benjamin Flower, 1807); William Robinson, ed., *Select Works of the Rev. Robert Robinson of Cambridge* (London: Heaton, 1861). Courtney S. Kenny, "A Forgotten Cambridge Meeting House," *Transactions of the Congregational Historical Society* 4 (1909-1910): 228. Andrew A. Smith, "Nonconformity in Green Street, Cambridge," *Journal of the Presbyterian Historical Society of England* 14:1 (1968): 64. Baptist Church Book, ff. 69, 4, 17. See also Josiah Thompson, ed., "History of Protestant Dissenting Congregations," 5 vols. (1772-) MSS. 38.7-11, microfilm, 1:151-80 (hereafter cited as "History"). In regard to the Dissenting ministers, see "A View of English Nonconformity," 5:209.

[41]*Lond. Chron.* (9-11 November 1775); *Lond. Eve.-Post* (11-14, 21-23 November 1775). The petition is printed in *Cam. Chron.* (9 December 1775).

[42]*Lond. Chron.* (16-18 November 1775); printed in *Cam. Chron.* (2 December 1775), HO 55/10/15. The address from the university was not agreed upon until November; *Gen. Eve. Post* (23-25 November 1775).

SOUTHAMPTON

At Southampton there also appears to be evidence that a local movement supporting independence coalesced with the American issue. The right to vote belonged to the freemen and inhabitants paying local rates, who numbered around 400, but the corporation still exercised a considerable amount of influence, and it was an unusually small body. Southampton was nevertheless somewhat open, and there was an independent party at odds with the Anglican-dominated corporation dating back to at least 1741. William Kingsbury, the Congregational minister at Southampton, was politically conservative. He petitioned in favor of relief from subscription to the Thirty-Nine Articles in 1772, but he voted for government candidates rather than the independent party's nominees in the elections of 1774 and 1790. The leadership of the Southampton independent party fell to the prominent Dissenting family of Bernard, a fact that is well illustrated in the general election of 1774.[43]

In preparation for this election, the sitting member of Parliament, Hans Stanley, worked in cooperation with the corporation and Lord North to form a coalition with John Fleming. Stanley and Fleming were opposed by Lord Charles Montagu, who won the favor of the independent voters. Montagu had been a supporter of Rockingham and was later appointed governor of South Carolina. When he decided to stand at Southampton in 1774, Lord North wrote to Dartmouth in an attempt to dissuade him. "I take it that either he is not apprised that these two gentlemen [Stanley and Fleming] have the wishes of government, or that he has not sufficiently considered how improper it is for a person in his situation to embark on any measure of opposition."[44] However improper his action may have been, Montagu refused to listen to North's advice. He went ahead with his opposition, voiced support for Wilkes, and demanded repeal of the Declaratory Act, but was badly defeated by both government candidates.[45] He received only 88 votes to his nearest opponent's

---

[43]*Commons, 1715-1754*, 1:253-54; *Commons, 1754-1790*, 1:300; the corporation consisted only of the mayor, sheriff, two bailiffs, and all who had served in those offices. "A View of English Nonconformity," 5:219; *The Poll* (Southampton, 1774), 11; *The Poll* (Southampton, 1790), 15. A. Temple Patterson, *A History of Southampton, 1700-1914. Volume One. An Oligarchy in Decline, 1700-1835* (Southampton: Southampton University Press, 1966) 65-68. Patterson ignores the place of Dissent in politics and thus misunderstands the nature of the opposition.

[44]*Commons, 1754-1790*, 3:152.

[45]Bernard Donoughue, *British Politics and the American Revolution* (London: Macmillan Co., 1964) 197. There is a story, which Namier discounts, that Montagu "had declared himself attached to the American cause and offered his services to Dr. Franklin in Paris, to take command of an army." *Commons, 1754-1790*, 3:153. The episode at Southampton suggests that Montagu may well have had sincere sympathies for America. Support for him continued among the electors through October 1775 when his petition for an undue election came before Parliament. See *Hamp. Chron.* (30 October 1775).

303, but of these 88, 19 were "plumpers"—single votes cast in a three-way contest in an attempt to secure the victory of the candidate of one's choice. Peter Bernard was a deacon in the Above Bar Congregational Chapel and an eminent member of the Bernard family. He, along with Joseph, Thomas, and William Bernard cast single votes for Montagu. After this election the Bernards continued to provide leadership for the independent party, for as late as 1790 the party was still engaged in its struggle against the corporation. When at the general election they attempted to bring in a candidate in opposition to the corporation and the government, Peter Bernard was elected the chairman of the Committee of Independence. The showing was much better in 1790 than it had been in 1774, but once again the party was defeated.[46]

The Above Bar Congregational Chapel was the largest Dissenting meeting in the borough. The Congregationalists erected a new building in 1803 that had seating for 500 people. There were also two Baptist chapels of unknown size; the first must have been small, since in 1773 it gathered only once a quarter. A General Baptist meeting house was built in 1775 and began services on 15 October. The conservatism of the Congregationalist minister, Kingsbury, is evident in his vote for government candidates, but the absence of his name on the conciliatory petition is also noteworthy, especially in light of the fact that it was signed by Samuel Trenoweth, an Anglican clergyman.[47] The Bernards, however, were as prominent in the agitation concerning America in 1775 as they had been in the election of 1774 and were to be in 1790.

In early October the corporation published advertisements calling for a meeting in Southampton to address his Majesty. The gathering assembled at the Audit-house, but during the meeting it became clear that some people opposed the plan of addressing the throne. When an address was finally agreed upon, the opponents called another meeting that evening at the Starr Inn. There, a petition from the city of Southampton that defended "the natural and Chartered Rights of our American Brethren" was set forth, and a committee

---

[46]*The Poll* (Southampton, 1774). Peter was a surgeon, Thomas and William were grocers, a second Thomas was a draper, and Joseph was a gentleman. See *Independence! or a Correct LIST of the Independent Commercial Gentlemen Tradesmen Who Voted for Mr. Dawkins on the 17th and 18th June 1790, in Support of the Glorious Independence of the Town of Southampton* (Southampton, 1790). Dawkins received 184 votes to his nearest opponent's 289. In addition to Bernard, there were at least two other Dissenters, Benjamin Johns, gentleman, and Thomas Adney Paine, attorney, who were on the twenty-three-member "Select Committee for Supporting the Independence of the Town of Southampton."

[47]Part of the register of the Above Bar Congregational Church is found in RG 4/610; 624, but the entire register in typescript used here is from the Society of Genealogists, Harrington Gardens, London. S. Stainer, *History of the Above Bar Congregational Church, Southampton, from 1622-1908* (Southampton: Southampton Times Co., 1909) 94. The Thompson List, 38.6, 14. *Hamp. Chron.* (9 October 1775). Trenoweth also "plumped" for Montagu in 1774.

was formed to oversee the collection of signatures. Within a single day, two opposing documents were advanced; the division between people was especially rancorous, leading to numerous exchanges in the press. As in other boroughs, there were charges made in the newspapers that the addressers were dependent upon the government, but opponents claimed that the petitioners belonged to the lower orders of society.[48]

The precise nature of the Bernard family's involvement in the agitation in support of peace is not known. Five of its members signed the conciliatory petition that gathered 117 signatures. In addition to signing the petition, Peter Bernard was active in the leadership opposing the coercive address for the county that originated in early November several weeks after the borough address. Bernard traveled from Southampton to the county hall in Winchester on 2 November and was one of the main speakers against the county address.[49] The borough address finally gathered only 56 signatures, but among the number were the mayor, the former mayor, two bailiffs, and the sheriff (that is, the entire corporation), and Matthew Woodford, agent of Hans Stanley, the government member of Parliament. It is also noteworthy that the conciliatory petition was presented to the Crown by John Sawbridge, member of Parliament and lord mayor-elect of London. The independent faction in favor of peace appears to have identified its local opposition to the government with American grievances, and possibly even London radicalism, just as the local corporation identified its own interests with the sovereign claims of the nation's great corporation, the House of Commons.[50]

BRIDGWATER

At Bridgwater the franchise was in the rate-paying inhabitants who numbered approximately 250. The corporation, local landowners, and the government all had an interest, and the Whigs normally controlled one seat in alliance with the corporation, with the other going to the landed interests. The corporation named the candidate in 1753 who was a government supporter, but by 1768 the corporation interest was already apparently turning away from the government, and the elections of 1768, 1780, and 1784 were contested. In the 1768 election Benjamin Allen was clearly moving into opposition, and Perceval and Allen both had the support of the corporation. Poulett, who remained on the government's side throughout this period, was the other

---

[48]Accounts in *Hamp. Chron.* (16 October 1775); *Sal. Win. J.* (16 October 1775); *Gen. Eve. Post* (14-17 October 1775); on the debate concerning the status of the petitioners, see *Hamp. Chron.* (16, 30 October, 6 November, 18 December 1775).

[49]*Hamp. Chron.* (6 November 1775); *Sal. Win. J.* (6 November 1775). William Andrews, attorney, may have been the leader of the petitioning movement in Southampton, and he does not appear to have been a Dissenter. The petition was left with him on 14 and 15 October, the days immediately preceding the official day set for its signing, *Hamp. Chron.* (16 October 1775).

[50]*Hamp. Chron.* (6 November 1775); HO 55/11/20; 11/19.

candidate. In the 1770s Allen first cultivated, then retained, the corporation's interest, and he was consistently opposed to North. Party rivalry, however, was not as clear-cut at Bridgwater as it was in other boroughs, and the shift in the corporation's orientation away from the government was not complete. In the election of 1780, when Charles James Fox and Benjamin Allen ran as opposition candidates, the corporation was divided with six votes going to the government and six to the opposition. In the same year Bridgwater was one of the boroughs to send a petition to Parliament concerning economic reform.[51]

The Whig orientation of the corporation and its movement into opposition during the American Revolution is undoubtedly related to the religious history of the borough. The Bridgwater Dissenters had started the century strong, and their influence on municipal affairs was remarkable. The large Presbyterian meeting later known as Christ Church Chapel had, in 1715, between 400 and 500 auditors, and it was ornamented at the upper end with an elevated seat for the mayor, a fact that did not escape the notice of Daniel Defoe in his tour through Somersetshire. A historian of Nonconformity later noted that the "Whole Magistracy of the Town and the principal Inhabitants" worshiped there through the end of Queen Anne's reign. But by 1773 the Presbyterian church had declined to a mere 150, and the Baptists were described as "few in number and poor in circumstances."[52] Despite this decline, however, the Dissenters still had access to local office, and the relationship between the Dissenters and the corporation seems to have remained close. The Presbyterian Robert Kennaway was collector of the customs in 1780, a lucrative and important post, and when the Dissenters rebuilt their chapel in 1788, it was once again furnished with a long pew for the use of the corporation.[53] Whether or not the capital burgesses actually attended the chapel remains uncertain, but if there was no relation between the chapel and the corporation, this provision for its presence would have seemed an empty gesture.

The strongly worded address in support of coercion appears to have circulated in the borough before the petition; in any case, it was presented to the Crown on 27 October, a week before the conciliatory petition reached London. The address and the petition divided local government in the same way that elections did, but with respect to America, most local officeholders favored conciliation. The petition was signed by Benjamin Allen and 149 other inhab-

---

[51]*Commons, 1715-1754*, 1:314; *Commons, 1754-1790*, 1:367; 2:17; 3:268. *The Poll* (Bridgwater, 1780). T. Bruce Dilks, *Charles James Fox and the Borough of Bridgwater* (Bridgwater: East Gate Press, 1907) 10.

[52]Daniel Defoe, *A Tour through the Whole Island of Great Britain*, 2 vols. (London: Dent, 1962) 1:270. Thompson, "History," 4:171. The register of the Presbyterian chapel has survived, and a handful of Quakers was resident in the borough. RG 4/142; RG 6/308.

[53]See RG 4/142 and *The Poll* (Bridgwater, 1780). Jerome Murch, *A History of the Presbyterian and General Baptist Churches in the West of England: With Memoirs of Some of Their Pastors* (London: R. Hunter, 1835) 181. It was opened 28 May 1788. George Evans, *Vestiges of Protestant Dissent* (Liverpool: F. E. Gibbons, 1897) 30.

itants, including the mayor and two-thirds of the twelve-member corporation, while the coercive address collected 100 signatures, including four members of the corporation. Whether or not there were Dissenters on the corporation at this time is unknown, but Thomas Watson, the Presbyterian minister, and Thomas Lewis, the Baptist minister, both failed to sign the conciliatory petition, even though Watson had signed the petition in 1772 asking for relief from subscribing to the Thirty-Nine Articles.[54] This is especially surprising in light of the fact that both ministers voted for Allen and Fox in 1780 and were active in leading the opposition to the government. In the 1780 poll book printed by the friends of Poulett and Acland, those who were instrumental in stirring up opposition to the government candidates are distinguished by an asterisk printed next to their name, and both Watson and Lewis are so distinguished.[55] Two Anglican clergy at Bridgwater petitioned in support of conciliation, though this must be balanced against the four clergymen who favored coercion. As at Cambridge, where a number of Dissenters were also involved in local government, the Dissenters at Bridgwater seem to have languished during the height of the agitation concerning America in 1775. But in both instances, they appear to have become more progressive in the late 1770s and early 1780s.

POOLE

Poole was a small freeman borough with about 100 electors. The corporation was influential, but it was dominated by a powerful merchant oligarchy that included many Nonconformists. A government interest was guaranteed by the presence of numerous placemen, and the borough was economically connected to the Newfoundland trade and the Carolinas. Between 1715 and 1765 government Whigs were consistently returned without a contest. The abiding influence of the Dissenters is seen in the political activity of the Presbyterian families of Henning, Tito, and Jolliff. In 1740 the mayor was R. Henning, and in 1741 he decisively influenced the return of Thomas Missing, a government Whig. Tito, who was an alderman in 1760 and whose recommendations for members of Parliament were carefully considered, declared in January 1761 that he and his friends "will vote for any person recommended by your Grace [the Duke of Newcastle] and for no one else."[56]

But in the reign of George III, the Dissenters turned against the government, and between 1765 and 1784 the borough was contested five times. Peter Jolliff, Jr., described in 1765 as having "the most interest of any person in this corporation," led a revolt against the government by attempting to bring in Joshua Mauger. He failed in 1765, but in 1768 he succeeded, and Mauger voted

---

[54]HO 55/11/34; 11/24. "A View of English Nonconformity," 5:277.

[55]*The Poll* (Bridgwater, 1780).

[56]*Commons, 1715-1754*, 1:235-36; *Commons, 1754-1790*, 1:267-71. *The History of Parliament* was unaware of the presence of the Dissenters at Poole. See W. Densham and J. Ogle, *The Story of the Congregational Churches of Dorset from Their Foundation to the Present Time* (Bournemouth: W. Mate and Sons, 1899) 191, 195.

consistently on the side of the Opposition through 1780. While Jolliff's parents were Dissenters and his birth is recorded in the Presbyterian register, his name does not appear again, and he cannot be placed firmly within the Dissenting fold.[57] It is clear, however, that the local independent party derived much support from the Nonconformists, and it remained opposed to the government throughout the American crisis. Isaac and Benjamin Lester, prominent merchants who signed the address in support of coercion, wrote to Lord Sandwich on 12 April 1776 to assure him of their attachment to the government. In exchange, they asked protection for their "persons and property," since the latter was "much injured both at home and abroad, by evil minded persons, enemies to Government," including an unnamed member of Parliament—"well known at our town"—presumably Mauger. As late as 1781 Benjamin Lester still complained of "a faction in the borough" that was opposed to the government.[58]

Three denominations subsisted at Poole during the American Revolution. The most opulent were the Presbyterians who met at Hill Street. The chapel could seat 800 auditors in 1721, and the facilities were expanded in 1767 and 1777. The drift of this congregation into Unitarianism led, in 1760, to the formation of Skinner Street Congregational Chapel, and the chapel records illustrate some continuing overlap between these two meetings. Many civic leaders of the town came from Hill Street and Skinner Street chapels, but a smaller Quaker community also had its share of wealthy merchant members.[59] The Dissenters were so actively involved in municipal politics that early in the eighteenth century they considered the possibility of rewriting the borough's charter in such a way that they could retain offices of trust without taking the oaths of allegiance to the sovereign, doubtless an illegal maneuver that was never actually attempted. In 1739 the Presbyterian pastor, Matthew Towgood, became impatient with the prevalence of conformity to qualify for office and preached a sermon against the practice, likening occasional conformists to dogs. This so incensed the more influential aldermen that they locked him out of the chapel and proceeded to secure another pastor.[60]

The borough gained some notoriety in February 1775 when it petitioned Parliament in support of the restraining bill and again in March in favor of keeping New England out of the Newfoundland fishery. Benjamin Lester spoke

[57]*Commons, 1754-1790*, 1:269-70; 2:120. RG 4/2270; the 1768 poll book has survived, but there are no poll books for the elections of 1774, 1780, and 1784.

[58]*Commons, 1754-1790*, 1:270.

[59]The Evans List, 32-34; The Thompson List, 38.6, 9. Densham and Ogle, *The Story of the Congregational Churches*, 190-92, 196, 198, 260. RG 4/464; 2270; 121; RG 6/1236; 278; 1340; 429.

[60]Densham and Ogle, *The Story of the Congregational Churches*, 191, 195. In this chapel the subscribers who contributed to the cost and maintenance of the building and the pastor's salary were not required to be members and they thus exercised great power.

in behalf of the latter petition. The Provincial Congress in Charlestown, South Carolina, interpreted these petitions from Poole as supporting the Coercive Acts. These acts added "to the heavy oppression under which the unfortunate and virtuous inhabitants of the four New England governments labour" and thus the Congress resolved that "this colony will not use or employ any shipping belonging to that port [Poole], or owned by any inhabitant there or carry on any transactions or hold any communications with that people." This resolution was printed in the *South Carolina Gazette* and subsequently reprinted in the English newspapers. The episode has been cited as an important example of the merchants' support of the government even to their own disadvantage.[61]

In the fall of 1775 Poole was one of the first boroughs in the county to address the Crown. On 20 September, in yet another vote of support for the government, the "Mayor, Aldermen, Burgesses, and Principle Inhabitants" agreed to an address in favor of coercive measures. It acquired fifty-seven signatures, including those of Isaac and Benjamin Lester and a number of corporation members.[62] A month later, following public notification, there was a second meeting at the Guildhall to petition the Crown in favor of peace, and Peter Jolliff, Jr., a sheriff, was elected chairman. The meeting unanimously resolved "that petitioning and addressing the throne, is the acknowledged privilege and undoubted right of the subjects of Great Britain, and that the proper exercise of this right is of the utmost importance, as the Sovereign is thereby informed of the real disposition of his subjects, and the true state of public affairs." Additional resolutions charged that the former petition and address to Parliament and the Crown in favor of coercion were "improperly obtained" and settled upon a petition in support of peaceful measures.[63] This petition was signed by 144 inhabitants, including two Dissenting ministers, Edward Ashburner and John Howell, and an Anglican clergyman. Here, as elsewhere, the laity also played a role in leadership.[64] It also appears that local government was divided in regard to America; though one sheriff signed the address, two others took the lead in the petition. The petition was presented to the king by the opposition member of Parliament, Joshua Mauger.

---

[61]*Parl. Hist.*, 35:164; *North. Merc.* (6 March 1775); *Lond. Chron.* (12-15 August 1775); *Sal. Win. J.* (21 August 1775); Dora Mae Clark, *British Opinion and the American Revolution* (New Haven: Yale University Press, 1930) 89-91.

[62]HO 55/8/2. The mayor, mayor elect, town clerk, town sergeant, a sheriff, five aldermen and nineteen burgesses.

[63]*Lond. Eve.-Post* (21-24 October 1775); *Sal. Win. J.* (30 October 1775).

[64]The meeting was held on 20 October. *Lond. Eve.-Post* (2-4 November 1775); RG 4/464. Samuel Fauconer, Anglican clergyman, also signed the petition, and the resolutions, noted above, claimed that the clergy of every denomination participated. See "A View of Nonconformity," 5:215; William Miller, Dissenting minister, did not sign; and regarding Jolliff as sheriff, see *Sal. Win. J.* (25 September 1775).

Newspapers provide evidence for the strength of feeling that divided this small but opulent community. In the popular mind there was far more than trade at stake in the American crisis. A wealthy Quaker, Thomas Nickleson, signed the coercive address, and he was charged by an anonymous author with deserting the pacifist principles of his denomination. In a signed essay, Nickleson argued the case for submission to the government with considerable cogency and concluded that the address was "signed by the Mayor, Aldermen, and principal inhabitants, who are Churchmen, Quakers, and Presbyterians, as their true sentiments."[65] A second signer of the address wrote that while "no man would wish to avoid such dreadful, hostile measures more than myself," if force was not used against the Americans, "we should have but a short period else this country should be subservient" to the colonies.[66] "Anti-Cataline" also wrote against the petition. He expressed concern regarding the connection between conciliation—an implied abridgment of the power of the legislative body—and contributing to popular discontent. Conciliation, in short, was bound to contribute to rebellion: "The dispute, sir, is no longer between America and Administration, it is a contention for power, with the people at large, and the meanest individual is deeply interested in the success of our troops."[67] In protest against the address supporting coercion, "a friend to Truth" recognized at length the value of trade to the port, but feared that "civil war, with all its horrors" and the "ruin of our constitution" were imminent unless the government's present measures changed in favor of peace.[68]

III

Although half or less of the petitioners in these boroughs were voters in parliamentary elections, by analyzing the behavior of those who both petitioned and voted, the political consistency of many individuals may be tested. This approach, unlike that of any survey of leadership, involves enough people to apply statistical measures of significance, and to that extent it holds more promise than traditional methods of analysis.

Early attempts to compare petitions to poll books were more impressionistic than exact. In his regional study of the west midlands, John Money discovered a notable correlation between voters in the Warwickshire election of 1774 and the loyal addressers of Birmingham in January 1775.[69] But the first

---

[65]*Lond. Eve.-Post* (3-5 October 1775).

[66]*Gen. Eve. Post* (7-10 October 1775).

[67]*Hamp. Chron.* (30 October 1775); *Sal. Win. J.* (30 October 1775); *Gen. Eve. Post* (7-9 November 1775).

[68]*Lond. Eve.-Post* (16-28 September 1775) and a second lengthy essay (7-10 October 1775).

[69]John Money, *Experience and Identity: Birmingham and the West Midlands, 1760-1800* (Manchester: Manchester University Press, 1977) 185. The first attempt to relate voters to petitioners was made by *Veritas* in *Lond. Eve.-Post* (7-9 February 1775). He compared a handful of voters in the Warwickshire election of 1774 to those who signed a counter petition.

statistical analysis made much better use of the data. In his examination of five large freeman boroughs that petitioned in the fall, John Phillips found a strong relationship between voting in favor of government candidates and addressing the Crown in support of coercive measures. At Coventry, Liverpool, and Nottingham approximately half of the electors voted for government candidates at the general election in 1774; but at Coventry, of those who voted for the government in 1774 and signed an address or petition in 1775, fully 93.4 percent signed the coercive address. At Liverpool and Nottingham the degree of consistency in political orientation was almost equally impressive (76.6 percent and 83.5 percent respectively). The figures for Bristol and Newcastle-upon-Tyne supported the same conclusion: even though a year or more separated the events of voting and petitioning, individuals behaved consistently in both political acts. Thus it seems reasonable to assume that they acted freely upon the basis of their own convictions.[70]

Large freeman boroughs were generally unencumbered by patronage or corruption, and the possibility of manipulating those who petitioned and voted was relatively slight. The same is not true, however, of smaller constituencies such as Cambridge, where the corporation had considerable influence, or Bridgwater, which was not above the influence of patrons. Yet similar patterns of consistency in political behavior over time are found in these boroughs as well (see Table 6.2).[71] Great Yarmouth and Southampton were subject to some influence, and yet the data from Great Yarmouth comports well with what was found in the larger boroughs. There appears to have been some inconsistency among the petitioners at Southampton; more conciliatory petitioners voted for the government candidates in 1774 than for the opposition candidate. However, while Montague was clearly in opposition to the government in 1774, America was not a major issue in the election. Moreover, it was always difficult to maintain a strict party vote in a three-way contest, since electors were reluctant to give up one of their votes. There was a small minority that did act consistently at Southampton; of the nineteen single votes cast for Montague in 1774, fourteen signed the pro-American petition the following year.

The statistics from Yarmouth and Southampton suggest that pro-American sentiment was held strongly, but nonetheless somewhat less consistently than the convictions of progovernment voters. The larger proportion of petitioners who split their votes at Southampton may also reflect more ambivalence on the part of pro-Americans than among those who supported the government. Even in the three small boroughs in Table 6.2 where one might

---

[70]Phillips, "Popular Politics," 618-20.

[71]Note that resident voters alone were counted. See nn. 23, 36, 46, 51 and 57 above for the poll books. Using x^2, the data from Great Yarmouth, Cambridge, Southampton, and Bridgwater yields a significant statistical difference at .01 level of probability. The figures for Poole are too small to be useful. The strength of the relationship between voting and petitioning in the first four boroughs, using Yule's Q, is .86, .77, .95, and .69 respectively.

expect to find more manipulation of political activity, there was some agreement between voters and petitioners—especially at Cambridge where America was an important issue in the election of 1774. The figures for Bridgwater and Poole are somewhat less clear, and this is what one would expect to find, given the nature of the local settings. The only borough in Table 6.2 that did not divide in 1774 was Bridgwater, and America was not a strong issue during the election for which a poll book survives. (There were opposition candidates in 1768 at Poole and in 1780 at Bridgwater.) The number of voters in Poole who were also petitioners or addressers was small, and the high percentage of split votes at both Bridgwater and Poole renders the comparison to the petitions less useful.[72]

An analysis of these five boroughs has pointed to a number of consistent patterns at the level of leadership and suggested strong parallels in terms of local disputes concerning patronage, officeholding, and social status. The Dissenters did not comprise the majority of petitioners in any of the boroughs, but the leaders were typically involved in a local struggle against Anglican-dominated corporations allied with the government, and they were repeatedly the losers in parliamentary elections. Among the laity, the Hurrys, the Bernards, and the Jolliffs took an active part in leadership, and at Cambridge this role fell to the Baptist minister, Robert Robinson. There appears to be considerable congruence from borough to borough between these independent, minority

TABLE 6.2

ELECTORS WHO VOTED AND PETITIONED COMPARED TO ALL VOTERS					
BOROUGHS AND DATE OF ELECTION	POSITION TAKEN IN ELECTION	PROPORTION OF ALL RESIDENT VOTERS		COERCIVE ADDRESSERS WHO VOTED	CONCILIATORY PETITIONERS WHO VOTED
Great Yarmouth (1777)	Government	502	71.6%	78	92.9%	27	34.6%
	Opposition	199	28.4%	6	7.1%	51	63.4%
Cambridge (1774)	Government	37	45.7%	23	88.5%	2	7.7%
	Opposition	41	50.6%	3	11.5%	22	84.6%
	Split	3	3.7%	-----	-------	2	7.7%
Southampton (1774)	Government	301	77.2%	40	93 %	37	48.7%
	Opposition	24	6.2%	1	2.3%	25	32.9%
	Split	65	16.7%	2	4.7%	14	18.4%
Bridgwater (1780)	Government	75	42.4%	38	73 %	20	25 %
	Opposition	68	38.4%	7	13.5%	46	57.5%
	Split	34	19.2%	7	13.5%	14	17.5%
Poole (1768)	Government	36	38.7%	7	25 %	1	11.1%
	Opposition	20	21.5%	7	25 %	3	33.3%
	Split	37	39.8%	14	50 %	5	55.6%

[72]At Poole thirty-seven addressers and petitioners who voted, however, do represent 40 percent of the electorate.

factions excluded from the perquisites of local office and their support of the American colonists. That their local struggle for recognition helped to motivate their sympathy for the colonists would seem beyond dispute, but this can only be established by further study of the petitioners at the individual level.

The data from subscription lists are useful in determining the seriousness of the petitioners' convictions, and poll books are valuable in establishing their political consistency more concretely. At least those petitioners who were subscribers and voters took their actions seriously. Subscribers dramatically underscored the intention behind their signatures with their financial contributions, and voters against the government could have expected nothing from the government in return for their actions. People seem to have understood their political statements as valid expressions of their opinion. No one will deny that some petitioners were influenced by the government or by local patrons, but sweeping negative evaluations of petitioning activity are clearly inappropriate. The organization of borough and county meetings, the geographical provenance of the petitions, the financial backing of coercive measures, and a comparison to electoral data all support the contention that many, if not most, signers of addresses and petitions acted on the basis of serious political conviction. These analyses, however, have served for the most part the negative purpose of answering charges that the documents had no relation to public opinion, or worse, that they actually misrepresented it.

If the question of the manipulation of popular opinion by direct external influence can be answered satisfactorily, much remains to be discovered about the inner motivation of the petitioners themselves. Even when combined, geography, subscription lists, and poll books do not tell us a great deal about why petitioners behaved consistently. To establish political consistency and strength of conviction is one thing; to explain this conviction requires an attempt to discern what lies behind a particular behavior. A few contemporary observers were reluctant to dismiss the petitioners, and they sometimes probed further than modern historians in an attempt to account for the petitioners' behavior. They showed a vital interest in the government influence of specific individuals, their socioeconomic status, and their religious affiliation. Answers to questions concerning the background of individuals will alone provide a satisfactory explanation of popular agitation with respect to America.

Petitioners and Addressers: Government Influence, Economic Status, and Religion

Chapter VII

The petitions to the Crown in 1775 offer twenty-four different locales in which to assess the background of individual petitioners.[1] This allows for a comparative analysis of the nature of the division in selected settings. Contemporary observers commonly focused upon three possible explanations for the petitioners' behavior: government influence, socioeconomic status, and religion. As with newspaper accounts generally, there was no attempt at a comprehensive survey along these lines, but the mass of data that is available for analysis invites further investigation. For the larger boroughs and counties the bulk of detail remains daunting, but medium-sized and small boroughs illustrate the same issues as those found in the large constituencies. A survey of the available records and the kinds of questions that contemporaries posed will serve as an introduction to an analysis of individual petitioners.

I

Government contracts and sinecures comprised an important form of influence that may have shaped the opinion of some who addressed the Crown. A comparison of large government contractors involved in provisioning and paying troops in America with the London merchants' address is readily made. Almost predictably, only one contractor was found on the conciliatory petition, while there were six who signed the coercive address.[2] Other boroughs also reveal an obvious connection between government officeholding and

---

[1] The signatures from the conciliatory petitions of Southwark, Worcester, and Bolton (Tables 3.1-3.2) are apparently no longer extant; of the counties, the signatures for Hampshire, Stafford, Cumberland, and Norfolk conciliatory petitions are missing (Table 3.3).

[2] *Commons, 1754-1790*, 1:136, provides a list of twenty-four large government contractors. The one is William Baker; the six are Richard Atkinson, William Devaynes, John Durand, Thomas Harley, John Henniker, and George Wombwell. The name John Stephenson appears in both lists. John A. Sainsbury, "The Pro-American Movement in London, 1769-1782; Extra-Parliamentary Opposition to the Government's American Policy" (Ph.D. dissertation, McGill University, 1975) Appendices A and B, does not distinguish between contractors and placemen and finds sixty-four altogether in two ministerial addresses.

expressions of support for the use of force in America. The land waiters of the port of Bristol, for example, subscribed £21 to the government fund; three customs collectors can also be identified as both signers of the coercive address and subscribers to the fund, and there were undoubtedly many more.[3] In most local settings, however, the normal channel for government patronage was the borough corporation, and it is therefore not surprising that critics sometimes dismissed all the coercive documents together as "corporation addresses."[4]

The most frequent point of interaction between national and local politics in the eighteenth century centered around the endemic conflict between corporation and anticorporation parties. When a corporation supported a government candidate for Parliament, a local anticorporation party often put forth an opposition candidate, and a national issue such as America was thus a natural attraction for anticorporation sentiment. The politics of eight large freeman boroughs turned on the conflict between corporation and anticorporation parties, and of these eight, it can hardly be coincidental that seven were deeply divided concerning America.[5] This phenomenon, however, was by no means limited to the larger boroughs. There are hints of such a connection at Portsmouth, where concern was expressed in 1775 over the "monopolizing" tendency of local government, and at Winchester, where the "constitutional club" suffered a defeat at the hands of the mayor.[6] Attention must therefore be given to how local politics, and especially corporations, interacted with parliamentary politics on the one hand, and popular politics on the other.

Studies that have interpreted the American crisis as merely a local issue have neglected the way in which the popular mind linked local matters to national crises. The outpouring of addresses and petitions testifies to the connection, but there are a number of instances where this implicit link was made explicit. The connection between corporations and the central government cannot be reduced to a matter of pecuniary interest; there was an ideological connection as well. At Bristol, for example, upon his resignation from the office of mayor, Charles Hoskin addressed the corporation in the following terms: "The internal policy here has very little to do with the business of the state, yet whatever may tend to strengthen the hands of authority either supreme or *subordinate* is surely an object worthy of the attention of the most respectable corporation this day in the kingdom. It was from this consideration, that I wished to see a dutiful, affectionate and loyal address presented to the throne from the magis-

---

[3]*Brist. J.* (30 December 1775; 6 January, 16 March 1776).

[4]*Lond. Eve.-Post* (21-23 September 1775); *Lond. Chron.* (4-7 November 1775).

[5]Colchester, Coventry, Liverpool, Nottingham, Worcester, Exeter, Leicester, and Norwich. Of these, the first five sent both coercive and conciliatory documents; Exeter was divided in 1776 and America may have played a role in this; on Leicester, see ch. 3 above. It is known that there was pro-American sentiment in Norwich in early 1775 and again in 1778. *Commons, 1754-1790,* 1:15, 253.

[6]*Hamp. Chron.* (20 November, 9 December 1775).

tracy of this opulent and flourishing city, and presum'd to call a house for that purpose."[7] In the American crisis, local government, just as the national government, had an obvious concern for the strengthening of authority.

Similar perceptions from an opposing perspective can be seen at Worcester. After the corporation sent up an address in favor of coercive measures, an application "by some respectable citizens" was made to the mayor for the use of the town hall, "that the citizens might deliberate on a dutiful and respectful Petition to the Throne." The mayor of Worcester refused this application, and at the meeting of petitioners at Tom's Coffee House that followed, it was resolved "that the Mayor of this city, in having refused to the Citizens the use of their Town Hall, for the purpose of deliberating on a dutiful Petition to the Throne, has, by such refusal, deprived the Citizens of their just rights." The injustice of the mayor's action, and the address of the corporation, which was said by the petitioners to be "smuggled" to the Crown as a "delusive" misrepresentation, were tied in the popular mind to the central government's producing "the present unhappy disturbances in America."[8]

The association of local corporate interests with support for the authority of the central government was not uncommon. The corporation of Bewdley, for example, not only addressed the Crown, but it followed this corporate act by electing Lord North a burgess of the borough "in consideration of his great and meritorious services in his administration of the public affairs of this country."[9] North was also the recorder of the borough of Taunton, and when the anticorporation party won a victory in 1775 over the corporation party's candidates in a contested election return, the Unitarian minister and historian of the borough, Joshua Toulmin, noted that "this determination gave great satisfaction to the county as well as to that part of the town, who had asserted their own privileges against the combined influence of the minister and the corporation."[10] Himself a signer of the petition for peace in 1775, Toulmin later wrote, "Corporate bodies have not, in general, proved themselves the most exact and faithful trustees," and with the corporation of Taunton and Parliament in view, he concluded: "The evils arising from a body of men being separated from the community, united by an independent interest or divided by mutual jealousies, the abuse of power connected with such constitutions, and the advantages which a corrupt minister may derive from their influence, have been, in many instances too visible to escape the observation of the most careless."[11] Just as local vested interests associated their values with Parliament and the Crown, local opponents to these interests at Worcester and Taunton were concerned

---

[7]*Brist. J.* (30 September 1775).

[8]*Lond. Eve.-Post* (9-11 November 1775); *Morn. Chron.* (30 October 1775).

[9]*Brist. J.* (25 November 1775).

[10]Joshua Toulmin, *The History of the Town of Taunton, in the County of Somerset* (Taunton, 1791) 90.

[11]Ibid., 64-65.

not only with their own rights, but also the rights of their fellow citizens across the sea.

The economic status of petitioners was a second major concern of contemporary observers. Essayists sometimes associated the addressers with property and the petitioners with the inferior orders, but it was equally common to point to the dependence of many addressers.[12] Was there, then, a class division underlying the political division? Rudé thought that pro-Americanism did not reach the lower orders and argued that the smaller craftsmen, journeymen, and urban wage earners were not yet supporters of liberty.[13] The American petitions provide the first real possibility of examining this thesis in detail. Unlike the Wilkes petitions, there were almost no marks in place of signatures in the petitions to the Crown concerning America, thus implying a higher level of literacy. But this fact is difficult to interpret and may simply reflect the urban orientation of the latter agitation.[14]

The most common means of distinguishing a person's economic status in the eighteenth century was his occupation. The coercive address from Newcastle-upon-Tyne, for example, listed the occupations of all but a few of the 168 signers, but it was the only document to do so. One interested party went to the trouble to determine the occupations and the annual rental paid by forty-five Middlesex addressers and twenty-two petitioners. The differences between the two are striking. The former paid an average yearly rental of £40 and the latter only £12.5.[15] It is impossible to know how representative this small four percent sample was, but on the surface it seems that there might well have been fewer respectable names among the pro-Americans. The movement for conciliation was in some ways far more radical than the pro-Wilkes movement; by the fall of 1775 a considerable amount of British property had been destroyed.

---

[12]Regarding the social status of petitioners and addressers at Middlesex, Cambridge, Lancashire, Westbury, Trowbridge, and Southampton, see *Lond. Eve.-Post* (3-5 October, 11-14 November, 26-28 December 1775); *Bath. Chron.* (21 December 1775); *Hamp. Chron.* (11, 18 December 1775). But in an equal number of cases, it was believed that the coercive addressers were poorer. See, for Poole, Winchester, Carlisle, Great Yarmouth, Southampton, and Southwark, *Lond. Eve.-Post* (5-7, 19-21 October 1775); *Cumb. Pacq.* (4 January 1776); *Pub. Adv.* (19 October 1775); *Sal. Win. J.* (13 November 1775); *Hamp. Chron.* (11 December 1775).

[13]George Rudé, *Wilkes and Liberty* (Oxford: Oxford University Press, 1962) 197-98.

[14]Rudé found 953 marks among the 37,224 county petitioners, and 157 marks among the 13,457 borough petitioners. *Wilkes and Liberty*, 211. The only petitions to have marks in the American agitation were the Bridgwater and Lancashire conciliatory.

[15]See *Pub. Adv.* (19 October 1775). "Numa" also listed the amount of estate in yearly value for the forty-five addressers, and the average is an impressive £221.69. This assessment was contested by a "Freeholder" who listed the occupations of twenty-nine addressers and pled for an objective view of which group was "more respectable." *Lond. Eve.-Post* (19-21 October 1775).

Some tentative steps have recently been taken to analyze the occupational standing of addressers and petitioners in two large urban settings. John Sainsbury determined the occupations of forty-six percent of the London merchants who addressed or petitioned by comparing signatures to directories and poll books, but he concluded there was no significant difference in occupational structure between the two groups.[16] This is not surprising since, of all the contrasting documents from a single setting, the address and petition from London alone purported to draw from a single occupational category, namely the merchants. Peter Marshall examined the Manchester directories of 1772, 1773, and 1781 in relation to the Manchester signatures of the Lancashire petition, and on the basis of occupations, he concluded that Manchester "divided along social and economic lines." People belonging to higher, more respectable occupational categories were found in greater numbers among the addressers than the petitioners.[17] These occupational analyses, however, are highly impressionistic and lacking in methodological rigor. Nevertheless, because of the paucity of extant tax assessments, occupational labels hold the most promise for social assessment of petitioners in most boroughs.

Finally, it was commonly believed in the eighteenth century that there was a religious division underlying the addresses and petitions.[18] The religious dimension of these documents may help answer why the colonial policy of George III and the Ministry was perceived in some quarters as a revival of Toryism. At the heart of the popular belief in a resurgence of Toryism was the question of religion. The fear of episcopal authority clearly influenced developments in the colonies, and it may have been this same fear that led low churchmen and Dissenters in England to view events at Westminster as especially menacing. The question of religion, however, has been neglected by modern scholarship and recently even discounted.[19] An exception to this neglect is Paul Langford's

---

[16]John A. Sainsbury, "The Pro-Americans of London, 1769-1782," *William and Mary Quarterly* 3rd ser., 35 (July 1978): 447.

[17]Peter Marshall, "Manchester and the American Revolution," *Bulletin of the John Rylands University Library of Manchester* 62 (Autumn 1979): 173.

[18]Concerning the belief that the Dissenters were behind the petitions, see *Lond. Chron.* (28-30 September 1775); *Gen. Eve. Post* (12-14, 26-28 December 1775); *Pub. Adv.* (4 November 1775); and *Cumb. Pacq.* (19 October 1775). Anglicans were viewed as behind the addresses; see *Bath. J.* (16 October 1775). For a brief statement of this traditional view, see Arthur L. Cross, *The Anglican Episcopate and the American Colonies* (New York: Longmans, Green and Co., 1902) and Carl Bridenbaugh, *Mitre and Scepter* (Oxford: Oxford University Press, 1962); and regarding the Dissenters, Dora Mae Clark, *British Opinion and the American Revolution* (New Haven: Yale University Press, 1930) 169, 258.

[19]It is said there appears to have been no "specific Anglican attitude towards the American War," *Commons, 1754-1790*, 1:115, and Sainsbury has downplayed any possible connection to Dissent, "The Pro-Americans of London," 450. In my earlier survey of the issue, I was also skeptical of the connection. See "Whigs and Nonconformists: Slumbering Radicalism in English Politics, 1739-1789," *Eighteenth-Century Studies* 9 (Fall 1975): 24.

essay on the coercive addressers and the rise of a new authoritarianism. Langford examined the rhetoric of the addresses and concluded that the high Anglican religious component of these documents was "deeply significant."[20] Just as corporations felt the need to uphold authority in a revolutionary setting, so did the Anglican Church. An anonymous letter dated 10 October 1775 at Bristol asked, "Can the clergy remain silent spectators, when the church is equally in danger with the State?"[21] It has long been recognized that since the Dissenters were handicapped in local officeholding by the Test and Corporation Acts, they were often the source of local anticorporation sentiment in parliamentary boroughs.[22] Thus the issue of religion brings us full circle to the question of corporate vested interests and government influence.

The Anglican clergy characteristically indicated their status in the addresses with the addition of "vicar," "curate," or more commonly "clerk" to their names. In the petitions from the eleven boroughs in Table 3.1, for example, there is a total of sixty-one Anglican clergy; of these, fifty-eight signed the coercive addresses and only three signed the conciliatory petitions. It is possible to locate twenty-nine Dissenting ministers in the same documents, and only two signed the addresses, while the remaining twenty-seven appealed for conciliation.[23] The lower Anglican clergy in the provinces added their voice to the majority of bishops in the House of Lords, and it is entirely likely that in the popular mind this provided the connection between the old Toryism and what was viewed as a new authoritarianism. Since the Dissenters were the quintessential Whigs, there appears to be some semblance of truth, at least from the local, popular standpoint, in the notion of the reality of a revived Toryism. But the crucial question in this regard has to do with the behavior of the laity. The laity's political orientation may be tested by comparing the signatures in the addresses and petitions to the Dissenters' nonparochial registers of births and baptisms. If the laity as well as the clergy divided on the basis of religion, then there may be some substance to the long-discounted claim of G. M. Trevelyan that local political rivalry and party continuity was largely a product of the religious rivalry of Church and chapel.[24]

---

[20]Paul Langford, "Old Whigs, Old Tories and the American Revolution," *Journal of Imperial and Commonwealth History* 8 (January 1980): 125.

[21]*Brist. J.* (18 November 1775).

[22]*Commons, 1754-1790*, 1:15, 19.

[23]These ministers' names are found in the petition sent to Parliament in 1772 for relief from subscription to the Thirty-Nine Articles. See "A View of English Nonconformity in 1773" in *The Transactions of the Congregational Historical Society* 5 (1911-1912): 205-385.

[24]G. M. Trevelyan, "The Two-Party System in English Political History," Romanes Lecture of 1926, in *An Autobiography and Other Essays* (London: Longmans, Green and Co., 1949) 199.

II

With the exception of Cambridge, all the boroughs examined in chapter six were port cities with numerous custom-house officials and revenue officers. Most government patronage was channeled through the corporation, local landed interests, or recognized government agents. Crewe's Act of 1782 disenfranchised customs officers, but before that date, officers could vote in parliamentary elections and they could obviously petition the Crown. Minor patronage was an important means of the central government's influence, and the charge was frequently made that progovernment addresses were supported mainly by placemen. A critic of the Yarmouth address, for example, noted that the proponents of coercion influenced everyone they could to sign it, "such as Placemen and those who are in want; of which we have a great many."[25] Since Yarmouth and Southampton corporations were unified concerning the American crisis, it would be highly useful to know how directly this unity was related to patronage. There is little information available for Yarmouth and Bridgwater, but all of the holders of minor government offices who signed the addresses at Southampton and Poole were listed in the newspapers.

An essay appeared in the *London Evening-Post* written by an inhabitant of Southampton (signed "S.R.") that listed the places, pensions, and family connections of thirty-six of the fifty-six signatories of the coercive address.[26] Twenty-seven people who signed the address (48%) were being paid directly by the government; these included nine customs officers (landwaiters, searchers, and surveyors); four captains and lieutenants in the navy, and an equal number of officers in half pay; two people with places in the Stamp Office; and an assorted group of commissaries, commissioners, and adjutants. In addition to these, there were two government contractors and five men who were relatives to these placemen and contractors. Only four persons in the list of thirty-six were not actually dependent in some way upon the government: Philip Lempriere was simply "a friend of Dr. Shebbeare's" (Shebbeare was a government pamphleteer); John Read, "a no pay colonel, wanting a fresh commission"; John Skerer "wanting a place in the Custom House"; and William Thring, "bull-dog to the present members for the town." The entire list appears to be accurate; five of the attributions can be confirmed from the poll book for 1774 and from the address itself.[27] The address, as previously noted, was signed by the corporation, but only the sheriff was a placeman.

A similar listing appeared in the *General Evening Post* for the coercive address from Poole. "A.B." of Poole found that nineteen of the fifty-seven ad-

---

[25]*Pub. Adv.* (19 October 1775).

[26]*Lond. Eve.-Post* (28-31 October 1775). An independent essay in *Hamp. Chron.* (16, 30 October 1775) refers to the addressers as pensioners, placemen, gentlemen in waiting, custom-house officers, and their dependents. See also *Sal. Win. J.* (13 November 1775).

[27]*The Poll* (Southampton, 1774); HO 55/11/19.

dressers, or thirty-three percent, were in government pay.[28] This included eleven who were landwaiters, coastwaiters, tide-surveyors and clerks in the Custom House, and the deputy controller. The address bore the signatures of the collector of the window tax, three half-pay officers in the navy and marines, two placemen, and one pensioner. In addition to these nineteen, Thomas Wise and Adam Wadham were said to be "wanting places." As noted above, ten corporation members signed this address and there was a good deal of overlap between placemen and the corporation; three of the five aldermen had places in the revenue, and a fourth received a government pension.[29]

In each of the boroughs examined, the corporation had connections with the government that made it natural for local placemen to find their security in the central government. It is not surprising to see addresses in support of Parliament's sovereignty and coercive measures emerging from these corporate bodies. Wherever there was an abundance of government patronage, a significant proportion of the addressers were probably on the government payroll, or were related to those who were. This may apply to the addresses from Yarmouth, Bridgwater, Kingston-upon-Hull, and Trinity House at Hull, Plymouth, Barnstaple, Huntingdon, and Rye, for in each case, the government had a strong local interest. The unsigned addresses from the corporations of Andover and Christchurch probably had the support of numerous local placemen.[30] Even in these cases, however, many—possibly more than half—of all addressers did not receive emoluments from the government, and these addressers must be accounted for as well. Few boroughs were as rich in government patronage as Southampton and Poole, and even the opinion of placemen cannot be dismissed as invalid or unimportant without further consideration.

Corporate interests, it is true, were anything but representative of English public opinion. It is equally true that corporations were least representative in those settings where the government gave lucrative gifts. The addresses from these corporations reflect not only a natural affinity of corporate bodies with Parliament, but a predictable link between government gifts and political conservatism. Corporations had the weight of property and respectability behind them, and in pursuing coercive measures against malcontents George III seemed clearly to be cultivating these conservative interests. It must also be emphasized, however, that the corporations of Cambridge, Bridgwater, and Poole were divided concerning America, and this suggests that there were complicating economic, religious, and ideological factors at work in the division of English

---

[28]*Gen. Eve. Post* (5-7 October 1775) dated 2 October 1775.

[29]Three of these attributions are confirmed from the address itself and a notice in *Sal. Win. J.* (25 September 1775). "A.B." 's list of names with places was never publicly contested, and the later public resolutions of 20 October claimed the same of the addressers, "nineteen are placemen or pensioners." *Lond. Eve.-Post* (21-24 October 1775).

[30]See Tables 3.1 and 3.6 above, and *Commons, 1754-1790*, 1:435, 367, 258, 251, 312, 453, 293, 294.

society. Government sinecures and corporate interests finally account for only a small proportion of the support George III received from the English people.

III

In none of the five boroughs is there anything approaching comprehensive tax records for the period of the American Revolution. A considerable amount of information concerning the occupations of inhabitants, however, can be derived from the poll books and baptismal registers. The historian who wishes to utilize such occupational data for the purpose of social analysis is confronted at the outset by two notoriously difficult problems. First, there is the issue of determining a small number of general occupational categories that can be related convincingly to social structure. Second, hundreds of specific occupations must be subsumed under half-a-dozen or so occupational categories. The question of occupational categories as indicators of wealth has recently received a great deal of attention, and there appears to be a growing consensus that such categories as merchant, shopkeeper, and artisan may validly be used to classify people in terms of wealth and social status.[31] The second, related question of which occupation belongs in which category will always lead to some disagreement, but differences can be minimized by a careful use of eighteenth-century trade manuals.

The studies of English social structure advanced by Gregory King in 1688, Joseph Massie in 1756-1765, and Patrick Colquhon in 1801-1803 are commonly used to determine general occupational categories. Of the three, the analyses of Massie have been the least studied, even though his estimates for

---

[31]Jackson T. Main, *The Social Structure of Revolutionary America* (Princeton: Princeton University Press, 1965) 68, was followed by the massive documentation of Alice H. Jones in *American Colonial Wealth: Documents and Methods*, 3 vols. (New York: Arno Press, 1977) in which the same clear relation between wealth and occupational category emerged (3:2007-14). With respect to England, the first study to link occupational data to probate inventories was Peter H. Lindert, "English Occupations, 1670-1811," *Journal of Economic History* 40 (December 1980) in which, through a comparison of parish registers and probate returns, Lindert concluded that the latter "give a clear and consistent wealth ranking to the major occupational groups" (694). See also Lindert, "An Algorithm for Probate Sampling," *Journal of Interdisciplinary History* 11 (Spring 1981): 663. John A. Phillips in *Electoral Behavior in Unreformed England: Splitters, Plumpers, and Straights* (Princeton: Princeton University Press, 1982) compared land-tax returns and poor-rate records to occupational categories in Norwich and Maidstone and here too there was a relation between economic and occupational rank (199). Most recently, L. D. Schwarz and L. J. Jones, "Wealth, Occupations, and Insurance in the Late Eighteenth Century: The Policy Registers of the Sun Fire Office," *The Economic History Review* 36 (August 1983): 371-72, demonstrated that there were distinctions in wealth between merchants and artisans.

the entire nation were recently judged more accurate than those of King.[32] Massie's accuracy and his proximity to the American Revolution make his assessment the most natural point of departure for this study. On three occasions between 1756 and 1765, he published estimates of the annual income and the taxes of families of different ranks, degrees, or classes. He did not utilize specific occupations, but he clearly thought in terms of occupational categories. Massie listed twelve categories, which in order of appearance are: 1. spiritual and temporal lords; 2. merchants; 3. tradesmen; 4. master manufacturers; 5. clergymen, law, and liberal arts; 6. civil and military officers; 7. innkeepers and ale sellers; 8. freeholders; 9. farmers; 10. manufacturers of wood and iron; 11. laborers; and 12. common seamen and soldiers.[33]

These categories can be readily reduced to six, and ordered hierarchically on the basis of the data that Massie gave for range of yearly income. Items one, five, and six can be combined on the grounds of contemporary usage that associated gentlemen with the professions. Freeholders and farmers may be put in a special category since so few agricultural occupations were encountered in this study. Master manufacturers and journeymen artisans are, under most circumstances, impossible to distinguish from each other, and so items four and ten are combined under the rubric *artisans*. Finally, all specific occupations found in Massie's works are subsumed under generic categories: innkeepers and seamen are put with categories three and eleven respectively. The resulting sixfold categorization of 1. gentlemen, professions; 2. merchants (wholesalers); 3. shopkeepers (tradesmen, retailers); 4. artisans (master and journeymen manufacturers); 5. laborers; and 6. other, including freeholders and farmers, is broadly compatible with most other studies of this period, though it is purposely organized to reveal economic rank, while other categorizations emphasize differences in types of manufacturing.[34] The impreci-

---

[32]Regarding Massie, see Peter Mathias, "The Social Structure in the Eighteenth Century: a Calculation by Joseph Massie," *Economic History Review* 10:1 (1957): 30-45. Mathias's positive but cautious assessment of Massie, 37-41, should be read in light of Lindert's research, "English Occupations," 688, 707.

[33]These are drawn from a broadside entitled *A Computation of the Money* (1760) in the University of Cambridge Library. Two of Massie's pamphlets set forth essentially the same categorization, though merchant and master manufacturer are missing from the first: *Calculations of the Present Taxes Yearly Paid by a Family of Each Rank, Degree, or Class*, 2d ed. (London, 1761); *Brief Observations and Calculations on the Present High Prices* (London, 1765). His estimates of wages changed slightly from pamphlet to pamphlet. For example, his London tradesmen's income ranged from £100-300 in his second edition of the *Calculations of the Present Taxes*, and from £100-400 in the broadside of 1760. This is obviously not related to any actual change in income, but reflects the roughness of his estimate. Mathias, "The Social Structure," 42-43 reproduces Massie's broadside somewhat less exactly.

[34]Regarding the professions, see Geoffrey Holmes, *Augustan England: Professions, State and Society, 1680-1730* (London: George Allen & Unwin, 1982). Massie clearly

sion of these categories should be fully recognized, but they may yet be useful in revealing wide economic differences between addressers and petitioners. Contemporaries believed one could generalize from occupational categories to socioeconomic rank. "A Lover of Truth" reacted to Edmund Burke and the Bristol petitioners by observing

> It is hereby offered to you and your partisans, that those who signed the Petition, and those who signed the Address, may put the addition of profession, trade and calling, to their respective names, that the public in general, who are strangers to our town, may be in some degree able to judge who are the tag, rag, and bob-tail of it, and who have a *real* interest in its tranquillity, trade, and commerce, and therefore most likely to give counsel or use arms for *honest* and *good* purposes.[35]

Recent research in voting behavior during the American Revolution has revealed little evidence that economic cleavage in the electorate impinged upon partisan choice. This contradicts the claim often made that voting behavior in the eighteenth century was related to socioeconomic status. In an examination of Maidstone, John Phillips concluded that there was no "measurable relationship linking an elector's social status and his choice of parties." At the 1780 election in Norwich, the middling ranks of society were more disposed toward the opposition than the elite, but not dramatically so. Though America was an issue in 1774 at Maidstone and in 1780 at Norwich, in neither borough was there any evidence of a link between partisan behavior and the lower ranks.[36]

This evidence of the failure of voters to divide on economic grounds in regard to the conflict with America is borne out by an analysis of the electorates of Yarmouth, Southampton, and Bridgwater. By arranging the electors by vote and occupation, the data from these boroughs confirms Phillips's findings (see

---

reflects contemporary usage in the distinctions he makes between generic categories, usage that is readily confirmed from such reference works as R. Campbell, *The London Tradesman* (London, 1747); Richard Rolt, *A New Dictionary of Trade and Commerce*, 2d ed. (London, 1761) see entries "apprentice," "merchant," "shopkeeper"; Wyndham Beawes, *Lex Mercatoria Rediviva: or, The Merchants Directory*, 4th ed. (London, 1783) 31; and Samuel Johnson, *A Dictionary of the English Language*, 6th ed. (London, 1785) entries on "manufacturer" and "artisan." J. F. Pound, "The Social and Trade Structure of Norwich, 1525-1575," *Past and Present* 34 (July 1966): 67-69; and Leslie A. Clarkson, *The Pre-Industrial Economy in England, 1500-1750* (London: Batsford, 1971) drawing upon Pound, 88-92. Lindert, "English Occupations," 688, Table 1, 663. The sixfold categorization is compatible with the studies that shed the most light on the eighteenth-century electorate; Phillips, *Electoral Behavior*, 321-22; Thomas R. Knox, "Popular Politics and Provincial Radicalism: Newcastle-upon-Tyne, 1769-1785," *Albion* 11 (Fall 1979): 237.

[35]*Gen. Eve. Post* (21-24 October 1775). Similarly, the occupations of twenty-nine Middlesex addressers and twenty-two of the Winchester corporation addressers are listed by critics to show the mean social standing of government supporters. *Lond. Eve.-Post* (19-21 October 1775).

[36]Phillips, *Electoral Behavior*, 263, 268, 270, 144, 145.

table 7.1).[37] In Yarmouth and Southampton America was raised as a political issue, though as with Maidstone and Norwich it was only one of several issues. At Yarmouth there was slightly greater support for the government candidates among the elite, and for the opposition candidate among the artisans, but this was hardly impressive and the differences are not statistically significant. The high proportion of split votes at Southampton renders the results somewhat

TABLE 7.1

OCCUPATIONAL STRUCTURE OF RESIDENT ELECTORATES					
	GOVERNMENT		OPPOSITION		SPLIT
Great Yarmouth, 1777					
1. Gentlemen, Professions	61	15.8%	7	4.6%	
2. Merchants	22	5.7%	11	7.2%	
3. Shopkeepers	53	13.7%	22	14.4%	
4. Artisans	149	38.6%	78	51%	
5. Laborers	101	26.2%	35	22.9%	
Cambridge, 1774					
1. Gentlemen, Professions	7	18.5%	2	4.9%	1
2. Merchants	13	34.2%	4	9.7%	1
3. Shopkeepers	10	26.3%	22	53.7%	1
4. Artisans	6	15.8%	11	26.8%	---
5. Laborers	2	5.3%	2	4.9%	---
Southampton, 1774					
1. Gentlemen, Professions	114	39.1%	9	42.9%	10	16.1%
2. Merchants	9	3.1%	0	0%	2	3.2%
3. Shopkeepers	54	18.6%	3	14.3%	26	41.9%
4. Artisans	88	30.2%	5	23.8%	21	33.9%
5. Laborers	26	8.9%	4	19%	3	4.8%
Bridgwater, 1780					
1. Gentlemen, Professionals	10	18.5%	9	16.7%	4	11.8%
2. Merchants	1	1.9%	5	9.3%	3	8.8%
3. Shopkeepers	23	42.6%	15	27.8%	14	41.2%
4. Artisans	16	29.6%	23	42.6%	11	32.4%
5. Laborers	2	3.7%	2	3.7%	1	2.9%
6. Other	2	3.7%	---	---	1	2.9%

[37]See, for the poll books, ch. 6, nn. 23, 36, 46, 51, and 57 above.

less revealing, and at Bridgwater the differences between occupational strata were even less.[38]

When we turn to Cambridge, however, there is some suggestion of economic stratification. Cadogan and Jenyns received half of their support from the upper two categories, while Byde and Meeke received more than three-quarters of their support from the lower three ranks. Cambridge was a smaller borough, but more important, the American issue was far more prominent at Cambridge in 1774 than it was at Yarmouth and Southampton. In fact, America was the central issue in the Cambridge election, and this suggests that the sharpness of focus concerning America as a political issue may be related to whether or not the electorate would polarize on economic grounds. On the whole, however, the weight of evidence from the poll books would support the notion that voters were not divided on an economic basis during the American crisis.

Just as with parliamentary elections, petitioning and addressing the Crown with respect to America was, in the eighteenth century, widely believed to be connected to one's economic status. An essayist who signed his work "x.s.k.q" claimed: "The Wind never divided more completely the Chaff from the Corn, than the present Addresses and Petitions have separated the Affluent and Independent from the misguided and prejudiced Rabble."[39] This thesis may be scrutinized by listing all petitioners and addressers who were also voters by occupational category. Since only voters who can also be identified as petitioners are counted, Table 7.2 tells us nothing about the numerous petitioners who were not voters. Yet it remains the case that all electors were free to sign addresses or petitions, and by utilizing the poll books, approximately forty percent of the petitioners' occupations can be determined.[40] The exceedingly high proportion of the elite group who signed the Southampton address requires an explanation in this regard. Some forty-seven people styled themselves "gentlemen" and fifty-eight referred to themselves as "esquires" in the 1774 Southampton election, and thirty-two (30%) of this elite group signed the address. While it is true that these self-designations may be somewhat inflated descriptions of a person's social standing, the accuracy of a number of the titles is at-

---

[38]Using x^2 the differences between occupational ranks were not significant at the .01 level of probability for Yarmouth, Southampton, or Bridgwater, but they were for Cambridge.

[39]*Pub. Adv.* (19 October 1775).

[40]A low proportion of 16.3% of the Cambridge conciliatory petitioners and a high of 78.6% of the Southampton coercive addressers can be identified from the poll books. The average for the remaining six addresses and petitions is 42%. The Poole poll book of 1768 does not list occupations; these are drawn from *Gen. Eve. Post* (5-7 October 1775). For the petitions and addresses, see ch. 3, Tables 3.1-3.2.

tested to from an independent source.[41] The election of 1774 did not polarize this elite along political lines; these gentlemen and esquires gave equal support to government and opposition candidates. But the American crisis of 1775 clearly divided Southampton voters according to socioeconomic rank.

The evidence from Great Yarmouth and Cambridge, and to a lesser extent also from Poole, confirms the pattern found at Southampton. By far the great-

TABLE 7.2

OCCUPATIONAL STRUCTURE OF PETITIONERS AND ADDRESSERS WHO WERE ALSO VOTERS

	ENTIRE RESIDENT ELECTORATE	CONCILIATORY		COERCIVE	
Great Yarmouth					
1. Gentlemen, Professions	11.5%	8	10.4%	44	50%
2. Merchants	5.6%	8	10.4%	15	17%
3. Shopkeepers	12.7%	20	26%	12	13.6%
4. Artisans	47%	31	40.3%	15	17%
5. Laborers	23.1%	10	13%	2	2.3%
Cambridge					
1. Gentlemen, Professions	12.2%	3	11.5%	11	34.4%
2. Merchants	22%	5	19.2%	12	37.5%
3. Shopkeepers	40.2%	8	30.8%	5	15.6%
4. Artisans	20.7%	9	34.6%	3	9.4%
5. Laborers	4.9%	1	3.8%	1	3.1%
Southampton					
1. Gentlemen, Professions	35.6%	6	7.7%	48	82.8%
2. Merchants	2.9%	5	6.4%	0	0%
3. Shopkeepers	22.2%	35	44.9%	4	7.4%
4. Artisans	30.5%	30	38.5%	2	3.7%
5. Laborers	8.8%	2	2.6%	0	0%
Bridgwater					
1. Gentlemen, Professions	16.2%	10	13.2%	6	13.6%
2. Merchants	6.3%	5	6.6%	4	9.1%
3. Shopkeepers	36.6%	28	36.8%	18	40.9%
4. Artisans	35.2%	27	35.5%	14	31.8%
5. Laborers	3.5%	3	3.9%	2	4.5%
6. Other	2.1%	3	3.9%	----------	----------

est support for coercion came from the elite, especially from gentlemen and those men in the professions. At Great Yarmouth and Cambridge the merchants as a group were more in favor of coercion than conciliation, but the evidence for this is not particularly strong at Yarmouth. Since Cambridge was not a port, it had virtually no connections with American commerce, and this may help account for the number of wholesalers there who favored coercion. Altogether, approximately two-thirds of those in favor of the government's measures at Yarmouth and Cambridge came from the upper two categories. Conversely, at Yarmouth, Cambridge, and Southampton, two-thirds to three-fourths of the support for conciliation came from the shopkeepers and artisans—the middling ranks of the English people.[42] Of the boroughs studied, Bridgwater and possibly Poole were exempt from this division. Equally noteworthy is the small number of laborers who petitioned compared with those who voted. This strongly suggests that the American issue stirred the upper and middle ranks of English society but not the rabble. In any case, the laborers who were also freemen were not as active concerning the American crisis as they were during parliamentary elections.

The most obvious characteristic emerging from these data is that voters from the ranks of the elite gave their support to the government concerning America, while those from the lowest rank, on the whole, were less involved in popular politics. It was predominantly the English shopkeeper—the grocer, stationer, and fishmonger—combined with the artisan—the ship carpenter, plumber, and glazier—who provided the bulk of support for conciliation. This may provide evidence of an economic dividing line between the politically literate public and those who were not yet ideologically alert. While a sizable proportion of unskilled laborers voted, they were universally recognized as the most susceptible to bribery, and they were evidently not involved in unsanctioned agitation against the government that could have been interpreted as treasonous. This contrasts quite impressively with the preponderance of support for conciliation that came from the shopkeepers and artisans.

The division among the merchants is particularly striking, although it is not out of keeping with recent studies of the subject. John Sainsbury has dem-

---

[41]Regarding the ascription of occupations at elections, see Phillips, *Electoral Behavior*, 5-6. Another reason for the high number of the elite at Southampton is that six Anglican clergy signed the address. The address itself distinguishes one "esquire," one "baronet," and three clergy. While there are five exact confirmations of the poll book in the essay in *Lond. Eve.-Post* (28-31 October 1775), many others can be inferred from this list. For example, Samuel Scott, a former lieutenant in the Navy, is styled "gentleman" in the poll book. R. Vernon Sadlier, a "contractor for the provisions at Nova Scotia," is also listed in the poll as "esquire." With the addition of this essay, the occupations of only two addressers remain unknown.

[42]Using x^2 the differences are significant for Yarmouth, Southampton, and Cambridge. There is little occupational data for the Poole conciliatory petition, but the coercive address seems to confirm patterns found elsewhere.

onstrated that the London merchants were thoroughly divided with respect to the use of force against the colonists.[43] The merchants at Bristol confirm the patterns found both in the metropolis and in the smaller boroughs. A comparison of the Bristol petition supporting peace with *Sketchley's Bristol Directory* reveals that certain American houses such as the Champions and the Harfords were indeed very prominent in the agitation supporting peace. Presently it is possible to identify only sixteen of these merchants as traders to America and the West Indies, and twelve of these signed the conciliatory petition, while four leading traders to the colonies signed the coercive address. But altogether there were at least forty-five Bristol merchants in favor of coercion, and only thirty-seven in favor of peace.[44] This requires significant modification of the traditional thesis concerning merchant support of the colonists.

Recent study of mass culture in the eighteenth century adds a further dimension to the support for conciliation that came from the middling ranks of society. John Brewer has shown how the provincial press played an important role in encouraging confidence in business and credit and that this emphasis was aimed especially at "the middling sort" of Englishman. While it remains unclear how such attitudes toward consumerism and its attendant benefits relate to a specific political viewpoint, a greater-than-usual interest among the middling ranks in the economic vitality and general well-being of American trade is not hard to imagine. The Westbury, Warminster, and Trowbridge petitioners, for example, pointed out that "the vital principle of trade is peace and confidence, not war and destruction."[45] Brewer's examination of the trademen's clubs seems to hold even more promise for our understanding of why pro-Americanism arose among the shopkeepers and artisans. The connection between club members and the printer who sold them political pamphlets as a commercial venture suggests a tie between increasing wealth and progressive politics. The moderate means of these groups compared to the laborers seem to account for their heightened political activity and interest in independence.[46] Clubs, of course, presuppose an element of leisure, and this too, as J. H. Plumb has documented, helps explain the political activity of the mid-

---

[43]Sainsbury, "The Pro-American Movement in London," Appendices A and B.

[44]James Sketchley, *Sketchley's Bristol Directory* (Bristol, 1775) isolates major Bristol merchants in a separate section of the Directory, 111-16. G. E. Weare, *Edmund Burke's Connection with Bristol, from 1774 till 1780* (Bristol: William Bennett, 1894) 4-5, has an additional list of large mercantile houses. These lists were compared to HO 55/11/64; 11/9.

[45]Neil McKendrick, John Brewer, and J. H. Plumb, *The Birth of a Consumer Society* (London: Europa Publications, 1982) 216-17. *Lond. Eve.-Post* (21-23 November 1775). See also Kent R. Middleton, "Commercial Speech in the Eighteenth Century," 280, in Donovan H. Bond and W. Reynolds McLeod, *Newsletters to Newspapers: Eighteenth-Century Journalism* (Morgantown WV: West Virginia University, 1977).

[46]McKendrick, Brewer, and Plumb, *The Birth of a Consumer Society*, 232-33, 253-59.

dling ranks.[47] How this relates specifically to their support of conciliation, however, remains problematic.

These observations on the middling ranks of society are of necessity rather crude. One could wish for finer discrimination, for example, between manufacturers who operated large-scale businesses and skilled but petty artificers who were only one step removed from the common laborer, but the nominal nature of the data does not reveal such distinctions. The greatest weakness of this attempt at analysis is, of course, that it does not treat those petitioners who were nonelectors. If electors who were laborers did not petition, it does not follow that nonelectors who were laborers abstained. Some further insights can be gained based on the data from the Dissenters examined below, but further research is needed in boroughs where additional records are available, since the social standing of petitioners who were nonelectors requires special attention. But the differences in occupational rank between addressers and petitioners in the boroughs studied thus far make it possible to conclude tentatively that socioeconomic status contributed directly to the political differences that divided the English populace concerning America.

IV

The Dissenting family of Hurry at Great Yarmouth, Robert Robinson at Cambridge, and the Bernards at Southampton provided aggressive leadership against the government in 1775, and in each of these boroughs a local tradition of opposition was kept alive largely through their efforts. Where the Dissenters were few, as at Bridgwater, or where they lacked outstanding liberal leaders, as at Poole, the resistance to the government over a period of years appears to have been less pronounced. It is a question of some interest whether or not the leaders were able to rally the average Nonconformist to the cause of independence and opposition to the government. This is readily addressed by comparing the nonparochial registers of the Presbyterians, Congregationalists, Baptists, and Quakers to the petitions and addresses. Table 7.3 demonstrates that a consistently greater proportion of Dissenters favored conciliation over coercion, especially at Yarmouth, Southampton, and Poole.[48] The Dissenting elite, whether clerical, as in the case of Cambridge and possibly Poole, or lay, as at Yarmouth and Southampton, was able to carry the majority of the laity with it. It may also be significant that at Bridgwater, the Dissenters were numerically weak, they lacked clerical leadership, and the ideology of the petition supporting conciliation was correspondingly more moderate. Bridgwater stands

---

[47]Ibid., 280-85.

[48]The denominational breakdown of Table 7.3 is unremarkable. Extensive Quaker registers subsist for only Yarmouth and Poole and, in both cases, the Presbyterians and Quakers responded to the situation similarly. The same pertains to Cambridge, where Baptists and Congregationalists acted together. The records for Southampton and Bridgwater are each drawn from a single congregation. For the nonparochial registers upon which these comparisons are based, see ch. 6, nn. 25, 37, 47, 52, and 59 above.

in contrast to Southampton where, of all the boroughs, the Dissenters were the most united, and the petition was more radically worded. Similarly, of the five boroughs, Bridgwater was the least divided on a socioeconomic basis, while the differences in occupational ranks between petitioners and addressers were greatest at Southampton.

The ratio of Dissenters who supported conciliation to those who favored coercion reveals a clear proclivity in support of peace among Nonconformists. Taking into consideration the consistently greater number of signatures on the conciliatory documents, the ratio of Dissenting signatures on the petitions to those on the addresses was as high as five to one at Southampton, about two to one at Yarmouth and Bridgwater, and a little less than two to one at Poole. With the exception of Cambridge, the uniformity of the Dissenters' opinion concerning America was impressive. When this is compared to the near unanimity of the Anglican clergy's response to the crisis, it is evident that the petitions and addresses divided the English public along religious lines.

While the Dissenting elite provided the leadership in advocating conciliatory measures, and while many laymen added their support, the fact that no more than one-quarter of the petitioners can be identified as Dissenters means that in each case the Anglican laity made up the majority of petitioners.[49] At Southampton and Bridgwater a few Anglican clergy added their voices to pleas

TABLE 7.3

NONCONFORMIST SIGNERS OF PETITIONS AND ADDRESSES					
	TOTAL SIGNERS	DISSENTING SIGNERS	% OF PETITIONERS	DISSENTING MINISTERS	ANGLICAN CLERGY
Conciliatory Petitions					
Great Yarmouth	344	66	19.2%	1	0
Cambridge	160	18	11.3%	3	0
Southampton	117	22	18.8%	0	1
Bridgwater	150	12	8%	0	2
Poole	144	38	26.4%	2	1
Coercive Addresses					
Great Yarmouth	228	20	8.8%	1	9
Cambridge	96	10	10.4%	0	3
Southampton	56	2	3.6%	0	6
Bridgwater	110	4	3.6%	0	4
Poole	56	9	15.8%	0	0

---

[49]There were undoubtedly a few more Dissenters who signed the petitions that were not, for one reason or another, recorded in the nonparochial registers. But it is highly unlikely that they made up more than half of the support for conciliation in any given borough.

in support of conciliation, thereby presenting a study in contrast to the politically quiescent Dissenting clergy in these two boroughs. This transdenomi-
national alliance, however, should not be viewed as extraordinary. In a number
of other boroughs there was an accepted arrangement between Dissenters and
low-church Anglicans during parliamentary elections. A party of Dissenters
and low-church Anglicans was repeatedly at odds with a high-Anglican party
at Exeter, Abingdon, Hertford, Bristol, and Shrewsbury. In these boroughs
this was no passing marriage of convenience, but a long-standing political arrangement upon which politicians came to depend.[50]

V

Both socioeconomic and religious differences contributed directly to the
emergence of these documents. Some people may well have signed petitions
for economic reasons, and others for religious and ideological reasons, but often
both elements were involved in the individual's political orientation. Further
evidence for the interaction of economic and religious causation is found in the
nonparochial registers, though only tentative conclusions may be offered on
the basis of the records that are now available. Table 7.4 shows that in each
case where it is possible to determine the social structure of an entire congregation, the socioeconomic standing of the Dissenters fell considerably below
that of the electorate (compare Table 7.4 to Table 7.1).

Table 7.5 compares all Dissenting petitioners and addressers in the five
boroughs to all other, presumably Anglican, petitioners and addressers.[51] These

TABLE 7.4

OCCUPATIONAL STRUCTURE OF NONCONFORMITY							
	GREAT YARMOUTH PRESBYTERIANS		CAMBRIDGE BAPTISTS		SOUTHAMPTON CONGREGATION-ALISTS		POOLE QUAKERS
1. Gentlemen, Professions	24	6.7%	10	11.5%	16	19.3%	2	3.4%
2. Merchants	30	8.4%	6	7.9%	1	1.2%	10	17.2%
3. Shopkeepers	34	9.6%	15	17.2%	11	13.3%	7	12%
4. Artisans	111	31.2%	30	34.5%	14	16.7%	21	36.2%
5. Laborers	156	43.8%	17	19.5%	40	48.2%	17	29.3%
6. Other	1	0.3%	9	10.3%	1	1.2%	1	1.7%

---

[50]John Evans, "List of Dissenting Congregations and Ministers in England and Wales
(1715-1729)," MS. 38.4, 31, 48, 49, 147. At Abingdon and Shrewsbury the Dissenters
are distinguished in the poll books. See *The Poll* (Abingdon, 1734 and 1754). For
Shrewsbury, see the manuscript poll book for 1747, S.P.L. Deed 19163.

[51]For Table 7.5 occupations for the Dissenting petitioners are drawn from the poll
books and from the nonparochial registers. This increases the numbers for which occupations can be found by about 50%.

data imply that the Dissenting petitioners, and at least those petitioners who were also voters, were drawn largely from the same occupational groupings.[52] A comparison of the strength of the relationship between religion and petitioning (Table 7.3) and between occupational status and petitioning (Table 7.5) shows that both elements were strong, though the latter was slightly stronger than the former.[53] If the occupational categories of Table 7.5 are regrouped into high (categories 1 and 2), middle (categories 3 and 4), and low (category 5), there is a clear correspondence between these ranks and the strength of the popular response to the government. In each of the three categories religion was important in determining whether or not one petitioned or addressed, but it was considerably more important among the elite than it was among the artisans and laborers.[54]

At the highest socioeconomic levels it appears that significant interaction between economic and religious motivation was common, and for the Anglicans this comports well with what is known of the connection between corporations and the government. On the one hand, a higher economic standing interacted with Anglicanism and officeholding, and this resulted in a strong conservative orientation. On the other hand, the same kind of connection worked the opposite effect among some of the Dissenters. Among those who supported peace, greater wealth was interactive with religious Dissent and exclusion from local office. There were a number of Dissenters who were evi-

TABLE 7.5

NONCONFORMIST PETITIONERS AND ADDRESSERS AND ALL OTHER PETITIONERS AND ADDRESSERS							
	DISSENTING PETITIONERS		ALL OTHER PETITIONERS		DISSENTING ADDRESSERS		ALL OTHER ADDRESSSERS
1. Gentlemen, Professions	18	16.2%	22	11%	9	24.3%	109	45.2%
2. Merchants	15	13.5%	13	6.5%	10	27%	37	15.4%
3. Shopkeepers	26	23.4%	75	37.5%	7	18.9%	53	22%
4. Artisans	42	37.8%	75	37.5%	5	13.5%	37	15.4
5. Laborers	9	8.1%	12	6%	6	16.2%	5	2.1%
6. Other	1	0.9%	3	1.5%	------	------		

[52]Using x^2 the difference between Dissenters and Anglicans who petitioned is significant, while that between Dissenters and Anglicans who addressed is not.

[53]Grouping all of the boroughs together, and thereby utilizing all the available data, the gamma for Table 7.3 is .40 and for Table 7.5 it is .61.

[54]The gammas for the high, middle, and low ranks are .76, .55, and .23 respectively; if occupational category 3 is left by itself, and 4 and 5 are combined, the gammas are .76, .45, and .38 respectively.

dently motivated to support peaceful measures, not because they were lower in occupational rank than other petitioners, but rather because they were higher. The greater proportion of Dissenting petitioners among the gentleman, profession, and merchant categories compared to all petitioners implies that they were reacting to a perceived inequality between their socioeconomic rank and the lack of social recognition.

Since support for conciliation came from the upper and middle rather than the lower ranks of Dissenters, these data suggest a genuine discontent with the restrictions that the Test and Corporation Acts imposed on potential office-holders. This certainly is likely in the case of a number of the lay Dissenting leaders, such as the Hurrys and the Bernards. Where Dissenters were excluded from corporations, as at Great Yarmouth and Southampton, there was greater consistency among Dissenters in their opposition to the government. At Cambridge and Bridgwater they were traditionally not excluded, and the opposition was correspondingly less strong. In the eighteenth century it is likely that in those cases where class divisions influenced political differences, they were almost invariably related first to religious issues and second to local structures of status and authority. Indeed, it may be that as early as the American Revolution, religion was the midwife of class.[55] But this observation will require further research and careful qualification.

The apparent connection between the middle ranks of society and the Dissenters in relation to petitioning poses a number of problems. The evidence from the nonparochial registers suggests that the petitioners for whom we have no occupational data were also drawn from the middle rather than the lower ranks. The occupations summarized in Table 7.5 provide the strongest evidence yet adduced that the lower orders in society were not engaged in extraordinary expressions of a political nature. When Table 7.5 is compared with Table 7.4, is is clear that even in the section of the population that was most enthusiastic in its support of opposition, namely the Dissenters, laborers were not heavily involved. Yet many laborers were active in sanctioned forms of political expression such as parliamentary elections.

The divisions in English society during the American crisis do bear some resemblance to commonly advanced notions of class conflict. If, on the one hand, urban laborers were not yet politically engaged, the artisans and shopkeepers were, and these were the very orders of society recently introduced to national issues through the public reporting of parliamentary debates. Such groups were clearly at odds with the gentlemen and those in the professions who were strongly progovernment in orientation. The agitation of 1775 may be construed as an intermediate phase of popular political development falling midway between the earlier radicalism of the Middlesex election affair and the

---

[55]The phrase is Harold Perkin's. In *The Origins of Modern English Society, 1780-1880* (London: Routledge & Kegan Paul, 1969), he sees this as a nineteenth-century phenomenon (196).

"new radicalism" of the 1790s in which laborers were involved. But it is also important to note that these divisions were, for the most part, latent. They only emerged in those parliamentary contests in which the American Revolution was a clear issue and in the petitioning agitation concerning the use of coercive measures. Finally, the division had a definite ideological component: Protestant Nonconformity in most cases added a progressive ideological element to the social divisions. It may thus be possible to posit a transitional stage in eighteenth-century popular politics involving conflict between those who had already attained a stake in society and the middle ranks who were hoping to acquire a larger place. The conflict was not sharp enough to lead to insurrection or revolt, but in the mid-1770s it did result in expressions of sympathy for those who were in rebellion.

Is it possible to argue that exclusion from office was the primary motivation behind the Dissenters' progressive politics? In other words, can the Dissenters' progressive outlook be reduced to material causes? The borough of Poole stands in the way of this conclusion, as do a number of other boroughs. Politically progressive ideology and local resentment over being excluded from office are of course highly compatible, as the various attempts to remove the Dissenters' legal restrictions demonstrated. The former should not be too readily dissolved into the latter, however, since many Dissenting clergymen, Robert Robinson preeminently, were articulate spokesmen of the Commonwealthman tradition in a setting where Dissenters were not excluded from officeholding. Nevertheless, lay leadership at Yarmouth and Southampton accomplished more in uniting the Dissenters against the government than clerical leadership and progressive ideology at Cambridge.

If the Dissenters' support for conciliation can largely be accounted for, first on the grounds of their exclusion from local office with all its attendant benefits, and second on the grounds of the ideological affinities with their brethren across the sea, there still remain a number of anomalies that require explanation. The relatively large proportion of Dissenting signatures on the coercive addresses (Table 7.3) must be explained. The American crisis divided the Anglicans, but it also divided Dissenters, and there is evidence to support the notion that wealth and place were as important to some Dissenters as ideological consistency was to others. A small minority of colonial Quakers broke from their brethren and became nonpacifists. This, however, was not clearly related to socioeconomic status: youth, kinship, and proximity to urban areas were more influential in dividing the Quakers than social standing. In any case, even in the colonies a handful of Quakers became Loyalists.[56] According to Table 7.5 the Dissenters who wished for coercion were evidently more well-to-do than

---

[56]Kenneth Alan Radbill, "Socioeconomic Background of Nonpacifist Quakers during the American Revolution" (Ph.D. dissertation, University of Arizona, 1971) 40, 75, 90. Radbill examines 420 Quakers from southeastern Pennsylvania disowned for bearing arms.

those who wished for peace (51.3% in the upper two categories compared to 29.7% among the conciliatory Dissenters). However, the Dissenters in the upper two categories fell considerably below all other addressers, and the relatively even distribution of Dissenters who favored coercion in all five categories must be given due weight.

Further details concerning specific occupations throw some light on this problem. There were, for example, numerous Presbyterians at Great Yarmouth in government pay, a fact that is candidly revealed in the baptismal register itself. John Constable and Thomas Askew were "officers in the excise"; William Calder was the "master gunner at the Fort" and John Fish was a tidewaiter. None of these four, however, signed either the address or the petition. But Gilbert Fairlie, a Presbyterian and a lieutenant in the navy, signed the address in favor of coercion, as did, inexplicably, a Dissenting minister, John Whiteside.[57] Among the ten Dissenters who signed the address in support of coercion at Cambridge were John Purchase and Joshua Finch, both aldermen, and Charles Finch and Stephen Harrison, successful Cambridge businessmen.[58] It seems that despite the pro-American political rhetoric of Robert Robinson, Cambridge Dissenters who were also officeholders or businessmen were not readily converted to a progressive political viewpoint.

At Southampton and Poole all of the Dissenters who favored the establishment can be identified. William Watson of Southampton was the deputy controller of the customs house and Walter Taylor, esquire, was a prominent citizen and a large supplier of block and tackle to the navy. Through his "liberality" Taylor was said to have sustained a number of charitable Dissenting institutions. He was the Dissenting minister's brother-in-law and enjoyed "the closest tie of friendship" with Kingsbury for forty years, also evidently sharing the minister's conservative political views.[59] We know that numerous Dissenters were involved in government work at Poole, both in the excise and in the service.[60] Of the five Quakers who signed the coercive address, three were big merchants in the Newfoundland trade, and the other two owned much prop-

---

[57]RG 4/1973. There is one other Dissenting minister known to have signed a coercive address: John Handasyds, of Newcastle-upon-Tyne. HO 55/12/6.

[58]Add. MSS. 5813 f. 131; 5855 f. 140. Harrison is called "rich" by William Cole, and Charles Finch was a trustee of St. Andrew's Street Baptist Chapel. Add. MSS. 5813 f. 252; Trust Deed of St. Andrew's Street Baptist Chapel (1795); J. Milner Gray, *Biographical Notes on the Mayors of Cambridge* (Cambridge: W. Heffer and Sons, 1922) 48, 51, 55-57.

[59]RG 4/610; 624; S. Stainer, *History of the Above Bar Congregational Church, Southampton, from 1662-1908* (Southampton: Southampton Times Co., 1909) 87, 101. Concerning Kingsbury's loyalty to George III, see 91.

[60]George Bigden, "an inferior officer in the customs," Samuel Hobbs, "formerly in the excise," and William Troke, "an extra man" in the customs. RG 4/121; David Young, Joseph Waldron, William Dean, and Thomas Linthorn were in the Royal Navy. RG 4/464.

erty. Thomas Nickleson's forthright public declaration of his Quaker principles and his support for coercion have already been noted. Of the four
additional Nonconformists, one was a landwaiter, one a coastwaiter, the third
simply a "burgess," and the last said to be "in considerable trade."[61] In each
case where it is possible to identify the occupation of a conservative Dissenter,
his political stance seems to be related to wealth, local officeholding, dependence upon the central government, or a combination of the three.

Does the ideological motivation of the Dissenters thereby finally collapse
into economic considerations? The evidence just cited seems to point in this
direction, and yet these establishment Dissenters were in a clear minority, and
there are additional bits of evidence that will not allow such sweeping generalizations. First, the Hurrys and Bernards were at least as wealthy as those Dissenters who supported coercive measures. The Dissenters at Yarmouth and
Southampton, however, were excluded from local office, and we have seen that
the questions of wealth and exclusion from local officeholding were dynamically related. Where Dissenters were excluded from corporations, the corporations were united in favor of coercive measures; this is evident in the case of
Yarmouth and Southampton where there were well-defined corporation and
anticorporation parties. But where a handful of Dissenters did hold local office
as at Cambridge, Bridgwater, and Poole, local government was divided with
respect to America. While this does not mean that all Dissenters were able to
transcend the lure of places and gifts, many were able to maintain their ideological commitments in spite of such benefits. There were numerous boroughs
where Dissenters were not excluded from corporate office and yet strongly
supported conciliation. In fact, in every known case where a corporation divided over America, a complement of Dissenters sat on the corporation. This
is true of Cambridge, Bridgwater, and possibly Poole, where the influence of
the Dissenters in dividing the corporation appears to have been indirect. But
at Bristol, Nottingham, Coventry, and Portsmouth, the Dissenters held local
office and thus enjoyed positions with considerable social status, and yet their
impact on the agitation in support of conciliation was direct and controlling.
This point will receive detailed attention in a subsequent study on religion and
revolution, but it requires brief notice here.

The presence of Dissenters on the corporation at Bristol was well known
and can be established from the nonparochial registers. At Bristol three aldermen, two sheriffs elect, the mayor elect, and eight common councilmen signed
the conciliatory petition, whereas the current mayor and sheriffs signed the
coercive address. While only three of these six conciliatory officeholders can
be identified as Dissenters, the connection between the traditional Whig pol

---

[61]*Gen. Eve. Post* (5-7 October 1775). The newspaper article notes the denomination
of two of the Quakers that are confirmed both with respect to denomination and occupation from the register. RG 6/1236; RG 4/2770; 464.

itics of the corporation and its openness to Dissenters is beyond dispute.[62] At Nottingham the alliance between Dissent and progressive politics was even firmer. Three aldermen and the mayor of Nottingham signed the conciliatory petition; in addition, the two sheriffs for 1776 also signed. All six of these leaders were Nonconformists, and eight of the nine common councilmen who signed were also Dissenters. The three remaining aldermen, one of whom was a Dissenter, signed the coercive address, but none of the remaining common councilors signed the address.[63] On 21 December 1777, two years after the petition was sent to the Crown, a local agent for Lord Sandwich, first lord of the Admiralty, described politics in Nottingham: "This town is without any exception the most disloyal in the kingdom, owing in a great measure to the whole corporation (the present mayor excepted) being Dissenters, and of so bitter a sort that they have done and continue to do all in their power to hinder the service by preventing as much as possible the enlistment of soldiers."[64]

The number and influence of Nonconformists in Coventry so impressed an anonymous observer in 1702 that he wrote: "The majority of the heads of the corporation and the magistrates are now in ye sober men, so it's esteemed a fanatick Town, and there is indeed ye largest Chapple, and ye greatest number of people, I have ever seen of ye Presbyterian way."[65] The Dissenting presence on the corporation throughout the eighteenth century is attested to by the designation of several people as aldermen in the nonparochial registers. Five of the borough's aldermen signed the petition supporting conciliation, one of whom can be identified as a Dissenter, while only one alderman can be discovered who signed the coercive address.[66]

---

[62]See references, for example, to Alderman Dampier, RG 4/2827; Levi Ames, alderman, RG 4/3507; John Page, esquire, and alderman Harris, RG 4/1829. Other Dissenters such as Isaac Elton and Isaac Baugh were sheriffs, RG 4/2497; and there are too many officers in the customs to note. HO 55/11/64; 55/11/9. Regarding William Barnes and T. Deane, aldermen, and John Noble, sheriff elect, the Dissenters who signed the conciliatory petition, see RG 4/1830; 2497, 3507.

[63]Mayor, John Fellows; aldermen, Humphrey Hollins, James Hornbuckle, Thomas Oldknow; councilors, W. Bilbie, George Dodson, James Foxcroft, John Foxcroft, Mark Huish, Jonathan Inglesant, Thomas Sands, Matthews Whitelock. E. L. Guilford, ed., *Records of the Borough of Nottingham*, 9 vols. (Nottingham: Thomas Forman and Sons, 1882-1956) 7:412. RG 4/1588; 137; 1586; 3664. Smith Churchill and Teritus Dale, both Dissenters and sheriffs for 1776, signed the conciliatory petition as well, HO 55/10/18. Cornelius Huthwait was the only Dissenting alderman for coercion, HO 55/11/27.

[64]*Commons, 1754-1790,* 1:355.

[65]T. W. Whitley, *The Parliamentary Representation of the City of Coventry* (Coventry: Curtis and Beamish, 1894) 117.

[66]Francis Perkins and John Clark are noted as aldermen in the register, RG 4/3315. It was noted that in 1735 eleven of the seventeen trustees of the Presbyterian Church were aldermen or councilors. Michael Watts, *The Dissenters* (Oxford: Clarendon Press, 1977) 483. See also Irene Morris, *Three Hundred Years of Baptist Life in Coventry* (Lon-

At Portsmouth the political influence of the Dissenters on the corporation was almost as controlling as at Nottingham. Another agent for Lord Sandwich wrote to him in November 1775 concerning the possibility of obtaining a loyal address from the Portsmouth corporation. Sandwich's agent thought it was ill advised, and even the leaders of the government party at Portsmouth were against it: "We have nobody that can speak at all, and the two Whites and Mr. Missing, the late recorder (who is a violent Presbyterian) would harangue our friends out of their senses. There are also two or three of our friends who would on such a question scarce support us, that is old Mr. Lowe, who is half a Dissenter, and Abraham Monasher, a whole one."[67] Accordingly, the plan was dropped, and Portsmouth sent up neither an address in support of coercion nor a petition in support of peace. Even Dissenters who were friendly to the government and held local office were known to turn against the government during the America crisis.

At Bristol, Nottingham, Coventry, and Portsmouth the Dissenters were well established and could by no means be considered oppressed, and yet they identified with the reported sufferings of the Americans and spoke in favor of conciliatory measures. It can hardly be doubted that these Dissenters were also motivated in part by the exclusion of their brethren from local office in places such as Yarmouth and Southampton. But even if this was in fact the case, such concerns cannot be dismissed as strictly economically motivated. The disaffection of some Dissenters may be traced to the failure of their ministers to obtain relief from subscription to the Thirty-Nine Articles in 1772. But religious and ideological interests seem to have been the controlling issues for many Dissenters. It is not surprising that those who were well-to-do and enjoyed the privilege of office wished to be free from the legal restrictions of the Test and Corporation Acts, however ineffective they were in practice. This inclination seems to have been almost invariably conducive to antipathy toward the government's American policy.

VI

In those settings where government patronage was extensive, support for coercive measures arose precisely from those in government pay. In settings where patronage was less important, wealthier people and those in the professions gave

---

don: Kingsgate Press, 1925) 26, and John Sibree and M. Caston, *Independency in Warwickshire* (London: Ward and Co., 1855) 57, 62. The five aldermen who signed the petition were John Clark, John Minister, Thomas Collett, Thomas Daken, and Joseph Craner. See *Lond. Eve.-Post* (21-24 October 1775) and *The Poll* (Coventry, 1774); the one alderman who signed the coercive address was John Hewitt (HO 55/11/65), but this was the second coercive address of October 1776.

[67]*Commons, 1754-1790*, 1:298. Concerning the prominence of the Dissenters on the corporation in the 1770s, see Richard J. Murrell and Robert East, eds., *Extracts from Records in the Possession of the Municipal Corporation of the Borough of Portsmouth* (Portsmouth: H. Lewis, 1884) 26, 296-304. In 1775, John Carter, Thomas White, and William White were Dissenters and aldermen.

their support to the government more readily than the middle ranks of society. A sizable group of Dissenters with government places or substantial personal wealth attests to the fact that economic and political security could, and often did, lead people to support the government's policy of force to restore colonial order. What, then, finally characterizes the loyal addressers? Old Tories who backed corporations that were known to be high-Anglican in orientation identified their interests with the greatest corporation of all, namely Parliament. The supporters of George III and Parliament were gentlemen, merchants, government placemen, loyal officeholders, and Anglican clergy—each of whom had an abnormal stake in due obedience to law. The small minority of Dissenters who agreed with the government were occasional conformists who, in many cases, were acting consistently with long-established custom.

The majority of Dissenters, however, and many Anglicans as well, signed their names to petitions supporting peace. Popular opposition to the government's American policy was often led by those who were excluded from local office, like the Hurrys of Great Yarmouth and the Bernards of Southampton. But opposition to the government cannot thereby be reduced to the complaint of the disaffected. If the Dissenters often provided the leadership for opposition to the government, in the nation at large they represented something less than four percent of the population, and in no constituency did they comprise the majority of petitioners.[68] The leaders appear to have been able to attract middle-ranking Anglicans to the cause of opposition, but the exact nature of this relationship requires further research. The religious dimension underscores in a dramatic way that the petitioners were not manipulated by either the Rockingham Whigs above or the rabble below, at least not the Dissenting rabble.

What, then, finally characterizes the petitioners? The Dissenters were the archetypical Whigs, and Dissenting ministers and laymen alike took the lead in protest against the government. Their prominence added substance to the claim that the government was moving toward a new authoritarianism that looked from the local angle like a revival of Toryism. The evidence from the boroughs studied here suggests that ideology in some cases counted for more than patron-client relations and socioeconomic rank, and in other cases it counted for less. But in either case it is impossible to avoid the conclusion that minor government patronage, economic differences, and religion were far more influential in dividing English society than the leaders who were supposed to have forced so many signatures. In the addresses and petitions taken as a whole, one can discern political consistency in that people petitioned in the same way they voted, and many people were willing to pledge monetary support in addition to their names. Economic differences played a predictable role in the division of English society, and ideological consistency can be seen in the way

---

[68]James E. Bradley, "Whigs and Nonconformists: Presbyterians, Congregationalists, and Baptists in English Politics, 1715-1790" (Ph.D. dissertation, University of Southern California, 1978) 142-43.

that Anglicans and Dissenters fell into a rational pattern of support and op-position. The cumulative nature of this evidence argues that external political manipulation was not a determining factor in most of these expressions of pop-ular opinion.

If the agitation for peace was not a product of political influence, can it be concluded that popular opposition concerning America was anything more than a series of unrelated local struggles for power? Was it the case in England, as Carl Becker said of New York, that the American crisis was not a question of home rule, but who should rule at home? American resistance to English au-thority did provide a focal point for local contests between established interest groups, whose identity and security were wrapped up in preserving the status quo, and independent groups excluded from the center of wealth and influ-ence. In many boroughs a corporation-anticorporation conflict, fueled by re-ligious and economic differences, was the center around which local and parliamentary politics revolved. But not all who voiced support for the gov-ernment were under the influence of the government, and not all who wished for lenient measures were excluded from power.

If radicalism was "inspired primarily by local, not national issues,"[69] how is it that hundreds of Dissenters and thousands of Anglicans all across the na-tion responded to the American crisis at the same instant? How is one to ac-count for the fact that counties as well as boroughs divided? Indeed, regions as well as counties were divided, and while the strong reaction against coercive addresses in the southwest might be interpreted as evidence that the American crisis was merely a regional issue, the response of the people in the midlands is less easy to dismiss. It is misleading to collapse the national issue into merely a series of local contests for power. Local issues were important, but the Amer-ican crisis provided the English people with something more than simply an-other opportunity to express opposition to the government. It gave them an opportunity to talk and write about their political principles, their interest in law and order, the supremacy of Parliament, and their commitment to their American brethren and peace. The signers of addresses and petitions believed they were saying something of transcendent importance to the king.

In a minority of cases the divisions produced by the American crisis cut across both religious and economic lines. When the government's policy di-vided the Dissenters, some conservatives such as Thomas Nickleson justified their support of the government on ideological grounds. Other wealthy Dis-senters, however, stood by progressive principles; these men enjoyed political power as mayors and aldermen, but this did not keep them from opposing the government's use of force. Similarly, the merchants were divided, and this forces one to seek explanations for their behavior that go beyond strictly eco-nomic concerns. More was at stake in the merchant's mind than the state of

---

[69]Ian Christie, *Myth and Reality in Late-Eighteenth-Century British Politics* (London: Macmillan Co., 1970) 285.

trade with America. For some, the colonial rebellion raised the political question of the necessity of law and the corollary of force in the proper ordering of
society; for others, the Americans' resistance raised issues of individual rights—
the right to be represented and the right to petition in the hope of redress. In
1775 many Englishmen believed that they were acting on the basis of political
principle. In the case of a minority of Dissenters and a large body of merchants, there is evidence to support their claim.

Skepticism concerning the ideological content of public opinion in eighteenth-century England has sometimes been grounded in the historian's un-
realistic view of human freedom. Religious and economic differences do account
for much of the division in English society. But expressions of high political
principle have occasionally been dismissed as mere rhetoric because they were
motivated by local, material, and even unconscious interests. Several well-re-
ceived analyses of eighteenth-century English politics have been written as
though self-interest and genuine ideological convictions are incompatible.[70] In
fact, it is doubtful whether the two are ever separable, and in the case of America they were certainly united.

Is it really plausible that the local time-serving placeman signed his name
and pledged his life in support of coercive measures without thought, or even
against his conscience? It would seem far more likely that the placeman's basic
ideological orientation toward the government was shaped in a conservative
mold long before America became an issue, and it was, on that account, certainly no less valid. Or is it possible to reduce the Dissenters' voices in favor
of peace to a self-interested statement concerning local oppression, rather than
an informed outlook on the rights and liberties of Americans? The ease with
which Dissenters could find fault with both local and central governments reflected a habit of mind developed over decades, even generations. For the
placeman, the merchant, and the Dissenter alike the American conflict provided an opportunity to make a statement that had a direct bearing on local
matters and at the same time reflected genuine conviction concerning a great
national issue. If local struggles for power and the lust for place stimulated and
sharpened people's involvement in national politics during the American crisis, these elements functioned in much the same way in later, more enlight-
ened times.

VII

The decline of the petitioning agitation was abrupt. Newspaper reports in
late November made public the administration's proposal to restrain trade, and
this involved indemnity for all British vessels that should seize or destroy rebel

---

[70]This is readily documented in the writings of Sir Lewis Namier. See *England in
the Age of the American Revolution*, 2d ed. (London: Macmillan Co., 1961) 18, 21, 23,
26-27, 41, 304. The attitude is pervasive in the biographies of the *History of Parliament*.
This perspective is brought to a pinnacle of refinement in J. C. D. Clark's recent publication, *The Dynamics of Change: The Crisis of the 1750s and English Party Systems* (New
York: Cambridge University Press, 1982) 14-15, 314, 456-57.

vessels. By 27 November it was known in England that the Americans had received word that their last petition had been rejected.[71] The same newspapers that noted the presentation in late December of the large petition supporting conciliation from Lancashire also told of the discouraging escalation of war in Canada.[72] The minority in the House of Commons continued to lose every division concerning America, and the American Prohibitory Bill, which passed into law on 22 December, seems to have crushed all hopes for reconciliation. The bill amounted to a declaration of war, and with it, even contributors to the *London Evening-Post* seem to have succumbed to despair: "The dies are thrown, and the game is lost. The addressers have won." On 30 May 1776 Burke wrote: "Our Session is over; and I hardly can believe, by the tranquility of everything about me, that we are a people who have just lost an Empire. But it is so."[73]

A few appeals for peace still went up to Parliament and the Crown. In March 1776 the city of London appealed to the Crown for peace and much later, in March 1778, yet another petition from the city recalled that when civil war was first threatened, petitions for peace from "many respectable public bodies in your kingdom" had been sent to the Crown, but to no avail.[74] Then, in February 1778 there was the massive petition to Parliament from Norfolk. But on the whole, the petitioning agitation concerning America had ceased to flourish by January 1776, and by the time of the trial of John Horne Tooke in July 1777 pro-American sentiment in the metropolis was evidently on the wane.[75]

For a brief moment in the fall of 1775 the English people were prodded by the royal proclamation to address the Crown, and in reaction to these addresses many Englishmen petitioned in favor of peace. These statements were but fleeting expressions of popular opinion and although they were momentary, they can be observed, measured, and evaluated. Is the absence of widespread continuing expression of opposition to be taken as the cessation of pro-American sentiment? Since we know that the same people who petitioned engaged in similar political acts at times well removed from the fall of 1775, it is possible to argue that the sentiment behind these momentary expressions was abiding. Expressions of opposition to the government as late as the parliamentary election of 1780 may have been merely the first opportunity an elector had to put long-held convictions to work. The decline of popular resistance to the government in the form of popular expressions does not mean that public sentiment shifted in favor of the government.

There is evidence that the divisions in English society concerning America were not only deep, but lasting. In each of the five boroughs studied here, op-

---

[71]*Sal. Win. J.* (27 November 1775).

[72]*Pub. Adv.* (21 December 1775); *Lond. Eve.-Post* (19-21 December 1775).

[73]*Lond. Eve.-Post* (19-21 December 1775); *Burke Correspondence*, 3:269 (Burke to Champion, 30 May 1776).

[74]*Lond. Gaz.* (19-23 March 1776); *Ann. Reg.* (13 March 1778).

[75]Sainsbury, "The Pro-American Movement in London," 166.

position to the government continued to be expressed, though explicit references were not always made to America. At Poole local conflict concerning America was still sharp in the spring of 1776.[76] The opposition at Yarmouth and Cambridge in 1775 can be tied directly to the agitation in support of reform in 1780-1782. We have also seen continuing expressions of opposition in Bridgwater and Southampton. Abiding divisions in London concerning America have been thoroughly documented, at least through July 1777.[77] At Bristol, as late as June 1777, advertisements appeared in the local newspapers criticizing the addresses of 1775; in 1778 there were general protests against the press gang made by local authorities. But opposition in Bristol to the American war was balanced by equally zealous efforts on behalf of the Ministry.[78] At Coventry, a year after the first address, a second, more strongly worded address was sent to the king. This document of October 1776 expressed "horror" at the "Distant Rebellion," but the citizens noted that this horror was "heightened by the unparalleled outrages of a Domestic Insurrection"—an apparent allusion to continued pro-American sympathy.[79] Nottingham was divided in 1777 and some were opposing the enlistment of soldiers. The citizens of Birmingham were much at odds regarding America as late as 1778.[80] The conciliatory petition from Norfolk presented to Parliament in February 1778 was put forth in reaction to the county muster that was recruiting servicemen and raising money in support of the government, but when this resistance began has never been documented. We know, however, that the resistance continued. In 1780 William Windham was chosen to stand at Norwich by the local opposition precisely because of his leadership in the petitioning agitation protesting the war in 1778.[81]

In Hampshire there was an attempt to give some permanence to opposition sentiment. Those who had met at Winchester to sign the county's petition supporting peace met at the George Inn in late November and formed themselves into a "Country Club" that began meeting in December.[82] Nearly a year after the corporation of Wallingford had petitioned the Crown in favor of peace, the Earl of Abingdon congratulated the members and reminded them of their

---

[76]*Commons, 1754-1790*, 1:270.

[77]Sainsbury, "The Pro-American Movement in London," 166.

[78]Peter Marshall, *Bristol and the American War of Independence* (Bristol: Bristol Branch of the Historical Association, 1977) 13-17. Marshall argues that political antagonisms in regard to the war were continually growing in this period, 17.

[79]HO 55/11/65.

[80]John Money, *Experience and Identity: Birmingham and the West Midlands, 1760-1800* (Manchester: Manchester University Press, 1977) 207 n. 69.

[81]HMC, *Dartmouth Manuscripts*, 3 vols. (London: Her Majesty's Stationery Office, 1887-1896) 1:419. Phillips, *Electoral Behavior*, 145.

[82]*Hamp. Chron.* (27 November, 4 December 1775).

"unanimous" petition.[83] Finally, at Manchester, where the conservatives in favor of coercion clearly dominated the city, opposition to the war bordering on violence erupted in the fall of 1776 and again in the summer of 1780. Peter Marshall found that only a "handful" of former petitioners became volunteers in the service and concluded that during the war there was little erosion of the "Whig" petitioners going over to the "Tory" side.[84] Further research may reveal additional places that were not supportive of coercive measures, and more detailed work is needed to illumine the local circumstances surrounding these divisions.

---

[83]*Amer. Arch.*, 5th ser., 2:808.

[84]Marshall, "Manchester and the American Revolution," 175, 182-83.

The Popularity
of the American War
in England

Chapter VIII

On 23 August 1775, the same day as the publication of the royal proclamation, John Wesley wrote to his patron, the Earl of Dartmouth. As an itinerant evangelist, Wesley had seen more of England than most politicians, his conservative convictions were well known, and his pamphlet, *A Calm Address to Our American Colonies*, would soon appear in defense of the government. His sole purpose in writing at this time was to refute those who claimed that the people of England were fully employed and generally satisfied with the government. Wesley reported that he had recently traveled across England, and he was convinced that there was nationwide opposition to the king. The ministry must not be led to believe the exaggerated accounts of popular support, for in fact, wrote Wesley, the people were "dangerously dissatisfied." "The bulk of the people in every city, town, and village where I have been, do not so much aim at the ministry, as they usually did in the last century, but at the king himself. He is the object of their anger, contempt and malice." The people, said Wesley,

> are full of the spirit of murder and rebellion, and I am persuaded, should any occasion offer, thousands would be ready to act what they now speak. It is as much as ever I can do, and sometimes more than I can do, to keep this plague from infecting my own friends. And nineteen or twenty to whom I speak in defense of the King, seem never to have heard a word spoken for him before. I marvel what wretches they are who abuse the credulity of the ministry, by those florid accounts.[1]

This viewpoint was confirmed by the highest authority. Two days later, on 25 August, Lord North wrote to the king: "The cause of Great Britain is not yet sufficiently popular."[2]

Almost immediately, dozens of addresses in support of coercive measures were sent up to St. James. But in the aftermath of these expressions, "a Free Citizen" wrote a public letter to North charging that the conflict with America was a "ministerial war." And, the citizen continued, "now you want to transfer it from

---

[1]HMC, *Dartmouth Manuscripts*, 3 vols. (London: Her Majesty's Stationery Office, 1887-1896) 3:220.

[2]Fortescue, 3:249 (North to George III, 25 August 1775).

administration to the people at large." On the basis of the "clandestine addresses" to the Crown, he said, "you have the assurance to avow, that it is a popular war, and conformable to the desire of the people, who must pay dear for this cruel butchery, or sportive pastimes of the Junto."[3] North not only claimed it was a popular war at the time, he later used the issue of popularity to defend the administration. In May 1783, looking back over the war years, North declared in a speech before the House of Commons, "It was the war of the people." He went on to claim that "it was popular at its commencement, and eagerly embraced by the people and Parliament." The Crown alone, said North, could not have procured such majorities in Parliament. "Or if the influence could have produced these majorities within doors, could it have produced the almost unanimous approbation bestowed without doors, which rendered the war the most popular of any that had been carried on for many years?"[4]

The fears expressed by Wesley were exaggerated, but the argument espoused by Lord North was nothing more or less than government propaganda. That the government made the question of public opinion a major line of defense for its policy is in itself significant. In an aristocratic age dominated by deference, Lord North hoped to find his ultimate justification in the voice of the people. The documents of popular protest presented here demonstrate a growing political consciousness among the people of England, and North's comment reveals a heightened awareness of this reality, even among the elite. But of the elite, Burke alone had a balanced perspective on the strength of popular opposition. In an attempt to convince Lord Rockingham of the value of petitioning the Crown before Parliament met, he wrote from Bristol: "I am persuaded that the movement of our City would be followed by that of twenty or thirty other places, and some of them of consideration."[5] Burke had his "twenty places" and more, but the Rockingham Whigs were unable to capitalize upon the agitation. The expressions of popular resistance that emerged resulted in no measurable change in the operation of the government; since they remained largely unknown, they had little if any impact on the emergence of modern democracy. But the number of people involved in popular politics, and the constitutional and political implications of their activity, call for a reevaluation of several traditional emphases.

A body of people equal to about one-fifth of the English electorate expressed their opinion on the American crisis. This petitioning activity shows that the English populace was interested in political issues and that America fits into a pattern of popular protest that intensified during the Wilkes affair in the late 1760s and extended throughout the American war. The documents concerning the use of force evince a picture of a politically literate public that

[3]*Lond. Eve.-Post* (14-16 November 1775).
[4]*Parl. Hist.*, 33:849 (7 May 1783). See also 255, 445 (5 December 1782; 17 February 1783).
[5]*Burke Correspondence*, 3:208 (Burke to Rockingham, 14 September 1775).

comports well with what we know from pamphlets, newspapers, and other forms of popular literature during the mid-1770s. A number equal to one-tenth of the electorate expressed opposition to the government's American policy, and this minority, while small, appears to be representative of even more widespread discontent with coercive measures. One form of social protest that has recently attracted attention is the anonymous letter; but with the petitions to the Crown, the anonymity of popular protest was clearly transcended. The "alternative political nation" brought to light by Edward Thompson, and illumined for the decade of the 1760s by John Brewer, was still politically engaged in the 1770s.[6] Clearly, as Sir Herbert Butterfield once wrote, greater masses of people were being brought to "a consciousness of their importance, a sense of their public rights, a habit of local self-help, and an interest in the destiny of their nation."[7]

Is the data provided by the petitions and addresses a valid sample of the English political nation as a whole? We have seen that each geographical area of England was involved in the agitation regarding America, and the geographic pattern and total numbers correspond roughly to the other popular protest movements of the decade. Most parliamentary borough types were involved in the agitation, and the American crisis provides us with the first signed petitions concerning a national issue from several large manufacturing towns that were not represented in Parliament. How representative these political responses were for the rest of the nation will, however, remain debatable. A comparison of the Englishmen who favored peace with the American Loyalists who resisted revolution may be instructive in this regard.

While it is possible to impugn the motives of the Americans in their various petitions to the Crown, it seems less advisable to question the motives of Englishmen who had little to gain by such expressions of opposition. English pro-Americans thus provide a study in contrast to the colonial Loyalists whose devotion to the Crown can hardly be doubted. Numerous American Loyalists emigrated to England or Canada, but there were many who remained in the colonies during the war, and attempts to identify the size and composition of this latter group are laden with problems.[8] Similarly, it may be assumed that those in England who actually signed petitions in favor of peace were only a small fraction of those who opposed the movement toward war. The same, of

---

[6]E. P. Thompson, "The Crime of Anonymity," in Douglas Hay et al., *Albion's Fatal Tree* (New York: Pantheon Books, 1975) 255-308; E. P. Thompson, *The Making of the English Working Class* (New York: Pantheon Books, 1963) 30; John Brewer, *Party Ideology and Popular Politics at the Accession of George III* (Cambridge: Cambridge University Press, 1976) 219-69.

[7]Herbert Butterfield, *George III, Lord North and the People, 1779-1780* (London: Bell, 1949) 9.

[8]William H. Nelson, *The American Tory* (Boston: Beacon Press, 1961); Mary Beth Norton, *The British Americans: The Loyalist Exiles in England, 1774-1789* (Boston: Little, Brown, and Co., 1972).

course, may also be said of those who favored coercive measures. How widespread, then, was the opposition's perspective on peace? In Parliament, Burke's plan in support of conciliation lost by a large majority, but it might not be far afield to suggest that that vote of 210 to 105 was an accurate reflection of the division in English society. It seems reasonable to conclude that as much as a third of the political nation opposed the government's American policy. Though a minority, the extent of this opposition would nevertheless warrant classifying the American conflict as England's least popular modern war.

The constitutional implications of the addresses and petitions will remain as controversial as the question of their representative nature. An important constitutional issue, for example, is raised by the frequent charge that in petitioning the Crown for peace, those who favored conciliation were acting more like Tories than their opponents, since they were, in effect, appealing to the king against Parliament.[9] In the fall of 1775, Charles James Fox attacked Lord North as a Tory. North responded by arguing that the Americans might with more justice be called Tories, since they appealed to the king's prerogatives, while the ministry upheld the authority of Parliament. At the Hampshire county meeting organized for the purpose of addressing the Crown, the clerk of the peace argued at length that in appealing to the king against Parliament, petitions supporting peace were at odds with the Revolution Settlement. With an eye on the Olive Branch Petition, the Middlesex justices of the peace exclaimed in their addresses to the Crown: "With the greatest professions of zeal for liberty do these infatuated people exalt the regal into arbitrary power, and from principles of law and logic, which are now for the first time advanced, contend that acts of the aggregate legislative body are of less force to bind the subjects than those of an integral part thereof." A number of other addresses made the same point concerning the petitioners' appeal to the Crown.[10] In reply to the king's proclamation of rebellion, the Second Continental Congress in December 1775 explicitly continued to allow "allegiance to the Crown," but discountenanced "allegiance to Parliament."

When, however, the entire petitioning movement is seen as a whole, the colonists' approach to British authority becomes far more explicable. The English people's line of appeal in seeking redress of grievances began with the House of Commons, moved to the House of Lords, and finally to the king himself. This avenue of appeal was unimpeachably Whiggish, grounded as it was in the Revolution Settlement and the Bill of Rights. It was exactly the same line

---

[9]Concerning the American reliance upon the Crown as a Tory posture, see Jerrylin Marston, "King and Congress: The Transfer of Political Legitimacy from the King to the Continental Congress, 1774-1776" (Ph.D. dissertation, Boston University, 1975), "The Whig Theory of Monarchy," 1-73.

[10]*Sal. Win . J.* (27 November 1775); *Lond. Gaz.* (17-21 October 1775). The text of the Olive Branch Petition is in K. G. Davies, *Documents of the American Revolution, 1770-1783* (Dublin: Irish University Press, 1976) 9:40-42. Regarding similar expressions from Oxford and Maidenhead, see *Lond. Gaz.* (11-14, 21-25 November 1775).

that the American petitions followed. The earlier petitions from New York, for example, had appealed to the king and Parliament, and they, like the English merchants' petitions, had been rejected by both Houses of Parliament. The eighth resolve of the First Constitutional Congress simply followed the Bill of Rights in insisting that the colonists "have a right peaceably to assemble, consider of their grievances, and petition the King." The Olive Branch Petition and other colonial petitions in support of peace must be read in the light of the intention of some 25,000 Englishmen who, in late 1775 through early 1778, still hoped for peace. These petitions supporting peace from Englishmen refute the charge that in appealing to the king, the colonists were more Tory in orientation than the ministry.[11]

Above all, the appeal to the Crown cannot be called a Tory appeal because of the religious dimension to the divisions in the contituencies. The central political issue raised by these popular protests centers around the question of local parties and party continuity. If there was a "new authoritarianism" in the government supported by an old authoritarianism in the constituencies, there was also a rising progressivism in the constituencies, and both elements had clear lines of continuity with the past. The so-called new authoritarianism and its connection with the "old Tories" has recently been thoroughly documented through a convincing analysis of the coercive addresses.[12] The counterpart to this conservative continuity is found in the role of Nonconformity in local Whig parties.

If there ever was a group that could be called faithful in its support of the government and jealous of the term *Whig*, it was the Dissenters. A half-century of steadfast devotion to the government could be cited to prove it. In those boroughs and counties where the Dissenters were prominent in politics, their religious ideology strengthened lines of party continuity, and this in turn gave the traditional party labels a lengthened life span. In 1759, when a certain Tory politician wished to make a show of his party loyalty in Essex, he equated the Whigs with the "Quakers, Presbyters," and "Devils." In 1761 at Maidstone, the Whigs and Dissenters in general were viewed as a party in contradistinction to the Tories. At Coventry the anticorporation party grasped for threads of continuity with the past and rhetorically stabbed at its opponents with the words, "Though they may have forgot the thing / Who was it murder'd Charles our King."[13] When George III was labeled a Tory by the Newcastle and Rockingham Whigs, and when affairs in America seemed to confirm their rhetoric,

---

[11]Concerning the Olive Branch Petition, see Ian Christie and Benjamin Labaree, *Empire or Independence* (Oxford: Phaidon, 1976) 264-65. Concerning appeals to the king, see Eric Robson, *The American Revolution in Its Political and Military Aspects, 1763-1783* (New York: W. W. Norton, 1966) 78-82, 88.

[12]Paul Langford, "Old Whigs, Old Tories, and the American Revolution," *The Journal of Imperial and Commonwealth History* 8 (January 1980): 106, 127.

[13]*Commons, 1754-1790*, 2:486; Sir Lewis Namier, *The Structure of Politics at the Accession of George III*, 2nd ed. (London: Macmillan Co., 1957) 118; T. W. Whitley, *The Parliamentary Representation of Coventry* (Coventry: Curtin and Beamish, 1894) 188.

the Dissenters found the charges eminently believable and well suited indeed to their local needs.

The Whig interpretation of the American Revolution, which viewed the king and his ministers as innovators and local Whig parties as loyal defenders of the Whig tradition, gains new relevance when viewed from the local angle—especially in those settings where religious differences remained strong. In 1775 the latent tendency toward two "parties" in the nation was strengthened, and just as Burke, Russell, Lecky, and Trevelyan believed, these "parties" were widely dispersed in the electorate and based largely on the age-old conflict between Church and chapel. The quantitative data provided by the petitions are less susceptible to biased interpretation than the literary sources of much Whig historiography, and yet the petitions strongly support the Whig interpretation of the revolutionary period. Commonwealthman ideology may be found to be nearly as important for England as it is for America, if the influence of religious ideology on political behavior is taken into account.[14]

Further work is needed regarding the economic dimensions of the division concerning America and how this is related to ideological differences. On the basis of what is already known, it seems likely that analysis of the larger boroughs and counties will lead to a new appreciation of both economic and ideological factors in motivating political behavior. The petitions supporting peace also raise fundamental questions concerning the inevitability of historical events. It is usually argued, for example, that as American resistance to English authority became more open, the English populace was naturally impelled to become more unified in its support of coercion.[15] The date for this hardening of opinion must now be shifted to the first months of 1776 at the earliest, since more conciliatory petitons appeared after Lexington and Concord than before those opening salvos. Charles Ritcheson has shown that as statesmen groped for a solution to the colonial problem, they haltingly and ever so slowly retreated from absolute parliamentary supremacy.[16] Now it can be demonstrated that a portion of the English population was also ready for this solution.

A minority of Englishmen did not accept the war as inevitable, even after Lexington and Concord. The rudimentary idea of a commonwealth was not lacking, even among the populace, though the leadership necessary to implement such an idea was. In most petitions in support of peace there was an implicit willingness to reconsider the claims of parliamentary supremacy. In some

[14]Colin Bonwick, *English Radicals and the American Revolution* (Chapel Hill: University of North Carolina Press, 1977) 10, 85, was unaware of the impact of ideology on behavior.

[15]Christie and Labaree, *Empire or Independence*, 216. Bernard Donoughue, *British Politics and the American Revolution: The Path to War, 1773-1775* (London: Macmillan Co., 1965) 198.

[16]Charles Ritcheson, *British Politics and the American Revolution* (Norman OK: University of Oklahoma Press, 1954) 202, 217-19, 225.

of the more radical statements, in which the rights of the Americans were defended, this willingness became explicit. Wallingford petitioners, for example, asked that Parliament "may permanently establish the limits of that subordination which it is no less their desire than their interest and duty to preserve." The pro-Americans at Nottingham were willing to defend only "the just, the useful and practicable rights of the English legislature."[17] From the people of England themselves emerged expressions that challenged constituted authority and pointed toward the future commonwealth.

The petitions lend credence to the neo-Whig interpretation of the Revolution insofar as they imply that the king and Parliament could have acted differently than they did. They demonstrate that popular support for conciliatory measures was not limited to radicals, and they require that a broader, more inclusive perspective be taken on pro-Americanism generally. Pro-Americans have in the past been equated with London coffee-house radicals, the intellectual elite, and a few progressive Dissenting clergymen. But the majority of those who signed the petitions supporting peace were not radicals, any more than the addressers who supported George III were Jacobites. The majority were not even Dissenters, and the leaders in the provinces were seldom radicals of the London Association stripe. Rather, the petitioners were concerned citizens drawn largely from the middle ranks of society who identified their interests with a tradition of liberal thought. There is some evidence to suggest that the lower ranks of society remained aloof from this agitation, but satisfying explanations concerning why they were not involved are yet to be advanced. The common people who are called upon to fight wars are seldom, if ever, indifferent to them; the petitions concerning peace may lend support to rumors of popular resistance to recruitment for the armed service that can be found in many newspaper notices of the era.

That the conciliatory petitions to the king finally counted for naught also tends to substantiate the neo-Whig conspiratorial interpretation.[18] The government was far more innovative than the opposition in the use of the press as propaganda. If J. C. D. Clark's skepticism concerning public opinion in the mid-eighteenth century has any validity for the 1770s, it is because expressions of opinion that opposed the government were not allowed to have any influence.[19] Though the impotence of public opinion is admitted, its reality cannot be denied. The way in which the government was successfully able to ignore popular opposition does reveal new dimensions of authoritarianism. To admit this is to admit the reality of the very thing Whigs feared and wrote about. Both

---

[17]HO 55/28/21; 10/18.

[18]Bernard Bailyn, *The Ideological Origins of the American Revolution* (Cambridge: Belknap Press, 1967) 148.

[19]J. C. D. Clark, *The Dynamics of Change: The Crisis of the 1750s and English Party Systems* (New York: Cambridge University Press, 1982) 3-4, 263-64, 314.

the reality of the opinion and the reality of its suppression are worth noting, though in the end the opinion proved ineffectual.

It is perhaps fruitless to speculate about what might have happened had the petitions supporting peace been taken seriously. The sheer bulk of parchment itself must have been ignored with difficulty, and one can only guess how the king reacted inwardly to the conciliatory documents as they passed before him at the levee. Evidently no minister had the courage to draw more attention to them. If the king had acted improvidently in 1769 concerning Wilkes, and again in 1784 at the dismissal of the Coalition, doubts about his handling of the American crisis may now be raised with more conviction than ever.[20] Herbert Butterfield once claimed that the House of Commons' unresponsiveness to the people led, by 1780, to a "quasi-revolutionary" situation in England.[21] It can now be shown that the Revolution was also stimulated in part by the unresponsiveness of the Crown. By the time of Dunning's resolution in 1780, a majority in the Commons acknowledged that the king's authority extended too far, though the same majority was not willing to press its advantage. But much earlier, even at the outset of the crisis, a minority of Englishmen out of doors sensed that Royal displeasure regarding petitions in support of peace would contribute to a disastrous war.

The numerous addresses in favor of coercion, however, meant that George III could legitimately claim that the nation was genuinely supportive of his measures. The king's willingness to recognize the petitions from the Corporation of London, and his refusal of those from the more radical Common Hall, was symbolic of where the government looked for support. The king and his ministers felt that more weight should be given to addresses from corporations and the respectable elements in society rather than from the English public at large. Since he knew that he had the support of Parliament and the majority of the civic leaders of the country, George III was confident in ignoring the petitions supporting peace. The evidence from the occupational data also suggests that the government had wealth and influence on its side. The large documents in favor of peace from London, Bristol, Newcastle-upon-Tyne, and Halifax, and the massive petitions from Hampshire and Lancashire, made little impression next to the equally large addresses from the same corporations and counties. Popular protest against the government was thus finally ineffective because the government chose to ignore it. Moreover, the king himself was deeply involved with matters of war and peace. This first widespread popular resistance to modern war was stillborn in large measure because the weight of

---

[20]Butterfield, *George III, Lord North and the People*, 3-17; John Cannon, *The Fox-North Coalition: Crisis of the Constitution, 1782-1784* (Cambridge: Cambridge University Press, 1969) xiii; Richard Pares, *King George III and the Politicians* (Oxford: Oxford University Press, 1953) 69-70.

[21]Butterfield, *George III, Lord North and the People*, vi; Cannon, *The Fox-North Coalition*, xi.

tradition supported the king as a leader in affairs of state who still had considerable influence on policy.

But the voice of the English people cannot thereby be dismissed. In the fall of 1775 a substantial minority of the common people believed that the war was "founded on unnatural principles" and that from it "nothing can be gained, tho' much must be lost." They felt certain that from "a most ruinous civil war" no good effects "may arise to these kingdoms." Some believed the government's policies were "disastrous measures" leading to "a fruitless and ruinous contest." Others shuddered "with horror when our brethren fall by the hands of brethren, in the unnatural and cruel conflict of civil war." Freeholders expostulated that they could "never be brought to imagine that the true remedy for such disorders consists in an attack on all other rights, and an attempt to drive the people either to unconditional submission or absolute despair." Inhabitants of boroughs complained that "in the present unnatural war with our American brethren, we have seen neither provocation nor object," and they pondered, "America may be laid low, but what laurels shall we reap by such a conquest?" In 1775 the people of England advised the king of England: "If this plan should continue to be enforced, it must be attended with great waste of blood and treasure to this country, without any well-grounded prospect of success, and may finally deprive these kingdoms of the valuable trade of America, and force the inhabitants of that county, against their inclination and interest, to set up an independent state."[22]

Given the reality of the popular response to the imperial crisis of 1775, the thoughts and actions of the English masses can no longer be likened to the "migration of birds" or the "plunging of hordes of lemmings into the sea."[23] The thinking of the people in 1775 was well informed, and their political actions were a natural reflection of their thought. The petitions in support of peace underscore the tragedy of the war rather than its inevitability. There are lasting ironies as well: the petitions prove that Englishmen at home were actually more free to express their opposition to the government than were Loyalists in the colonies who opposed the Revolution.[24] And, though it is possible to call the leadership to account for losing its last real opportunity for compromise, given

---

[22]Staffordshire, *Lond. Eve.-Post* (12-14 December 1775); Cambridge, *Cam. Chron.* (9 December 1775); Wallingford, HO 55/28/21; Poole, *Lond. Eve.-Post* (2-4 November 1775); Berkshire, HO 55/12/9; Newcastle-upon-Tyne, HO 55/28/19; Coventry, HO 55/8/6; Southwark, *Pub. Adv.* (4 December 1775).

[23]Namier was explicitly dealing with the English nation of 1770-1778 when he wrote this. *England in the Age of the American Revolution*, 2nd ed. (London: Macmillan Co., 1961) 41. "There was," wrote Namier, "no free will in the thinking and acting of the masses."

[24]Richard Buell, Jr., "Freedom of the Press in Revolutionary America: The Evolution of Libertarianism, 1760-1820," in Bernard Bailyn and John B. Hench, eds., *The Press and the American Revolution* (Worcester: American Antiquarian Society, 1980) and Janice Potter and Robert M. Calhoun, "The Character and Coherence of the Loyalist Press" in the same volume.

the number and weight of the addresses favoring coercion, it might be concluded that the king did act in good conscience. But contrary to the opinions and actions of the masses, the king and ministry were able to maintain the picture of a nation united in abhorrence of the rebellious colonists. Only now is it possible to say that the people of England were divided concerning the use of force against their American brethren. For many Englishmen, the American Revolution was not an unnatural rebellion, but a tragic, unnecessary, and unnatural civil war.[25]

---

[25]Newspapers noted the report that the coercive addresses were ordered to be printed and sent to America, "there to be distributed" in order to set those "misled people right." *Lond. Chron.* (19-21 September 1775); *Man. Merc.* (19 September 1775); *York Cour.* (26 September 1775). However, none are known to have been printed. Broadsides of the London petition of 5 July 1775 were, however, printed at Boston, Salem, Watertown, and New York, and there were probably accounts of the petitions in some colonial papers. Charles Evans, *American Bibliography*, 14 vols. (Chicago: Blakely Press, 1903-1959) 5:149.

Appendix 1

The petitions and addresses to the Crown regarding America are retained in the Home Office papers at the Public Record Office. The official government organ, the *London Gazette*, published all but one of the English addresses found in the Public Record Office (the address from Coventry), and it printed twenty-six documents in favor of coercion that are no longer extant. These twenty-six documents include six from English boroughs and towns, three from English counties, (see Tables 3.1-3.6 above) and eleven from Scottish burghs and towns, and four Scottish counties (see Appendix 2). The *London Evening-Post* did equally well as far as publishing petitions in support of peace; it listed all of the conciliatory petitions found in the Public Record Office and, in addition, it mentioned three others and printed the text of seven more that are no longer extant. These eight English boroughs and towns, and two counties, are found in Tables 3.1-3.3, with references. A comparison of the manuscripts with the printed documents in the *London Gazette* and in the *London Evening-Post* reveals that both the texts of the documents and the signatures were transcribed and printed with great care. No errors were detected in a survey of hundreds of names.

There are eight lists of signatures in the Public Record Office that have been detached from the narrative part of the petitions and are listed as "unknown." I have been able to identify HO 55/7/2 and 55/10/19 as part of the Lancashire coercive address and HO 55/8/6 is positively identified as the Coventry conciliatory petition, but it has only about half of the signatures. The text of the Coventry petition and all of the signatures were printed in the *London Evening-Post* (19-21, 21-24 October 1775). It has not been possible to locate those who presented the petitions from Colchester, Southampton, Lymington, Leeds, Middlesex, and Berkshire. The documentary history of the Revolution entitled *American Archives*, "prepared and published under authority of an act of Congress," printed the texts without signatures of all but two of the English coercive addresses to the Crown as they appeared in the *London Gazette*—the addresses from Cirencester and the county of Hereford alone were missing (*London Gazette*, 11-14 November, 12-16 December 1775). With the exception of Manchester and four other instances in Tables 3.5 and 3.6 above, these were printed without signatures appended. It printed the texts without the signatures of the conciliatory petitions from ten places in England (two from Nottingham), and the petition from Cork, but even these petitions have not been studied in secondary works. The texts of the conciliatory petitions available in *American Archives* are: London Merchants, Bristol, Coventry, Newcastle-upon-

Tyne, Nottingham inhabitants, Nottingham mayor and burgesses, Worcester, Taunton, Bridgwater, Westbury-Warminster-Trowbridge, Berkshire, and Cork. See *American Archives*, 4th ser. 3:1010-11, 816-17, 981-82, 1201-202, 1115-16, 1113-15, 1519-20, 803-804, 1189; 6:71; 3:1383-84; 6:402-403. The fifteen documents in this Appendix have not been printed since 1775.

In the body of each petition, capitalization has been brought into conformity with modern usage, the less-familiar archaic words, "betwixt," "burthen," and "shew" have been modernized, ampersands changed to "and," and punctuation has been added where it is absolutely necessary for the sake of clarity. Otherwise, the texts are exact reproductions of the original manuscripts in the Public Record Office or, where the originals are no longer extant, from the first source noted.

SOUTHWARK

To the King's Most Excellent Majesty.

The humble Address and Petition of the Electors of the ancient Town and Borough of Southwark, assembled at a General Meeting at the Town Hall.

May it please your Majesty,

We your Majesty's dutiful and loyal subjects, the electors of the ancient town and borough of Southwark, beg leave humbly to approach your Majesty, with our unfeigned sentiments on the present dangerous and alarming situation of affairs, respecting the mother country and her colonies in America.

We should not have presumed, at this time to have troubled your Majesty with assurances of our unalterable zeal, love, and attachment to your Majesty's person and Government, the sincerity of which we have manifested on all occasions, and which we have embraced from education and principle, if the intention of some amongst us to encourage, as we apprehend, an unnatural civil war between us and our fellow subjects in America, had not made a declaration of our opinions absolutely necessary.

Britons who are happy in the enjoyment of the freest constitution in the world have at all times manifested the strongest attachment to the right of representation, and have cheerfully submitted to the heaviest burden of the state, whilst they have enjoyed that great privilege entire. The Americans, we humbly conceive, are entitled to all the rights of our excellent constitution, and till lately have always exercised the privilege of granting their own money.

Happy in the possession of that privilege, we have seen them ready to assist the mother country with men and treasure for the general good, and cheerfully submitting to a restraint of their commerce, by which this country has reaped the greatest advantage.

If the justice of the attempt was better founded than we humbly conceive it to be, we cannot see the wisdom of persisting in a plan of governing an immense continent by force, against the general sense of a people, who profess their dutiful attachment to Great Britain as their common parent, and every dependence on it, confident with their privileges as freemen.

If this plan should continue to be enforced, it must be attended with great waste of blood and treasure to this country, without any well-grounded prospect of success, and may finally deprive these kingdoms of the valuable trade of America, and force the inhabitants of that country, against their inclination and interest to set up an independent state.

Permit us therefore, royal Sire, humbly to request that a stop may be put to war and bloodshed, and that your Majesty would be pleased to render happy our American fellow-subjects, by a restoration of those measures and mode of Government, which experience has shown to have been productive of the greatest advantage to them and us, and which alone can render flourishing and united the great empire over which we hope your Majesty and your royal descendants will reign to the latest posterity.

Signatures: 756

Presented: 29 November 1775 by Nathaniel Polhill, attended by Sir Joseph Mawbey, Richard Carpenter Smith, Samuel Bennett Smith, Thomas Fawcett, James Burt, and Edward Henshaw

Original: No longer extant

Text alone printed:

Pub. Adv. (4 December 1775)

COLCHESTER

To the King's Most Excellent Majesty.

The humble Address of Many of the Gentlemen, Merchants, Freeburgesses, and Traders of Colchester and places adjacent.

Most Gracious Sovereign,

We your Majesty's dutiful and loyal subjects, gentlemen, merchants, freeburgesses and traders, inhabitants of the ancient borough of Colchester and places adjacent, think it our incumbent duty, at the present alarming crisis, to assure your Majesty of our most loyal, unfeigned and unshaken attachment to your Majesty's person, family and government, being fully sensible that the happiness of your subjects consists in a firm adherence to your royal person and family, and in an allegiance to your Majesty's Government, according to the most excellent constitution of the British monarchy; which we cannot but esteem of all others as the wisest and best; being fully reminded that to be a subject of Great Britain, with all its consequences, is to be the freest member of any civil society in the known world.

Deeply affected with the calamitous and destructive differences that at present subsist between Great Britain and her colonies, we beg leave to express our warmest wishes that such conciliatory measures may be adopted and pursued as shall have a happy tendency to put a speedy period to the same.

That this most desirable event may take place, may the Almighty guide your Majesty, as the father of your people, and direct your councils to measures best cal-

culated to that important end, is the sincere prayer of, Sire, your ever faithful and most affectionate subjects.
Signatures: 511
Presented: 29 January 1776
Original: HO 55/9/4
Text alone printed:
  Cam. Chron. (3 February 1776).

GREAT YARMOUTH

To the King's most Excellent Majesty.

The humble Address and Petition of the Merchants and Inhabitants of the Borough of Great Yarmouth, in the County of Norfolk.

Most Gracious Sovereign,

At this alarming crisis, when many of your Majesty's subjects come with addresses to offer their sentiments with respect to the unhappy differences with our fellow subjects in America, we should think we failed in our duty to your Majesty, our country and ourselves, did we, by concealing ours, tacitly admit them to be what they are not.

Permit us, Sire, to approach your Throne with hearts full of gratitude for the many blessings the subject enjoys under your Majesty's Government in Great Britain.

At the same time we lament the evils that threaten this kingdom, from the present measures taken with the Americans. Should the extensive British settlements in North America be compelled by force to submit to claims which they appear united to oppose, we fear the many scenes of bloodshed which must precede that event (if ever it should take place) will totally alienate the minds of our fellow-subjects there; and that this kingdom will not, for a long continuance, enjoy the advantages arising from those establishments, which a reconciliation will be most likely to render durable.

We therefore most humbly beseech your Majesty to lend an ear to petitions for peace; and instead of coercive measures, to adopt such gentle means as may bring about a reconciliation with America. Happy shall we be to see all parts of the British empire vie with each other in the strengthening union between them, and enjoy the advantages of a mutual increasing commerce, its grand support.

Signatures: 344
Presented: 17 November 1775 by Sir Edward Astley and Wenman Coke
Original: No longer extant
Printed with signatures:
  Norw. Merc. (2, 9 December 1775)
Text alone printed:
  Lond. Eve.-Post (21-23 November 1775)

SOUTHAMPTON

To the King's Most Excellent Majesty,

The humble Petition of many of the Burgesses, Gentlemen, Merchants, and Traders of the Town and County of Southampton.

We, your Majesty's most dutiful and loyal subjects, the burgesses, gentlemen, merchants, and traders of the town and county of Southampton, beg leave with the utmost humility to approach your Majesty, to declare our unfeigned attachment and loyalty to your Majesty's royal person and family, and to represent our dreadful apprehensions of those operations of force at present adopted against our fellow subjects in America.

The regard we entertain for the just rights of all our fellow subjects, and the great anxiety with which we behold the present unhappy contest, rendered still more destructive by the effusion of the blood of your Majesty's subjects, oblige us to lay ourselves at your royal feet, humbly to implore your Majesty, that the natural and chartered rights of our American brethren may be preserved inviolate, the system of force laid aside, and that some measure may be adopted to promote a just, happy, and constitutional reconciliation between Great Britain and her colonies, that this distracted empire may be again united in firm bonds of peace and amity and continue indissoluble under the auspicious Government of your Majesty and the illustrious House of Brunswick to the latest posterity.

And your petitioners as in duty bound shall ever pray.

Southampton
October 13th, 1775
Signatures: 117
Presented: 27 October 1775
Original: HO 55/11/20
Text alone printed:
    Lond. Eve.-Post (2-4 November 1775)

CAMBRIDGE

To the King's most Excellent Majesty.

Most gracious Sovereign,

We, the mayor, bailiffs, burgesses, and principal inhabitants of the town of Cambridge, do humbly beg leave to approach the Throne, with the most respectful assurances of our attachment and affection to your Majesty's royal person and family, and of our zeal for the support and dignity of your Government, the glory of your reign, and the peace and prosperity of your empire.

With the utmost affliction, and the most anxious apprehensions, we behold a most ruinous civil war begun in America, which, we fear, if pursued, must totally alienate the affections of our fellow subjects in the colonies, and in the prosecution of which we can foresee no good effects that may arise to these kingdoms; even were your Majesty's arms victorious, desolated provinces and an exasperated people must be the only consequence of a continuance of this war.

We beg leave most humbly to assure your Majesty, that no part of your Majesty's subjects wish more earnestly to preserve the constitution of this country than the town of Cambridge; but we humbly conceive that healing concessions are more likely to restore the confidence and affections of the colonies, than the exertion of force, which can only tend to their destruction and desolation.

We find ourselves under the indispensable necessity of making, with the utmost respect, this dutiful representation of our sentiments to your Majesty, lest our silence might make it supposed we consented to the wishes of coercive measures expressed in some of the late addresses. We assure your Majesty we are men of peaceable dispositions, and detest the thought of recommending force and rigour against any part of your Majesty's people. We wish for the return of that peace and tranquility which marked the happy period of your Majesty's reign before these distressful disputes were agitated with the colonies. We have every assurance to believe that they wish nothing more earnestly than to return to that allegiance and affection, so essentially necessary to the commercial interests and happiness of this country; and we trust in your Majesty's wisdom to reconcile the differences that unhappily subsist, and to restore those days of peace and mutual confidence, to which we look back with gratitude and satisfaction.

By this dutiful representation of our sentiments we have endeavoured to discharge our consciences to the almighty Governor of all things, to our Sovereign, and to our country, and to clear ourselves from having to share in producing the calamities that may fall upon this nation, praying God to avert them, that he may please to make your Majesty's reign glorious and happy.

Signatures: 160
Presented: 29 November 1775 by Samuel Meeke and Thomas Plumer Byde
Original: No longer extant
Printed with signatures:
   Cam. Chron. (9 December 1775)

POOLE

To the King's Most Excellent Majesty.

Most Gracious Sovereign,

We, your Majesty's truly loyal and dutiful subjects, the gentlemen, clergy, freeholders, merchants, traders, and inhabitants of the town and county of Poole, in the Guildhall assembled, duly sensible of the many important privileges and blessings which, under the present happy and wise form of government, we enjoy, beg leave most humbly to approach the Throne, professing our zealous attachment to your Majesty's person and Government, and most ardently solicitous to see the Crown of these realms acquire additional lustre, as it is continued to be worn by your illustrious House; deeply interested in whatever may affect your Majesty's person, family, or

Government, we cannot but painfully feel these dissensions and alarming contests which have lately arisen between Great Britain and the colonies; which, from their inauspicious beginnings, and alarming progress, without your Majesty's gracious and benevolent interposition, may terminate in the loss or diminution of the lustre of the most precious jewel belonging to your Majesty's Crown, and in the greatest of all national evils, the unspeakable horrors, misery, and destruction of civil war; by which the external supports, and internal strength of this mighty empire, must be violently and dangerously shaken, if not totally destroyed, and become an easy prey to our natural and avowed enemies.

Influenced by no interested motives, actuated by no partial views, but inspired alone by the duty and affection we bear to your Majesty, the love of our country, and that great and godlike principle of humanity, which suffers when even an enemy falls, but shudders with horror when our brethren fall by the hands of brethren, in the unnatural and cruel conflict of civil war. Zealous for our national honour and reputation, as well as the extensive renown of your Majesty's glory and fame, we humbly pray that your Majesty, in your wonted goodness and princely benignity, as the father of his people, would be pleased most graciously to interfere, suspend the operations of war, and direct such mode of application to be made, as may abate the jealousies, remove the contests, and compromise the differences now fatally subsisting between Great Britain and the colonies. That the precious blood of subjects, which ought never to be spilt but for the maintenance of the honour and dignity of your Majesty's Crown, and the sacred rights of the people, may cease to flow, and that peace and harmony may be restored to this divided empire, from which alone the prosperity of these realms, the happiness of this great people, and your Majesty's own glory and felicity can be derived; and upon which the stability and permanency of this Government absolutely depend; and by which the happy prospect, and auspicious hopes, that the sceptre of these kingdoms will be ever swayed by one of your illustrious family, can be best secured to your faithful subjects, and the zealous friends of the House of Hanover.

That your Majesty may adopt such measures, and pursue such counsels as may lead to so desirable, important, and glorious an end, is the most earnest and zealous prayer of your Majesty's most loyal and dutiful subjects.

Signatures: 144
Presented: 31 October 1775 by Joshua Mauger
Original: No longer extant
Printed with signatures:
    Lond. Eve.-Post (2-4 November 1775)

LYMINGTON

To the King's most Excellent Majesty.

The Humble Address and Petition of the Principal and Other Inhabitants, Merchants and Manufacturers of the town of Lymington, in the County of Southampton.

Most Gracious Sovereign,

At this truly interesting period, when 'tis confessedly of the last importance, that your Majesty should be made acquainted with the real voice of your people; we presume with all dutiful humility, and constitutional freedom, thus to lay our sentiments at your royal feet.

Sensible of the manifold blessings we enjoy, under your Majesty's auspicious reign, we beg leave to testify our unfeigned and zealous attachment to your royal person and family; nor would we wish to be thought less tender, of the honour, dignity, and just prerogatives of the Crown, than the natural and chartered rights of the subject.

Inspired with the highest veneration for both, we cannot without the most painful and alarming apprehensions anticipate, the dreadful consequences of the present unhappy national contest; and therefore with earnest supplication most devoutly pray, that some lenient and constitutional measures, may be yet happily adopted, by your Majesty's great wisdom, and innate goodness of heart, together with the efforts of your national council, directed by divine influence, not only to prevent the further effusion of human blood, but restore and perpetuate, an indissoluble tie of amity, and mutual confidence, between Great Britain and her colonies, during a long, happy, and prosperous reign, in your Majesty's sacred person, and to the latest posterity of the illustrious, and Protestant House of Brunswick.

Signatures: 135
Presented: 17 December 1775
Original: HO 55/11/56
Never previously printed

ABINGDON

To the King's most Excellent Majesty.

The humble Address and Petition of the Gentlemen, Manufacturers, and others, Inhabitants of the Borough of Abingdon, in the County of Berks.

Most Gracious Sovereign,

We your Majesty's most dutiful and loyal subjects, the gentlemen, manufacturers, and others, inhabitants of the borough of Abingdon, in the county of Berks, justly sensible of the many important blessings we enjoy under your Majesty's Government, beg leave, with all humility and respect, to approach your royal presence, where the wisdom of this well-attempered constitution hath taught the faithful subject to hope for success in every time of public calamity and distress.

Anxiously solicitous for the welfare and prosperity of this nation, for the honour and security of your Majesty's person, family, and Government, we must be alarmed at every appearance of events that may endanger the public peace, or disturb your Majesty's repose, and therefore most earnestly deplore the present unhappy and unnatural dissensions between Great Britain and her American colonies; dissensions that, if not speedily brought to a period, must be attended with consequences exceedingly dangerous, if not entirely destructive, to the sacred union that has so long happily subsisted between them, the valuable lives of thousands of your Majesty's faithful subjects, and the commercial interest, strength, and glory of the whole empire.

These considerations, among many others, deeply affecting to the hearts of true citizens, compel us most earnestly to supplicate your Majesty, as the father of your people, to adopt such measures as may speedily effectuate an happy and lasting reconciliation, upon such constitutional principles as the wisdom of your Majesty's councils, under the influence of justice and benevolence, shall suggest, that your loyal and peaceful people may no longer hear of the horrors and devastations of civil war.

Your Majesty, in your late speech from the throne to both Houses of Parliament, was pleased graciously to declare your "anxiety to prevent, if possible, the effusion of the blood of your subjects, and the calamities which are inseparable from a state of war;" and also, "that your people can have no cause in which your Majesty is not equally interested." In these paternal and constitutional declarations we rejoice; and relying upon your Majesty's royal clemency, as well as these public declarations, we encourage ourselves in hope, that as the present state of our public affairs is so extremely critical and serious, and the fate of this great empire seems to depend upon the manner in which they are conducted; your Majesty will see reason to adopt the pacific plan; and that this our loyal address and petition, which a sense of duty to your Majesty, as well as love to our country, hath prompted us to thus humbly to present, will be graciously received.

That the valuable blessings of peace and union may be restored and established; that the liberty, both civil and religious, which your Majesty's illustrious House was raised up by the divine Providence to support and defend, may be still preserved; that your Majesty may long live to reign over a free and happy people; and that for these important purposes the crown of these realms may be established in the royal line of Brunswick and the sceptre never depart from it till time shall be no more, are the sincere and fervent prayers of your Majesty's most dutiful and loyal subjects.

Signatures: 117
Presented: 17 November 1775 by the Earl of Abingdon
Original: No longer extant
Text alone printed:
Lond. Eve.-Post (18-21 November 1775)

WALLINGFORD

To the King's most excellent Majesty.

The humble Address and Petition of the Mayor, Aldermen, Burgesses and Inhabitants of the Borough of Wallingford in the Country of Berks.

We your Majesty's faithful and loyal subjects the mayor, aldermen, burgesses and inhabitants of the borough of Wallingford deeply impressed with that just allegiance which is due from a free people to their lawful Sovereign and venerating the happy constitution under which we live, beg leave to approach your Majesty, and to express with great sincerity our sentiments on those disastrous measures which are now pursuing with respect to your Majesty's colonies in America.

We presume not to enter into a nice and useless discussion of points long since abandoned in theory and reprobated by practice; nor to define in what instances rights may be claimed without exercise, or exercised without oppression; but we humbly entreat your Majesty's attention to these plain and serious truths—That the sudden and unnecessary departure from established systems in Government is ever dangerous, and frequently unjust. And that the complaints of subjects who think themselves aggrieved, deserve the most candid and liberal construction.

We lament the infatuation of our fellow subjects, who not content with the exclusive commerce they enjoy with America and the certain profits they derive from that source, have been deceived into an opinion, that, their own burdens would be relieved in proportion to the taxes which may be raised on our brethren in America and are urging your Majesty by their addresses to persevere in these destructive measures. But we should be wanting in our duty to your Majesty, ourselves, and our posterity, if we did not embrace this occasion of bearing our cordial testimony against such proceedings, which can have no other tendency than to encourage your Majesty to exhaust the blood and treasure of your subjects in a fruitless and ruinous contest, and to entail on our brethren in America the miseries of a civil war; in which if it were possible to prevail, there is reason to apprehend, that foreign mercenaries, whose assistance hath been offered or solicited, in a work to which Britons are neither equal nor inclined, will conquer for themselves and not for Britain; and it is but too obvious that a people alienated in their affections from the parent state by such unexampled rigour, will never return to that due obedience which is professed to be the object of these unnatural exertions. Nor is it less manifest that a commerce of a country thus desolated, when forced from its proper channel by weak and impolitic management, or destroyed by the violence of arms will never again be restored to that fullness and extent, which it is the glory of your Majesty's reign in better days to have experienced. We forbear to wound your Majesty's ear by reciting what must be the consequence of disappointment and defeat, when success itself must be our ruin.

From these considerations of prudence, justice, and humanity, we most earnestly implore your Majesty to recommend to your Parliament an immediate inquiry into the true causes of this unfortunate controversy, by which the peace of your Majesty's empire hath been so deeply affected; that, availing themselves of the present season of public business, and of that benevolent disposition which we are persuaded your Majesty must feel to prevent the further effusion of the blood of our fellow subjects, they may apply themselves with temper and with effect to the redressing of those real grievances of which our fellow subjects in America complain and may permanently establish the limits of that subordination which it is no less their desire, than their interest and duty to preserve.

That the blessings of peace and the advantages of commerce may again be restored to the whole empire, is the anxious and earnest prayer of your Majesty's most dutiful subjects.

Signatures: 80
Presented: 17 Nov. 1775 by the Earl of Abingdon
Original: HO 55/28/21
Text alone printed:
  Lond. Eve.-Post (18-21 November 1775)

LEEDS

To the King's most Excellent Majesty.

The Humble Address and Petition of the Gentlemen, Merchants, Manufacturers, and Traders, of the Town and Neighborhood of Leeds in the County of York.

Most Gracious Sovereign

We think it our duty in the present alarming situation of affairs, to assure your Majesty of our unfeign'd affection to your Majesty's person and Government. We have been educated from our earliest youth in a faithful adherence to the principles of our excellent constitution, as it was established at the Revolution, and confirmed by the auspicious accession of the illustrious House of Hanover to the Throne of these kingdoms. Our own happy experience has born full testimony to the wisdom of our ancestors, and hath convinced us how deeply we are interested in the preservation of an authority under which we enjoy such invaluable blessings.

We are therefore bound to allegiance by a conviction of duty, as well as by a habit of affection, and shall always with the greatest cheerfulness exert ourselves to the utmost of our power, in opposition to the attempts of all your Majesty's foreign and domestic enemies. But at the same time, in justice to your Majesty, in justice to our selves, and in justice to all our fellow subjects in your Majesty's extensive dominions, we are obliged to declare with all the honest freedom of faithful and affectionate subjects, that we cannot approve the sanguinary measures, which have been recommended to your Majesty, in some recent addresses on the present unhappy disturbances in America.

We acknowledge with gratitude the integrity and fidelity of our American brethren in their connections with us, and are therefore deeply affected when we reflect on the unhappy misunderstanding which hath interrupted this beneficial intercourse, the effects of which some of us already sensibly feel, and which we are apprehensive will in a short time be still more severely and generally felt.

Permit us therefore, most gracious Sovereign, humbly and earnestly to entreat your Majesty to commiserate the anxieties of your faithful subjects, and to pursue such conciliatory measures, as shall in your Majesty's wisdom seem most likely to remove these threatening evils.

Signatures: 594
Presented: 9 November 1775
Original: HO 55/21/39
Text alone printed:
  York Cour. (14 November 1775)

HALIFAX

To the King's Most Excellent Majesty.

The humble and dutiful Petition of the Gentlemen, Clergy, Merchants, Manufacturers, and other Inhabitants of your Majesty's commercial and extensive parish of Halifax, in the West-Riding of the county of York.

Most gracious Sovereign,

Always zealous to express our unfeigned attachment to your Majesty's royal person and family, and our desire of promoting tranquility, as well at home as in every part of your Majesty's dominions, we therefore supplicate your royal interposition for an amicable termination of all differences between the mother country and her colonies whereby, we, as well as all other of your Majesty's most faithful subjects are essentially affected.

Firmly relying on your Majesty's wisdom and prudence, we humbly beseech your Majesty to accept this humble and loyal petition, as proceeding from motives solely tending to the re-establishing of that mutual confidence which ought always to subsist between the legislative body and the subject.

Signatures: 1,865
Presented: 7 November 1775 by Sir George Savile
Original: HO 55/16/3
Text alone printed:
   York Cour. (14 November 1775); *Lond. Eve.-Post* (4-7 November 1775);
   Lond. Chron. (7-9 November 1775).

BOLTON

To the King's Most Excellent Majesty.

The humble Address and Petition of the Gentlemen, Clergy, Traders, and other Inhabitants of the Town and Neighbourhood of Bolton, in the County of Lancaster.

May it please your Majesty,

We, your Majesty's most loyal and dutiful subjects, the gentlemen, clergy, traders, and other inhabitants of the town and neighbourhood of Bolton, desire to approach the Throne at this interesting period, as persons who would not yield to any of your Majesty's subjects, in affection to your royal person and illustrious family, and in earnest wishes for the firm support of your Majesty's Government, and the dignity of your Crown, and who are desirous of expressing those sentiments by every exertion which it is in their power to make.

We find it difficult to express to you, Sir, the sentiments of grief with which our hearts are penetrated, when we reflect on the unhappy situation of affairs in your

American dominions. The strength and glory which the British empire has derived under your Majesty's Government, and that of your royal ancestors, from the union which subsisted between the mother-country and her colonies, are now we fear in danger from the spirit of dissension which has gone forth, and proceeded to such amazing lengths.

We cannot be unconcerned spectators, Sir, of the miseries which threaten our native country; and we have the highest abhorrence of the principles and practices of those who contribute to them, and earnestly wish that your Majesty's wisdom and humanity may direct you to the pursuit of such measures as may disappoint the designs of your Majesty's enemies, and those of your kingdom, and cause all your friends to rejoice in the recovery of peace, union, and tranquility, amongst all your Majesty's subjects.

Your Majesty will pardon your loyal and dutiful subjects, if the interests of trade and manufactures, the principal subsistence of this town and neighbourhood, engage some part of our attention. The present unhappy divisions between your subjects at home and in America threaten the utter destruction of trade in general, and of the trade of this country in particular; and though some accidental causes have, as yet, prevented our feeling this calamity, yet we apprehend the time cannot be very remote, when the temporary supplies of traffic failing, we shall bitterly feel, and in vain lament, that these channels in which our trade has so long and so happily flowed, are for ever dried up.

We are well persuaded, Sir, that your royal heart is possessed with sentiments of humanity and compassion, and that the best interests of your subjects are ever your concern; and these will be stronger arguments with you to listen to the petition we now with humble duty present, than any we can use to enforce it. And we hope we shall not be guilty of a criminal presumption, if we add, that the dignity of your Crown, and the glory of your Government, will be more effectually secured by the timely exertion of your royal clemency, than by any successes or any advantages which the prosecution of coercive measures may afford. And how doubtful the success of them is, and how they may be in their consequences, is but too well known.

Upon all these accounts, we request of you, most gracious Sovereign, that you wou'd receive this our humble petition, as a tribute of loyalty to your royal person. Let your Majesty's great goodness incline you to cause all hostilities with your American subjects to cease, and to recall them to the enjoyment of peace and tranquility, and to secure their willing subjection to your Government in future years, (and may they be many and happy) by a return and steady adherence to those measures, which long experience has shown to be of mutual advantage to this nation and its colonies.

Signatures: 751
Presented: 16 December 1775 by Lord George Cavendish
Original: No longer extant
Text alone printed:
    Lond. Eve.-Post (14-16 December 1775)

MIDDLESEX

To the King's most excellent Majesty.

The humble Address, Petition and Remonstrance of the Freeholders of the County of Middlesex

Impressed with an awful sense of the dangers which surround us, feeling for ourselves and our posterity, anxious for the glory of a country hitherto as much renowned for the virtues of justice and humanity as for the splendour of its arms, we approach your throne with sentiments becoming loyal subjects at so alarming an hour, and at the same time with that respect which is due to the monarch of a free people and prince of the illustrious House of Brunswick, to which we feel ourselves in a peculiar manner attached by all the ties of gratitude and affection.

It is with inexpressible concern that we have heard your Majesty declare in your speech to both Houses of Parliament your intention of persevering in a system of measures which has proved so disastrous to this country. Such a declaration calls for the voice of a free and injured people. We feel the respect due to Majesty, but in this critical and awful moment, to flatter, is to betray.

We cannot but repeat what we have before expressed to your Majesty, our unvaried abhorrence of this contest with our American brethren, especially when we look back to the real objects which produced it and to the precious opportunities which proffered very early to prevent or stop it before the breach was rent thus wide. Yet discontented as we have been, like patient subjects we have sat still and have born our share of the very oppressive burdens with which this nation has been loaded, hoping that infatuation would soon run its length, and what was unjustly and unwisely rushed into might obtain in the revolution of events a termination in due time which might reconcile all in amity.

But when a second army has been captured; when the consumate valour of the first officers in Europe and the tried bravery of the first troops in the world have been insufficient to make more than momentary impression, or to save themselves from captivity in the end—when the most sanguine expectation can hardly look for less defeat where every position that is taken by your Majesty's troops is by the invitation of war, and the mode of it, surrounded at best with timid friends and desperate enemies—when every possible exertion hath been made at home, every requisition of your Majesty's ministers in Parliament for fleets and armies hath been most amply indulged beyond all imagination of the neighbouring states of Europe, and all examples of former times; when disastrous experience hath brought us to a moment like this of knowing that the combat is too unequal to our strength, we cannot forbear imploring your Majesty's consideration for us and our posterity.

What we feel from this detestable war is matter of too much notoriety for the most artful tongue to gainsay. The trade of this country has suffered irreparable losses and is threatened with final extinction.

The manufactures in many valuable branches are declining and their supply of materials rendered precarious by the inferiority of your Majesty's fleet to that of your enemies in almost every part of the globe.

The landed property throughout the kingdom has been depreciated to the alarming degree.

The property of your Majesty's subjects vested in the public funds has lost above one third of its value.

Private credit has been almost wholly annihilated by the enormous interest in the public loans above what is allowed by law in any private contract.

And amidst these cruel diminutions of our resources your Majesty's subjects have been loaded with a burden of taxes which even if our victories have been as splendid as our defeats have been disgraceful, if our accession of dominion had been as fortunate as the dismemberment of the empire has been cruel and disastrous, could not in itself be considered but as a great and grievous calamity.

O' Sire, suffer not this once great and flourishing nation to experience the utmost measure of calamity, which can flow from ill-fated councils. Look back, we beseech your Majesty, to that fatal period in the Spanish history when contending for a length of years with impracticable provinces, the glory of that monarchy and the whole vigour of that nation sustained a blow, from which to this hour they have never recovered.

We do therefore most earnestly entreat your Majesty to relinquish entirely and for ever the plan of reducing our brethren in America to obedience by force and to improve the present moment while your Majesty has a degree of force still left and possessions still remaining in the western world, towards bringing forward a peace with that people.

And as a most probable opening to these views and also as a pledge both to them and us of your Majesty's fixed determination to abandon a system incompatible with the interest of your Crown and the welfare of your people, we further beseech your Majesty to dismiss from your presence and councils all the advisers, both public and secret, of the measures we lament, that their influence being removed, they may meet that fair and just trial of their conduct, which their injured country has a right to demand.

Signatures: 1,033
Presented: 21 October 1775
Original: HO 55/13/2
No other copy located

LANCASHIRE

To the King's Most Excellent Majesty.

The humble Address and Petition of the Gentlemen, Clergy, Traders, and Freeholders of the County Palatine of Lancaster.

May it please your Majesty,

*We your Majesty's most dutiful and loyal subjects, the gentlemen, clergy, trad-
ers, and freeholders of the county Palatine of Lancaster, beg leave to approach the
Throne with the most respected assurances of our inviolable attachment and affection to your Majesty's royal person and illustrious family, and our unaffected zeal
for the firm support of your Majesty's Government, the dignity of your Crown, and
the prosperity of this once happy and united empire.*

*In the present alarming and critical situation of public affairs, it becomes every
man, who glories in the name of Briton, to drop every inferior consideration and
distinction, and sedulously endeavor to avert those calamities which threaten your
Majesty's dominions.*

*Animated with these sentiments, we humbly and earnestly implore your Maj-
esty, to indulge the natural propensities of your heart in the exerting of your royal
influence for the re-establishment of peace and harmony between Great Britain and
her colonies in America, by such means as may immediately put a stop to the dreadful
and destructive consequences of a most unnatural civil war. These sentiments we feel
ourselves constrained to lay before your Majesty, with all humility, lest by our silence, it might be imputed to us, that we were consenting to the opinions and wishes
of severity and coercion, which have of late been repeatedly expressed to your Majesty in certain addresses to the Throne; such addresses, however well-intended, we
cannot approve, because we apprehend the measures therein recommended, may be
very doubtful in their success, and fatal in their consequences.*

Signatures: 4,014
Presented: 17 December 1775 by Lord George Cavendish
Original: HO 55/9/3
Text alone printed:
    Man. Merc. (14 November 1775); *Lond. Eve.-Post* (19-21 November 1775)

STAFFORD

To the King's Most Excellent Majesty.

*The humble Address and Petition of the Gentlemen, Clergy, Freeholders, Traders,
and Manufacturers of the County of Stafford.*

*We, your Majesty's most dutiful and loyal subjects, the gentlemen, clergy, free-
holders, traders, and manufacturers of the county of Stafford, humbly beg leave to
lay before your Majesty our apprehensions with respect to the present critical state of
this great empire.*

*With inexpressible concern, we see a war commenced between this country and
America; a war founded on unnatural principles, by which nothing can be gained,
tho' much must be lost.*

*We deplore the unhappy measures which have brought this country into this sit-
uation.*

*We feel for the distresses of your Majesty's troops now at Boston, and wish they
were employed in a better cause.*

We feel also for our brethren, against whom they are sent, who appear deter-mined to give up every worldly interest, and to endure the worst extremities, in this contest. They think they are fighting in the sacred cause of liberty; and, if mistaken, they ought on that account to be considered by Englishmen with indulgence.

We look back with regret to the harmony which subsisted between this kingdom and America during former reigns; and we lament the late deviations from the plan of government then pursued; a plan which made every part of your Majesty's do-minions happy, and which might have continued us a great and flourishing people for many ages to come.

But we now see a dreadful cloud gathering round us; our trade and manufac-turers threatened with ruin; desolation and carnage begun; Britons sheathing their swords in the bowels of their fellow-subjects; this great empire likely to be dismem-bered; and its very being made to depend on the peaceable disposition and forbear-ance of our natural enemies.

In circumstances so alarming, and with apprehensions so painful, it is impossible for us to be silent; and trusting in your Majesty's paternal goodness, we pray, that your Majesty would be pleased to adopt such measures as may have a tendency to restore this kingdom to its former state of safety—to heal the breach between Great Britain and America, and prevent the further effusion of the blood of our fellow-subjects.

Signatures: 900

Presented: 11 December 1775 by Robert Piggott, accompanied by Thomas Wooldridge and Thomas Rogers

Original: No longer extant

Text alone printed:

Lond. Eve.-Post (12-14 December 1775)

Appendix 2

Most of the addresses from Scotland, Ireland, and Wales were printed by the *London Gazette* and are retained in the Public Record Office.[1] Thirty of the thirty-three Scottish counties sent loyal addresses to the Crown, but none of them were circulated for the purpose of collecting signatures and, of the forty-one Scottish burghs that addressed, only four were signed: Dundee (with 371), Dumfries (122), Perth (166), and Sanquhar (76).[2] The Scottish burgh addresses came typically from the "Provost, Magistrates, and Town Council" of the burgh, and many of them add explicitly "in common council assembled." They are thus not intended to be representative of popular opinion. The only

---

[1]The *Lond. Gaz.* failed to publish only four addresses from Scotland found in the PRO: the addresses from the Scottish burgh of Forres, and the counties of Caithness, Roxburgh, and Edinburgh (PRO, HO 55/11/62; 8/36; 11/57; 11/59). However it retained coercive addresses from eleven Scottish burghs and towns and four Scottish counties that are no longer extant: Irvine, Leith, Aberdeen, Stirling, Dumfermline, Ayr, County Argyll, Angus, Perth, County Dumfries, Burntisland, Cuper, County Orkney, County Wigtown, Sanquhar (*Lond. Gaz.*, 10-14, 14-17, 28-31, 31 October–4 November, 4-7, 7-11, 11-14 November, 12-16 December 1775; 13-17 February, 19-23 March 1776). The *Lond. Gaz.* also retains the addresses of two groups of ministers: the ministers and elders of Angus and Mearns and the ministers and presbytery of Irvine (4-7 November, 12-16 December 1775). *Amer. Arch.* 4th ser. printed two Scottish addresses not found in either *Lond. Gaz.* or in the PRO: the address of the ministers and elders of the Provincial Synod of Glasgow and Ayr, 10 April 1776 (5:835) and the Address of the Provincial Synod of Dumfries, 17 April 1776 (5:959).

[2]The three counties that did not address are Buteshire, Inverness-shire, and Selkirkshire. For the Scottish counties, see PRO, HO 55/8/11, 12, 14, 17, 20, 21, 26, 28, 31, 32, 35, 36, 37, 43; 11/10, 16, 35, 44, 45, 48, 50, 51, 57, 59; 12/1; and the references to *Lond. Gaz.* in n. 1. For Dundee, Dumfries, Perth, and Sanquhar, see HO 55/8/24; 11/38; 8/18; and *Lond. Gaz.* (19-23 March 1776). Dundee and Perth sent two addresses each; compare HO 55/8/24 with 11/21 and 55/8/18 with the *Lond. Gaz.* (4-7 November 1775). For the remaining burghs, see HO 55/8/8, 13, 15, 16, 18, 19, 22, 24, 25, 27, 29, 33, 38, 39, 40, 41, 42; 11/5, 8, 11, 18, 29, 36, 38, 39, 42, 46, 47, 49, 55, 60, 62, and n. 1 above. Thirty-seven of the forty-one burghs belong to one of the fourteen groups of parliamentary burghs; in addition, there were addresses from Leith, Jedburgh, Paisley, Aberbrothuck. This left only twenty-eight parliamentary burghs that did not send addresses. See *Commons, 1754-1790*, 1:498-512. *Amer. Arch.* printed all of the Scottish addresses but those from the burgh of Irvine and the counties of Clackerman and Edinburgh (*Lond. Gaz.*, 10-14 October, 14-18 November 1775; and HO 55/11/59). See *Amer. Arch.* 4th ser. 3:756-1704; 4:153-980; 5:461.

exceptions are the four that collected signatures noted above and three others: the addresses from Leith and Elgin claim to come from the "inhabitants," and that from Fortrose says it is from "all the principal inhabitants," but none of these are signed.[3] These addresses are uniform in their expression of loyalty to George III, their abhorrence of rebellion, and the promise of their lives and fortunes in reestablishing constitutional authority in the colonies. The addresses from the counties, like those from the burghs, represent small numbers: most Scottish counties had electorates of less than 100, and many of these voters were nominal. The addresses from Scotland, however, do represent vast landed influence. Since the assemblies that met to agree on the addresses were arranged similarly to head court meetings that preceded parliamentary elections, further study is certainly warranted.

The addresses and petitions from Ireland and Wales have also been almost completely neglected. In Ireland, Dublin, Cork, and the county of Dublin addressed the throne; in Wales, Haverfordwest, Carmarthen, and the county of Carmarthen addressed.[4] All six of these coercive addresses have signatures appended, with 1055, 160, 21, 207, 167, and 160 signatures respectively. On the three counter petitions for peace, Dublin had 2,986 signatures, Cork 500, and Belfast was apparently unsigned.[5] Two addresses from the Isle of Man (one from the clergy and the other from the House of Keys) and another from the island of Guernsey should be mentioned here. The first two were signed by thirty-eight combined, the latter by fifty-nine.[6]

---

[3]See *Lond. Gaz.* (14-17 October 1775); HO 55/8/24; 11/49. On the nature of the Scottish county representation, see *Commons, 1754-1780*, 1:38-46, 521. Only four counties had an electorate of more than 100, and most of them were dominated by patrons.

[4]HO 55/12/10; 11/61; 11/66; 10/30; 11/14; 11/30.

[5]See, for Dublin, HO 55/7/4 dated 9 November 1775 and *Lond. Eve.-Post* (5-7 September, 21-23 December 1775); for Belfast, R. B. McDowell, *Irish Public Opinion, 1750-1800* (London: Faber and Faber, 1944) 44; for Cork, dated 10 May 1776, *Amer. Arch.* 4th ser. 6:402-403. McDowell, *Irish Public Opinion*, 41-44 has a brief discussion of the Irish petitions, but he mentions nothing concerning their size, nor the loyal addresses. Maurice R. O'Connell, *Irish Politics and Social Conflict in the Age of the American Revolution* (Philadelphia: University of Pennsylvania Press, 1965) mentions only a loyal address of the Irish Catholics in September 1775 and another loyal address from Newry in 1778 (33, 70).

[6]HO 55/8/7, 8; 11/22.

Bibliography

Manuscript Sources

British Library, London.
Additional Manuscripts:
    Hardwicke Papers, 35626.
    Cole Papers, 5813, 5823, 5855.
Public Record Office, Chancery Lane, London.
Nonparochial Registers:
    Bridgwater RG 4/142, RG 6/308.
    Bristol RG 4/2827, 3507, 1829, 2497, 1830.
    Cambridge RG 4/3870.
    Coventry RG 4/3315.
    Great Yarmouth RG 4/1973, 2473; RG 6/1570, 1473, 1410, 689, 597, 1482, 558, 507.
    Nottingham RG 4/1588, 137, 1586, 3664.
    Poole RG 4/2270, 464, 121; RG 6/1236, 278, 1340, 429.
    Southampton RG 4/610, 624.
Public Record Office, Kew, Surrey.
Home Office Papers: 55/7/1—55/31/6.
Dr. Williams's Library, London.
Evans, John. "List of Dissenting Congregations and Ministers in England and Wales (1715-1729)." MS 38.4 microfilm.
Thompson, Josiah. "List of Protestant Dissenting Congregations in England and Wales (1772-1773)." MS 38.6 microfilm.
Thompson, Josiah, ed. "History of Protestant Dissenting Congregations." 5 vols. 1772- . MSS 38.7-11 microfilm.
Society of Genealogists, Harrington Gardens, London.
    Register of the Above Bar Congregational Chapel, Southampton.
Bristol Central Library, Bristol, Gloucestershire.
    Bristol Elections, 1774-1790. Addresses, Squibs, Songs. Ref. B6979.
Cambridge County Record Office, Shire Hall, Cambridge.
    St. Andrew's Street Baptist Church Book.
St. Andrew's Street Baptist Church Archives, St. Andrew's Street, Cambridge. Trust Deeds of 1764 and 1795.
Dorset County Record Office, County Hall, Dorchester.
    Calcraft Manuscripts: MS poll book of the 1768 Poole election.

University of Nottingham, Nottingham.
   Portland Papers.
Shropshire Record Office, Shrewsbury, Shropshire.
   S.P.L. Deed 19163.

Printed Primary Sources

Poll Books

Institute of Historical Research, University of London.
   Poll books of the elections at Bridgwater, Bristol, Colchester, Coventry,
   Nottingham, Southampton, and Worcester.
Guildhall Library, London.
   The Poll (Abingdon, 1768).
Cambridge Central Library, Cambridge.
   The Poll (Cambridge, 1774, 1776, 1780).
   The County Poll (Cambridge, 14 September 1780).
Norwich Central Library, Norwich.
   The Poll (Great Yarmouth, 1777).
Oxfordshire Record Office, Oxford.
   The Poll (Abingdon, 1754).

Newspapers and Periodicals
Annual Register
Bath Chronicle
Felix Farley's Bristol Journal
Cambridge Chronicle
The Crisis
Cumberland Pacquet
General Evening Post
Gloucester Journal
Hampshire Chronicle
Kentish Gazette
Leeds Mercury
London Chronicle
London Evening-Post
London Gazette
Manchester Mercury
Middlesex Journal
Morning Chronicle and London Advertiser
Northampton Mercury
Norwich Mercury
Creswell's Nottingham and Newark Journal

Public Advertiser
Reading Mercury and Oxford Gazette
Salisbury and Winchester Journal
Shrewsbury Chronicle
Sussex Weekly Advertiser
Berrow's Worcester Journal
York Courant

Books and Pamphlets

Addresses, Remonstrances, and Petitions to the Throne, Presented from the Court of Aldermen, the Court of Common Council, and the Livery in Common Hall Assembled: Commencing the 28th October, 1760, with the Answers Thereto. London: Benjamin Pardon, 1865.

An Appeal to the People of England, on the Present Situation of National Affairs; and to the County of Norfolk, on Some Late Transactions and Reports. London, 1778.

Beawes, Wyndham. *Lex Mercatoria Rediviva: or, The Merchants' Directory. Being a Complete Guide to All Men in Business. . . .* 4th ed. London, 1783.

Blackstone, Sir William. *Commentaries on the Laws of England. . . .* 4 vols. Joseph Chitty et al., eds. London: W. Walker, 1826.

Campbell, R. *The London Tradesman. Being a Compendious View of All the Trades, Professions, Arts, both Liberal and Mechanic, Now Practiced in the Cities of London and Westminster.* London, 1747.

A Collection of Papers, Addresses, Songs etc., Printed on All Sides during the Contest for Representation in Parliament for the Borough of Liverpool. Liverpool, 1780.

Copeland, Thomas W., ed. *The Correspondence of Edmund Burke.* 10 vols. Cambridge: Cambridge University Press, 1958-1978.

Davies, K. G. *Documents of the American Revolution, 1770-1783.* Vol. 9. Dublin: Irish University Press, 1976.

Defoe, Daniel. *A Tour through the Whole Island of Great Britain.* 2 vols. London: Dent, 1962.

Flower, Benjamin, ed. *Miscellaneous Works of Robert Robinson.* Harlow: Benjamin Flower, 1807.

Force, Peter, ed. *American Archives: A Documentary History of the English Colonies in North America.* 4th ser., 6 vols; 5th ser., 3 vols. Washington: M. St. Clair Clarke and Peter Force, 1840-1853.

Fortescue, Sir John, ed. *Correspondence of King George the Third from 1706 to December 1783.* 6 vols. London: Macmillan Co., 1927-1928.

Greene, Donald J. *Samuel Johnson's Political Writings.* New Haven: Yale University Press, 1977.

Guilford, E. L., ed. *Records of the Borough of Nottingham.* 9 vols. Nottingham: Thomas Forman and Sons, 1882-1956.

Guttridge, G. H., ed. *The American Correspondence of a Bristol Merchant, 1766-1776: Letters of Richard Champion.* Berkeley: University of California Press, 1934.

Hansard, T. C., ed. *The Parliamentary History of England . . . to the Year 1803.* London: T. C. Hansard, 1806-1820.

Historical Manuscripts Commission. *Dartmouth Manuscripts.* 3 vols. London: Her Majesty's Stationery Office, 1887-1896.

——————. *Tenth Report, Appendix, Part 6.* London: Her Majesty's Stationery Office, 1887.

Independence! or a Correct LIST of the Independent Commercial Gentlemen Tradesmen Who Voted for Mr. Dawkins on the 17th and 18th June, 1790, in Support of the Glorious Independence of the Town of Southampton. Southampton, 1790.

Johnson, Samuel. *A Dictionary of the English Language.* 2 vols., 6th ed. London, 1785.

The Journals of the House of Commons.

Labaree, Leonard W. and William B. Willcox, eds. *The Papers of Benjamin Franklin.* 23 vols. New Haven: Yale University Press, 1961-1983.

Laprade, William T. *Parliamentary Papers of John Robinson, 1774-1784.* London: The Royal Historical Society, 1922.

Lewis, W. S., ed. *Horace Walpole's Correspondence.* 48 vols. New Haven: Yale University Press, 1937-1983.

Massie, Joseph. *Brief Observations and Calculations on the Present High Prices. . . .* London, 1765.

——————. *Calculations of the Present Taxes Yearly Paid by a Family of Each Rank, Degree, or Class.* 2d ed. London, 1961.

——————. *A Computation of the Money that Hath Been Exorbitantly Raised upon the People of Great Britain by the Sugar Planters, in One Year from January 1759 to January 1760; Shewing How Much Money a Family of each Rank, Degree or Class Hath Lost by that Rapacious Monopoly, After I Laid It Open. . . .* 1760.

Norton, J. E., ed. *The Letters of Edward Gibbon.* 3 vols. London: Macmillan Co., 1956.

Pickering, D., ed. *The Statutes at Large from Magna Carta to . . . 1761; Continued (to 1806).* Cambridge, 1762-1806.

The Proceedings and Tryal in the Case of the Most Reverend Father in God William, Lord Archbishop of Canterbury, and the Right Reverend Fathers in God. London, 1689.

Robinson, William, ed. *Select Works of the Rev. Robert Robinson of Cambridge.* London: Heaton, 1861.

Rolt, Richard. *A New Dictionary of Trade and Commerce*. 2d ed. London, 1761.

Sketchley, James. *Sketchley's Bristol Directory*. Bristol, 1775.

A Speech Intended to Have Been Delivered to the Right Honorable the Lord Mayor, Aldermen, Recorder, and the Rest of the Body Corporate of the City of York; Endeavouring to Show the Necessity of an Address to His Majesty, on the Present Affairs in America; Interspersed with Remarks on the Reasons Advanced in Opposition to it; Particularly Those Handed about, and Signed by Some Members of the Corporation. York, 1775.

Steuart, A. Francis, ed. *The Last Journals of Horace Walpole*. 2 vols. London: John Lane, 1910.

Taylor, William S. and John H. Pringle, eds. *The Correspondence of William Pitt, Earl of Chatham*. 4 vols. London: John Murray, 1838-1840.

Toulmin, Joshua. *The History of the Town of Taunton, in the County of Somerset*. Taunton, 1791.

Secondary Sources

Books

Adams, Thomas R. *The American Controversy: A Bibliographical Study of the British Pamphlets about the American Dispute, 1764-1783*. 2 vols. Providence: Brown University Press, 1980.

Alden, John R. *The American Revolution, 1775-1783*. New York: Harper and Row, 1954.

Ayling, Stanley. *George the Third*. New York: Alfred A. Knopf, 1972.

Bailyn, Bernard. *The Ideological Origins of the American Revolution*. Cambridge: Belknap Press, 1967.

_____ and John B. Hench. *The Press and the American Revolution*. Worcester MA: American Antiquarian Society, 1980.

Balderston, Marion, and David Syrett, eds. *The Lost War: Letters from British Officers during the American Revolution*. New York: Horizon Press, 1975.

Bancroft, George H. *History of the United States of America from the Discovery of the Continent*. 6 vols. Boston: Little, Brown and Co., 1876.

Billington, Ray Allen, ed. *The Reinterpretation of Early American History*. San Marino CA: The Huntington Library, 1966.

Black, Eugene C. *The Association: British Extraparliamentary Political Organization, 1769-1793*. Cambridge: Harvard University Press, 1963.

Bond, Donovan H. and W. Reynolds McLeod. *Newsletters to Newspapers: Eighteenth-Century Journalism*. Morgantown WV: West Virginia University, 1977.

Bonomi, Patricia U., ed. *Party and Political Opposition in Revolutionary America*. Terrytown NY: Sleepy Hollow Press, 1980.

Bonsall, Brian. *Sir James Lowther and Cumberland and Westmorland Elections, 1754-1775*. Manchester: Manchester University Press, 1960.

Bonwick, Colin. *English Radicals and the American Revolution.* Chapel Hill: University of North Carolina Press, 1977.

Brewer, John. *Party Ideology and Popular Politics at the Accession of George III.* Cambridge: Cambridge University Press, 1976.

Bridenbaugh, Carl. *Mitre and Sceptre: Transatlantic Faiths, Ideas, Personalities, and Politics, 1689-1775.* Oxford: Oxford University Press, 1962.

Brooke, John. *King George III.* London: Constable and Co., 1972.

Burton, K. G. *The Early Newspaper Press in Berkshire (1723-1825).* Reading: University of Reading, 1954.

Butterfield, Herbert. *George III and the Historians.* London: Collins, 1957.

——————. *George III, Lord North and the People.* London: Bell, 1949.

Cannon, John. *The Fox-North Coalition: Crisis of the Constitution, 1782-1784.* Cambridge: Cambridge University Press, 1969.

——————. *Parliamentary Reform, 1640-1832.* Cambridge: Cambridge University Press, 1973.

——————, ed. *The Whig Ascendancy: Colloquies on Hanoverian England.* New York: St. Martin's Press, 1981.

Cartwright, William H. and Richard L. Watson, Jr., eds. *The Reinterpretation of American History and Culture.* Washington: National Council for the Social Studies, 1973.

Christie, Ian. *The End of North's Ministry, 1780-1782.* London: Macmillan Co., 1958.

——————. *Myth and Reality in Late-Eighteenth-Century Politics and Other Papers.* London: Macmillan Co., 1970.

——————. *Wilkes, Wyvill and Reform.* London: Macmillan Co., 1962.

—————— and Benjamin Labaree. *Empire or Independence.* Oxford: Phaidon, 1976.

Clark, Dora Mae. *British Opinion and the American Revolution.* New Haven: Yale University Press, 1930.

Clark, J. C. D. *The Dynamics of Change: The Crisis of the 1750s and English Party Systems.* New York: Cambridge University Press, 1982.

Clarkson, Leslie A. *The Pre-Industrial Economy in England, 1500-1750.* London: Batsford, 1971.

Colley, Linda. *In Defiance of Oligarchy: The Tory Party, 1714-1760.* Cambridge: Cambridge University Press, 1982.

Cranfield, G. A. *The Development of the Provincial Newspaper, 1700-1760.* Oxford: Clarendon Press, 1962.

Cross, Arthur L. *The Anglican Episcopate and the American Colonies.* New York: Longmans, Green and Co., 1902.

Davidson, Philip. *Propaganda and the American Revolution, 1763-1783.* Chapel Hill: University of North Carolina Press, 1941.

Deane, Phyllis and W. A. Cole. *British Economic Growth, 1688-1959: Trends and Structure.* 2d ed. Cambridge: Cambridge University Press, 1967.

Densham, W. and J. Ogle. *The Story of the Congregational Churches of Dorset from Their Foundation to the Present Time.* Bournemouth: W. Mate and Sons, 1899.

Dickinson, H. T. *Liberty and Property: Political Ideology in Eighteenth-Century Britain.* New York: Holmes and Meier, 1977.

Dilks, T. Bruce. *Charles James Fox and the Borough of Bridgwater.* Bridgwater: East Gate Press, 1907.

Ditchfield, P. H., ed. *The Victoria History of Berkshire.* 4 vols. London: A. Constable and Co., 1906-1924.

Donoughue, Bernard. *British Politics and the American Revolution: The Path to War, 1773-1775.* London: Macmillan Co., 1964.

Downie, James A. *Robert Harley and the Press: Propaganda and Public Opinion in the Age of Swift and Defoe.* Cambridge: Cambridge University Press, 1979.

Eisenstein, Elizabeth L. *The Printing Press as an Agent of Change.* 2 vols. New York: Cambridge University Press, 1979.

Emden, Cecil S. *The People and the Constitution, Being a History of the Development of the People's Influence in British Government.* 2d ed. Oxford: Clarendon Press, 1956.

Evans, Charles. *American Bibliography.* 14 vols. Chicago: Blakely Press, 1903-1959.

Evans, George. *Vestiges of Protestant Dissent.* Liverpool: F. & E. Gibbons, 1897.

Frothingham, Richard. *The Rise of the Republic of the United States.* Boston: Little, Brown and Co., 1872.

Gipson, L. H. *The Coming of the Revolution, 1763-1775.* New York: Harper and Row, 1954.

Gray, J. Milner. *Biographical Notes on the Mayors of Cambridge.* Cambridge: W. Heffer and Sons, 1922.

Greene, Donald J. *The Politics of Samuel Johnson.* New Haven: Yale University Press, 1960.

Gunn, J. A. W. *Beyond Liberty and Property: The Process of Self-Recognition in Eighteenth-Century Political Thought.* Kingston and Montreal: McGill-Queen's University Press, 1983.

Guttridge, G. L. *English Whiggism and the American Revolution.* Berkeley: University of California Press, 1963.

Hanson, Lawrence. *Government and the Press, 1695-1763.* Oxford: Oxford University Press, 1936.

Hartog, Hendrik. *Public Property and Private Power: The Corporation of the City of New York, 1730-1870.* Chapel Hill: University of North Carolina Press, 1983.

Hay, Douglas, et al. *Albion's Fatal Tree*. New York: Pantheon Books, 1975.

Hinkhouse, Fred J. *The Preliminaries of the American Revolution as Seen in the English Press, 1763-1775*. New York: Columbia University Press, 1926.

Holmes, Geoffrey. *Augustan England: Professions, State and Society, 1680-1730*. London: George Allen & Unwin, 1982.

Hurry-Houghton, Thomas. *Memorials of the Family of Hurry*. Liverpool: C. Tinling and Co., 1926.

Jacobson, David L., ed. *The English Libertarian Tradition*. Indianapolis: Bobbs-Merrill Co., 1965.

Jones, Alice Hanson. *American Colonial Wealth: Documents and Methods*. 3 vols. New York: Arno Press, 1979.

Kammen, Michael G. *A Rope of Sand: The Colonial Agents, British Politics, and the American Revolution*. New York: Vintage Books, 1974.

Keir, Sir David L. *The Constitutional History of Modern Britain since 1485*. 9th ed. London: Adam and Charles Black, 1969.

Lambert, Sheila. *Bills and Acts: Legislative Procedure in Eighteenth-Century England*. Cambridge: Cambridge University Press, 1971.

Langford, Paul. *The First Rockingham Administration, 1765-1766*. London: Oxford University Press, 1973.

Laprade, William T. *Public Opinion and Politics in Eighteenth-Century England to the Fall of Walpole*. New York: Macmillan Co., 1936.

Lutnick, Solomon. *The American Revolution and the British Press, 1775-1783*. Columbia MO: University of Missouri Press, 1967.

McDowell, R. B. *Irish Public Opinion, 1750-1800*. London: Faber and Faber, 1944.

McIlwain, Charles H. *The American Revolution: A Constitutional Interpretation*. Ithaca NY: Cornell University Press, 1923.

McKendrick, Neil, John Brewer, and J. H. Plumb. *The Birth of a Consumer Society*. London: Europa Publications, 1982.

Mackesy, Piers. *The War for America, 1775-1783*. London: Longmans, 1964.

Maier, Pauline. *From Resistance to Revolution: Colonial Radicals and the Development of American Opposition to Britain, 1765-1776*. New York: Alfred A. Knopf, 1972.

Main, Jackson T. *The Social Structure of Revolutionary America*. Princeton: Princeton University Press, 1965.

Marshall, Dorothy. *Eighteenth Century England*. 2d ed. Thetford, Norfolk: Longmans, 1974.

Marshall, Leon S. *The Development of Public Opinion in Manchester*. Syracuse: Syracuse University Press, 1946.

Marshall, Peter. *Bristol and the American War of Independence*. Bristol: Bristol Branch of the Historical Association, 1977.

Medley, Dudley J. *A Student's Manual of English Constitutional History.* 5th ed. Oxford: B. H. Blackwell, 1913.

Mekeel, Arthur J. *The Relation of the Quakers to the American Revolution.* Washington: University Press of America, 1979.

Miller, John C. *Origins of the American Revolution.* Rev. ed. Stanford: Stanford University Press, 1959.

Money, John. *Experience and Identity: Birmingham and the West Midlands, 1760-1800.* Manchester: Manchester University Press, 1977.

Morgan, Edmund S. *The Stamp Act Crisis: Prologue to Revolution.* New York: Collier Books, 1963.

Morris, Irene. *Three Hundred Years of Baptist Life in Coventry.* London: Kingsgate Press, 1925.

Murch, Jerome. *A History of the Presbyterian and General Baptist Churches in the West of England: With Memoirs of Some of Their Pastors.* London: R. Hunter, 1835.

Murrell, Richard J. and Robert East, eds. *Extracts from Records in the Possession of the Municipal Corporation of the Borough of Portsmouth.* Portsmouth: H. Lewis, 1884.

Namier, Lewis B. *England in the Age of the American Revolution.* 2d ed. London: Macmillan Co., 1961.

——————. *Personalities and Powers.* London: Hamish Hamilton, 1955.

——————. *The Structure of Politics at the Accession of George III.* 2d ed. London: Macmillan Co., 1957.

—————— and John Brooke. *The House of Commons, 1754-1790.* 3 vols. London: Her Majesty's Stationery Office, 1964.

Nelson, William H. *The American Tory.* Boston: Beacon Press, 1961.

Norton, Mary Beth. *The British Americans: The Loyalist Exiles in England, 1774-1789.* Boston: Little, Brown and Co., 1972.

O'Connell, Maurice R. *Irish Politics and Social Conflict in the Age of the American Revolution.* Philadelphia: University of Pennsylvania Press, 1965.

O'Gorman, Frank. *The Rise of Party in England: The Rockingham Whigs, 1760-1782.* London: George Allen & Unwin, 1975.

Olson, Alison G. *Anglo-American Politics, 1660-1775.* Oxford: Clarendon Press, 1973.

Owen, John B. *The Eighteenth Century, 1714-1815.* London: Thomas Nelson and Sons, 1974.

Palmer, Charles John. *Memorials of the Family of Hurry.* Norwich: Miller and Leavins, 1875.

Pares, Richard. *King George III and the Politicians.* Oxford: Oxford University Press, 1953.

Patterson, A. Temple. *A History of Southampton, 1700-1914*. Vol. 1: *An Oligarchy in Decline, 1700-1835*. Southampton: Southampton University Press, 1966.

Perkin, Harold. *The Origins of Modern English Society, 1780-1880*. London: Routledge & Kegan Paul, 1969.

Perry, Thomas W. *Public Opinion, Propaganda, and Politics in Eighteenth-Century England: A Study of the Jew Bill of 1753*. Cambridge: Harvard University Press, 1962.

Peters, Marie. *Pitt and Popularity: The Patriot Minister and London Opinion during the Seven Years' War*. Oxford: Clarendon Press, 1980.

Phillips, John A. *Electoral Behavior in Unreformed England: Plumpers, Splitters, and Straights*. Princeton: Princeton University Press, 1982.

_____. *Nominal Record Linkage and the Study of Individual-Level Voting Behavior*. Iowa City: University of Iowa; Laboratory for Political Research, 1976.

Plumb, J. H. *In the Light of History*. New York: Dell Publishing Co., 1972.

Pocock, J. G. A., ed. *Three British Revolutions: 1641, 1688, 1776*. Princeton: Princeton University Press, 1980.

Pole, J. R. *Political Representation in England and the Origins of the American Republic*. New York: Macmillan Co., 1966.

Rea, Robert R. *The English Press in Politics, 1760-1774*. Lincoln: University of Nebraska Press, 1963.

Read, Donald. *The English Provinces, c. 1760-1960: A Study in Influence*. London: E. Arnold, 1964.

_____. *Press and People, 1790-1850: Opinion in Three English Cities*. London: E. Arnold, 1961.

Ritcheson, Charles R. *British Politics and the American Revolution*. Norman OK: University of Oklahoma Press, 1954.

Robbins, Caroline. *The Eighteenth-Century Commonwealthman*. New York: Atheneum, 1968.

Robson, Eric. *The American Revolution in Its Political and Military Aspects*. New York: W. W. Norton, 1966.

Royle, Edward and James Walvin. *English Radicals and Reformers, 1760-1848*. Lexington: University of Kentucky Press, 1982.

Rudé, George. *Paris and London in the Eighteenth Century: Studies in Popular Protest*. New York: The Viking Press, 1973.

_____. *Wilkes and Liberty*. Oxford: Oxford University Press, 1962.

Russell, Lord John. *The Life and Times of Charles James Fox*. 3 vols. London: Richard Bentley, 1859.

Schutz, John A. *Thomas Pownall: British Defender of American Liberty*. Glendale CA: The Arthur H. Clarke Co., 1951.

Schwoerer, Lois G. *The Declaration of Rights, 1689*. Baltimore: Johns Hopkins University Press, 1981.

Sedgwick, Romney. *The House of Commons, 1715-1754*. 2 vols. London: Her Majesty's Stationery Office, 1970.

Sibree, John and M. Caston. *Independency in Warwickshire*. London: Ward and Co., 1855.

Sims, John, ed. *A Handlist of British Parliamentary Poll Books*. Riverside CA: University of Leicester History Department and University of California, Riverside, 1983.

Stainer, S. *History of the Above Bar Congregational Church, Southampton, from 1662-1908*. Southampton: Southampton Times Co., 1909.

Sutherland, Lucy S. *The City of London and the Opposition to Government, 1768-1774*. London: University of London, Athlone Press, 1959.

Thomas, P. D. G. *British Politics and the Stamp Act Crisis: The First Phase of the American Revolution, 1763-1767*. Oxford: Clarendon Press, 1975.

——————. *The House of Commons in the Eighteenth Century*. Oxford: Clarendon Press, 1971.

Thompson, E. P. *The Making of the English Working Class*. New York: Pantheon Books, 1963.

Trevelyan, G. M. *An Autobiography and Other Essays*. London: Longmans, Green and Co., 1949.

Vincent, J. R. *Pollbooks: How Victorians Voted*. Cambridge: Cambridge University Press, 1967.

Ward, William S. *British Periodicals and Newspapers, 1789-1832: A Bibliography of Secondary Sources*. Lexington: University Press of Kentucky, 1972.

Watson, J. Steven. *The Reign of George III, 1760-1815*. Oxford: Clarendon Press, 1959.

Watts, Michael. *The Dissenters*. Oxford: Clarendon Press, 1977.

Weare, G. E. *Edmund Burke's Connection with Bristol, from 1774 till 1780*. Bristol: William Bennett, 1894.

Werkmeister, Lucyle. *The London Daily Press, 1772-1792*. Lincoln: University of Nebraska Press, 1963.

Whitley, T. W. *The Parliamentary Representation of the City of Coventry*. Coventry: Curtis and Beamish, 1894.

Wickwire, Franklin B. *British Subministers and Colonial America, 1763-1783*. Princeton: Princeton University Press, 1966.

Williams, E. Neville. *The Eighteenth-Century Constitution, 1688-1815: Documents and Commentary*. Cambridge: Cambridge University Press, 1970.

Wright, Esmond, ed. *Causes and Consequences of the American Revolution*. Chicago: Quadrangle Books, 1966.

Wrigley, E. A., ed. *Identifying People in the Past*. London: E. Arnold, 1973.

Dissertations

Bradley, James E. "Whigs and Nonconformists: Presbyterians, Congregationalists, and Baptists in English Politics, 1715-1790." Ph.D. dissertation, University of Southern California, 1978.

Fryer, Charles E. "English Church Disestablishment: A Statistical and Sectional View, Being Mainly a Study in the Development of the Political Influence of Dissent since 1688." Ph.D. dissertation, Harvard University, 1906.

Hayes, B. D. "Politics in Norfolk, 1750-1832." Ph.D. dissertation, Cambridge University, 1958.

Kinnear, Mary. "Pro-Americans in the British House of Commons in the 1770's." Ph.D. dissertation, University of Oregon, 1973.

Marston, Jerrilyn. "King and Congress: The Transfer of Political Legitimacy from the King to the Continental Congress, 1774-1776." Ph.D. dissertation, Boston University, 1975.

Radbill, Kenneth A. "Socioeconomic Background of Nonpacifist Quakers during the American Revolution." Ph.D. dissertation, University of Arizona, 1971.

Sainsbury, John A. "The Pro-American Movement in London, 1769-1782: Extraparliamentary Opposition to the Government's American Policy." Ph.D. dissertation, McGill University, 1975.

Schiavo, Bartholomew Peter. "The Dissenter Connection: English Dissenters and Massachusetts Political Culture: 1630-1774." Ph.D. dissertation, Brandeis University, 1976.

Underdown, Peter T. "The Parliamentary History of the City of Bristol, 1750-1790." M.A. thesis, University of Bristol, 1948.

Wallace, Charles I., Jr. "Religion and Society in Eighteenth-Century England: Geographic, Demographic, and Occupational Patterns of Dissent in the West Riding of Yorkshire, 1715-1801." Ph.D. dissertation, Duke University, 1975.

Articles

Aspinall, A. "The Reporting and Publishing of the House of Commons Debates, 1771-1834," in Pares, Richard and A. J. P. Taylor. *Essays Presented to Sir Lewis Namier*, 227-57. London: Macmillan Co., 1956.

Bargar, B. D. "Matthew Boulton and the Birmingham Petition of 1775." *William and Mary Quarterly* 3rd ser. 13 (January 1956): 26-39.

Benson, Lee. "An Approach to the Scientific Study of Past Public Opinion." *Public Opinion Quarterly* 31 (Winter 1968): 522-67.

Bonwick, Colin C. "An English Audience for American Revolutionary Pamphlets." *The Historical Journal* 19 (June 1976): 355-74.

_____. "English Dissenters and the American Revolution," in H. C. Allen and Roger Thompson, eds. *Contrast and Connection: Bicentennial Essays in Anglo-American History*, 88-112. Athens OH: Ohio University Press, 1976.

Bradley, James E. "Religion and Reform at the Polls: Nonconformity in Cambridge Politics, 1774-1784." *Journal of British Studies* 23 (Spring 1984): 55-78.

_____. "Whigs and Nonconformists: 'Slumbering Radicalism' in English Politics, 1739-1789." *Eighteenth-Century Studies* 9 (Fall 1975): 1-27.

Brewer, John. "The Misfortunes of Lord Bute: A Case-Study in Eighteenth-Century Political Argument and Public Opinion." *The Historical Journal* 16 (March 1973): 3-43.

Butterfield, Herbert. "George III and the Constitution." *History* 43 (February 1958): 3-43.

Cam, Helen. "Quo Warranto Proceedings at Cambridge, 1780-1790." *The Cambridge Historical Journal* 8:2 (1945): 145-65.

Clark, Dan E. "News and Opinion Concerning America in English Newspapers, 1754-1763." *Pacific Historical Review* 10 (March 1941): 75-82.

Fraser, Peter. "Public Petitioning and Parliament before 1832." *History* 46 (October 1961): 195-211.

Ginter, Donald. "The Loyalist Association Movement of 1792-1793 and British Public Opinion." *The Historical Journal* 9:1 (1966): 179-90.

Gipson, L. H. "The Great Debate in the Committee of the Whole House of Commons on the Stamp Act, 1766, as Reported by Nathaniel Ryder." *Pennsylvania Magazine of History and Biography* 86 (January 1962): 10-41.

Hershberg, Theodore and R. Dockhorn. "Occupational Classification." *Historical Methods Newsletter* 9:2 (1976): 59-98.

Ippel, Henry P. "British Sermons and the American Revolution." *The Journal of Religious History* 12 (December 1982): 191-205.

Jenson, Richard. "How Democracy Works: The Linkage between Micro and Macro Political History." *Journal of Social History* 16 (Summer 1983): 27-34.

Katz, Michael. "Occupational Classification in History." *Journal of Interdisciplinary History* 3 (Summer 1972): 63-88.

Kelley, Paul. "Radicalism and Public Opinion in the General Election of 1784." *Bulletin of the Institute of Historical Research* 45 (May 1972): 73-88.

Kemp, Betty. "Crewe's Act, 1782." *English Historical Review* 68 (April 1953): 258-63.

Kenny, Courtney S. "A Forgotten Cambridge Meeting House." *Transactions of the Congregational Historical Society* 4 (1909-1910): 223-29.

Kinnear, Mary. "British Friends of America 'Without Doors' during the American Revolution." *The Humanities Association Review* 27:2 (1976): 104-19.

Knox, Thomas. "Popular Politics and Provincial Radicalism: Newcastle-upon-Tyne, 1769-1785." *Albion* 11 (Fall 1979): 224-41.

_____. "Wilkism and the Newcastle Election of 1774." *Durham University Journal* 72 (1979-1980): 23-37.

Langford, Paul. "Old Whigs, Old Tories and the American Revolution." *The Journal of Imperial and Commonwealth History* 8 (January 1980): 106-30.

_____. "William Pitt and Public Opinion, 1757." *English Historical Review* 88 (January 1973): 54-80.

Langton, John and Paul Laxton. "Parish Registers and Urban Structure: The Example of Late-Eighteenth-Century Liverpool." *Urban History Yearbook* (1978): 74-84.

Laprade, William T. "Public Opinion and the Election of 1784." *English Historical Review* 31 (April 1916): 224-37.

Lindert, Peter H. "An Algorithm for Probate Sampling." *Journal of Interdisciplinary History* 11 (Spring 1981): 649-68.

_____. "English Occupations, 1670-1811." *Journal of Economic History* 40 (December 1980): 685-712.

Lowe, William C. "The House of Lords, Party, and Public Opinion: Opposition Use of the Protest, 1760-1782. " *Albion* 11 (Summer 1979): 143-56.

Maier, Pauline. "John Wilkes and American Disillusionment with Britain." *William and Mary Quarterly* 3rd ser. 20 (July 1963): 373-95.

Marshall, Peter. "Manchester and the American Revolution." *Bulletin of the John Rylands University Library of Manchester* 62 (Autumn 1979): 168-286.

Mathias, Peter. "The Social Structure in the Eighteenth Century: A Calculation by Joseph Massie." *Economic History Review* 10:1 (1957): 30-45.

Money, John. "Birmingham and the West Midlands, 1760-1793: Politics and Regional Identity in the English Provinces in the Later Eighteenth Century." *Midland History* 1 (Spring 1971): 1-19.

_____. "Taverns, Coffee Houses and Clubs: Local Politics and Popular Articulacy in the Birmingham Area, in the Age of the American Revolution." *The Historical Journal* 14:1 (1971): 15-47.

O'Gorman, Frank. "Fifty Years after Namier: The Eighteenth Century in British Historical Writing." *The Eighteenth Century* 20 (Spring 1979): 99-120.

Phillips, John A. "Achieving a Critical Mass while Avoiding an Explosion: Letter-Cluster Sampling and Nominal Record Linkage." *Journal of Interdisciplinary History* 9 (Winter 1979): 493-508.

_____. "Popular Politics in Unreformed England." *Journal of Modern History* 52 (December 1980): 599-625.

_____. "The Structure of Electoral Politics in Unreformed England." *Journal of British Studies* 19 (Fall 1979): 76-100.

Pound, J. F. "The Social and Trade Structure of Norwich, 1525-1575."*Past and Present* 34 (July 1966): 49-69.

Sainsbury, John. "The Pro-Americans of London, 1769-1782." *William and Mary Quarterly* 3rd ser. 35 (July 1978): 423-54.

Schwarz, L. D. and L. J. Jones. "Wealth, Occupations, and Insurance in the Late Eighteenth Century: The Policy Registers of the Sun Fire Office." *The Economic History Review* 36 (August 1983): 365-73.

Short, K. R. M. "The English Indemnity Acts, 1726-1867." *Church History* 42 (September 1973): 366-76.

Smith, Andrew A. "Nonconformity in Green Street, Cambridge." *Journal of the Presbyterian Historical Society of England* 14:1 (1968): 62-74.

Speck, W. A., W. A. Gray, and R. Hopkinson. "Computer Analysis of Poll Books: A Further Report." *Bulletin of the Institute of Historical Research* 48 (May 1975): 64-90.

Thomas, P. D. G. "The Beginnings of Parliamentary Reporting in Newspapers, 1768-1774." *English Historical Review* 74 (October 1959): 623-36.

_____. "John Wilkes and the Freedom of the Press (1771)." *Bulletin of the Institute of Historical Research* 33 (May 1960): 86-98.

"A View of English Nonconformity in 1773." *Transactions of the Congregational Historical Society* 5 (1911-1912): 205-385.

Wilsher, J. C. " 'Power Follows Property'—Social and Economic Interpretations in British Historical Writings in the Eighteenth and Early Nineteenth Centuries." *Journal of Social History* 16 (Summer 1983): 7-26.

Index

Aberbrothuck, 235

Aberdeen, 235; American issue in, 85

Abingdon, 54-55, 58, 67, 70, 75, 99, 134, 136, 142, 144, 193; petition of 1775, 224-25

Abingdon, Willoughby Bertie, 4th Earl of, 54, 68, 147, 205, 225, 227

Acland, John, 168

Acland, Sir Thomas Dyke 52, 146

Addresses, 26; Administration's support of merchant addresses, 23; American addresses compared to Middlesex addresses, 72; county addresses and the peerage, 53; ideological content, 72-74; in relation to corporations, 78-80, 83. *See also* Corporations, George III, Government contractors, Patronage, Tories

Administration, 5-8, 15, 17, 19-20, 23, 25-27, 35, 43, 49-53, 55, 67-68, 70-71, 89, 92-93, 98, 104, 117-18, 134-35, 145, 154, 171, 179, 204-205, 207-208, 210, 214, 216; approach to petitions, 42-43; coherent use of popular expressions, 57; use of press, 118-19. *See also* Government contractors

Allen, Benjamin, 166-68

American documents published in England: "Declaration of the Causes and Necessity of Taking Up Arms," "The Twelve United Colonies to the Inhabitants of Great Britain," 96. *See also* Olive Branch Petition

American Prohibitory Bill, 11, 204

American Revolution: colonists viewed as in rebellion, 33, 35, 39-40, 47, 50, 70-72, 97, 99-100, 106; independence, 8; interpretation, 7-9; as issue in parliamentary elections, 60, 86-87

Andover, 79, 132, 182

Anglican: bishops in the House of Lords, 42, 180; church, 125, 129, 157-58, 164, 174, 180; clergy, 88, 124, 165, 170, 180, 189, 192, 193; clergy who were also justices of the peace, 107; high Anglican, 125, 129, 147, 180, 193, 201; low churchmen, 161, 165, 168, 170, 179, 193; petitioners, 147; subscribers and clergymen, 154; support addresses, 178-80; support petitions, 193, 201. *See also* Corporations, Tories

Angus, 235

Anne, 167

Annual Register, 93, 118

Appleby, 106; American issue in, 84-85

Archer, Andrew, 2d Baron, 149

Argyll, Co., 235

Arundel, 78, 131

Ashburner, Edward, 170

Association movement, 2, 4, 10, 48, 161; compared to American petitions, 135; economic-reform petitions, 3, 13-14, 122, 126-29, 132, 144, 167; number of signatures, 136-37

Astley, Sir Edward, 130-31, 220

Atherstone, 21

Axbridge, 77-78

Ayr, 235

Bacon, Edward, 28

Bagot, William, 146

Baker, William, 26, 28, 35, 54, 148

Baptists, 128, 159, 161-62, 165, 167-68, 191, 193

Barclay, David, 38-39

Barnstaple, 52, 78, 142, 182

Barrington, William Wildman, 2d Viscount, 53

Bateman, John, 2d Viscount, 53

Bath Chronicle, 110, 136

Bath Journal, 111, 116

Bathurst family, 53

Bayley, T. B., 56